21世纪法学系列教材

基础课系列

英美法导读
（第二版）

Learning Anglo-American Law:
A Thematic Introduction
(Second Edition)

李国利 著

北京大学出版社
PEKING UNIVERSITY PRESS

图书在版编目(CIP)数据

英美法导读:第2版 = Learning Anglo-American Law:A Thematic Introduction:2nd Edition:英文/李国利著.—2版.—北京:北京大学出版社,2010.8
(21世纪法学系列教材)
ISBN 978-7-301-16683-3

Ⅰ.①英… Ⅱ.①李… Ⅲ.①英美法系-高等学校-教材-英文
Ⅳ.①D904

中国版本图书馆 CIP 数据核字(2010)第 156968 号

书　　　名:英美法导读(第二版)
　　　　　　Learning Anglo-American Law:A Thematic Introduction(Second Edition)
著作责任者:李国利　著
责 任 编 辑:李燕芬
标 准 书 号:ISBN 978-7-301-16683-3/D·2658
出 版 发 行:北京大学出版社
地　　　址:北京市海淀区成府路205号　100871
网　　　址:http://www.pup.cn
电　　　话:邮购部 62752015　发行部 62750672　编辑部 62752027
　　　　　　出版部 62754962
电 子 邮 箱:law@pup.pku.edu.cn
印 刷 者:北京虎彩文化传播有限公司
经 销 者:新华书店
　　　　　　730 毫米×980 毫米　16 开本　26.5 印张　471 千字
　　　　　　2005 年 8 月第 1 版
　　　　　　2010 年 8 月第 2 版　2023 年 2 月第 3 次印刷
定　　　价:39.00 元

未经许可,不得以任何方式复制或抄袭本书之部分或全部内容。
版权所有,侵权必究
举报电话:010-62752024　电子邮箱:fd@pup.pku.edu.cn

内容简介

本书主要以美国的法律和法律体系为阐述对象，采用体系化的研究方法，在体例及内容上力求构建一个有机的英美法体系。本书力图强调英美法体系的组成部分、整体面貌及其个性特征。为正确理解英美法，本书以专题形式从诉讼、法律推理、法律研究、法律资源等方面来阐述美国法，向读者展现一个良好法律体系的构建过程。本书浓墨重彩之处在于法律制定、废除、修改的过程及具体操作，阐明了判决如何确定，判决制订者如何相互作用，以及法律规则如何最终形成等。本书系导读性著作，但又有一定的深度，作者采用英文写作，语言简练易懂，可读性强，为读者创造了一个良好的英美法语境。本书可供大学师生学习英美法使用，也可供科研人员、法律实务人员参考。

作者简介

　　李国利教授，男，1935年生于山东烟台，1959年毕业于台湾大学法律系。1963离开台湾赴加拿大深造，在麦吉尔大学空间法研究所、图书馆信息科学院攻读，并于1968年分别取得这两个专业的硕士学位。此后在麦吉尔大学空间法研究所、麦吉尔大学法学院执教，直到2000年退休。

　　李国利教授对空间法、国际法和法哲学都有浓厚的兴趣。在这些领域发表了很多文章，并著有最全面的多卷本世界空间法百科全书。

Revised Edition Preface

This publication is a revised and updated version of the first edition that is based on the contents of lectures given by me at the school of law, Yantai University. Some of the lectures are based on a number of books on the subject matters included. These books are given in the general references at the end of the book. Other lectures included in this book are the results of my own findings and views. As such, the subject matters of these lectures are not normally found in books on Anglo-American law. But in my opinion, these lectures are very much an integral part of Anglo-American law. The main focus of the contents of this book is on the law and legal system of the United States. This is primarily due to the fact that not only the United States has adopted the Common Law tradition as opposed to the codified system of law as found in civil law countries but also that the United States has the most rich and vibrant law and legal system in the world, and has an unprecedented and unsurpassed influence internationally.

Most if not all existing books on the foundation of the Anglo-American law including the Common law and those of an introductory nature are, to a significant extent, of a non-systematic nature; Not only their forms of presentation lack any organization and structure, the material components included in these foundation or introductory texts are largely an agglomeration or a grab bag of materials, and devoid of any meaningful systematic connectedness.

They unduly attend too much to the individual trees while losing sight of the forest. It is not unreasonable to say that this unfortunate state is largely due to a lack of a proper conception of what counts as law in general and as Anglo-American law in particular. Another weakness is that the authors of these books confuse the sources of law as the real law—the law in action—as well as that they neglect to tackle the most interesting and dynamic authoritative and effective decision-making process through which the law in action ultimately emerges. Another contributing factor for this weakness is that these earlier publications failed to draw attention to the interactivity and the mutually informing and shaping nature of law between elite powers in the political moral arena.

The lectures found in the present book purport to emphasize the systemic components, features, and characteristics of Anglo-American law. This is evident from the contents of the lectures. No subject components of any substantive law, especially those of a private law nature are included. Thus, little or no discussion of and citation to cases or judicial decisions are included. Wherever private law subjects or matters are touched upon, these are dealt with in the broader context of the legal system.

Instead, the emphasis is on real life happenings and issues, namely, juridical case or cases in a much broader sense, if you will. One of such cases is the on-going economic meltdown, financial and banking crises as well as the regulatory programs, bailout plans, and rescue or nationalization attempts. Here the issues and problems involved include the fierce debates over big government versus small government, liberalism versus conservatism, regulatory guidance and control versus laissez-faire free market capitalism, state powers versus social forces, and public versus private. The study also stresses the overwhelming primacy of legislative and executive decisions and negligible role of the judiciary. Above all, we emphasizes the life drama of the interactitivity of mutual informing and mutual shaping of elite powers both within the state realm and with elite participants in the non-state sectors, and the relationship and distinction between authority and efficacy.

What are generally missed or overlooked by other introductory works on Anglo-American law have been particularly chosen to strengthen the systematic nature of Anglo-American law properly understood. Thus, one finds in this work a chapter on Anglo-American law and You, The building of a good legal system, United States law in action and legal reason. Even in the discussion of some of the conventional subjects, issues or matters of a system or process nature are specially chosen.

The systematic emphasis of the lectures particularly stresses the process and operation of the making, unmaking, and remaking of the law rather than the inanimate and rigid nature of substantive rules and the general and pliable (elastic) legal principles. The emphasis is on how decisions are made, how decision-makers interact, and how a rule of law finally emerges. The central theme of the emphasis is the interactivity between sources and decision-makers. We believe how and why decision-makers interact and how and why the law finally emerges should be the central focuses in any studying of Anglo-American law.

For ease of learning and locating any specific text and information, a detailed table of contents is deliberately structured and provided. In addition, catching headings and distinct paragraphs are specifically created. The unique way of the structure of the table of content also serves to reveal at a quick glance the thematic presentation of lectures and the contents thereof. Instead of a subject index normally featured in books of this nature, it is believed that a detailed table of contents is a better means for quick and easy accessing the substantive contents of the lectures found in this book. In a few instances, text of a more or less similar nature is found in more than one place. This is deliberately done to maintain the holistic structure of the topics concerned.

Thus, this is not just an introductory text. The comprehensiveness, the details and the unique characteristics of the contents, and its thematic structure and in-depth analysis should serve hopefully as a valuable source for information, ideas, insights, perspectives for readers doing advanced research and study in a field of law concerned.

Since the publication of the first edition in 2005, important developments in the law of political morality have happened. Many of such developments have been added to further illustrate the systemic and interactive nature of the Anglo-American law.

In addition to the revision and improvement in the text on substantive issues, correction, change, and improvement in style, spelling, grammar, and syntax have also been made.

The mistakes, defects and weaknesses in the text of the first edition materialized was primarily due to both the negligence on the part of author and the fact that the author was not able to review the text before printing.

In addition to the many books that inform these lectures, an amply number of footnote references have been provided. Footnotes have also been completed and standardized wherever called for. There are still a few places where bibliographical information is not completely given. It is to be hoped that in the advanced age of digitalized world, it is more profitable to resort to online sources, proprietary or those in the public domain, to identify a case, article, or monograph than a printed source that in general is not be readily accessible, especially for students studying outside North America. Ditto the citation of cases to the established format of printed law reports, as these are no less easy to get hold of. Whereas, it is a growing trend for governmental bodies, especially courts to publish their decisions and other information of public interest on their official websites.

In order to keep the book within a manageable size, Chapter nine on Civil litigation and Chapter ten re Legal research and legal materials have been deleted from this second edition. Please refer to the first edition for discussion.

There have always been voices that the law should be written in the common, everyday language and that legal writings should be equally popularized. Coming from students whose mother tongue is in a language other than English, such voice is quite understandable. However, the language of law has always been drafted, written, and spoken in a sort of normal language heavily informed by certain special terms, concepts, and complex syntaxes which would be extremely cumbersome, if not difficult to be translated into common, ordinary everyday language. Even text that appears to be in popular language may carry a heavy dosage of special, technical meaning. The requirement in some jurisdiction for jury instruction to be given by the presiding judge in plain English is one notable exception. So, the author tries wherever feasible to make the text easily comprehensible; it is highly advisable that one should also try to internalize unique, if not esoteric, language of law.

Fortunately, common language has in fact already found its way in legal text. The legal rules made by judges are factual based and written in plain language. Recently, a strong stream of bright light may soon begin to shine through one of the most important legislation. President Obama's new, no short of a revolutionary nature, proposed overhaul of the financial sectors will five regulators the power to set tough new rules so that companies compete by offering innovative products that consumers actually want and actually understand. Those ridiculous contracts he said—pages of fine print that no one can figure out—will be a thing of the past. You'll be able to compare products, with descriptions in plain language, to see what is best for you.

However, in order to further easy comprehension, we include in this edition a brief introduction for each chapter and a few review and reflective questions at the end of each chapter. Furthermore, many of the hard-to-understand words, terms, concepts, etc., have been translated into Chinese and included in the text.

Special thanks must go to teachers Wang Lujuan, Wang Hongping, Pengjie, Zhang Limin, Shan Chun, who have kindly agreed to participate in the translation project. With their help and participation, the value and importance of this book are considerably enhanced.

Should there be any mistakes, gaps, omissions, inaccuracies, these are the sole responsibility of the author and should not be attributed in any manner and fashion to any institution that is associated with or individual who assisted the author.

Kuolee Li
April, 2010, Toronto, Canada

修订版前言

本教材是根据我在烟台大学法学院的授课内容编写的,是对第一版的修正和更新。其中部分内容参考了相关问题的一些著作,参考文献在本书最后列出。书中其他内容是本人的观点和研究成果,这些在大多数英美法书籍中是没有涉及的,但我相信它们是英美法整体中密不可分的一部分。本书的研究对象主要是美国法和美国法律制度,这是因为美国不仅沿用了与大陆法系国家成文法系统相对的普通法体系,并且美国拥有世界上最丰富和最有影响力的法律和法律制度,它的国际影响是前所未有、无法逾越的。

目前大多数以普通法为内容的英美法专著在一定程度上说是缺乏系统性的,因而实际仅仅是对英美法的简介,其行文没有组织结构,内容很大程度上是一堆相关材料的堆集和罗列,全无有意义的体系构建和前后联结。

这些书可谓只见树木,不见森林。可以说,这样的书之所以不成功主要是由于没有对法律整体以及英美法做适当的概念界定。另一个问题在于这些作者误认为法律渊源是真正的法律,同时,他们也忽视了探寻诉讼中的法律所最终呈现出最具意味的权威有效的动态裁判过程。此外,早期专著没有正确地在政治和道德层面上剖析法律的本质与精英权力之间的互动关系。

本教材中的内容着力于英美法的构成和特征,书中许多地方都表现了这一点,而实体法的内容尤其是私法方面没有涉及。因此,书中几乎没有这方面的讨论,当谈到私法命题时,更多的是从法律制度这一宏观的角度来探讨的。

相反,本教材的重点放在了现实发生的热点问题上,比如司法判例或更广泛领域的一些案例,其中包括正在发生的经济衰退、金融危机以及监管方案、紧急援助计划和国有化与救市计划。这些焦点和问题囊括了各种对立概念的激烈交锋,如大政府与小政府、自由主义与保守主义、控制监管导向与自由放任的资本主义市场经济、国家权力与社会力量、公共权威与私人力量之间的关系和相互作用等。这些研究也强调了立法、裁判执行和司法消极性的基础性地位,最主要的是我们通过现实在国家权力和社会参与两方面阐述了精英权力的本质和影响,以及权力和效力的关系和区别。

其他的英美法导论书籍往往不注重强调对英美法系统性的理解。因此在本书中我们有叫做"英美法与你"的专章讲述良好的法律制度的构建、美国法和法律推理。即使在一些争议性问题上,我们也选择了体制和程序性的问题进行探讨。

　　本教材的重点在于造法、法律废除与法律修改的操作过程而非死板无趣的实体法律规范本身或是大而化之的基本原则。我们应当关注裁判如何作出，裁判者与法源如何相互影响以及通过判决最终形成法律规范的过程。其中，中心议题就是法律渊源与裁判者的交互作用。这一点以及法律规范的最终形成就构成了学习和研究英美法的关键。

　　为便于了解和定位具体章节和信息，我们给读者编排了详细的目录，还特别设置了醒目的标题和明确的段落。这种目录结构的特别之处有利于迅速浏览主题介绍及其内容。比起这类书籍所常用的论题检索，这种方式更有助于读者定位和查找教材中的相关内容。教材中有些相似的内容会出现在不止一个章节中，这也是为了该命题以及整本教材的完整性和体系性。

　　因此，这不仅仅是一本导论，它的内容、细节、文章特点、命题结构以及深度的分析可以作为读者获取信息、观点、内涵、前景，以及进一步研究和学习相关法律领域的宝贵来源。

　　本书自从2005年第一版出版以来，政治和道德领域方面又有了很多重要的发展。我们收录了一些新的发展内容来进一步探寻英美法的内在特性和体系。

　　本书第一版中的错误、瑕疵及不足之处主要是由于作者的疏忽以及作者未能在交付印刷时对文章做全面检查。

　　除了教材中的参考文献外，相关的大量脚注也在教材中需要的位置做了规范的标注。还有部分文献我们没有标出，这主要是因为，在这样一个数字时代，对读者来说，尤其是非北美地区的学生，比起使用常规的不易获取的印刷材料，上网利用私人或公共资源检索案例、文章、专题报告无疑是更简便易行的办法。照抄那些法律报告上现成的案例是再容易不过的了，现今政府机关尤其是法院确常常将它们的判决及其他有关公众利益的信息公布到官方网站上。

　　为了控制篇幅，第二版中删除了第九章"民事立法"及第十章"法律检索和法律资源"，相关内容请参见第一版。

　　人们总是希望用日常语言来表述法律，从而使之被广泛地接受和理解，对于英语是第二语言的学生来说这种想法是可以理解的。然而当起草法规、撰写文书及口头陈述的时候，我们往往使用特定的规范性词汇、术语概念和句式，这就使得法律语言无比晦涩难懂，更别说翻译成普通的日常语言了。即使有的文章看起来是用日常语言书写的，文章的含义和内容也还是十分复杂和专业。当然，有时候主审法官要用通俗易懂的语言指导陪审团的情况除外。因此，作者尽可能地使本书的内容易于理解，建议读者尝试从内在理解这种特殊的而非难懂的法律语言。

可喜的是，日常语言已经出现在法律写作中，法官造法实际上来源于用日常语言表达，近来这种现象已出现在重要的立法之中。奥巴马总统对金融行业革命性的新一轮检视将敦促权力机关颁布严厉的法规，从而使商家在为消费者提供他们真正需要、真正理解的新产品的层面上竞争。他说，那些厚厚一叠却不知所云的荒唐合同将成为过去，你可以通过日常语言缩写的说明来比较产品，看哪个是适合你的。

不过为了更便于读者理解，我们在第二版中的每一章都增加了简介，并在章末附上了复习及提问。此外，我们将一些难懂的单词、术语、概念翻译成中文附在文中。

特别要感谢参与本书翻译工作的王鲁娟老师、王洪平老师、彭婕老师以及张丽敏、单纯，他们的参与使本书的价值得到了提升。

若书中出现任何错误、缺失、疏忽及不准确之处，由作者本人负责，与协助作者的其他人员无关。

李国利

2010年4月于加拿大多伦多

Preface

This publication is the revised text of the content of lectures given at the Faculty of Law, Yantai University. Some of the lectures are based on a number of books on the subjects included. Other lectures included are the results of my own findings and views. As such, these are not normally found in books of this nature. But in my opinion, they are very much an integral part of the subject matter, Anglo-American Law. The main focus of the lectures is on the law and legal system of the United States. This is primarily due to the fact that not only the United States has adopted the Common law tradition, it has the most rich and vibrant law and legal system in the work and has an unprecedented and unsurpassed influence internationally.

The lectures purport to emphasize the systemic components, features, and characteristics of Anglo-American Law. This is evident from the content of the lectures. No subject components of any substantive law, especially private law are included. What are generally missed or overlooked by other introductory works on Anglo-American Law have been particularly chosen to strengthen the systematic nature of Anglo-American Law properly understood. Thus, one finds in this work a chapter on Anglo-American Law and you, the building of a good legal system, United States law in action, legal reason, legal research and legal materials.

The systematic emphasis of the lectures is purported to stress the process and operation of the making, unmaking and remaking of the law rather than inanimate nature of substantive rules. The emphasis is on how decisions are made, how decision-makers interact and how a rule of law finally emerges. The central theme of the emphasis is interactivity between sources and decision-makers. How and why decision-makers interact and how and why the law finally emerges is believed to be an important element in studying Anglo-American Law.

For ease of learning and locating any specific text and information, a detailed table of content is deliberately structured. In addition, catching headings and distinct paragraphs are specifically created. The unique way of the structure of the table of content also serves to reveal at a quick glance the thematic presentation of lectures and the content thereof. Instead of a subject index normally featured in books of this nature, it is believed that a detailed table of content is a better means of access. In a few instances, text of a more or less similar nature is found in more than one place. This is deliberately done to maintain the holistic structure of the topic concerned.

In addition to the many books that inform these lectures, an amply number of footnote references have been provided. However, should there be any mistakes, gaps, omissions, inaccuracies, they are the sole responsibility of the author and should not attributed to any institution or individual that is associated with the author.

Kuo-Lee Li
Center for Study of Anglo-American Law
December 28, 2004
Yantai University, China

TABLE OF CONTENTS

Chapter One: Anglo-American Law and You   *1*
  Section One: A Political and Moral Perspective—I Am the Law   *1*
  Section Two: Anglo-American Law Defined   *3*
    A. Common law(共同法或习惯法、普迪法) Countries   *5*
    B. The Subjects of Common law   *6*
  Section Three: Study of Anglo-American Law—Why, What, and How   *6*
    A. What is or Counts as Foreign Law—Definition and Clarification   *7*
    B. Why for the Study of Anglo-American Law   *8*
    C. Reasons for Study—A Summary   *10*
    D. Implications of Globalization of Law: International Trade, Commerce, and Private Law—Unification and Uniform Application   *11*
    E. Similarity of Private Law Worldwide   *13*
  Section Four: Factors and Considerations Affecting Choice of Foreign Law   *15*
    A. Foreign law chosen on the basis of shared history and tradition   *15*
    B. Foreign law chosen on the basis of superior human value conditions   *15*
    C. Foreign law chosen on the basis of special relationship   *15*
    D. Foreign law chosen on the basis of superior legal structure and framework   *16*
    E. Foreign law chosen on the basis of the rationality of the substantive content of its laws   *16*
  Section Five: Methodology and Approach of Foreign Law Study   *17*
    A. How Should Anglo-American Law Be Studied   *18*
  Section Six: Importance of Knowledge of Legal Research and Legal Materials   *21*
  Section Seven: Need for the Study of Foreign Law in Vernacular   *22*
  Section Eight: The "What" (the Subject Matter) of Study   *22*
    A. Hot Topics and In-demand Subject or Issue: Reactive Research   *22*
    B. Topics or Issues for Scholarly and Theoretical Research   *24*
    C. Study the Common Law as a Unique Legal System   *24*
    D. Study the Philosophical Ideas Informing Anglo-American Law   *25*

Section Nine: Sources, Texts, and Materials of the Study of
    Anglo-American Law   27

Section Ten: Conditions and Factors Determinative of the Need and
    Viability of Legal Transplant   27

Chapter Two: Sources of Law in General   30

Section One: Codes(法典) and Statutes(制定法)   30

Section Two: Regulations(规章,条例), Decrees(判决,裁定), and
    Administrative Directives(行政命令、行政规章)   31

Section Three: Binding Nature or Significance of Administrative Directives   32

Section Four: Judicial Decisions   32

Section Five: Non-state or Unofficial Sources of Law   33
    A. Reason as a Source   33
    B. Fundamental Importance of Doctrine or Legal Writing: Scholarly Law   34
    C. Interdisciplinary Research and Works as Sources   35
    D. Intelligence, Idea, Proposal, and Recommendation as Source   35

Section Six: Legal Pluralism and Legal Centralism—Written Law(成文法)
    vis-a-vis Unwritten Law(不成文法), Express vis-a-vis
    Implicit Law, Law in Book vis-a-vis Law in Action   37
    A. Pre-(state) Law(国家成立前的法律)   37
    B. Relative Insignificance of Judicial Law (Settlement of Disputes)   38
    C. Implicit Law, Unwritten or Autonomous Ordering   38

Section Seven: Custom   45

Section Eight: Sources of American Law Worthy of Special Mention   48
    A. Statute Law   48
    B. Constitution as a Source   50
    C. Treaties(条约) and International Agreements   50
    D. Administrative Law(行政法)   51
    E. Compilations and Consolidations of Laws   52
    F. Court Rules   52
    G. Uniform State Law   52
    H. Secondary Authority   53
    I. Restatement of Law: Nature and Status   54
    J. View of Formalism(形式主义) versus Realism(现实主义) as to What
        Counts as Law   55

K. Authoritative and Effective Decision as a Source 55
L. Integration of All Sources of Law-Generating Actions and Decisions 57
Section Nine: Reason as a Source (of Law) 58

Chapter Three: The Common Law 61
Section One: Historical Development of the Common Law 61
    A. First, The Anglo-Saxon Period(盎格鲁—撒克逊时代)(Preceding the Norman Conquest, 1066) 62
    B. Second, Formation of the Common Law (1066-1485): From Writs(令状) to Actions on the Case 62
    C. Third Period: Growth of Equity(衡平法) (1485-1832) 64
    D. Fourth Period: The Modern Period 67
Section Two: Special Characteristics of English Law of English Law 69
    A. Distinct Characteristics of English Common Law 69
    B. Courts Decide Fate of Statutes through Interpretation 73
    C. Courts Apply Principles Derived from Statutes 73
Section Three: Certain Characteristics of the Common Law Authority 73
Section Four: Sources of the British Common Law 75
Section Five: Importance of Legal Structure, Defining Categories and Concepts 75
Section Six: English Judicial Organization 76
Section Seven: Judicial Authority in England 78
Section Eight: Form and Content of English Judgments 79

Chapter Four: Legal System and Foundation of Law of the United States 81
Section One: General Remark 81
Section Two: Reasons for Choice of Focus 82
Section Three: Spirit and Fundamental Characteristics of American Law and Society 83
    A. Liberty, Rights, and Government by Consent 84
    B. Individualism, Competing Values, and Personal Choice 84
    C. Distrust of Government: Separation and Limitation of Powers, Checks and Balances(政府机关彼此之间的相互制衡), Political Accountability, and the Bill of Rights 84
    D. Pragmatism in Law(法律的实用主义) 86
    E. Government under the Rule of Law 87
    F. Tolerance 88

            G. Optimism   89

            H. Unity out of Diversity(差异带来的统一或联合)   90

            I. Diversity as Divisiveness(差异引起的分歧): Disquieting Factors and
               Troubling Voices(不安定因素和声音)   91

            J. American Greed   91

            K. Corporate Bonuses, Compensations and Other Perks and Imprudence   92

            L. A Nation of Excessive and Cheap Credit and Voracious Debtors   93

    Section Four: Basic Constitutional and Political Structure   93

    Section Five: Division and Limits of Legal Authority of the United States   95

            A. Originality of American Law   96

            B. Place of Statute in American Law: the Abnormal or Excessive Attitude toward
               Statute   96

    Section Six: Allocation of Legal Authority between Federal and State
               Governments   97

            A. Inherent Legal Authority of the States   97

            B. Jurisdiction of Federal Law versus Jurisdiction of State Law   97

            C. Supremacy Clause   99

            D. Preemption Controversies(优先适用争议)   99

            E. Derivative Principle of Preemption Clause(优先适用条款的派生原则) 100

            F. Continued Importance of State and Local Law   100

    Section Seven: Judicial Organization   100

            A. Organization of Courts   100

            B. Administrative Agencies and Tribunals(行政机关和行政法庭)   101

            C. State Courts(州法院)   102

            D. Jury   102

    Section Eight: Allocation of Judicial Authority   103

            A. General Allocation   103

            B. Two Primary Bases of Federal Jurisdiction   103

            C. Structure Parallel Systems of Adjudication: Judicial Dualism(司法二元主义) 104

            D. Foreign Sovereign Immunities Act(外国主权豁免法), 28 U.S.C,
               Para. 1330   104

            E. Jurisdiction of the Supreme Court   105

    Section Nine: Reception of the Common Law in the United States   106

            A. Ignorance and Slight of the Common Law   107

B. Influence of the Codification Movement	*107*
C. Triumph of the Common Law	*108*
Section Ten: Is There a United States Common Law or a Distinct Common Law for Each State Individually	*109*
A. Different Social and Economic Conditions Produced Diverse Common Law	*109*
B. The Common Law Develops Along the Same Line and Way as Legislation: Federal and State	*110*
C. Complicating Factors	*110*
Section Eleven: The Cohesion and Unity of American Law	*112*
Section Twelve: Unifying State Common Laws—Role of State and not Federal Courts	*116*
Section Thirteen: Codification of American Common Law	*117*
Section Fourteen: A Systematic Statement of the Common Law	*118*
Section Fifteen: Protection from the Burdens of Multi-State Legal Authority	*118*
A. Tradition of Uniform Laws	*118*
B. Constitutional Limit on the Reach of State Court Jurisdiction and Choice of Law	*120*
C. Negative Commerce Clause	*121*
Chapter Five: Case Law: Form, Nature and Function of Judicial Decisions	*123*
Section One: Form and Content of Judicial Decisions	*123*
Section Two: The Judicial Function	*124*
Section Three: Meaning and Scope of the Rule of Precedent in British Law	*125*
Section Four: Doctrine of Stare Decisis and its Justification	*126*
Section Five: The Doctrine of Stare Decisis and Ratio Decidendi or Holding of a Case	*126*
Section Six: Transforming Facts into Binding Legal Rules	*127*
Section Seven: In Search of an Ideal Holding or Ratio Decidendi of a Case	*128*
Section Eight: Rule of Precedent and Statute Law	*129*
Section Nine: Obiter Dictum: Definition and Clarification	*130*

Section Ten: Ratio, Obiter, and Principle: Distinction or Confluence
(Conflation)   *130*

Section Eleven: Doctrine of Stare Decisis in United States Law   *132*

Section Twelve: The Overriding Importance of the Opinions of the
Appellate Courts   *133*

Section Thirteen: Factors Likely to Figure in Distinguishing Decisions   *133*

Section Fourteen: Opposing Treatments of Precedents   *134*

Section Fifteen: To Distinguish or to Overrule(推翻先例)   *135*

Section Sixteen: Multi-legged Holding   *136*

Section Seventeen: The Retroactive Effect(追溯力) of Application of
Judicial Decisions   *136*

Section Eighteen: Contradiction and Tension between Predictability and
Hard Cases(疑难案件)   *140*

Section Nineteen: More Characterizations of the Common Law   *141*

Section Twenty: Is the Common Law a Living Law   *143*

Section Twenty-one: The Common Law—Vitality, Staying Power, and
Continuing Relevance   *144*

Section Twenty-two: Common Law in the Welfare State of the Twentieth
Century—the Age of Statutes   *146*

**Chapter Six: United States Law in Action(诉讼中的): the Operative
and Interactive Dynamics**   *148*

Section One: The Defining Character and Spirit of Anglo-American Law   *149*

Section Two: The Contrast between Law in Action and Law in Book   *149*

Section Three: Sites, Sources, and Manifestations of Law and Legal
System in Action: State and Non-state   *154*

Section Four: The Life of Law in Common Law America: Selective
Accounts of the Interactive Dynamics of Elite Power
Decisions   *159*

  A. Check and Balance: The Overriding Principle of Interactivity(互动性原则)   *160*

  B. Exemplary Interactive Relationships Between the President, the Congress,
the Court and the States   *160*

  C. Life and Fate of Legislation   *165*

  D. Judicial Attitude toward Legislation: The Legal Standing or Status of
Legislation in the Legal System   *167*

E. Place of Statute in American Law　　168
F. Transforming Statutes into Common Law: The Life of Statute Takes on the Form of the Common Law　　169
G. Nature and Content of the United States Code　　170
H. Constitutional Activism of the Judiciary　　170
I. Measures Taken to Counter Anti-democratic(反民主的) or Unpopular Judicial Review　　175
J. Life and Fate of a Common Law Rule or a Common Law Case　　177
K. Role of Lawyers in Shaping Judicial Law　　179
L. Transforming Judicial Law by Legislative Decision or Executive Action　　180
M. Judges and Judge-made Law versus Legislatures and Legislation　　181
N. Scholarly Rendering and Exposition of Legislation　　183
O. Formation of Leading Cases(援引的判例): the Role and Contribution of Jurists　　184
P. Scholars and Scholar's Law versus Judges and Judicial Law　　184
Q. Inherent Self-contradiction and Internal Creative Destruction of Legislative, Executive and Judicial Authority　　187
R. Some Anecdotal Observations of the United States Legal System in Action　　188
R. The Democratic Process of United States Law in Action　　190
S. Conclusion—Some Tentative Ideas on What Count as Law in General and Anglo-American Law in Particular　　192

Section Five: Some Critical Observations on the Law of the United States in Action: Phenomenon of Idealization of Law(法律的理想化), Juridification Saturation(法律的饱和) of Society and Hypertrophying of Law and Legal Reason　　193

Section Six: Modes and Levels of Dispute Resolution　　195

Section Seven: Critique of the Efficiently Processed Dispute Theory and its Notorious Conclusions　　197

Section Eight: In Search of an Emerging Law　　201

Chapter Seven: Good Legal System, Good Laws, and Good Decision-makers Lawyers　　212

Section One: Legal System and System of Law Distinguished　　212

Section Two: Good Legal System Produces Good Laws　　214

A. The Formal and Procedural Requirements for a Good Legal System　　215

  B. Legal Proceduralism   *216*

 Section Three: Good Law Informs Good Legal System   *218*

  A. Substantive Moral Requirements for a Good Legal System   *218*

  B. Democratic Foundation and Spirit of Law and Legal System   *221*

  C. Democratizing Law-making (Authoritative and Effective Decision) Process   *224*

  D. Open and Transparent Decision-making   *227*

  E. Right to Know and Freedom of Access to Information   *231*

  F. Elite Powers and Democracy   *233*

  G. Equality before the Law: Equal Protection of the Law   *234*

  H. Timely Access to the Court   *238*

  I. Non-retroactive Application of Legislation   *241*

 Section Four: The Virtue of Legal Simplicity   *242*

  A. General   *242*

  B. Some Defining Elements of Legal Simplicity   *249*

 Section Five: The Falsity of Legal Complexity   *249*

 Section Six: Private Ordering versus State Law   *256*

 Section Seven: Transnational Components of the National Legal System   *260*

 Section Eight: Human Elements of a Good Legal System and Good Law   *264*

  A. Rule of Law versus Rule of Man   *264*

  B. Good Lawyer, Good Legal System and Good Laws   *271*

  C. American Law Schools and Legal Education   *276*

  D. The Conditions and Requirements of A Good Judge   *286*

  E. Condition and Requirements of A Good Politician   *299*

  F. Condition and Requirements of A Good <u>Legal Scholar</u>(法学学者) or Jurist   *318*

  G. Conditions and Requirements of a Good Citizen   *321*

  H. Conditions and Requirements of a Good Corporate Citizen   *329*

Chapter Eight: Legal Reason and Executing Decision   *340*

 Law and Legal Reason   *343*

  A. Nature of Legal Reason   *344*

  B. Content or Material Bases of Legal Reason   *346*

  C. Distinctive Nature and Superior Status of Reason   *349*

  D. Reason and Discretionary Decision   *353*

  E. Allure and Rick of Legal Reason   *354*

  F. Evaluation and Balancing of Reason   *357*

G.	Authoritative and Effective Decisions and Justifying Reason	*359*
H.	Truth and Myth of Judicial Reason	*360*
I.	Moral, Epistemological Pluralism, and Incommensurability	*365*
J.	Limits of Legal Reason and Limits of Knowledge	*368*
K.	Reason Runs out	*369*
L.	Subjective versus Objective Reason	*372*
M.	Reason, Faith, and Other Belief Systems	*373*
N.	Belief in Disguise of Reason	*376*
O.	Legal Reason is a Noble Scam: The Self-Referential Nature of Law and Legal Reason	*378*
P.	Beyond Reason, beyond Law; without Reason, without Law	*381*
Q.	Law, Reason and Deep, Divisive Social Issues	*384*
R.	Critique of Cynicism, Defeatism and Self-denial of Law and Reason —"As If Jurisprudence"	*386*
S.	Doubters' Law and Legal Reason	*387*
T.	Truth in Law and Reason	*388*
U.	Emotion Figures Large in Political and Moral Decision-Making Process	*393*
V.	Defending and Redeeming Reason	*394*
W.	Re-imagine and Re-conceptualize Law and Reason	*397*

Chapter One: Anglo-American Law and You

Introductory Note

To study Anglo-American law, one must first have a political and moral stance and perspective. Who you are and what you want to accomplish determine very much why, what and how Anglo-American law should be studies.

Therefore, in the very beginning of this book, we stress the importance of perspective, examine the why, what and how, the choice of Anglo-American law as foreign law, the subject matter, and even the philosophical ideas informing Anglo-American law.

简介

在学习英美法前,学习者应当有一定的政治和道德的立场和视角。学习者对自己的定位和想要达到的目标对于为什么要来学习英美法,要学习英美法的哪些内容及如何学习英美法起着至关重要的作用。

因此,在本书的开篇,我们再次强调一下不同视角的重要性,并审视自己为什么要将英美法作为国外法的学习对象,要学习哪些内容、如何来学习英美法,以及了解相关讨论的主题,甚至从哲学的角度来思考英美法。

Section One: A Political and Moral Perspective—I Am the Law

You are the center of the legal universe. Anglo-American law is part of that universe, same as your domestic law. This is true whether you take the nationalist perspective of law or the internationalist perspective of law. How do you live through your experience with Anglo-American law will inform, define, and shape that normative universe—a universe that aspires to and cherishes liberty, democracy, equality, justice and other highly regarded values of political morality. This legal normative universe is a shared and collaborated one: you share it with all citizens who take an internal view of it in conduct guidance and criticism. What form, content, character, objectives and functions of this shared and collaborated normative universe will take depends very much on your intelligence, imagination, efforts, devotion, and commitment. You are the protagonist and active agent of this inclusive, shared, and evolving normative universe. You are its master.

Your response to the idea above may be fast and sharp. You would retort by saying that this is incredible, unrealistic, and even fantasy; I am not even the master of my house, or the legal universe of my own country, let alone the master of the Anglo-American law world. From where I am to where I could be, it is a long and difficult journey if it is possible. The prospect looks like an ever-fading horizon.

Aim high and hit low. While there is a will, there is a way. You are the creator of your destiny and world. First, you must have a right perspective. You have to mobilize the power of intention, efforts, devotion, and commitment. The power of intention and a heart-felt and life-long commitment would bring you to the destiny of your free will. Your perspective may be that of a nationalist or an internationalist. You may take a stance from an external or an internal point of view. These perspectives and stances will and must converge at a proper time in the future and form a unity, if not in reality, at least in your conception of the legal normative world.

There is no law other than the living law in action that is the law operating in the real world in our daily lives.

From the insightful perspective of Justice Oliver W. Holmes[*], it is the exalted status of the moral self, the "I", who creates the outside world, defines truth, and bets on what will be "the prevailing can't help of the majority." The word "I" is one of the first words uttered in human development. Above all, individuals are social and normative agents of change. President Obama's election campaign of change would not be authoritative and effective without the blessing and supporting actions of the nation at large in terms of both power elites and individual citizens.

Empowered by the modern digital world of self-projecting, self-making and remaking as well as mutual informing and shaping, the innovative concept that I am the law is not presumptuous, outrageous or unreasonable. After all, we have iTune, iPod, iPhone, iReport, iTrade, and many other empowering possibilities. The concept is highly creative, theoretically and realistically rich; it is extremely and

---

[*] 霍姆斯大法官,美国联邦最高法院大法官,任职期间为 1902—1932 年。

unprecedentedly powerful and challenging; its impact is far-reaching and significant. Whatever social economic, political circumstances and conditions we find ourselves in and whatever difficulties, constraints, and predicaments that come along, we strive to conduct our lives and make necessary decisions. It is "I" who finds, evaluates, accepts, rejects, criticizes, predicts, guides, and projects. Along with republicanism, there is liberalism, in collectivity, we find individuality, and to counter a conditioned self, we assert our context-breaking free soul.

This is just to individualize the functions of intelligence, recommendation, invocation, interpretation, application, evaluation, appraisal, and termination in the comprehensive processes of authoritative and effective decision-making of the polite, locally, nationally and internationally as advocated in the seminal works of Myres McDougal and Harold Lasswell and associates at the Yale School of Law. Only when cast in terms of such functional jurisprudence(法理学), can we really start to fully appreciate the innovative, liberating, powerful, and challenging nature of the idea that "I am the law." Just think how the idea that "I am the law" would apply to the role, functions, and possibilities of a judge, a lawyer, a politician, a legislator, a scholar, or a plain citizen.

At the same time, do not let yourself be disarmed and incapacitated by the finiteness of life and the feeling and the sense of frustration and powerlessness as experienced by Holmes. For in many instances and to a significant degree, the feeling and experience of constraint and powerlessness are self-imagined and self-imposed. Instead, we see the political moral self in action even in such instances. Through internalizing barriers, constraints, hardship, and value-deprivation, we set ourselves free, and feeling liberated and empowered.

Remember that you are not alone. You together with many like-minded as a collective political moral force may just be able to change the legal normative world of your image.

Section Two: Anglo-American Law Defined

Broadly speaking, Anglo-American law may be understood to signify the entire body of the law of the English-speaking world. Such a view would include the Common law, all the established sources of law and much more. Narrowly defined, it mainly refers to the Common law tradition. The Common law system as it was conceived by and evolved first in England and later received or adopted in all other countries belongs to that tradition.

The sources of the Anglo-American law world include much more than the Common law—a body of law that was originally derived from the decisions of the royal courts of England as well as the principles developed from these decisions. In its broad conception, Anglo-American law signifies the decisions of the court as well as other established sources of a primary nature. In addition, it encompasses all of the secondary sources of law. Moreover, any broad and realistic conception of the sources of law would extend much further to include all law generative events and phenomena. Thus, any comprehensive study of Anglo-American law has to cover the Common law which in modern terminology refers to the law of judicial decisions or judicial law, legislation, and other sources of authoritative and effective decisions, state and non-state.

The main feature of Anglo-American law is that it is a body of law based on judicial decisions—judge made law. More specifically, it adheres to the basic concepts, principles, and values originated from that version of the law as it arose and developed in England. But this should be understood as true as far as private law and a few other subjects are concerned. ①

Some believe that the Common law before anything else is reason. Today, in England, law remains primarily a work of reason distinct from legislation or statute. For example, one does not think of the Common law as a system of "national law"; it is much more; it is "the common heritage of the English-speaking peoples.

In modern welfare states, judicial decisions are not what people are mostly concerned with. What primarily affect their life are legislative, administrative, regulatory decisions, and even rules, regulations, and decisions made in the non-state sectors. It is also important to point out that whatever the traditional view and attitude of lawyers and jurists had toward legislation, legislation has been widely recognized as a major component of Anglo-American law. As a matter of fact, the significance and impact of legislation are of a predominant feature for the life of citizens in all modern welfare states of liberal democracy, including most if not all Common law countries.

The distinction between private law and public law is no longer significant and

---

① P. S. Atiyah and R. S. Summers, *Form and substance in Anglo-American law: a Comparative Study of Legal Reasoning, Legal Theory, and Legal Institutions*, Oxford, N. Y., Clarendon Press, 1987.

even valid. It is not just that the subject matters belonging to the public law field are enormous and multi-purpose and vary greatly in nature and content. The comprehensiveness, inclusiveness, and interrelationship of the laws of a public nature in modern time simply defy easy classification. The nomenclature presently used to signify the nature and subject matter of the law, such as public, private, constitutional, labor, or legislative, judicial, regulatory, is just playing a catching game.

All these areas mentioned above and much more are an integral part of the subject content of Anglo-American law. As judicial decisions potentially cover the entire spectrum of the corpus of the law, all subject matters of the law regardless of their nature, content, and policy goal may take on a judicial law form over times.

Since concept, terminology, open-ended decision-making process, analogous reasoning, fact-based legal rules, judicial review are some of the most notable distinct characteristics of the Common law tradition, these may very well be taken as representatives of the spirit and essence of the Anglo-American law. And even the specific exclusion of certain matters from the jurisdiction of the court may not last forever.

What is of particular significance is that Anglo-American law, for that matter, law in general, has both its static components and its dynamic aspects. In addition to rules, principles, precepts, concepts, there are functions and operations. Law including Anglo-American Law is best understood as a comprehensive process of authoritative and effective decision-making in terms of participant, objective, conditional factor, past trends of decisions, strategy, and outcome.

A. **Common law(共同法或习惯法、普通法) Countries**

Generally speaking, all the countries of the former British colonies belong to the Common law system. Regardless of this shared common legal tradition, however, each country has its own distinctive nationalist legal order, characters, institutions, and structure. This is mainly due to their differences in political structure, historical background, economic and social condition, institution design, and value systems as well as moral view (s) and aspiration. These differences are increasingly and primarily defined through legislation, regulation, policy statements, and other normative manifestations at the various levels of society.

It is fair to say that today, except the major principles, precepts, methodology of reasoning, and other distinct characteristics of the Common law that continue to play an active role in different Common law countries, the Anglo-American law is mainly a national law in terms of substantive content. Today, even the substantive rules of the Common law are no longer commonly applicable throughout the so-called Common law countries. Except on rare occasions, the judicial decisions(司法裁决) of one common law country are not even judicially noticed in another.

B. The Subjects of Common law

Traditionally, the Common law is exclusively a private law—the core of the Common law subject includes Contract(合同法), Tort(侵权法), Property, and Restitution(赔偿法). Understood primarily as an integral body of a judge-made law that is developed on the foundation of the doctrine of stare decisis* and of related judicial techniques, the subject content of the Common law would have to be broadly conceived. In this sense, the term Common law can no longer be limited to private law matters but has to be extended to include all areas of the law, including constitutional law and other public law matters. In this case, the Common law refers more to the comprehensive substantive content of the law as developed by the court of a country belonging to the Common law system than to the decision-making techniques, methodology, process, and other characteristics of the Common law tradition.

Section Three: Study of Anglo-American Law—Why, What, and How

Anglo-American law may be studied as a legal tradition, that is, a study done from the perspective of a country that belongs to the Common law system. Or it may be studied from a perspective of a country belonging to the Civil law system or other legal systems, when Anglo-American law is studied as a foreign law or a foreign legal system. In fact, even countries belonging to the same legal system treat the law of each other as foreign law. On the other hand, Anglo-American law may also be studied by anyone taking an internationalist point of view as an integral part of the legal tradition of the world that includes the domestic law of one's own country.

---

* 遵循先例原则,或称 Doctrine of Precedent,较高级的法院在处理某一类事实确立一项法律原则后,在以后该法院或同级、下级法院在处理案件中同类事实时应遵循该已确立的法律原则。

Whatever the stance is, one should always attempt to design the most effective way or methodology to achieve one's objectives.

What are the objectives of the study of Anglo-American law? Regardless of one's standpoint or perspective, there are basically two major shared objectives. The study is either for reason of authority or for authority of reason. In many instances, the study may be for both, considering the intractable relationship between them. If one's reason for study is to ascertain authority, then one must be fully aware that authority without reason is like a de-robbed or naked emperor.

What is to be included in ones' study? With respect to the choice of subject, topic, issue, etc, it all depends on ones' interest, purpose, need, mandate, and other considerations. Should one study the Anglo-American legal system as a first priority? Could one successfully study any subject, issue, etc, without a good knowledge of the system and its operation? To study the Common law as a unique system, one must pay special attention to its special nature, features and characteristics.

How should Anglo-American law be studied? In other words, what are the approach, technique, methodology, and even materials to be used and applied? This is another priority question.

A detailed discussion of the why, what and how involved in the study of Anglo-American law is undertaken in the sections below.

A. What is or Counts as Foreign Law—Definition and Clarification

Definitive Criteria and Issues

What counts as foreign law? Is Anglo-American law a foreign law? Is nationalism or sovereignty the exclusive criterion? Should foreign law be defined in terms of factors such as political and geographical boundaries, legal tradition, legal system, political, economic, and social linkage or relations, and even institutions? If law is defined as a universal normativity(规范标准) of political morality based exclusively on the dictate of reasons, rationality and morality, then the distinction between national law and foreign law begins to blur. Some go so far to suggest that the term "national" in national law has a restrictive connotation that is appropriated by xenophobes and cultural purists.[②] In other words, all national laws are subsets of

---

[②] R. Macdonald, "National Law Programme at McGill", 13 *Dalthousie L J* 211, 251 (1990).

the international legal order. The concept of foreign law is better understood as a misnomer.

B. Why for the Study of Anglo-American Law

The Need, Reason, and Purpose for the Study of Foreign Law (in our case Anglo-American Law)—Some general insights.

Legal science would become rather provincial, closed, and static, when scholarship and legal study are confined within national political boundaries. This is a wretched and unseemly state.③ The influence of foreign law rings well with Watson's insightful observation that "the native element in the law of any country is relatively slight; law develops mainly by borrowing. Our vision is culturally blinkered; our expertise built on sand or unsystematic, incomplete foundation, a thing of shreds and patches."④ Patrick Glenn views law from the perspective of adoption. In his view, transplantation of law has always been a common phenomenon worldwide.⑤

In this sense, could any enlightenment-conscious student of law who takes an activist role in legal development and reform afford not to study the law of other countries? It is increasingly plain that with globalization having penetrated virtually every corner of our lives and interdependence has become and inescapable force, the law of other countries, domestically or internationally based, must be treated as either reason or authority by every student of law and especially those who are active across national borders.

(1) The Practical Perspectives and Considerations: the Reason of Authority

The need for the study of foreign law is obvious and well known. It is necessitated by globalization in virtually all aspects of the modern life of man—political, economic, social, trade and commerce with its increasing intensification and reach brought upon by interdependence and constant worldwide communications. The demand for expertise and specialists in foreign law is fierce and unprecedented.

All ambitious law schools should and many do in fact aspire to this laudable goal

---

③ Rudolf von Jhering, *Geist des Romische Rechts*, 16th ed., Aalen, 1968, p. 15.
④ *The Making of the Civil Law*, Cambridge, 1981, p. 181.
⑤ Patrick H. Glenn, *Legal Traditions of the World: Sustainable Diversity in Law*, 2nd ed., Oxford, New York, Oxford University Press, 2004.

of foreign law study through the offering by college and university at both undergraduate and graduate levels of programs in some of the most pertinent and important subject areas. Competent and effective lawyering and legal research in foreign law are especially important in an increasingly globalization of law practice and legal culture. To fulfill these objectives would entail a comprehensive and systematic study of international transactions and arrangements, intensive use of policy analysis of insights and experience that may be derived readily from foreign law study and research, and an in-depth exploration of foreign legal system.⑥ This perspective encompasses primarily the searching for binding intrinsic authority. In fact, studying American-Anglo law for practical reasons and considerations falls within the task of identifying, invoking, and applying binding authority in foreign law.

What constitutes binding authority is a practical assessment taking all the relevant information and factors into consideration. Because of the dynamics and complexity involved in the identification, analysis, and project of what is or counts as authority for the issue or problem in question, subjectivity and prediction are bound to play an important role in these exercises. Practical authoritative reasons are quite inclusive, highly variable, and multiple. These may be for doing business, personal and professional need, and diplomatic and international relations, to give just a few examples.

(2) The Theoretical and Juridical Perspective: The Authority of Reason

The search for and study of the authority of reason is not simply for academic or intellectual enlightenment; it may be very well for legal reform and modernization. This is mainly the concern for comparative law study. Comparative study of foreign law is looked upon as a method of epistemic (intellectual) search for just and rational rules, principles, etc., and the underlying reasons. Lon Fuller's moralistic search for best conduct-guiding norms, Roderick Macdonald's study of the imperatives in a polyjurial (多法) normative universe, and even Hans Kelsen's monist view of law all speak strongly and favorably to this perspective. Viewing law as an inter-culture communication and collaboration also serves as an additional impetus and reason for this view.

---

⑥ See, Robert C. Clark, "Building a World Law School: International and Comparative Studies at Harvard", 42(2) *Harvard L Bull* 5 (1991).

C. Reasons for Study—A Summary

Foreign law may be studied from either a nationalist perspective or the internationalist perspective, or both.

Whatever ones' perspective, need, reason, or purpose, the study of foreign law may be divided into the following headings:

(1) Study foreign law as persuasive authority for rational rules and principles serving as normative standards for critical analysis, study, and insight of domestic law for law reform, modernization and progressive development. Teaching foreign law as a subset of an international legal order founded on the basis of a universalistic polyjuriality(多法化) as opposed to a practical stance of studying foreign law as authoritative decisions, given/accepted without doubt. To study foreign law as persuasive authority is to study for authority of reason.

(2) Study foreign law as intrinsic and binding authority for commercial, trade, personal or other practical reasons. This would require a good knowledge of the legal system and the law as it is widely accepted and generally practiced in the foreign country. This is to study for reason of authority.

(3) Study the law, legal structure, and institutions of a country that shares the same legal system for the purpose to nourish and enrich one's own received and cherished legal tradition. For example, for Canada and Quebec, the study of British common law and French civil law falls into this category.

(4) Study foreign law as a subset of the international legal order. From the perspective of Kelsen's monist view of legal order that considers national legal order as a subset of the international legal order, to study foreign law would be even more compelling. The relationship between the international legal order and the national legal order is according to this view comparable to the situation between the state order and the national order within a country constituted on a federal basis.

However, no matter how closely countries within the same legal system, civil or common, are related to each other, and how much common features and characteristics they share, significant differences exist in both substance and operations. These differences and dissimilarities are primarily due to the diversity and variation in their political, economic, social and other value systems. These diversities and variations form the unique characteristics of a country's legal structure and institutions.

(5) Training of Critical Reasoning Faculty: There is another important and distinct purpose for studying American-Anglo law. This is for the training of critical reasoning faculty. The Common law has a unique reasoning and decision-making or legal method. The well-known case method of teaching has been found to be particularly fitting for the training and developing critical reasoning faculty. Common law reasoning is a comprehensive, practical, open-ended and fact-based configurative way of thinking things through. Its breadth and in-depth factual analysis is unmatched and outstanding. It entails a comprehensive, extensive, and comparative study and analysis of past trends of decisions and conditioning factors. And it culminates in a normative and objective-oriented generalization and statement of relevant facts and events. Its reasoning based on precedents and history ensures certainty and predictability, and commands respect.

D. Implications of Globalization of Law: International Trade, Commerce, and Private Law—Unification and Uniform Application

The idea of comparative law study in terms of borrowing, adoption and transplant of law and the idea that law is a subset of a commonly shared international legal order all lend to the phenomenon of the globalization of law.

The increasing and close contact and communications of people worldwide necessitates the need and importance for unifying the provisions of international private law and for ensuring their uniform application. This phenomenon strongly lends support to the perspective of the internationalists.

The development of international community and that of international trade and commerce are closely linked. Both help strengthen the interdependence and the idea of international brotherhood among people of the countries worldwide. The establishment and healthy development of the World Trade Organization and many other international and regional economic and trade structures and arrangements further accelerate the interdependence and globalization of law in trade and commerce especially.

The raison d'etre(存在的理由) for unification and uniform application is not just crucial for the promotion of international transaction, exchange, and communications, but also for the upholding of the fundamental principle of fairness and equal treatment that all players on the international stage are subject to the same set of rules.

All these developments move from the nationalist perspective of law toward an internationalist perspective of law. The prospect of this trend of harmonization, unification, and globalization has proved beyond doubt that Kelsen's notion of considering a national legal order as a subset of the international legal order is a rare and significant insight.

What is ironically interesting and even unfortunate is that due to the excessive influence of the United States in military, economic, technological, and many other fields of human concern, globalization of law has become Americanization of law. As a consequence, the cosmopolitan, universalistic perspective of the normative enterprise of world law has been viewed as an imperialistic attempt of the United States for dominance and control.

Recently, there is a call for a reduction in the number of made-in-Canada regulation respecting rules governing how crops are grown, how foods are labeled, how drugs are approved and how industrial projects are assessed for environmental impact. Some argue that Canada should develop its own regulatory requirements only when they are necessary in order to meet national goals and values. Critics warn that this in fact will mean the widespread adoption of U. S. standards.

In a market based economy flourishing on the soil of free competition, one commands by superior knowledge and sets standard by avant-garde advanced technology. Viewed from this perspective, the phenomenon of Americanization of many fields including law is just a natural development and nothing to be alarmed about. For an example, it has been observed that there are lots of industries where China's market is leading, like cellphones and DVDs. And it is natural for Chinese companies to emerge as leaders in setting standards in those areas. That elite power decides and sets standards is simply a fact of life, internationally and nationally.

One of the latest attempts to coordinate and unify national laws internationally is the following example:

In response to the global economic meltdown and the collapsing of the international financial system, a number of economic summits have been organized by major countries attempting to forth ahead certain coordinated and collective regulatory approaches to deal with the situation. There are two distinct, competing, and even opposing philosophies of political economy. One that favored by members of the European Union including the British calls for the set up of strong, strict rules and frameworks. United States and Canada, on the other hand, advocate a strong nationalist approach with international coordination.

Sensing the urgent need for a strong and timely regulatory action in response to the global financial meltdown and banking crisis, the International Money Fund or IMF urged a new system of government oversight of big hedge funds, private-equity firms and other financial firms whose failure poses a major or systemic risk to the global economy, along with other moves to dramatically widen the scope of international financial regulation. Specifically, IMF suggested that governments adopt a "binding code of conduct across nation" to coordinate how and when they would intercede in troubled firms, and how to share losses from major financial institutions that operate across borders. The IMF proposals are aimed at influencing the April 2, 2009 summit in London of the so-called Group of 20 members. The IMF plays a huge role in the international co-ordination of regulatory policy only. Each of the G-20 nations would have to enact its own rules comparable to the others for any enhanced regulations to operate effectively across borders. The White House and the U.S. Congressional leaders also want to reach a "conceptual agreement" on how to regulate systemic risks in time for the G-20 session. The IMF is endorsing a previous G-20 idea to have the regulation of major financial firms overseen by "colleges of supervisors"—essentially regulators from a financial firm's home country and other countries where it does business. Surely, regardless of the merits of an idea, there is always some dissenting voice. A former official of the Bush Administration alleged that such restrictions could backfire by limiting growth of innovative companies, and could reduce the flow of capital to higher-risk developing nations. ⑦

E. Similarity of Private Law Worldwide

Comparative law study and the resultant mutual adoption and transplant of law among countries along with coordination, cooperation, and unification of law, private and regulatory internationally are directly responsible for the convergence of private law among countries. Thus, it has been said that regardless of the difference in political and social structures, there is a surprising similarity of private law among countries.

Max Rheinstein, the eminent comparative law scholar, once remarked that it was an impressive experience to realize how little the private law systems of the world differed from one another. This is so, notwithstanding the fact that wide divergences

---

⑦ Bob Davis. "IMF Seeks 'Binding Code of Conduct' to Oversee Global Financial Players", *The Wall Street Journal*, later reported in The Global and Mail, March 6, 2009, B7.

might exist in public law between countries of democracies and even authoritarian regimes, between private property and market-based economies and central-planned socialist systems, and even between those belonging to the same political or economic systems. ⑧

Similar private law rules surprisingly flourish in different place, time and people, regardless of the belief that culture, society and law are intractably linked and that uniqueness and particularities in culture and society would entail concomitant characteristics and features in social rules, legal structure and institutions. Civil law code multiplies around the world in defiance of any difference in political, social, and economic condition and development. Legal rule outlasts changes in society and government. The strength and influence of the Common law in many parts of the world also attests to the truth of this view.

Some <u>jurists(法学家)</u> who like to see the Common law as practiced and developed in the United Kingdom, the United States, Australia, New Zealand, India and Canada for example include many of the variations present respectively in these countries as a mutually reinforcing normative system. This is a thesis advocated by unificationists. One wonders whether it would be equally appropriate and valid to view the private law that prevails in countries belonging to the Romano-Germanic* legal system in the same light.

Such view could also be deemed as a universalistic and a polyjurial approach to the study of law. This view rests on the assumption that law arises from principled and rational decisions. Both Justice O. W. Holmes and Professor Frederick Pollock discussed the universality of the Common law in some of their works.

The trend of legal universalism has been further strengthened and supported by the ease of publishing, world-wide dissemination of legal information and writings, by inter-university exchange and reciprocal visiting of legal scholars and lawyers, and by the unification movements of private laws at the international level. What is most interesting and enlightening is the increasing and intensifying trend of publishing the law text by countries on the Internet. This no doubt constitutes a revolutionary and unprecedented strong facilitating force. Political and economic regionalization further solidifies the integration of private laws worldwide. In this respect, the European

---

⑧ Marriage Stability, *Divorce and the Law*, University of Chicago Press, 1972, p.6.

* 罗马—日耳曼体系,又称大陆法系(Continental Law System)或成文法系(Written Law System),发源于罗马法。

Union represents a powerful and shinning beacon. All these go a long way toward stimulating productive transplant and informed practical and theoretical dialogues.

Section Four: Factors and Considerations Affecting Choice of Foreign Law

A. Foreign law chosen on the basis of shared history and tradition

Comparative legal study for the purpose of seeking out persuasive authority in foreign law usually flourishes on the bedrock of shared history and tradition, especially in countries with similar social, political, and economic conditions, and institutions, and with commonly cherished value systems.

However, fidelity to legal tradition is purely due to the impulse of blindly obedience to the founding constitutive moment, a formal authoritarianism(独裁主义). This is increasingly evident as the founding text has been subject to ceaseless, constant and multiple bombardments and changes in its home country and has long lost its originality, and its present face and content are formed and transformed by the contemporary and changing conditions of a social, political, and economic nature in the home country. Thus, to require fidelity to a legal tradition for an adopting country with a completely different conditions and circumstances becomes even more untenable. The only rational thing to do is to regard legal tradition as authority of reason like any other authority informed primarily by its substantive content.

B. Foreign law chosen on the basis of superior human value conditions

From the perspective that law reflects the value quality and conditions embodied in authoritative and effective decisions, it would seem reasonable and natural that the law of some of the most successful and powerful countries in the political, social, economic, military, environmental, or human rights field should be chosen. The assumption is simply that countries that excel in most of these important areas of human dignity values would most likely enjoy a more just and effective legal system and a healthy corpus of good laws.

C. Foreign law chosen on the basis of special relationship

Special relationship in this connection may be political, military, economic, social, etc. Due to the dynamics of international relations, the special bilateral relationship between countries may change quickly. And this would also be against the basic belief that private law is founded on the basis of rational and principled decisions. Moreover, the increasing integration and interdependence of countries of the world would make the factor of special relationship largely irrelevant and insignificant. Also it seems that at least the political structures and system of a country have nothing much to do with the legal system the country adopts. Countries belonging to the Common law system differ significantly in constitutional and political setup. So are countries belonging to the civil law tradition.

D. Foreign law chosen on the basis of superior legal structure and framework

Here the concern goes beyond the question of legal system considerations. Its main focus is on the constitutional design and structure and on the organization of political powers, the division and allocation of legal powers as well as judicial powers. In other words, the attention concentrates on the question: Does the foreign country enjoy a superior legal system in a broader sense? The presumption is that a good or superior legal system is more likely than not to have good or superior laws.

Undoubtedly, the criterion of a superior legal structure and framework refers to the formal quality and features of the legal system, not so much to the moral content. One of the most important qualities and features of a legal system is procedural justice(程序公正) or in the terminology of Lou Fuller's "internal morality of law." The qualities that come readily to mind include equality, fairness, consistence, efficacy, public accessibility, non-retroactivity, etc.

To some extent, to choose foreign law on the basis of superior legal structure and institution is similar to the choice of foreign law on the basis of superior human values conditions, though in an inverse sense.

E. Foreign law chosen on the basis of the rationality of the substantive content of its laws

Law is an instrumentality of political morality. Law is social engineering. As such, it seems reasonable to assume that the superior value and material conditions of a country should fairly closely reflect the high rationality of the content of its laws. If such conditions of a society are only an indirect and even an incomplete measurement of the rationality of its laws, what are the direct or unmediated criteria for evaluating a law's rationality? Of course, one possible and even reasonable explanation is that there are glaring, startling disconnects between the law and the social and material conditions.

Morality of law is a subjective notion. It belongs to the realm of natural law. In the section on authority of reasons as a motivation for studying foreign law, we mention the need for an epistemic (intellectual) search for just and rational rules and the underlying reasons, Lon Fuller's moralistic search for best conduct-guiding norms, and Roderick Macdonald's idea of imperatives in a polyjurial normative universe.

Are there credible and reasonable criteria of a practical or realistic nature that can be employed by most, if not all, countries to judge the rationality of the substantive content of the laws of a foreign country? Could it be possible that democracy, principles of equality, such as equal opportunity and chance, fairness and equal concern, non-discrimination on any ground, and human rights fit the bill? Are these the widely shared fundamental values of human dignity?

The great social theorist Max Weber recognized the correlation between a developed capitalist economy and a highly developed legal system. Security, certainty, and predictability are extremely important values for voluntary economic activity, such as property, contracts, and commercial transactions. It is therefore not surprising that one finds that the most highly developed legal systems and rational laws are in the most advanced capitalist countries of Europe and North America.

<u>Marxists</u>(马克思主义者), <u>anarchists</u>(无政府主义者), and other radicals of various persuasions all hold the view that the law of a capitalist society serves as a tool of oppression and a protector of inequality and special interests. But oppression, inequality, and special interests exist in countries around the world regardless of the nature of economic system, capitalist, socialist, market-based, or central-planned. Such criticism simply does not in any way derogate from the truism that law closely relates or reflects the values and material conditions of society.

Section Five: Methodology and Approach of Foreign Law Study

What approach and methodology should one adopt in order to ascertain either intrinsic authority or extrinsic authority in Anglo-American law? Does purpose or reason affect the choice of materials, methodology, and approach?

Certainly, if reason of authority, that is, the extrinsic binding decision, is the object, to verify the validity and the authority of the law must be of a primary concern. For this reason, some of the research finding tools, materials, and methodology for up-dating the status of authority as well as the expository and critical works on the subject or issue must be consulted. Conversely, if authority of reason is what one looks for, tools and materials used for up-dating status of authority may not be as important and necessary. Instead, works of an expository and critical nature in both the subject area and its related fields could be very well sufficient.

In identifying and ascertaining reason of authority, one must carefully distinguish sources of law from law in action. Here not only the materials to be used may be different, the methodology and approach could also be different. When law or legal authority in action is sought, one must look beyond the established sources of law and research tools and focus attention on the authoritative and effective decision-making process and the interactivity of mutual informing and shaping between elite powers. The emphasis is on the empirical over the theoretical, operational dynamics over conceptual in-animated rules, principles, etc.

A. How Should Anglo-American Law Be Studied

(1) Macro versus Micro Perspective

First, one may take a macro view and study a particular legal system in its entirety; in this case, history, development, and the trends of past and future decisions respecting the legal system all have to be considered. Also at the macro level, one may regard entire corpus of the law of a country as a comprehensive, if not complete, entity of its normative enterprise. In this sense, one could in a way view the constitution as the root, the laws in the various subject areas, such administrative, labor, etc., as the multiple trucks, and the individual laws as leaves and flowers. Here, one examines the structure, internal connectedness, consistency, etc. Second, at the micro level, one's concentration may be very well limited to a particular topic, issue, subject, subject area, concept, or institution, etc.

How the two types of study and perspective are mutually informing and strengthening should be of particular concern. This is especially true for a comprehensive study of the entire life story of the law in the chosen subject. Thus, how the legal system of the country operates in reality must be attended to when studying any particular issue, problem, subject matter, etc.

As the legal process of authoritative and effective decisions encompasses a number of distinct functions, such as intelligence, interpretation, application, prescriptive, appraisal, and termination, a study may be selective as to a specific function or inclusive as to all functions of the entire process.

Here again, the distinction between sources of law and law in action must be born in mind and the approach for the identification and ascertainment of the law in action must be employed.

(2) Scope Delimitation in Time and Space

In all cases, one may attempt to refine one's study further. In the case of legal system study, scope may be confined within a particular country, or a group of countries. To study a particular issue, subject, or institution, etc, one may similarly delimit the scope to a single country, group of countries, or to include the study internationally.

As to the temporal scope of one's study, it all depends on the goal and extensity of study. The subject matter studied may also have time implication as it has continuous interest and concern. There is no doubt that any comprehensive study is required to include the historical origin and development, past trends of decisions, conditioned factors, present and contemporary situation and state, and potential future development and prospect.

(3) Study of Foreign Law from the Bad Man's Perspective and Standpoint: for reason of authority largely from an external point of view

For practical purpose, it is necessary to ascertain and study the binding authority of a foreign law on the subject, issue, or point in question. A simple textual or literal analysis of the meaning of applicable legal rules and principles would not be sufficient. Even careful reading of expository and critical works on the subject matter and issue would be not adequate. A bad man's perspective requires first of all the ascertainment and study of all applicable legal rules and principles found in authoritative and binding judicial decisions, and then a close analysis of the benefits of compliance and the costs or value-deprivation for violation or non-compliance. A so-called "bad man" or a pragmatist perspective, formally speaking, would care more for authority and especially the coercive power behind the law than the rationality and substantive moral content of the law. What is mostly likely to happen in application, interpretation, and implementation? What are the immediate and near term practical value impacts of an authoritative and effective decision is the main if not only focus of attention.

Authority recognized from this perspective easily collapses into the concept of efficacy. This is what H. L. A. Hart called "being obliged." What motivates the actor and decision-maker is not moral righteousness and compulsion, justice, fairness, or other intrinsic virtues of a similar kind, but the indulgence or deprivation of human dignity values.

(4) Study Foreign Law from the Internal Perspective/Standpoint: for authority of reason

Comparative study purports to capture the truly internal statement of the law of a country for study or the spiritual essence or moral quality of its law. As such, it must be comprehensive in scope, in-depth in inquiry and investigation, and thorough and extensive in analysis. For a study of this nature and magnitude, simple reading of expository works would not be sufficient. Nor would critical or reformist scholarship be fully satisfactory. What is needed is an extensive and in-depth analysis of the entire spectrum of the life of the law studied as well as everything that figures in the process of the authoritative and effective decisions. In other words, what is needed is a comprehensive approach to the making, unmaking, and remaking of authoritative and effective decisions from the perspective of the so-called "internal statement of law", a concept of law that is vigorously discussed and advocated by Herbert L. A. Hart in his seminal work "The Concept of Law."

Internal statement of law manifests the moral imperative of invoking and applying law for authoritative and effective decisions in the strong sense of an obligation. To study law from this standpoint, one must put oneself in the shoe of the citizens of a foreign country. In other words, one must immerse oneself completely in the political, moral milieu of the country. One must invoke and apply the rules, principles, standards, etc as a compulsory guide for one's own action as well as using the same as a standard for criticism.

From an internal point of view, legal authority may be recognized in a number of ways. Authority so recognized could be what is called authority of reason as well as reason of authority, such as that of a parental, expertise, intellectual, religious, political nature.

Foreign law, in our case, Anglo-American law, can also be studied from an internal perspective of an internationalist. This is similar to Hans Kelsen's insight of treating foreign law as a subset of the international legal order in which one partakes in terms of both authority and reason. Such a critical study of foreign law is made for the purpose of assessing and evaluating whether and to what extent international standards or obligations have been complied with or been violated. Such a study may be taken by individual scholars, international governmental bodies, international non-governmental organizations, or even by the government of one's home country. For an example, the United States publishes a report every year dealing with a host of areas of concerns, particularly human rights, in which compliance, violation, achievement and regression are noted.

Section Six: Importance of Knowledge of Legal Research and Legal Materials

A good lawyer is not the one who knows all the laws—this is virtually impossible—but one who knows how to find the law. No one has either the ability or time to acquire all the knowledge on the law, let alone to up-date the applicable rule found.

Therefore, to be accurate, complete, and up-to-date in the study and analysis of authority, binding or persuasive, one is required to have a good knowledge on the important materials and techniques used in legal research. A foundation course of this nature should be designed precisely for this purpose.

What are the source materials for authority and for reason respectively? How can one be sure that the authority one has identified has in fact the authoritative status and continues to be so? Are different sets of materials, research tools, and methodology required for the ascertainment of authority as opposed to reason? To cast the net even wider, are legal rules, principles, policies, social change and trends, and other related factors all legitimate objects of inquiry and study? Should and to what extent research and study be expanded to include source materials belonging to other disciplines or fields? Inter-disciplinary study readily comes to mind. Should one follow the insight of Myres McDougal and Harold Lasswell of the Yale Law School, the scope of the material sources for authority or reason would be much more inclusive indeed.

Because of its importance, we devote the whole chapter ten to legal research and legal materials. In fact, what constitute the sources of law determines to a great extent the material bases of research.

Section Seven: Need for the Study of Foreign Law in Vernacular

This need is based on the belief that law and legal propositions and statements, like other normative pronouncements, discourses and rhetoric, are full of minute details, and complex or extensive arguments made from an internal point of view. Unless one is sufficiently familiar with the language in which the law and legal materials are written and talked about, one would be hard put to capture correctly the richness, spirit, complexity, subtlety, etc of the law of a foreign country.

Requirement of English Language—English is the common and shared language in all Common law countries. A good knowledge of the English language is the first and prime requirement for the study of Anglo-American law. The complexity and the technical nature of its legal language, its unique terminology and often arcane and esoteric legal concepts constitute an additional hurdle to be overcome. Often many of these terms, notions, and concepts defy translation and can only be correctly comprehended in English language.

Section Eight: The "What" (the Subject Matter) of Study

Law and its life embrace much more than the static and inanimate formulaic rules and their substantial content. They extend by nature and implication to application, interpretation, implementation and other effecting measures and actions. What are equal if not more important are operation and the interaction between elite decision-makers.

A. Hot Topics and In-demand Subject or Issue: Reactive Research

It is no surprise that the study of foreign law may be undertaken in timely response to legislative, regulatory or other instrumentalist or reformist demands or needs. Such demands and needs are often resulted from social, economic, political, ethical, environmental or other change and concern. Hot topic or in-demand research is usually limited in time, jurisdiction(管辖权), subject matter, and/or even material scope. It may even only involve specific source, aspect, and operation of the law. Yet, unlike the task of identifying, invoking, or applying foreign binding authority, responsive research usually expands its horizon to analysis of authority of reason as well. Research of this nature may be embarked on by lawyers, judges, jurists, and even scholars in other related subject fields.

(1) **Codification(法律编纂) of Private Law**

Codification is a major intellectual undertaking in law. In its proper sense, codification is a systematic "juridification(法规化)" and formulation of laws to be included all together in one particular code format as a one-time project. This is unlike the situation where laws on different subjects that have either already been promulgated or will be enacted and put into effect in the future, are consolidate, classified, and published into a codified form. In this way, the distinctive characteristics such as the logical structure and systematic arrangement of the materials as found in a civil code of a country belonging to the civil law system feature equally in the codified laws in the sense of systematic consolidation.

It is reasonable to assume that to codify the private law of a country is an extremely complex, difficult, and deliberated intellectual undertaking. It may be regarded as a reactive research of a special or unprecedented sort. Yet, to ensure the thoroughness and completeness of the project, research and study of a fundamental and scholarly nature is required. As well, in such an undertaking, comparative law study and legal borrowing play a significant role.

Civilians are proud of the greatness of their codes for their organic structure, systemic wholeness, coherence, and elimination of inconsistencies and unequal treatment of similar sets of facts. Substantive harmonization is another virtue of a code. The hallmark of codes is their intellectual rationality and the expunging of special, arbitrary legislative provisions of historical or political origin.

Yet, no code is ever complete, let along perfect. For example, the German civil code includes a long list of losses for uniformity of the law. Many provisions of a comparably stable nature and systematic principles remain outside of the basic codification and difficult to fit into the existing codification without endangering its clarity and integrative quality.[9] Special codification has to be undertaken, even for laws of a civil nature. In addition, change of social conditions and circumstances,

---

[9] F. Bydlinski, "Civil Law Codification and Special Legislation" In: *Questions of Civil Law Codification*. Budapest, Institute for Legal and Administrative Sciences, Hungarian Academy of Sciences, 1990. p. 31.

the rise of new needs, and the enactment of special legislation all have made the undertaking of an ideal civil code extremely challenging. In France, we have similar problems of disintegration. The 1804 Code long lost its integrative value. The system of the codification would be exploded if an attempt were made to incorporate into the code the manifold activities of the French Parliament and government.

B. Topics or Issues for Scholarly and Theoretical Research

In opposing to reactive research, there is the so-called comprehensive study of the legal science or law that is comparable to basic scientific research. The primary objective of this type of study is the discovery of the truth. Truth search in law refers to the pursuit for immanently just and rational norms. Thus, comprehensive, theoretical research is relatively neutral as to subject, issue, jurisdiction, or material. Political or reformist agenda concern or instrumentalist value is not of a prime consideration. Comprehensive study is normally undertaken by legal scholars voluntarily funded or not by public money.

Depending on one's interest, specialization, need, or purpose in pursuing comparative law study, it seems that no subject matter, issue and problem should, by nature or other reason, fall outside of the realm of scholarly and theoretical research. Therefore, the choice of subject matter, etc is mostly a personal judgment.

C. Study the Common Law as a Unique Legal System

What is particularly important to note is that the Common law has a number of distinct and special characteristics and features that are worthy of study and emulation. It is reasonable to assume that the robust and highly influential nature of the Common law approach and methodology worldwide rightly reflects its superior quality and strength.

It would be shortsighted and xenophobia not to learn from foreign substantive law through comparative study. It would be likewise irrational and even irresponsible not to inquire into the unique and special characteristics of another legal system to see if any of its notions, concepts, institutions, techniques, approaches, or processes can be adopted to enhance and strengthen one's own legal system.

Suffice it to say here, the following characteristics or special features desire special mention:

The concept of judge-made legal rules;

Open-ended system of the Common law;

Fact-based and characterized legal rules;

Unique judicial attitude toward legislation;

Process justified decision-making;

The adversary system of adjudication, the prominence of lawyers in the finding of just and reasonable rule;

The relatively retiring role of the judge;

The concept of stare decisis;

The judicial technique of distinguishing cases; and

Judicial review of law(司法审查) and administrative action.

D. Study the Philosophical Ideas Informing Anglo-American Law

Philosophical ideas are ideas of political morality. At the state level and in public spheres, it is political ideology. Philosophy informs policy. Policy takes the form of law that emerges out of the political market place of political, moral philosophy. Explicitly or implicitly, human action is informed and shaped by certain philosophical ideas. Even a newspaper's editorial board has its philosophical underpinning. The editor of the Globe and Mail admitted that it was socially liberal, economically conservative, loudly protective of civil liberties, and generally tilting to the moderate centre-right. ⑩

Law as a social artifact is similarly informed and shaped. So is the Anglo-American law. The last example in the U.S. is that both political parties are trying their best to harness the massive Katrina rebuilding effort to propel their own ideological agendas. Democrats(民主主义者) view this as a once-in-a-generation opportunity to try to reduce poverty and racial inequality, touting more investment in public school construction and housing vouchers. On the opposite side, Conservatives(保守派) see some of their handiwork on the Administration's initial proposals for job-training accounts and private-and parochial-school vouchers, as well as decision to suspend rules requiring federal contractors to pay "prevailing wages" in the region. In enacting the Patriot Act and related laws, "Congress and the White House appear to be moving toward costly command-and-control mandates to get the counter-terrorism protection they deem necessary. The irony is that a

---

⑩ "Agonizing Over Decisions is All Part of an Editor's Job", *The Globe and Mail*, June 19, 2004. p. A2.

corporate leadership seemingly as devoid of a cooperative spirit, patriotism and vision as it is of ethics is driving the movement."

Whether or not federal money should be used to fund stem cell research is greatly influenced by political moral philosophy; The Bush conservatives opposed it for reason of the sanctity of life and man should be play God, while the Obama democrats belief that science and truth should prevail.

No doubt, at the constitutive, political level, natural law exerts an overwhelming influence on the fundamental principles enshrined in the constitution. On the other hand, at the practical level at least, the elite powers in both government and society primarily ascribe to the positive law stance by default. This is especially true for lawyers.

Yet, with the rise of post-modernism(后现代主义), decisions and actions(诉讼) are increasingly informed by many of the emerging schools of law. Whether the claims made by many of these schools are descriptive or prescriptive is still subject to debates. For example, it has been claimed that we are all realists. Many of the treatises on the subjects of private law, such as contract or tort, contain a section on economic analysis. Economics of law scholars think that all laws are informed and can in fact be analyzed by criteria of benefits and costs*. When examining the practice of a government within or outside its national boundaries, one has no difficulty in discerning the evidences of the influence of either legal instrumentalism or policy sciences.

Inquiry into the philosophical idea of law collapses necessarily into the choice of methodology and approach. As a matter of fact, the questions of why, how, and what are closely linked. In this connection, it would most advisable that if possible all the major treatises written by established theorists in law should be intensively studied. And in time, somehow one may be able to really capture the philosophical ideas underpinning the law in action. This book expounds a particular philosophical insight developed through a life-long study of the ideas of western theorists of law. Some of these ideas are articulated throughout the book wherever it is relevant and important.

---

* 法律经济学的观点认为所有法律问题都可用"成本—收益"的标准作为分析工具,其代表人物是罗纳德·科斯。

Section Nine: Sources, Texts, and Materials of the Study of Anglo-American Law

There are different texts and materials, primary as opposed to secondary, official as opposed to unofficial. Leaving aside the questionable nature of such distinctions, different texts and materials serve different needs and purposes, though none is completely adequate for all circumstances.

Generally speaking, when searching for binding text of authority, official primary text must be consulted and referred to. Secondary materials and nonofficial publications serve to further understanding. These types of materials would seem to fulfill all the needs for the exploration of authority of reason, such as in the case of comparative study.

Yet, for a number of reasons, neither the primary official texts nor the non-official secondary sources would provide a correct reading of the law in some circumstances. This is not only true for areas of law where deep intractable social or moral issues are involved, such as same-sex marriage, abortion, physician-assisted suicide, etc., but also for subject matters that seem well established. This is due to the undeniable fact that neither the official text nor the secondary, particularly expository works truly and sufficiently reflects the actual law prevalent in society, that is, the law in action. In such cases, original and comprehensive research is called for just as foreign citizens who take an internal view of own law must do. For this purpose, authoritative and effective decisions beyond the established categories must be resorted to. This is a daunting project indeed.

To a significant extent, the discussion on sources of law should provide a good starting point serving as an indication of the nature and scope of the materials needed for the different types of research, ranging from a simple responsive or reactive task on a particular problem, issue or conflict to a comprehensive scholarly undertaking.

Section Ten: Conditions and Factors Determinative of the Need and Viability of Legal Transplant

Under normal circumstances, when comparative study of foreign law is embarked on, legal transplant（法律移植）or adoption, if considered desirable, should follow naturally. However, there may be factors and conditions existing in a country that would decline any adoption or transplant deemed largely unsuitable or not viable, even though a need for transplant exists.

Legal structure, institutions, and operation are intractably linked with the constitutional philosophy, setup, and prescription of a polity. To a considerable extent, social conditions, economic development and cultural tradition also play a role. For example, wherever power is largely centralized, it would simply be untenable to attempt at transplanting the institution of the independence of the adjudicative or regulatory body and process. For an example, when choosing the United States Federal Reserve as a model for streamlining a country's central bank system, one must give the banker all the necessary powers to determine and adopt monetary policy independently.

Legal Borrowing and Transplant: Need, Desirability And Timing

Legal borrowing and transplant is one of the logic goals of comparative law study for authority of intrinsic reason. They are normally and should be done after an extended period of deliberation, public consultation and careful consideration of its advantages and disadvantages. Only in times of colonization, revolution, and foreign invasion and occupation, borrowing and transplant are done involuntarily, forced, and other-imposed.

The need and the importance for borrowing and transplanting foreign law are normally discovered and recognized as a result of globalization and interdependence in all aspects of modern life. Whether or not borrowing and transplant are undertaken is more a matter of political philosophy or practical considerations. It goes much beyond legal nationalism and xenophobia. In many cases, it is the political morality maturity rather than need and importance that is decisive.

The object of borrowing and transplant may include an entire legal system, a particular segment of the legal system, a particular subject area of the law, or a specific legislation.

Review and Reflective Questions

1. Enumerate all the possible reasons for studying the law of the U.S. as foreign law.

2. For comparative study, why the law of the U.S. may be considered as the most relevant and important choice?

复习及提问

1. 列举出学习美国法的所有理由。
2. 在比较学习过程当中,为什么美国法是最为重要及具有参考意义的?

Chapter Two: Sources of Law in General

Introductory Note

Sources of law are standard features of most introductory books on law. As expected, this chapter contains both the general, established sources of law as well as sources of Anglo-American law in particular.

In addition, the philosophical ideas informing this book necessitate an inquiry of the importance of commonly and unfortunately neglected sources of an informal, unwritten nature and origin. The relatively insignificance of much emphasized judiciary decision is also noted. Moreover, the realistic nature and significance of what is called "authoritative and effective decision" is particularly illustrated.

简 介

每本法律入门书籍基本上都会介绍到法律渊源这一部分。本章将介绍一般的、公认的法律渊源,并着重介绍英美法的法律渊源。

另外,这本包含哲学思想的书,强调了那些经常被忽略的非正式、不成文的法律渊源的重要性。这其中还谈到了相对不重要但被过分重视的行政裁决。除此之外,本章将重点讨论"权威、有效的判决"的现实特点和重要意义。

Section One: Codes(法典) and Statutes(制定法)

Unlike the civil code and other codes in the civil law countries, codes in countries belonging to the Common law system generally refer to consolidations of statutes already enacted. Such consolidations may be either general in scope or subject-based.

The importance and the special significance of statutes in any modern regulatory and welfare states are patently obvious. This is equally true for the Common law countries. It is apparent that most, if not all, aspects of our lives are regulated by legislation. Even some of the traditional Common law areas have already invaded by statutes. This has been criticized as "juridification" saturation of society.

English statutes have a casuistic character or case-by-case approach not found in continental legislation. On the other hand, rules and principles expressed in a statute are not fully recognized by English jurists(法官,法学家) and therefore not truly integrated in the Common law until they have been applied, reformulated and developed by the decisions of courts. And then a statute is accepted only to the extent to which such application and interpretation have taken place. And the statute so applied and interpreted only makes corrections and adjuncts to judicially established principles or render them more specific.

This traditional view of legislation and its strict interpretation face increasing challenge and have to change. It could be said that a public officer's law laying special emphasis on statutory law as opposed to the traditional lawyers' law is on the rise. The overwhelming influence and significance of statutes including codes must be carefully attended to and appreciated along with the realization of the insignificance of judicial decisions in the large scheme of thing.

Section Two: Regulations(规章,条例), Decrees(判决,裁定), and Administrative Directives(行政命令、行政规章)

In modern states, the legislators themselves cannot provide all the necessary regulations, rules, and other directives as these are extremely more complex and specialized. All that can be expected of legislation, at least in many areas, is a statement of principles and more or less general rules. For the more detailed directions, permissions, prohibitions, and requirements, more specific and pointed regulations are necessarily required same as the reliance on the activity and decision of administrative or regulatory authorities that are staffed with experts and specialists in their respective fields. This is done by providing for the implementation of legislation and by delegating the power to make such regulations to administrative or regulatory bodies and agencies. The control of regulation and regulatory decision, the guarantee of the supremacy of statutory law, and the conformity of regulatory provisions in its application with statutory requirements are in the hands of both the legislature and the court. Judicial review of administrative action serves the overseeing function. Balancing the all-powerful legislators and their overburdening responsibility and unsatisfactory legislation, administrative and regulatory agencies entrusted with the responsibility of administrating legislation have enjoyed quite a considerable autonomy.

Section Three: Binding Nature or Significance of Administrative Directives

The binding nature and effect of administrative directives are largely due to the internal regulations and instructions that various administrative bodies distribute to their officers as agents. In themselves, these instructions have only a "doctrinal" value, not normative in character, and are not considered as sources of law by those who support the principle of legislative positivism. The Sociological school of law considers them as sources of law par excellence, because in the immense majority of cases, it is certain that civil servants will observe the instructions received as these are their only means of knowing the law. It is no less certain that in most cases private persons will accept the application of the law as laid down in such administrative directives. In modern regulatory and welfare states, it would rather be unrealistic and even unproductive to believe that administrative decisions, whatever their nature and function are not on the same scale as legislation or regulation in terms of importance and impact.

Section Four: Judicial Decisions

One measure of the significance and influence of judicial decisions is the collection and publication of law reports and digests of case law. Not compiled for the use of legal historians or sociologists or for the pleasure of their readers, judicial decisions are to be used by lawyers in practice for advising clients and pleading cases before the court. This view of Rene David and J. E. C. Brierley is unnecessarily narrow. By excluding historians, sociologists, and others who take an internal view of law from the law-making process, David and Brierley consequently underestimate the special significance and contribution of historians and sociologists, and others as they relate to, and interact with, judges and their decisions.

Many different views exist as to the importance and law-creating nature of judicial decisions. In the Common law family, contentious questions surround the primacy of statutory law and the proper and right role of the court in the law making process. The sweeping power of judges to force legislative change, the immediate and lasting impact of judicial decisions on elite decisions and society in general are particular subjects of concern. In this respect, the continuous debates on the merits of judicial activism are of particular relevance. More and detailed discussion of judicial activism and the significance of judicial decisions are to be found in many of the sections below.

Section Five: Non-state or Unofficial Sources of Law

Non-state or unofficial sources of law refer to self-regulation or autonomous ordering in the social sectors. Customs is a typical example of a non-state source. What is debatable and generally ignored, especially by legal positivists is the authoritative and effective decisions made by social elite powers and entities within their respective areas of competence. Why, for example, are not considered as law the decisions made by schools and universities, commercial establishments and business, clubs, and other corporate entities? What are the ultimate criteria for state law to count as law to the exclusion of such private sources? A logical extension of this broader conception of law would allow the stance that the decision and action of any activist citizen in the political moral arena of the polity should be no less treated.

A. Reason as a Source

Reason helps to fill the gaps of the English legal system as well as to guide its evolution. The case-by-case approach of the Common law necessarily results in production of gaps. And the development of new legal rules is based on judicial reasoning through distinguishing cases and new fact-situations. Law before anything else is reason, the so-called authority of reason. Today in England, law remains primarily a work of reason and distinct from legislation. For example, one does not think of the Common law as a system of "national law"; it is much more; it is "the common heritage of the English-speaking peoples." Being such, it cannot be anything other than reason. While in principle, it seems hardly refutable that reason underlies all laws and decisions, it is nevertheless undeniable that reason in either its practical sense or its technical legal connotation is often general, vague, elusive, subjective, often controversial and highly debatable. What are the sources of reason is a quarry difficult to snare. Ronald Dworkin expounds the virtue of principles in deciding hard cases. H. L. A. Hart resorts to discretion when in difficulty. Both approaches are closer to reality and more rational and honest. Could it be possible that the general, abstract, supple principles or the subjective, elusive discretion would hold up under rational persuasive scrutiny without underlying reason?

Legal reason is the body and mind of law. This declaration seems quite pure, sound, and innocuous. Yet, critics of law brand legal reason as nothing more than assertion, pretense, violence, and power in disguise. In essence, reason or legal reason represents interest, value, belief, and faith.

For a more detailed discussion of legal reason, its nature, sources, function, power, limitation, and many other issues, please refer to Chapter Eight of this publication.

Why should dissenting judicial opinions or minority judgments that are published along with the majority opinion be equally significant as a source of potential law? A good explanation for this view is: It is the quality of the reason given in support of these opinions and judgments that are compelling in terms of justice, morality, reasonableness, etc. It is not the authority of the court. Nor that much should be attributed to the status and prestige of the judges concerned.

B. Fundamental Importance of Doctrine or Legal Writing: Scholarly Law

The historical role of jurists in universities in the development of the law cannot be denied. Neither the impact of the establishment of democratic ideas nor the advent of codification has really changed much of this role. Doctrine is a living source of law. It creates the legal vocabularies and ideas that legislators use and establishes the methods by which law gets understood and statutes interpreted. The real relationship between legislation and doctrinal commentary is much similar to that between judicial decisions and scholars. This can hardly be ignored. To further examine the role of doctrinal writings of legal scholars and to understand the dynamic relationship between scholar's laws and laws derived from the various official sources, we must study the on-going, comprehensive process of authoritative and effective decisions. More discussion of scholars' role and contribution to law are found in sections in Chapter Six.

In England, certain legal texts that were written mostly by judges were treated as sources of authority. The works of Glanvill, Bracton, Littleton and Code have enjoyed such a prestige that they are considered in the courts to be the most authoritative exposition of the law of their time and were endowed with a status that Europeans would only accord to legislation itself.

A closely related scholarly activity is the intelligence and recommendation functions. The latest example of the influence and authority of legal scholars involves the Prime Minister of Canada, Stephen Harper's request for the Governor-General to prorogue the Canadian Parliament in order to avoid the fate of his imminent defeat and resignation in the face of a scheduled non-confidence vote of the opposition parties. It has been reported that on this extraordinarily important issue of Canadian constitution the Governor-General specially solicited the opinion of Professor Peter Hogg, the author of a definitive scholarly work on the constitution law in Canada.

C. Interdisciplinary Research and Works as Sources

In his seminal work "The Concept of Law". H. L. A. Hart distinguishes between an internal statement of law and an external view. Internal statement is made by citizens who take the norms or rules embodied in the corpus of the law as a standard for both conduct guiding and criticism. On the other hand, external statement is the view of an outsider observing externally patterns of conduct and trend of decision.

Such distinction seems innocuous enough. What is problematic and controversial is should such internal statement be limited to judges, lawyers or legal scholars of the legal community? Conversely, to accept interdisciplinary works and research as sources of law, as we propose, would require the recognition of the normal statements of a political moral nature made by, for example, scholars in disciplines other than law as no less internal to law. Are historians or sociologists or even ordinary people taking an internal view of the law when making critical, reformist normative statement? If so, what are the sources of manifestation of such internal views other than their published works, findings, actions, or decisions publicized, disseminated, or otherwise known whatever the sources?

D. Intelligence, Idea, Proposal, and Recommendation as Source

The policy science school of law at Yale as expounded by McDougal, Lasswell and associates in their widely read works lists first the intelligence and recommendation functions along with invocation, application, appraisal, and termination in the comprehensive process of authoritative and effective decision-making.

Law without justifying reason, whatever its origin and nature is the most crude, naked coercive power. Unless one stubbornly adheres to the dictate of legal positivism which regards exclusively and only as sources of law prescriptions or other normative statements of a state and its institutions and other entities, and blindly insists that sources must be dressed in certain officially recognized or prescribed forms, such as statutes, regulation, judicial decisions, etc., one must count as sources of law all reasons advocated for authoritative and effective decisions as advanced by such entities as law reform bodies, legal scholars, think-tanks, lobbying and advocacy groups.

This is a natural and logical extension of the view that law without morally, politically, socially, environmentally, etc., compelling reasons, is not law at all. This view is also built on the bedrock of the intrinsic and intractable relationship between the notion of reason of authority and that of authority of reason. Law and reason are in practice synonymous in the comprehensive process of authoritative and effective decision making of a polity, national as well as international.

The policy paper entitled Change for American: "a progressive blueprint for the 44th President" is the most recent example of such source issued by the Center for American Progress (CAP). It has been reported that much of the content had already been adopted by Barack Obama, the President-elect at the time of this writing for the legislative agenda of his government. These days, CAP's issue papers are a must reading, its briefings standing-room only, jammed with advocacy-group representatives, lobbyists and reporters looking for advance insight into Obama's probable policies.⑪

Unfortunately, intellectual ideas may do good as well as evil. Bush and Cheney took up the neo-conservatives' ideas only to turn them into foreign policy disasters.

The massive government intervention in order to rescue the global economy from collapsing is said to find its support in Keynesian economy.

To regard reason as law, one must jettison the legal positivist's(法律实证主义) claim that the only litmus test for what counts as law is the official stamp of a legislature, a court, or a governmental official. Instead, one embraces the universally upheld realistic, inclusive standard of what in fact guides conduct in the political, moral arena.

---

⑪ Lynda Hurst, "U. S. Politics: The Ideas Factory in Obama's Washington", *The Toronto Star*, November 22, 2008. pp. ID3, ID7.

Section Six: Legal Pluralism* and Legal Centralism —Written Law(成文法) vis-a-vis Unwritten Law(不成文法), Express vis-a-vis Implicit Law, Law in Book vis-a-vis Law in Action

Law works best in silence and state law occupies merely an insignificant portion of the entire realm of legal landscape. This insight is slowly catching on. It may be submitted that the existing fixation of laypersons and officials alike solely on the law of the state is be largely attributed to the ignorance, neglect, fault, if not intentional distorting, of the normative picture of the law by members of the legal profession.

A. Pre-(state) Law(国家成立前的法律)

Law and many of its juridical concepts long existed before the rise of nation states. The pre-law research has proved beyond doubt that law, emanated from and existed in, social relations, customs, and practices. The law of the state does not exhaust or entirely appropriate the legal universe. There is more to law than that which emanates from the state. State law is a modern phenomenon that is contingent and temporary, and may very well transitory and replaceable. State law is in essence very much declaratory of pre-existent order of things. The Common law arises on the back of custom and local order.

"In the Homeric state, the law is not something that is distinct or set aside from other human activities... Law has the potential to pervade all such activities, to exist immanent in rather than above and apart from that which it governs."⑫. "Law is not conceived as some specifically formulized or institutionalized set of practices but simply as those forms of social regulations which have somehow come to be embodied in custom, tradition or even myth... characterized by the multiplex acts of seizure, interdiction, execution which consolidate simultaneously an autonomous power and as a priori magico-religious power."⑬"The nature of juridical relations is nascent. The efficacy of legal sanction evolved originally not from the fear of physical threat but rather out of the fear of a mystical power lurking behind the law... the mysterious

---

* 法律多元主义,两种或更多种的法律制度在同一社会领域中的共存状态。

⑫ L. Garnet, "Droit et societe Dans la Grece Ancienne". Paris, Sirey, 1955, p. 18.

⑬ Les temps dans les fores de la Grece antique, Paris, Maspero, 1968, pp. 261 at 265.

character of the letter and writing possess."⑭ "The private delict (taking the law into one's own hands) evolved as a totemic interfamilial law pertaining to the status, power and honor of the family, clan, not a legal concept in any modern sense but a legitimate form of social regulation... the familial network and the informal or tacit structure of social interrelationship"⑮

B. Relative Insignificance of Judicial Law (Settlement of Disputes)

It has long been statistically established that relatively insignificant number of disputes ever arose has been referred to the court for resolution. Judicial decisions being fact-specific are limited in impact and effect to the immediate case in question only. The precedent authority of a decision if it ever earns can only be proclaimed at the very point of its subsequent application. It is one thing to proclaim that something is the law of the land and quite another to have it empirically established beyond doubt that it is such. A great majority of cases are easy and routine concretization[s] of established law. No two cases are the same on all four. In hard cases, applications of rules in book may very well be forced or overreaching. Moreover, change in time and space along with change in social, economic, political circumstances, conditions, and value and belief systems simply tends to make the precedent value of any case highly uncertain, questionable and susceptible to being distinguished, rejected, overruled or just fall to desuetude. The indetermination argument advanced by the Critical Legal Study (批判法学) proponents is no exaggeration. The meaning and application of any law are in a state of dispute most of the time. Rules are knowingly ignored, rejected, contravened, or violated routinely in the process of decision-making. We all are Holmes' "bad man". We are constantly changing and shaping the meaning and application of legal rules to suit our specific interest, need, or value-belief.

C. Implicit Law, Unwritten or Autonomous Ordering

One of the most distinguished jurists who advocates the importance of un-formulated or implicit law emerging from autonomous ordering in social interactions is

---

⑭ Huvelin, P. Magie et droit individuel. 10 L'Anee sociologigue 1 at 38 (1905-1906).
⑮ Neil Duxbury, "Foundations of Legal Tradition; the Case of Ancient Greece", 9(3) *Legal Studies*, pp. 241, 247 (1989).

Lon L. Fuller*. The concept of unwritten law permeates throughout his writings. Fuller offers a non-definition of law as the enterprise of subjecting human conduct to the governance of rules. One has no difficulty in perceiving in this definition the immanence of implicit law.

One typical example is customary law (rules) which has never been and probably will never be officially or otherwise "juridified" in formulaic forms. The crucial question is where, when, and how to ascertain this type of law. The sources of implicit law are clear; they are found in social interactions and autonomous orderings. Courts applied customary law in disposition of disputes. In international law, customary rules are one of the officially recognized sources. It has even been submitted by a number of reputable international jurists that international law is mainly consisted of customary rules.

Could it be said that implicit laws are invoked and followed wherever and whenever the law of the state does not figure in decisions and actions? Writings on the concept of "without the law" tell a great deal about the significance of unwritten law along with the insignificance of state law. The ascendancy of unwritten law goes in direct proportion with the decrease in the importance of state law.

At the international level, there is a well-established new concept called "international soft law." This refers to rules which are not recognized by states as having binding authority and offered to states for their voluntary adoption and guidance. But such rules are in written form nonetheless. It is certainly true that not all authoritative decisions are found or accessible in written form. On what basis could one persuasively argue that when such soft law guides in effect the decisions and conduct of states, it is still not law in the sense of the conventionally received categories? Many of the resolutions or declarations adopted by international bodies, state or non-state, such as, e. g. the United Nations Conference on Trade and Development, are known to have been incorporated into the domestic law of many developing countries. Multinational corporations doing business in these countries must comply with these resolutions and declarations as incorporated in conducting business.

Legal Centralism posits that law lies at the center of events, that law is neutral, and that it is unsullied by any close identification with contending interests or classes

---

* 朗·富勒,美国法学家,第二次世界大战后新自然法学派主要代表之一,曾长期任哈佛大学法理学教授。主要著作有《法在探求自己》、《法理学》、《法的道德性》、《法的虚构》和《法的自相矛盾》。

or political philosophies. Law engages the power and prestige of the state. Law commands, people obey, and the course of future of events is fixed. Law is knowledge. Legal knowledge is disseminated to those who understand it the least by those who know it best.

Yet the formal or centralist paradigm fails to explain why law-like patterns of social behavior occur even though they lack some of the apparently essential characteristics of the formal law. Nor does the paradigm take account of the frequent inability of the formal law to achieve the results it is designed to do.

It has been said that instead of the vantage-point atop the lofty structures of the central legal system, it is from the ground level that law must be viewed, if we are to take its true measure.

Unless one can firmly and persuasively establish the ground or base for privileging the rules or norms posited by the state, legislative, regulatory, or judicial, any arguments for the authority of state law at the sacrifice of norms, orders emerging from social sectors are built on sand. Some of the constitutive notions advanced by legal positivists, such as Kelsen's "basic norms", H. L. A. Hart's "rules of recognition", or "validity", equally apply to "non-law" sectors. On the other hand, the self-referential and infinite regressive nature of these notions has already done enough damages to the myth of the authority of state law.

No actions or decisions that are more important and have heavier impacts and consequences on the society at large than those made by elite powers in the economic and business fields. And it is not unreasonable to say that legislation and judicial decisions are to a large extent confirmation and application of the economic or business norms already established. Economic policy and business decisions are made on the ground of risk management and wealth maximization rather than rules. This is true for the making of the Federal Reserve's interest rates policy. It is also true for the business and financial decisions made by corporate elites. Judicial decisions are made not on precedents(判例) but on judicious characterization of facts or discretion. In essence, they are just "juridification(法规化)" of a declarative nature. Then why we are continuously preoccupied with state law and loyally engaged in the analysis and study of the opinions of appellate courts? Could the critics be right that we are simply enchanted with state law?

Legal Pluralism—In contrast, social scientists have proposed that law consists primarily of rules by which persons in society order their conduct, and that norms of decisions developed by the courts and of legislation enacted by the state are of a secondary nature. For example, civil adjudication(判决、裁定) in 19th century England was shared among a myriad of special tribunals administering special law for special groups. Local and special court systems fell into three categories, namely, 1) there were centralized courts of the Common law, sometimes with special procedural arrangements, 2) courts that applied special customary law rather than the Common law, and 3) courts with broad discretionary powers(自由裁量权) and de facto autonomy exercised in such a way as to establish a local variant of the general law. In the case of courts of requests, lay judges, local mayors, aldermen, or stewards of the manor presided over the proceeding operating with extremely simple formality in which parties themselves testified, and decision was made according to equity and good conscience.⑯ The source of the Common law should not be located in doctrinal propositions which purport to state legal rules but in social propositions which include propositions of conventional morality, policy, experiences.⑰

The large majority of laws are often unwritten yet well understood codes defining standards of behavior in industrial enterprises and business transactions, among neighbors, and within universities, churches, or public bureaucracies. These ongoing processes by which different manifestations of law came into existence cannot be ignored. We must accept that law is much more diverse in its content, causes, and effects than the legal centralism proposes. Roderick Macdonald seems to follow Fuller's step in saying that the manifestation of normative order needs not necessarily explicit and formulaic. J. D. Whyte's threshold test of the existence of normative order is a prior standard for action.

Industrialization and urbanization brought about an awakening consciousness of the need for an integration of national legal system. The rise of the modern welfare state and the ascendancy of legal instrumentalism necessarily strengthen the hand of state law. But the normative ordering of society is simply a fact of life in despite of state law.

To many lawyers, the very idea of legal pluralism is a contradiction in terms. In the world of positivist lawyering, legal pluralism is relegated to a nether world of

---

⑯ H. W. Arthurs, *Without the Law: Administrative Justice and Legal Pluralism in Nineteenth-Century England*, Univ. Toronto Pr., 1985, p. 17.

⑰ M. A. Eisenberg, *The Nature of the Common Law*, Harv. Univ. Pr., 1988.

qualifying adjectives and unnatural synonyms: indigenous, or informal law, systems of social control, normative systems or folkways as opposed to the positive, state, formal or exogenous of lawyer's law. This is a short sight and an unnecessarily restrictive view of the functions of lawyers in the normative ordering of society.

There is more to law than state law. Lawyers and judges themselves are often the authors of corporate structures, contractual regimes, informal understandings between disputing parties and other private arrangements that operate upon behavior more immediately than formal codes or case law. Nor are they strangers to aggressiveness, intransigence, negotiation, mediation, arbitration, domestic adjudication or political devices such as voting or the organizing of consensus, which round out the repertoire of dispute-settling arrangements encountered in organizations, groups, and less formal business or social networks.

Pierre Schlag(美国法学家施拉格), a critic of law and legal reason, shares the same view. "[F]or every dispute that ripens into even the possibility of a lawsuit or an arrest, millions of frictionless legal transactions take place, most of them blissfully free of any conscious knowledge on the part of the participants that they are in any sense partaking in legal interaction. For every dispute involving some sort of formal legal action, there are dozens of conflicts where legal action was considered that were resolved without recourse to it. For every civil lawsuit(诉讼) resulting in a formal courtroom disposition, there are between thirty and fifty suits that are settled prior to this point. And for every lower court disposition of a case that results in an appellate court(上诉法院) opinion, there are many more that do not."⑱ Why then the decisions and opinions of the appellant courts continue to a main source of discourse in law? The answer is that lawyers go where the money is and legal scholars find there a rich source of reasoning already provided.

Few human interactions generate disputes; most disputes never see the inside of a law office or courtroom; and parties usually vindicate, compromise, or abandon their claims without reference to "law" at all.⑲

It is of particular significance that for centuries, businessmen had eluded the welcoming embrace of the central legal system, organized their affairs according to law that was their own, and settled their disputes in forums they controlled according to decisional norms and procedures which they consciously contrasted with those of the

---

⑱ Paul E. Campos, *Jurismanias, The Madness of American Law*. Oxford Univ. Pr., 1998, p. 58.
⑲ Ibid.

superior courts(高级法院). Rules for buying and selling, lending and borrowing, shipping and carrying are generated primarily by regimes of private ordering. It is extremely doubtful that more than the tiniest fraction of these transactions is made with conscious reference to formal rules and common or statute law. Private ordering through negotiation tends to yield a variety of non-adjudicated(未作出判决的) and indeterminate outcomes: satisfaction, acquiescence, renegotiated terms, or compensation. Nor does the failure of negotiation necessarily signal the advent of formal legal intervention. Arbitration and other types of domestic adjudication dispose of a significant number of disputes. Finally, we should not forget that only a small proportion of disputes set down for formal determination actually sees the inside of a courtroom.[20] Implicit in all of these attempts to create or legitimate distinctive forums for the adjudication of commercial disputes was a tacit acceptance of the pluralistic nature of English law.[21] By Code's time it was accepted that the law merchant was part of the domestic law of England.

Law in action is manifested wherever and whenever people act or decide without the evocation and application or on the basis of state law (statute, judicial decision, or regulation or regulatory decision) either as reason or justification. Seemingly, examples of law in action are readily identified or identifiable upon close observation wherever one looks. For example, new drugs or new use whereof must be blessed with the governing agency's stamp of approval before being marketed or prescribed. Yet in many instances where life saving is at stack, drugs well tested for effectiveness have been regularly prescribed before or pending such approval. No wonder that it has been suggested that the works and documents of lawyers and law firms should be studied in this context. The source of the Common law should not be located in doctrinal propositions which purport to state legal rules but in social propositions which include propositions of conventional morality, policy, experiences.

On the other hand, it can be convincingly argued that whatever the centrifugal forces, national states remain largely unchallenged in their power, impact, and effectiveness in agenda setting, resources-mobilization and strategic communications when making value-impact decisions and actions. After all, it is still the state policy and decision that dictate economy, not the other way around. This is true not only in times of economic and financial crisis as we are witnessing right now, but also during

---

[20] Arthurs, op cit at 50-51.
[21] Id., at 52.

period of normal market economy.

What is most ironical and paradoxical is that legal centralism per se conceives legal pluralism. It has been insightfully observed that public regulation and personal control are two sides of the same coin. The individual's capacity to control is governed and empowered by a pre-existing regime of property relations; property owners are petty sovereigns. Every lawful economic power becomes a type of political power and every economic inequality poses a question of political inequality. Property so viewed is "private government"[22]. Yet, this invisible government is not a single coherent unit. It is a cluster of different groups and persons who hold sway in different fields. Thus the entire economic system must be regarded as "one vast structure of minority dictation" under the protection of the law. What Friedman calls freedom from coercion is for Hale counter coercion. The freedom of market is essentially a freedom of individuals and groups to coerce one another with the power to coerce reinforced by agencies of the state itself. To an autonomous moral agent taking committed public moral action, this is a double-whammy.[23] A closely related phenomenon to legal pluralism is the flourishing of informal justice, an integral part of alternative dispute resolution. Informal justice may be state-sponsored or initiated by the private sectors. State informal justice is a double-edge sword. "It appears to be simultaneously more and less coercive than formal law, to represent both an expansion of the state apparatus and a contraction. When accused of being manipulative, it can show its non-coercive face; when charged with abandoning the disadvantaged, it can point to ways in which informal justice extends state paternalism. It is essential to unravel these contradictions if we are to grasp the full significance of recent legal innovations.[24]

Richard Falk seems to believe that the phenomenon and expansion of the multinational corporations may lead gradually to the erosion of state power on the international plane as well as domestically. It is hardly disputable that the wealth and power of these corporations have exerted some unprecedented impact on our life. The increasing pace and trend of privatization of state enterprises in countries worldwide and contracting out of state services of various nature to the private sectors all may

---

[22] Hale, Robert, "The Constitution and the Prize System", 34 *Columbia L R* 401, 402 (1934).
[23] Robert Hale, "The Economy of Legal Force", 53 *Modern L R* 421, 434-435 (1990).
[24] Richard L Abel, "The Contradictions of Informal Justice" In: *Politics of Informal Justice*. Vol.1. Ed. R. L. Abel. Academic Pr., 1982, pp.267, at 307.

lead in the future to a small government and consequently a resurgence of private autonomous ordering. Unfortunately, privatization in the name of efficiency and economy of state enterprises and services tend to enrich certain well-connected people at the sacrifice of the general public.

Non-state sources include actions, conducts on the part of people, single-handed individually or collectively, organized. The nature and variety of such actions or conducts are potentially infinitive. Some indications of these can be found in Section three of Chapter six: Sites, sources and manifestations of law and legal system in action.

Section Seven: Custom

Any normative order that is just and lasting must be built upon and sustained by certain established and widely shared (internalized) value systems and moral precepts. Because of its implicit, informal, unwritten nature, customary law is elastic, flexible, evolutionary, vigorous, and dynamic. What constitute customary law are committed actions and effective decisions in the public domains which have been repetitively made and survived for a relatively long period of time. It is generally believed that for any such acts and decisions to be accorded the status of customary law, they must be also generally regarded as law—this is the well-known psychological element in international law as opposed to the material element of the repetitively committed acts for a long period of time. Upon further reflection, such requirement for both the material element and the psychological element in constituting customary law appears to be patently confusing if not self-contradictory, for the psychological requirement evidently and effectively renders the material element of the long-duration repetitively committed act superfluous. This is one of the main reasons that led Ben Cheng, a well-known international jurist, to concoct the notion of "instant customary law". Rather than a static entity, customary law is constantly evolving and changing and yet its essential content and characteristics remain constant.[25] The idea of customary law could also be attributed to the important role of anthropology in law-generation.

According to a sociological concept of the sources of law, custom plays a

---

[25] Moore Sally Falk, *Social Facts and Fabrications: Customary Law in Kilimonjaro 1880-1980*, Cambridge Univ Pr., 1986.

preponderant role in all legal systems and in developing or applying the law. Legislators, judges and jurists are, as a matte of fact, more or less consciously or unconsciously guided by the public opinion and by the general custom of the community. Customary law could be analogous to one of the fundamental tenets in the Marxist thinking: the material conditions of production. Customary law is the infrastructure upon which the law is built.

The Common law borrowed many rules from the varied local customs formerly in force, but the process of building the Common law itself was the fashioning of a judge-made law, based on reason, which replaced the customary law of the Anglo-Saxon period. The sphere in which custom may be considered as a truly living source of the present law is very limited except in areas where a custom could be established to have existed as early as 1189. Though the requirement of "immemorial" does not apply to commercial custom. It suffers the same loss of its customary character after being absorbed by either statutes or judicial decisions.

The real importance of custom in England really exists in the sense of the "convention of the constitution." Without a written constitution, these conventions nevertheless continue to dominate English political life. Also in many areas of criminal law(刑法), customs have the value of a usual practice. For example, in certain cases, custom definitely obliges a judge to make use of jury trial(陪审团审判).

For example, the origins of the Uniform Commercial Code lie in the law merchant, a specialized body of usage or customs that governed contracts dealing with commercial matters until the seventeenth century. Large amounts of this law were carried into the English common law of negotiable instruments and insurance. Lord Mansfield, one of England's most noted judges, made it a point to ascertain and apply the usage of the trade.

The practical role of custom in ascertaining the meaning of law is well established.

Legislation itself, in order to be understood, often has to appeal to custom for the necessary clarification of the intent of the legislators(立法者). Without such a reference it cannot be said, for example, when a person has committed a fault, whether a certain mark constitutes a signature, whether an object is a family keepsake, whether a person has acted within a reasonable delay, etc. Its diminished role is due largely to the long-standing primary importance attributed to written law.

God and Religion as a Source of Law

In all states founded on imperialism, oligarchy, dictatorship, totalitarianism, etc., the words and acts of an individual or group of individuals, whatever entitled, are sources of law. In modern age, states founded on or otherwise heavily influenced by religious fundamentalism, the God, the Bible, or the Koran is often referred to as the source, ground, or justification for the decision or action of the man in control. The draft constitution of Iraq emerging after the U. S. -led invasion has unequivocally enshrined Islam as the source of all laws: No legislation can be enacted in contravention of the basic teachings and principles of the Koran. The church has laws. According to canon law, people who persist in manifest grave sin are to be denied Holy Communion. It doesn't matter whether the bishops agree with this or not. It is the law of the church. They are obligated to enforce the law.

Authority and Efficacy of Law

One of the most challenging and fundamental questions ensued from the above critical observations is how to distinguish and separate the law of the state (legal centralism) from all the non-state sources (legal pluralism). On what basis could one possibly say that the king or queen's decree, the law of the church (canon law), Joe Cabill's order, or a gunman's demand differs from the enactment of the legislature or the decision of the court. H. L. A. Hart, a preeminent legal theorist, attempts to answer this challenge on the basis of the dichotomy between being obligated and being obliged. In the same vein, some jurists have tried very hard to snare the quarry by exploring the bases of obligation. In domestic law, a contract is <u>voidable</u> <u>(可撤销的)</u> due to unconsciencousebility. Yet at the international level, unequal or coerced treaties are very much a part of valid international law. Unfortunately, on this fundamentally crucial question, the jury is still out.

Fundamentally, the notion of sources of law collapses in the final analysis onto the concept of law that in turn collapses onto the twin notions of authority and efficacy. The notion of obligation or being obligated by nature and logic originates from the notion of authority, while the notion of being obliged or being compelled arises from the notion of efficacy. The success of distinguishing or separating being obligated from authority being obliged relies solely on the possibility and reasonableness of dichotomizing authority and efficacy. Authority may be said to be psychological, emotive and relates to the political, the moral and a sense of fairness, justice, righteousness, etc. On the other hand, efficacy is material in nature, politically, morally, and value neutral; it is mainly pragmatic and factual. Authority is also normative, prescriptive, subjective, intentional, and voluntary. Efficacy on the contrary is descriptive, objective, and taking what is given.

Yet, there is an intractable and complex relationship between authority and efficacy. Authority without the support of efficacy becomes at best potential, theoretical, and presumptive. Before long, authority without efficacy would loose its legitimacy. Efficacy without becoming authoritative is just naked power and violence. And forced and imposed efficacy may eventually acquire its authority status upon acceptance.

Section Eight: Sources of American Law Worthy of Special Mention

A whole series of factors has contributed to making enacted law particularly important in the United States ever since the Declaration of Independence. And the most important of these are the existence of a federal Constitution(联邦宪法) and its Bill of Rights(权利法案), the very basis of many American institutions and civil rights.

The issues respecting the sources of law are in fact more complex in a composite state. The vertical character of the sources of law gives way to a more elaborated formula in which the hierarchical order within each legal structure is maintained, while the relations between the sources of law also fit one into the other on a horizontal plane. Laws enacted by a lesser community at a sub-national level may have the same value as national law. In some countries (including the United States) the formal principle of hierarchical subordination operates along side by side with the principle of competence to take into account the plurality of the territorial organizations and thus the multiplicity of the authorities vested with legislative and regulatory competence.[26]

A. Statute Law

(1) The Need for and Growth of Legislation and Regulation

The increasing complexity of commercial and social life creates a growing need

---

[26] F. Delperee, "Constitutional Systems and Sources of Law" In: *Law in the Making: a Comparative Survey*, Ed. A. Pizzorusso, 1988, pp. 88 at 92-93.

for intervention and regulation by government. The drafting and promulgation of legislation by a central authority can tackle a whole field of problems and attempt to advance a unified set of solutions. Judicial decision-making is, by nature, designed to resolve immediate and particular claims made by a party under existing law, and its slow and fragmentary resolution of individual disputes simply does not suit well for the general and comprehensive needs of modern regulation states. Judicial decisions are reactive, piecemeal, particular, concrete, fact-based, retrospective, declarative, while legislation signifies just the opposite; legislation is proactive, wholesale, general, universal, prospective, prescriptive, and transcending facts.

(2) **Legislative Process**

The United States Congress is a bicameral body consisted of the House of Representatives and the Senate. Originated from either the Executive branches, the constituents as individuals, organized bodies, or member of the House, a proposed law is presented in the form of a bill. A bill may be introduced in either house, but only by a member of that House. With rare exceptions, the bill will be referred to one of the Standing committees of the House where it is introduced. The majority party has the larger member in the committee. A member of the majority party serves as the chairman. In some cases, subcommittees are created. Much of the serious work is done in committee and subcommittee. Once a bill is in the committee, it will be studied by the experts on staff in the committee and departments of the executive branch may be requested to submit their views in writing. If the bill is of sufficient importance, there may be public hearings at which interested parties are heard. Finally the committee members vote to determine the fate of the bill. They may report it favorably with or without comments or amendments to Congress with its recommendations. In the report, the purpose of the bill, its need and legislative history will be provided. The report contains a section by section analysis, an estimate of its cost, reports and comments from appropriate governmental agencies and departments, and minority views. Debates in the House are ensued and further amendments may be proposed. Or the committee may postpone its consideration of the bill by tabling it, which normally prevents further action upon the bill. A large percentage of bills die in committee. If the bill is approved by a majority vote, it then goes to the Senate to undergo a similar procedure. Should the versions passed by both houses be identical, its goes directly to the President for signature. If there are minor differences, they may be accepted by vote in the house where the bill originated. But should the differences be substantial, they will be adjusted by a conference committee consisting of members of both houses followed by the approval of the compromised version by a majority vote of each house. The President has veto power over federal legislation. If he does not sign it within ten days, the bill becomes law automatically without his signature. The President returns his vetoed bill with reasons to the House where it originated. A two-thirds vote of each House is then necessary to override the veto and enact the bill into law.

B. Constitution as a Source

The United States Constitution defines its own primacy at the apex of American sources of law. Article VI of the American Constitution, enacted in 1787, is inspired by the ideas of the Natural law school. It put into operation the concept of social contract, by not merely spelling out the organization of the country's political institutions but also more importantly by tracing the limits of the powers of the federal authorities in their relationships with individual states and citizens. These same relationships have been even more specifically enunciated by the first 10 Amendments (1789) which make up the Bill of Rights and the 13th, 14th, and 15th Amendments which guarantee that certain "natural rights" of citizens will not be violated or frustrated by state authorities.

Interpretation of the Constitution as Source

There were no official records of its proceedings at the Philadelphia Constitutional Convention(美国制宪会议), 1878. But James Madison and other delegates kept extensive notes of the debates at the State conventions. The Federalist, with essays by Madison, John Lay, and Alexander Hamilton, is considered an essential source of contemporaneous opinion. According to the present day interpretative theories, the Supreme Court is the keeper of the Constitution. In other words, judicial interpretation of the Constitution constitutes the prime source of law just as the Constitution itself.

The Constitution has been interpreted through the years with great flexibility and teleologically. The whole development of American law, the distinction between federal law and the law of the states, and even American history itself, were influenced by the Court's interpretation of Constitutional provisions.

C. Treaties(条约) and International Agreements

The Supremacy Clause(最高权力条款) of the Constitution (Article VI, section 2) declares that "the Constitution, laws of, and treaties made by, the Unites States shall be the supreme law of the land, and the judges in every state shall be bound thereby, any thing in the constitution or laws of any state to the contrary notwithstanding." This clearly put the status of treaties as a source of US law on the same footing as the Constitution and the law.

From the perspective of Kelsen's monist view of legal order that considers national legal order as a subset of the international legal order, to regard treaties and other international agreements as a source of national legal order is equally compelling. The relationship between the international legal order and the national legal order is according to this view comparable to the situation between the state and the national order within a country constituted on a federal basis.

However, the exact status of treaties in the US legal order depends primarily on the kind of the treaty in question. In the United States, treaties are generally classified into self-executing, non-self-executing, and executive agreements. For a more detailed discussion on this, please consult B (1) of Section five in Chapter six.

D. Administrative Law(行政法)

Within the broad framework of administrative law, there is a large variety of boards, agencies, commissions, and tribunals, etc. especially in the social and economic fields. These are established and empowered by the Congress to make regulations and decisions for the application and implementation of statutes and to settle disputes in their respective areas of responsibility.

The birth of the modern welfare state has witnessed an unprecedented upsurge of massive mundane programs with great impact on the social, economic life of people. Along with the establishment and administration of the legislative mandates come multitude of bureaucracy and arbitrariness. Regulation by administrative decisions and rulings as well as deregulation by regulation will continue to flourish. Public or elitist discourse about administration and regulation will continue to concentrate on subject matter, such as validity, rationality of legal instrumentalism and optimum models of regulation. There does not appear to be any novel, paradigm breaking idea on the horizon to bring about a revolutionary or drastic change to the social, economic, and other related structures and institutions associated with the modern welfare state.

E. Compilations and Consolidations of Laws

With the continuing increase and proliferation of statutory law (legislation and regulation), the need to arrange by subject matters and consolidate them become obvious. At the federal level, there are the Official United States Code, the privately published United States Code Service, and United States Code Annotated. At the state level, Civil codes similar to the Romano-Germanic type have enacted in California, N. Dakota, S. Dakota, Georgia, and Montana. Many states also have codes of civil procedure and some codes of criminal procedure. In all states there are codes of criminal law.

F. Court Rules

The judiciary itself generally promulgates court rules dealing with procedural issues under the authority of either a constitutional or a statutory provision.

The United States Supreme Court(美国联邦最高法院) has congressional authority to issue rules of criminal and civil procedure for courts of appeal and district courts(联邦地方法院). Today, major national rules in these areas include: 1) the Federal Rules of Appellate Procedure (1968); 2) the Federal Rules of Civil Procedure (1938); 3) the Federal Rules of Criminal Procedure (1946); and 4) the Federal Rule of Evidence (1975).

Federal cases interpreting these rules are reported in Federal Rules Dicisions since 1940 and in Federal Rules Service since 1949. The annotated versions of the U.S. Code by West and Lawyers Co-op carry case abstracts.

The U.S. Supreme Court and specialized federal courts have their own rules. The U.S. Code and its two annotated versions contain all the national court rules. The Federal Rules Service publishes local court rules.

State court rules are published in state statutes.

G. Uniform State Law

The proliferation of enacted law poses a particular problem for the United States. The danger of states to enact statutory provisions to correct or supplement the Common law may destroy the uniformity of American law. Thus from a practical point of view, it is eminently desirable to propose uniform or model laws on certain subjects. First, there was the National Conference of Commissioners for Uniform

State Laws that later works in cooperation with the American Law Institute, to produce the Uniform Commercial Law in 1952 that has been revised many times since. Uniform laws also exist in many other private law areas. However, even so, uniformity cannot always be guaranteed due to divergent interpretations in each of the enacting states.

Nevertheless, with the increasing authority of the Federal government and its intervention in areas having general national interest and transnational implications, some success may finally be achieved in the realm of the uniformity of laws in the United States.

H. Secondary Authority

Treatises, legal periodicals, encyclopedias, and other finding tools are useful for its collection of citations, organizations of the subject matter, statement of legal rules, original analysis, criticism, and proposals for improvement. They are persuasive, and no judge is bound to follow. In practice, they are frequently cited in opinions. The authority of such second source depends on esteem of writer and intrinsic worth.

Treatises and Textbooks are carefully reasoned scholarly expositions of a field with explanation of the reasons behind the rules and criticisms of the present state of the law.

Encyclopedias(百科全书) are concerned mainly with the exposition of the law rather than with critical analysis. Usually unsigned and done by publisher's permanent staff.

Practitioner's texts are mainly concerned with the present state of the law.

Legal periodicals-university law reviews, edited by top-ranking students contain student notes and comments, signed leading articles and book reviews. Legal essays are apt to be more original, argumentative and critical. Most are general in nature and scope. Some are devoted to a special field. Some edited by faculty. There are also law journals published by bar associations, learned societies, and specialized groups.

There are many indexes to law reviews and other periodical publications. The most important ones include Index to Legal Periodicals, Current Law Index, and Legal Resources Index. Legal Resources Index lists newspapers and newsletters as well. Legaltrac and the CD-ROM version of Legal Resources Index are the most comprehensive periodical indexes in electronic format.

Loose-leaf services are published by BNA, CCH or Prentice-Hall and are mostly in regulatory fields.

I. Restatement of Law: Nature and Status

The American Law Institute was established in 1923. One of its objectives is "the clarification and simplification of the law." It identified two main defects in American law—uncertainty and complexity that caused wasteful delay and expense as well as impossibility to advise persons, and the inexhaustible store of cases. It vows to bring order into the chaos of case law(判例法).

Drafted by one or more reporters, eminent law teachers, in collaboration with a group of advisors—teachers, practitioners, and judges, the Restatement of law is the most significant and influential work in American common law.

Divided into sections and subdivisions, each Restatement contains black-letter statements of principles or rules, followed by comments that explain their purpose and scope and by illustrations of their application. Reporter's notes cite cases and other authorities and may mention conflicting views.

The Restatement is neither an exposition of the law as it is, nor a prescription of what it ought to be. Rather it is the considered opinion of some of the country's foremost legal scholars as to the law that would be applied by an enlightened court today. The Restatement is cited by appellate courts at a rate of over 4000 times a year as recorded in Restatement in the Courts, and can exercise an important influence toward unification when a new question arises. The Restatement is not intended to aim at codification.

Though being looked upon very favorably by jurists of countries with codified systems, because for them the Restatement is seen as a precious tool that provides a systematic exposition of American law in a form not dissimilar to their own codes. The Restatement is no more than a kind of systematic digest in which one only finds the judicial decisions on point. ㉗

㉗ David Rene & John Brierley, *Major Legal Systems of the World Today*, London: Stevens, 1985, pp. 438-439.

J. View of Formalism(形式主义) versus Realism(现实主义) as to What Counts as Law

To the formalists, the law is what an authoritative decision-maker says it is. They would construct a hierarchy of the sources of law. For example in Oklahoma, the United States Constitution is at the top and the state common law at the bottom.[28]. However, the dominant perspective among law-trained persons is one of realism. When sources and the law are in dispute, it is what a judge says the law is that ultimately matters (Holmes' dictum). Judicial interpretation thus prevails over the interpretation of the police or other public officials. In this view, the appellate case becomes the most important source of law. The range of realism in American law depends on the degree of one's skepticism about the instrument of language as a mode of communication. It also depends on one's belief about the general quality of judges and their willingness to purposely subvert the obvious meaning of a text to accomplish some political aim. The core meaning and penumbral or interstitial interpretation (H. L. A. Hart) versus the indeterminacy and politicization of legal norms of the Critical Legal Studies serves as the ammunition to the debate; there are no easy legal questions and answers; all are hard. There are only legal arguments and the final decision of the court.

K. Authoritative and Effective Decision as a Source

Law in book is not necessarily the law in actual fact. Sources of law are not law strictly speaking, otherwise, the distinct between law and sources would be redundant, superfluous, and works only to create confusion.

Law in its most realistic and inclusive sense is an authoritative and effective decision. Political power is legal power. Law is politics moralized in public or public morality politicized. Law results through a dynamic system of checks and balances, and the mutual informing and shaping process of authoritative and effective decision-making. It is the outcome of a continuing communication and dialogue between the legislature, judges, governmental officials, lawyers, legal scholars, corporate entities of various kinds, and citizens who take an internal standpoint of the law. This view of what is law supports and mutually reinforces the role of man or human

---

[28] *Example Found in Introduction to the Law of the United States*, Edited by David S. Clark and Tugrul Ansay, Kluwer, 1992, p. 34.

element in informing and shaping the establishment of a good legal system and good law. Chapter Seven, Section Eight of this book has an extensive discussion on this view.

From the discussions above with respect to the historical development of the Common law in England, we understand how the kings and their royal officials, the Parliament, the Lord Chancellor, the jurists, and the common people all interacted in the process of shaping the course of the Common law.

On the road leading to the final triumph of, and the establishment of the cohesion and unity of, the Common law in the United State, a number of individuals and landmark decisions were involved in the process. The following are the most noticeable:

The Calvin's case 1608;

The David Dudley Field and Jeremy Banthem's unsuccessful attempts for codification, The works of James Kent, Joseph Story, and Sir William Blackstone;

The rejection by many state legislatures to apply the Common law and legislation of England after 1776;

The Judiciary Act 1789;

The decision of Swift v. Tyson 1842;

Justice Brandeis' opinion in Erie Railroad Co. v. Tompkins 1938;

Countless jurists and scholars expounding on the virtue of the Common law;

The pressure exerted by generations of lawyers and their influence and impact on the authoritative decision-making process of various kind; and

The appreciation by both federal and state court judges as responsible members of the juridical community of the importance of their role and contribution to the promotion of a cohesive and united version of the American common law.

Further illustrations of the dynamic relationship between authoritative decision-makers in the United States is found in the collision and interaction of the legal powers of the executive branch, the legislative, and the intervention of the judiciary. However, to regard judges as the ultimate oracles of the law is to view law as a static normative state. The law (the legal rule) that the judge announced controls primarily the immediate dispute seized by the court. Even the precedent authority of a legal rule is limited to similar future cases at most. Only an insignificant number of actual disputes among people are adjudicated by the court of law. The fact that precedents are subject to being rejected, overruled, distinguished, or not followed in later cases further erodes or diminishes their value.

Therefore, the question of what is law ultimately rests with the internal statement and judgment of the individual and his or her choice. What commands attention is either authority of reason in terms of morality, obligation, and other normative notions, or reason of authority considering the consequences of value deprivation or value enhancement.

Authoritative and effective decisions are the foundation of law in the most realistic sense that they initiate the generation and establishment of social norms. Social norms are legal norms. The concept that law is an internal statement that projects externally onto both one's own decision and action and those of others and society at large. From the private, social and non-statist perspective, law operates as a standard of criticism backed by group and community pressure, and social approval and disapproval.

The concept of authoritative and effective decision is realistic, innovative, inclusive and universal. It necessitates a fresh way of thinking and understanding of what, how and why we consider as law. The concept of authoritative and effective decision gives a new meaning to life, liberating and empowering at the same time.

Lon L. Fuller advocates principles of social orders and the implicit laws embodies in patterns of actions and decisions discernable in the social fields. From the realistic perspective of the law in action, social orders and patterns of action and decision manifest authoritative and effective decisions and are the raw materials of the law. The financial and stocks markets reflect the collectivity of individual investors' actions and decisions. The authoritative status and the nature of their efficacy reside in the strength of the rise and fall of the markets. Because of their implicit nature, these orders and patterns need to be formalized or "juridified(法规化)"—a sort of sublimation to the privileged status of law. This comes to be known as the insight of the formal existence of law.

L. Integration of All Sources of Law-Generating Actions and Decisions

In view of the great variety of sources given above, one is tempted to ask, is there a term or concept that would include and integrate all of them?

How do we identify all the law-generating and law-shaping forces and elements without perpetuating and becoming apologist for the status quo of the received notions, categories, assumptions, paradigms and normative structures? And at the same time, one would have no difficulty to embrace the non-state, private, and un-formulated categories. One way to do it is not to overstress and use blindly any of the received categories, concepts, and language to identify, describe and evaluate the phenomena of social normativity. We submit that to effectively capture the true meaning and essence of what counts as law, a new legal paradigm has to be innovated. And that paradigm is the law of authoritative and effective decisions, a concept that has been repetitively advocated in the text of this work.

Section Nine: Reason as a Source (of Law)

The idea of authority and reason and their distinction are interesting, intriguing, and potentially, misleadingly complex. Law is authoritative. Yet the authority of law deprived of or lacking supporting or justifying reason becomes a naked emperor. We accept the authority of law precisely because of its justifying reason. In general, normal practice, it would be reasonable to assume that reason is immanent in authority; reason simply remains implicit and unarticulated. Reason is the sine quo non of authority and efficacy.

Are the propositions above potentially a slippery slop? Would they lead to legal cynicism or nihilism? We submit that the fear is unfounded. Any normative propositions advanced in the political moral field must pass the litmus test of authority and efficacy. The trepidation is not totally rational. After all, the material bases or constituent elements of reason are potentially infinite and fairly inclusive. Reason may be factual, logical, dialectical, religious, fictional, imaginary, tangible or intangible. Reason, in other words, is a grab-bag. Even so, we stress that the fear is still unfounded.㉙

Of exceedingly interest and significance in this connection is the invocation of the law of nature as reason of law. Darwin's law of natural selection and adaptation （达尔文的自然进化论） is particularly relevant. Darwin and his scientific breakthroughs have been tied to everything from the evolution of modern capitalist economies to asset management, hedge fund trading models and stock selection. Financial firms, in fighting for their survival at a time of unprecedented transformation and upheaval in global markets are reaching out to him more than ever. Hedge funds are using his name to assure worried customers that their ability to

---

㉙ A detailed discussion of reason is found in Chapter Eight of this book.

adapt and profit from difficult markets over full cycles is the way to reduce volatility and risk. Politicians are invoking his name to oppose bailouts for failing corporations. And money managers are proffering lists of stocks that fit the adapt-or-perish theme. There is a book entitled "Financial Darwinism: Create Value or Self-Destruct in a World of Risk."

Billionaire George Soros together with several other wealthy philanthropists, horrified at the neo-conservative ideology(新保守主义思想) at work in the Bush White House, set out to reinvigorate the Democratic alternative by establishing a liberal, ideas-oriented think-tank called the Center for American Progress or CAP. Its goal is to fill an intellectual black-hole in the Democratic party and to create a progressive agenda for its eventual return to power. With Barack Obama's victory, it's being saluted as the most influential "ideas factory" in the US. CAP issued a policy paper entitled "Change for America: A Progressive Blueprint for the 44th President." In it, 67 leading policymakers, scholars, authors and former government officials offer practical, often innovative, advice to the President. These days, CAP's issue papers are must readings, its briefings standing-room only, jammed with advocacy-groups representatives, lobbyists and reporters looking for advance insight into Obama's probable policies. Taking its lead from the Conservative think tank Heritage's playbook, CAP quickly became an effective liberal counterweight in the marketplace of ideas. Chief Justice Holmes's prediction theory coined for judicial law is no less applicable to predicting the decision or trends of decision in the field of authoritative and effective decisions. The decisions and actions taken and to be taken by the Obama Administration are exactly of this nature.

Review and Reflective Questions

1. Law is what we internalize as the right reason and externalize in action. Besides sources of an official, state nature, there are sources of an informal, unwritten origin. Discuss in detail why such unwritten normativity should be considered as sources.

2. Could you make sense of both the official, state sources and those implicit, non-state normative activities from a broader, more inclusive perspective?

复习及提问

1. 法律内化为正确的理性,外化为具体的行为。法律渊源除了正式的成文的形式,还存在非正式的不成文形式。具体讨论为什么不成文规范应当被作为渊源看待。

2. 你能否从一个更广的视角来理解正式的、书面的法律渊源和那些非正式、非书面的规范？

Chapter Three: The Common Law

Introductory Note

The origin of Anglo-American law is Common law. To examine the historical development of the Common law must be included.

Since The Common law originates in England, the distinct characteristics of English common law, its authority, and its sources are discussed. Also included are the British judicial organization and the form and content of English judgments.

简 介

英美法起源于习惯法,本章主要探究习惯法的历史发展。

习惯法起源于英国,本章将讨论英国习惯法的显著特点、权威性及法律渊源。同时涉及英国的司法机构及英国法院判决文书的形式和内容。

Section One: Historical Development of the Common Law

The Common law system came into being, historically, in England largely as the result of the activity of the royal courts(国王的法院) of justice after the Norman Conquest*. In England, first, there were Germanic laws(日耳曼法) during the period of Anglo-Saxon law. Though, England was ruled by a single monarch, the law in force was still made up of strictly local customs. With the Norman Conquest, the period of tribal rule was finished and feudalism installed. Gradually, through the institutionalization of the royal courts and the extension of their jurisdiction, a body of laws called the Common law applied to the whole country came into being. There is also a dissenting view that Common law is also royal law; the basic characteristics of much of the Common law can be traced back to royal legislation.

---

* 诺曼征服:1066 年,法国诺曼底公爵对英格兰的入侵和征服。

There are four distinct periods:

A. First, The Anglo-Saxon Period(盎格鲁—撒克逊时代)(Preceding the Norman Conquest, 1066)

This is the period when different tribe of Germanic origins (Saxons, Jutes, Danes and Angles) divided up England. These tribes applied local customs for dispute resolution.

B. Second, Formation of the Common Law (1066 - 1485): From Writs (令状)* to Actions on the Case

The Norman Conquest brought about a strong and centralized administrative organization. With it, the period of tribal rules was finished and feudalism installed. The highly organized character of English feudalism prepared the way for the development of the Common law. The following are some of most important developments.

(1) County and Local Courts

The hundred local or county courts that applied local custom were gradually replaced by new feudal courts that still applied the same local customary law. But how could the highly organized character of the feudal system of government and the establishment of feudal courts help the development of the Common law since the new feudal courts applied also local customary law? What was done is that in either case, the applicable law or rule was extended to all the people in the jurisdiction.

(2) Jurisdiction of Royal Courts—restricted reach

The creation of the comune ley**, an English law truly common to the whole of England, was to be the exclusive work of the royal courts of justice.

At first, the King only exercised "high justice(大法官)." The Curia Regis(国王的法院), from which the King dispensed justice assisted by his closest officials and highest ranking persons, was a court for only the most important personalities and disputes.

Feudal barons resisted the jurisdiction of royal courts. Certain parts of the Curia Regis gradually became autonomous bodies and established their seats at

---

* 令状是指国王发给的一种书面命令,同意赋予法院审判案件的权力,英国早期国王集立法司法行政于一身,人民是否能进入国王法院必须获得相应的令状,然后根据一定的程序进行诉讼。

** 普通法,也称 common law,同地方习惯相反,是整个英国普遍适用的法,建立这一体系,是英国王室法院的任务。

Westminister.

Royal courts had jurisdiction only over Royal finance, ownership and possession of land, and serious crimes.

(3) Extension of Royal Jurisdiction

Reasons for extension include: more cases meant more fees for the kingdom, people viewed the royal courts superior to feudal courts, only royal courts had the means to summon witnesses and to enforce judgments, and only the King, apart from the church, could require the swearing of an oath. Royal courts followed modern procedures and availed of the verdict of a jury(陪审团的裁决)*.

(4) Writs

Until 1875, the royal courts remained special courts to which the citizen had no automatic access. The person who pressed a claim had first of all to address his request to an important royal official, the Chancellor, asking him to deliver a writ. A writ is simply another terms for a court order. The effect of a writ was to enable the royal courts to be seized of the matter upon the payment of fees. It was not automatic that a writ would be issued. The judges had to be convinced to take up the matter complained. Each instance had to be individually examined. The list of established situations where writs were granted automatically was slow to grow

Nonetheless, the list grew and increased over times. Neither should the extension of royal jurisdiction be measured by such increase nor was caused by the passage of the Statute of Westminister II** of 1285. That statute authorized the Chancellor to deliver writs in consimili casu(同类案件) (in instances having great similarity to others for which the delivery of the writ was already established). The reasonable explanation for the extension over times is to accommodate increasing social needs.

(5) Actions on the Case

What is significant and decisive is the appreciation by the royal courts of the significance of the declaration made by the plaintiff(原告) explaining the details of the facts of the case. And this led to the admission by the royal courts of their jurisdiction over new factual situations or instances because of the compelling nature of the moral and justice issues. In time, these admissible actions multiplied and were

---

* 除非法官在某些特殊情况下撤销陪审团的裁决,否则一般情形下法官会依据陪审团的 verdict 作出终审判决。

** 《威斯敏斯特第二法》,准许大法官对同类案件发给令状。

given special titles in the light of the facts which justified them—actions of assumpsit (损害赔偿之诉), deceit, trover(侵害遗失物之诉), negligence, and so on. These actions may be generally classified under three headings: trespass(侵害之诉) to land, trespass to goods, and trespass to the person. Trover is defined as a Common law action to recover the value of personal property illegally converted by another to his or her own use. In old French, trover means find.

C. Third Period: Growth of Equity(衡平法) (1485 – 1832)

(1) Emergence of Equity

The strict compliance with formalist procedure exposed the Common law to two dangers: that of not developing with sufficient freedom to meet the needs of the period and that the dangers of becoming paralyzed because of the conservatism of the legal world of the time.

Unfortunately, these shortcomings of the royal courts could not be rectified or corrected by other courts that had general jurisdiction(一般管辖权), for these courts were themselves in decline and gradually disappeared from the scene.

The situation led to the eventuality that in a number of cases, no just solution could be found. In seeking another way of obtaining redress, a direct appeal to the King, the fountain of all justice and favor, was the logical and natural option.

In cases of no solution or shocking solution, people addressed the King asking him to intervene as an act of royal grace to satisfy conscience and as a work of brotherly love. As the King's confessor, the Chancellor had the responsibility of guiding the King's conscience and would, if he thought it appropriate, transmit the request to the King for judgment in his council.

In other countries, the judges themselves could supply the required remedy by prohibiting the abuse of a right or fraud, or by applying the principle of public order and good morals; such remedies were possible on the European continent within the very framework of the legal principles. In England, however, the royal courts did not have the same freedom of action because they had never had the same general jurisdiction and were bound to observe rigid procedures.

This recourse to the royal prerogative, perfectly justifiable and unopposed so long as it remained exceptional, could not fail to give rise to a conflict when it became institutionalized and developed into a system of legal rules set up in opposed to the Common law.

Gradually request for intervention by the Chancellor became more frequently; the practice became institutionalized. At the time of the Wars of the Roses (1453-1485), the Chancellor became a more and more autonomous judge deciding alone in the name of the King and his council. Decisions were made on the basis of "the equity of the case." Equitable doctrines grew out of the chancellor's decisions. These worked to add to and correct the legal principles applied by the royal courts.

After 1529, the Chancellor no longer served as confessor to the sovereign and was not an ecclesiastic but examined the petitions addressed to him as a real judge and observed a written procedure inspired by Canon law. The substantive principles he applied were also largely taken from Roman law and Canon law rather than the very often archaic and outmoded Common law rules.

A number of legal institutions (the principal one being the trust) and concepts such as misrepresentation(虚假陈述), undue influence*, specific performance(强制履行), and subrogation(代位求偿权) were developed in the Chancellor's equitable jurisdiction.

In all of these matters, the intervention of the Chancellor is discretionary. He only intervened if it was considered that the conduct of the defendant(被告) was contrary to conscience, and if the plaintiff had no cause for reproaching himself; he, on his side, had to have "clean hands"** and must have acted without undue delay in asserting his right.

The English sovereigns favored the chancellors' jurisdiction due to their concern for justice and good administration. The procedure of Chancery was private, written and inquisitorial in nature and also preferred by a monarch of authoritarian disposition.

As the chancellor applied Roman law, this worked to reduce the law to a simple private law and lawyer's work. And all these features helped give a greater scope to royal absolutism and executive discretion.

The risk is that the success of the Chancellor's equitable jurisdiction and the decay of the Common law carried potentially the seed of a danger that disputing parties would eventually abandon the Common law court.

---

* 不当影响,在英国法中,指一种影响、压力或控制力,使得一方当事人由此而不能自由、独立地就自己的行为作出选择。它作为衡平法的原则,是推定欺诈原则的组成部分。

** 净手,指某人在其起诉他人之事项上,其行为是正当的、合法的。

(2) Conflict and Compromise between Common Law and Equity

The royal courts and the Common law lawyers resisted the encroachment by the Chancellor on their jurisdiction and the Chancery's continuing expansion.

To defend their position and work, and to support them against royal absolutism, the Common law courts also found an ally in Parliament(国会). The poor organization of Chancery, its congestion and venality (that is, association with corruption or bribery) were also used as effective weapons.

A compromise was finally reached and pronounced by James I. The Common law courts and the court of the Chancellor worked side by side in a kind of equilibrium of power.

Specifically, no new encroachments at the expense of the Common law courts by the Chancery were allowed. The Chancellor would continue to adjudicate according to its precedents, not morality alone and arbitrarily, and thus escape from the criticism that it was arbitrary. The King also agreed he would no longer use his prerogative to create new courts independent of the established Common law courts. The Chancellor, as a legal or political figure, was no longer seen as judging on the basis of morality alone and tended to act more and more as a true judge. Further, after 1621, the control of the House of Lords(上议院) over the decisions of the Court of Chancery was admitted.

Over the centuries, the rules of Equity became as strict and as legal as the rules of the Common law. Today, the body of rules developed in Equity is an integral part of English law. The reasons formerly justifying the intervention of the Chancellor no longer exist; if English law is in need of remedial measures, there is Parliament. The security of legal relations and the supremacy of the law would be threatened if judges were allured to bring the rules of established law back into question under the pretext of equity.

Yet, key distinctions between law and equity remain important today. Among the distinctive features of a suit in equity as opposed to an action at law were:

- The absence of a jury—the judge instead of a jury is the exclusive decision-maker in equity,
- Court of equity follows a more flexible procedure,
- It enjoys a wider scope of review on appeal,
- While the law courts were generally restricted to the award of money damages as a relief, equity operated on the person of the defendant (equity acts in

personam). The court of equity could, for example, issue an injunction(禁止命令), forbidding a particular breach of promise of an obligation, or it could decree specific performance, ordering performance of the obligation. A defendant who disobeyed could be punished by fine or by imprisonment for contempt of court until compliance,

- In the beginning at least, the Chancery was not considered a court, it did not appear to be deciding "in law,"
- Even the terminology adopted by the Chancery's court(衡平法院) bears witness to the distinction. The procedure before the court is a "suit," not an "action"; one invokes "interests," not "rights"; the Chancery grants a "decree," not a "judgment"; he may award "compensation," not "damages."

D. Fourth Period: The Modern Period

(1) Duality versus Unity in Action: Fusion or Merger of the Common Law and Equity

Before 1873-1875, in any one dispute, it might have been necessary to institute two actions: one before a Common law court, the other in Chancery. Such, for example, was the case, if in addition to the specific performance of a contract (a remedy obtained in Equity), damages for the delay in the performance of the contract (a remedy obtained at Common law) were also wanted.

The 19th and 20th centuries are periods of fundamental transformation. Legislation brought about reform and modernization. Adjudication is free of formalistic procedural framework of forms of action(严格的诉讼形式). Greater attention is devoted to substantive law. Rules of established law are systematic and re-organized.

Judicial organization was greatly changed by the Judicature Acts of 1873-1875, which removed the formal distinction between Common law courts and the court of the Chancellor. The Acts did not change the law as it stood before but merely enabled Common law and Equity to be administered concurrently by the same courts. By virtue of the Acts, all English courts became empowered to apply the rules of Common law as well as those of Equity.

Equity is a body of rules that were given effect by the Chancery to correct English law in the course of history. Today, it is an integral part of English law. In the High Court of Justice, some judges sitting in the Queen's Bench Division decide according to the oral and contradictory procedures of traditional Common law, and others sitting in the Chancery Division, decide cases according to the written, inquisitorial procedures derived from the old Equity proceedings.

The same barrister does not plead in both divisions; the tradition of being either a "common lawyer" or an "Equity lawyer" persists.

As to the assigning of subject matters to one or another of the divisions of the High Court, the historical origin of the law to be applied is no longer of any importance. What is decisive is which of these two procedures is most appropriate in the circumstances. Equity now includes that a series of subjects in which it appears appropriate to proceed by way of written procedures; whereas the Common law comprises those in which the oral procedures of the past are retained.

Generally speaking, today, in order to know whether one is within the area of the Common law or that of Equity, it is more important to know which branch of law is involved rather than what sanction is available. These two branches of law are made up of a certain number of subject matters and characterized by the use of a definite procedure and marked by their own juristic attitude. Common law thus comprises criminal law, the law of contract and torts; but the common lawyers apply equally doctrines as misrepresentation, undue influence and estoppel. Equity includes the law of real property, trusts, partnerships, bankruptcy, the interpretation of wills and the winding up of estates.

The United States adopted the dual system of law and equity along with the general principles of the Common law system. The courts at both the federal level and the state level perform the dual function of law and equity.

(2) Landmarks in the History of the Development of English Law

13th century was the formative period of the Common law;

16th century is the formative period of Equity;

17the and 18th centuries is the period of Harmonization;

18th and half century is the absorption of the law merchant.

(3) Lessons Learned from the Historical Development of the Common Law in England

Many conclusions may be drawn from the study of historical development of the Common law in England. The following observations are offered as a starter for further analysis and study.

- The way of the birth and growth of the Common law in England appears to reflect the general trend of political development of most societies in the West during that period. This is manifested in the acquisition of a superior and dominant status by the royal courts of the kingdom at the sacrifice of feudal courts and tribal courts as well as a law that is generally and commonly applicable to people throughout the kingdom.

- The system of law as demonstrated in the emerge of the court of equity and its fusion with the Common law court into one hierarchical structure and the development of a scheme of procedure and remedies to meet the different and growing needs serve to satisfy the expectations of justice, fairness and equality.

- We witness the progressive development of the law over time. Both the legal system and the system of laws make themselves more complete and perfect.

Section Two: Special Characteristics of English Law of English Law

The special character of English law consists in its emphasis on the importance of Adjective Law. The rules that relate to matters of procedure, evidence, and enforcement of judicial decisions are collectively known as adjective or adjectival law. This differs from the traditional concentration of the civil law and continental jurists on substantive law. This special character is vividly illustrated by the distinct characteristics of English Common law. The following are some of the most representative ones.

A. Distinct Characteristics of English Common Law

(1) Remedies Precede Rights

Different writs entail or put into operation different procedures and involve different forms. English jurists concentrated on matters of form and questions of procedure. The Common law, in its origin, was made up of a number of procedures—forms of action. The first and foremost consideration for the litigant was to select the correct form of action or writ by which court could be seized, and then, to carry through with the formalistic procedure laid down. The emphasis was on the various formalistic procedures rather than substantive principles of justice.

The procedures provided the framework within which the English law developed and was organized. The law appears to have been "secreted in the interstices of procedures. " (Sir Henry Maine) For example, the chronicles known as the Year Books concentrate principally on matters of procedure and omit altogether whatever solutions given in the disputes.

(2) Wasting Away of Private Law

Enlarging the jurisdiction of the royal courts and their intervention was justified in the interests of the Crown and kingdom. Other courts dealing with private interests were in decline. In this sense, all the cases that were submitted to the English royal courts had the appearance, as it were, of being public law disputes.

The writ was not simply the plaintiff's authorization to act. Technically it was an order given by the King commanding his officers to order the defendant to act according to the law by satisfying the claim of the plaintiff.

If the defendant refused to obey the order, plaintiff's action against the defendant before the court was taken not so much because of the opposition to his claim but the defendant's disobedience of an order of the administration.

The trial centered essentially on a debate as to whether an administrative act, the writ, issuing from the royal chancery, was properly issued and whether the order it embodied to the defendant was to be maintained.

(3) Review of Decision-making Process; Procedural Fairness, Manner of Application and Interpretation rather than Substantive Justice and Merits of Dispute

English law is not a law of the universities. Nor is it a law of principles; it is a law shaped by proceduralists and practitioners. Judges are elevated from the profession of barristers, not from the university professor and judges need no university degree but trained in the daily work of a law office. Judging involves the determination of the proper form of action and follows strict rules of evidence for jury to render verdict. Though substantive law has been considerably enriched and principles of law are learned in universities, this traditional state of mind perpetuates and continues to be very much part of present day attitudes.

A correlated feature is the review of judgments by high court on procedural requirements, not on merits. Disputes in England are mostly handled by lower courts, administrative boards, tribunals, or by commissions or private arbitrators. The control exercised by the superior courts over these bodies concerns, in many instances, primarily with the manner in which they have interpreted and applied the law. And very often, especially in the case of administrative boards, commissions, rental boards, and arbitration, such reviews will only deal with the manner in which the procedures were carried out, not with attempt to verify whether on the merits the decision is justified or not. The focus is more on the observation of a fair procedure during which whether all the interested parties had been heard, and whether the conclusion had had in possession of all material facts. This is what the English means the concept of a fair trial.

(4) **Enforcement of Judicial Decisions: Enforcement of Mandamus Order**

This is another characteristic of adjective law. It is considered quite natural for the courts to issue orders to the various branches of the government (in order) that the law be respected in addition to quashing an illegal administrative act. Such order is known as a mandamus order. Specifically, it commands that that the legally required administrative step is taken. The vigor and the effectiveness of English enforcement procedures are impressive. Ignoring court orders resulting in the contempt of court is fundamental. This differs from the functions of the bailiff or court bailiff, who as an officer of the court, serves, processes, and enforces orders, especially warrants authorizing the seizure of a debtor's goods. Mandamus is defined in law as a judicial writ issued as a command to an inferior court, administrative or regulatory body or a person to perform a public or statutory duty.

(5) **Concept of Judge-Made Legal Rule—Case Law (facts-based legal rule)**

The rules of English law are, fundamentally speaking, the rules that are found in the ratio decidendi(判决理由) of the decisions rendered by the English superior courts. To the extent that he gives opinions not strictly necessary for the solution of the case before him, the English judge is speaking obiter. The legal rule is situated at the level of the case for which, and only for which, it has in fact been found and enunciated. It is thus not really understood and its significance cannot be measured unless one knows all the facts of the case in which it was enunciated. This is completely unlike the rules prescribed in codes of the Romano-Germanic family designed to direct the conduct of citizens in a range of cases without necessarily any reference to a particular dispute. No wonder, the French calls English legal rules applications, while the English calls rules in civilian codes principles of law, or like general moral precepts rather than true legal rules.

(6) Open system of the Common Law Rules vs. Closed Nature of Code: Discover a New Rule versus Interpret Existing Rules

The laws of the Romano-Germanic family are coherent but closed in which any kind of question can, and must at least in theory, be resolved by an interpretation of an existing rule of law. The English law provides rather a method of resolution. The technique is not one of interpreting legal rules; it consists, beginning with those legal rules already enunciated, of discovering the legal rule—perhaps a new legal rule—that must be applied in the instant case. This is accomplished by paying a very great attention to the facts of each case and by carefully studying the reasons that may exist for distinguishing the factual situation in the case at hand from that in a previous case. To every new fact situation there corresponds—there must correspond in the English legal mentality—a new legal rule. The function of the judge is to render justice, not to formulate in general terms a series of rules, the scope of which may well exceed the terms of the dispute before him. Often the judge's statements and comments are substantially broader than what is strictly necessary for a decision in the instant case. The emphasis is more on orbiter dictum than ratio decidendi. This fact is what has prompted the technique of distinguishing cases.

(7) Abnormal Character of Legislative Rules—Judicial Attitude toward Legislation

In the eyes of an English jurist, law, which is legislative in origin, has traditionally appeared as somewhat abnormal in character. Legislative provisions are not fully assimilated into the English legal system until they have been taken up and affirmed and sometimes even distorted by the courts in the course of the normal working processes of the Common law. It has been said that codes promulgated in the US or India, for example, have not become the basic legal structures the way the Napoleonic codes have in France.

In fact, the United States Code (USC) differs markedly from the civil codes of countries belonging to the civil law system as well as the criminal codes enacted worldwide. They differ not only in form and substance but also in nature and character. The USC resembles more or less the consolidated statutes found in some countries, e.g. Canada. Thus, the USC is consolidated and composite in form rather than the organic and holistic nature of a typical civil code. The USC is all-inclusive in content; it includes every legislative enactment during a specific period that is still in force at the date of consolidation; new edition or consolidation may be published after a lapse of certain years. The new edition or consolidation supersedes all previous ones. In the case of the civil code, it is a one-time ever-lasting undertaking; though specific articles, parts or portions of the code may be replaced by later enactment, the whole code remains intact.

B. Courts Decide Fate of Statutes through Interpretation

In principle, a statute cannot be altered by judicial decisions. In practice it is within the power of the court through interpretation to give free rein to the statute or to hobble it. Orthodox judicial attitude regarded legislation, as it is, exceptions are to be applied strictly and narrowly so as to confine it to the cases that it expressly covered.

The restrictive attitude fortunately no longer prevails in United States. Courts in the United States routinely incorporate legislative innovations and policies into Common law principles. It has always been the duty of the Common law courts to perceive the impact of major legislative innovations and to interweave the new legislative policies with the inherited body of Common law principles.

How is this done? If this is done by means of interpretation, restrictive, expansive, or distorted, the traditional attitude regarding legislative rules as abnormal still stands.

C. Courts Apply Principles Derived from Statutes

There are two classes of cases in which courts traditionally have derived general principles from statutes; illegal contracts that courts refused to enforce, and losses or injuries resulted from a violation of a statute, for which courts allowed recovery. (The violation of the statute is said to be negligence as a matter of law.)

There are also many other cases in which court have been willing to reason by apply general principles derived from statutes.

Section Three: Certain Characteristics of the Common Law Authority

These characteristics sprang from the judiciary's institutional position and conceptual orientation. They are subtle and complex.[30]

---

[30] For detailed characteristics, see Melvin A. Eisenberg, *The Nature of the Common Law*, Cambridge, Mass., Harvard University Press, 1988.

A. Common Law Authority is Trans-political: Generally speaking, the Common law is regarded as embodying a set of transcendental principles: nowadays it is regarded as trans-political. Though no longer universally true, it doest reflect a widespreading consensus that it crosses existing political boundaries and thus becomes indigenous. Viewed from this perspective, it would be safe to say that the rules and principles embodied in the private law codes of countries belonging to the civil law family certainly are of a similar nature and quality. All these appear to confirm the insight that the private laws worldwide are similar. This refers to the immanent and fundamental nature of the Common Law.

B. Common Law Authority is Principle-based: Due to its counter majoritarian difficulty or the concern as raised by Alex Bichel, judicial law-making can only be legitimized by the view that judges discover and apply general principles based and found in prior cases rather than express their own policy preference. Or unless, according to the popular progressive view, any effective power holders (socially allocated) can make law. Her, it refers to the essential quality of the Common Law at the process and operation level.

C. Common Law Rules Rest on the Bedrock of Facts: Judges develop and make law incrementally within the limits of the range of cases presented to them. These facts create the horizon of the judges' legitimate decision-making power. Facts permeate the structure of English law and often accede themselves to the rank of legal rules.

D. Common Law Authority Founded on Precedents: The mode of argument of judicial decision is process justification—This entails first, the characterization of facts; second, the comparison of the facts so characterized with conclusions of prior cases, third; the identification of similarities and differences, and finally, conclusion.

E. Common Law Authority Feeds on Elite Political Morality: Gradually in modern welfare states, policy arguments displace analogous reasoning. If principles are merely transcending the political, they may be likewise embodied in sources other than judicial decisions, such as statutes, regulations, and even public opinion and other sorts of authoritative and effective decisions. All authoritative and effective decisions are informed by and represent a particular vision of political morality. Judicial decisions are no less political than decisions made by other branches of government or by non-state entities and individuals in the public domain. The only meaningful difference between judicial decisions and other authoritative and effective decisions is the decision-making process, the participants, factors, and the scope, depth of other elements considered. Only through input of such an inclusive nature would the Common law be able to reflect the broadest social and political developments and trends and thus ensure its flexibility, continued vitality, and staying power. [31]

Section Four: Sources of the British Common Law

The famous Magna Carta(英国大宪章) of 1215, Anglo-Saxon customary rules and principles, Northern French practices and procedures familiar to the governing Anglo-Norman elite, customs of the law merchant, decisions of the royal courts, and today, the decisions of all the Common law courts of England all are sources of British Common law.

The sources of the Common law should not be located in doctrinal propositions which purport to state legal rules but in social propositions which include propositions of conventional morality, policy, and experiences. [32]

The word "common" in Common law represents customs common to the whole kingdom as opposed to those that prevailed only locally or within a particular colony. The identification of the Common law with the general customs of the nation was certainly exaggerated. Yet, much of it consisted of a blending of Anglo-Saxon customary rules and principles with northern French practices and procedures familiar to the governing Anglo-Norman elite.

The Common law is a collection of individual authoritative decisions, a body of principles and concepts of public policy expressed and repeated by judges from one generation to another.

Section Five: Importance of Legal Structure, Defining Categories and Concepts

The essential in law is not so much the individual rules enunciated at any given moment in decisions but rather in the structure of the law, its classifications, the

---

[31] E. L. Rubin, "The Concept of Law and the New Public Law Scholarship", 89 *Mich L R* 792, (1991).
[32] M. A. Eisenberg, *The Nature of the Common Law*, Harv Univ Pr., 1988.

concepts it makes use of and the type of legal rules upon which it is based. Beyond the ever-changing rules, there is a framework of the law that is relatively stable. It is essential for a law student to learn a vocabulary and to become familiar with certain constant concepts that will well equip him to study any question of law. While rules may change, new rules are explained within an organizational framework in doctrinal works that has little changed over the centuries.

There are many distinct and untranslatable categories and concepts unique to the Common Law. For an example, there are concepts such as trust, bailment, estoppel, consideration and trespass that mean nothing to the civilian mind. Even terms and concepts that look and sound the same are not—contract, equity, administrative law, civil law, etc. The importance of legal categories relates closely to the need for specialization, that is expertise in relatively fewer subject fields of law.

Section Six: English Judicial Organization

There is a fundamental distinction between "superior" courts and all other courts. Particular interest attaches to the decisions of the superior courts because it is from them that decisions having value as precedents are drawn, and it is through the study of the decisions of the superior courts that the state of English law on a particular point can be established—the overriding authority of the decisions of superior courts.

Superior Courts: the Supreme Court(最高法院) of Judicature

Throughout English history there have been many superior courts:

The Courts of Westminister (Court of King's Bench (K. B.), Court of Common Pleas (C. P.), Courts of Exchequer (Ex) administering the Common law;

The Court of Chancery administering Equity;

The Court of Admiralty for most maritime law matter;

The Court of Divorce for subjects falling within Canon law; and

The Court of Probate in respect of wills.

The Judicature Acts of 1873 abolished and grouped them within a single superior court. The Supreme Court of Judicature (SCJ) over which the Appellate Committee of the House of Lords exercises a final appellate jurisdiction. Presently, the SCJ is organized in three sections: the High Court of Justice, the Crown Court and the Court of Appeal.

High Court of Justice(高等法院)—Queen's Bench Division(后座庭) (Q. B.). (An Admiralty court, or a Commercial court), The Chancery Division(大法官庭). (A Companies court or a Bankruptcy court), and the Family Division(家事庭) and Subdivisions that signify special expertise.

The Crown Court(王权法院) hears cases in criminal matters. If the accused pleads not guilty, judge will be dispose of the case with the assistance by a jury.

The Court of Appeal(上诉法院) is the second level of jurisdiction having 16 Lord Justices presided over by the Master of the Rolls. Cases are in principle heard by a bench of three judges and each expresses his own opinions separately.

The House of Lords

From the decisions of the Court of Appeal, a further appeal may lie to the Appellate Committee of the House of Lords. In the House of Lords, there are the Lord Chancellor(司法大臣), the 11 lords of Appeal in Ordinary who have been especially created (non-hereditary) peers for this purpose and certain other lords. Cases are heard usually by a bench of five and not less than three lords. The appeal is brought in the form of a petition. Each judge expresses separately his opinion technically called a speech.

The Judicial Committee of the Privy Council(枢密院司法委员会)

This body is composed of judges from the Lords sitting either alone or with others from overseas. It hears appeals from decisions of the Supreme Courts of those British overseas territories or commonwealth states that have not yet abolished its jurisdiction. The decisions of the Judicial Committee—which in theory merely gives advice to the Sovereign in the exercise of his or her prerogative—have an authority more or less equal to those of the House of Lords in Common law matters.

Lower Courts

The vast majority of cases that arise are heard before a large number of lower courts.

In civil matters the principal court is the County Court. Judges (260 total in number) are, as in the High Court, selected from among experienced practitioners. More minor affairs may also be handled by the judge's auxiliary, the Registrar or be referred to Arbitrators(仲裁员). The arbitrator will often be the registrar or the judge if the case is significant or some other person agreed upon by the parties.

In criminal matters, the petty or summary offences are judged by magistrates(治

安法官), members of the community who enjoy the title "justice of the peace" but receive no remuneration. They have no legal training but are assisted by a legally trained clerk. In London and several other large cities, the justices of the peace are replaced by full-time, paid stipendiary, namely, paid professional, magistrates. For all major or indictable offences, it falls to the magistrates to decide whether there are sufficient grounds to send the suspected person to trial before the Crown Court. A great majority of such accused opts to be tried before the magistrates whose sentences are less severe. Magistrates also have a limited jurisdiction(有限管辖权) in civil matters, such as family law and in some claims for debt. Appeals when permitted from decisions of the County Courts are taken directly to the Court of Appeal. Appeals from decisions of the Magistrates' Courts, after authorized, proceed either before the Crown Court or before the Queen's Bench Division.

Quasi-Judicial(准司法的) Disputes and Bodies

In administrative matters and for problems arising under certain statutes, different bodies known as boards or commissions or tribunals have a quasi-judicial jurisdiction. They are many such bodies and their scope of activity is extremely wide. A Council on Tribunals created in 1958 to oversee the operations of some of these bodies now has authority over 2,218 tribunals of 41 different types which in 1978 decided well over a million cases. Most of these bodies are connected to a branch of the government administration; some are independent. Their composition, attributions and powers vary; the enabling statute for each body must be consulted for detail. All such bodies do at least in theory come under the supervisory jurisdiction of the High Court of Justice

Section Seven: Judicial Authority in England

The eminent position of English superior court judges is really on the same level as the legislative and executive authorities. Responsible for the development of the Common law and Equity historically, superior courts created the law of England in its very foundations. Courts themselves were the champions in the struggle for the affirmation and protection of English rights and freedoms. Today, they continue to serve as a counter-balance to the consummated alliance that now exists between Parliament and the government. The principle that there is no decided case that can escape the supervisory jurisdiction of the superior courts in the exercise of their inherent jurisdiction may now be taken as a rule of established constitutional usage. The existence of a full independent and highly respected judicial authority is seen as indispensable to the proper functioning of English institutions.

The indicators of the scope of power and importance attaching to the authority of the superior courts include:

All disputed cases are in principle to be adjudicated by the Supreme Court of Judicature. Just as masters in the creation of the law, the superior courts are also masters in its administration. The procedural rules for practice before the court are the work not of Parliament but of a commission upon which judges are the dominant influence.

The superior courts have the effective means for ensuring that their decisions are respected; they can address orders (prerogative orders) to public officers and through contempt of court procedures. This procedure is known as the so-called Mandamus order as mentioned earlier under the section "The Special Characteristics of English Law."

Absence of Minister Public

There is no procurator's office or ministry of justice in England. These are considered irreconcilable with the autonomy and dignity of judicial authority. The real power and authority of the judiciary is also demonstrated, historically, in the fact that the education and admission to practice as a barrister was controlled through the Inns of Court.

Section Eight: Form and Content of English Judgments

An English decision is no more than a single resolution or order making known the judgment in the dispute. English judge is not obliged to give reasons to justify his decision in the eyes of the parties. They do so primarily to instruct law students, the future barristers who traditionally received their legal education through attendance at court and through participating in the practical handling of cases. Often the judge's statements and comments are substantially broader than is strictly necessary for a decision in the instant case. The emphasis is more on orbiter dictum* than ratio decidendi. This fact is what has prompted the technique of distinguishing cases.

---

* 法官的附带意见,指法官在作出判决的过程中就某一与案件并不直接相关的法律问题所做的评论,它并非为本案判决所必要,因此不具有判例的拘束力。

The application of the rule of precedents in the Common law involves an analysis of these opinions or comments accompanying the decisions. The judge himself does not state what the ratio decidendi or obiter dictum is in that case; it is for a judge in a later case to do so in order to decide whether the earlier decision applies in the matter he must decide. Such practice undoubtedly gives judges in later cases amply opportunity to distinguishing earlier decisions. The technique involved here is either to narrow or to broaden the ratio decidendi of cases invoked, interpreted and applied. The persuasive value of an obiter dictum depends on the prestige of the judge who made such remarks, the acuteness of his analysis and the circumstances of the case.

Review and Reflective Questions

1. How do you think that the historical development of the Common law influences the form and content of Anglo-American law today?

2. You many take account of the characteristics and authority of the Common law in developing your thought in the question above.

复习及提问

1. 你认为普通法的历史发展是如何影响当今英美法的内容和形式的?

2. 在回答上述问题时,你可以从普通法的特点和权威性角度出发来思考以上问题。

Chapter Four: Legal System and Foundation of Law of the United States

Introductory Note

The law of the United States is commonly regarded as representative of Anglo-American law. Our choice is thus both logical and necessary. Struggling free from England to build a new model nation, America stresses and favours certain important characteristics and spirit. These are discussed. The United States is founded on a federal system. The political and legal authority between the federal government and state government must be distinguished and discussed. How the United States has been building a harmonious common law instead of a disparate system is of particular significance and interest.

The allocation of legal power between the federal government and the state government undoubtedly carries certain inherent burdens for business and citizen alike. We talk what have been done to overcome or ameliorate them.

简介

美国法被认为是英美法的典范。所以我们对于美国法的研究就是合理而必要的。美国独立过程中,展现了自己的一些重要特征和精神。美国是一个联邦制国家。本章将讨论在联邦体制下,联邦政府与州政府的政治及司法权威的关系,以及美国是如何建立起一套运作良好的普通法体系的。

联邦与州政府的分权无疑给国内的民众及各行业带来了不少麻烦。我们将讨论美国是如何来克服和改善这些问题的。

Section One: General Remark

The foundation of the law of a country should be the first thing to study. The foundation includes the legal system of a country, its constitutional and legal structure and process, its elite or authoritative decision-makers and other participants in the law-making, application and interpretation processes, judicial (court) structure, the allocation of legal and judicial authority, sources of law such as legislation, regulation, judicial decision among others. The role and the function of judges, legal education, legal scholars, and the legal profession are also an integral part of the foundation. What is of equal importance is to study how the various sources of law and the authoritative decision-makers interact, and how the system operates at the practical level.

Section Two: Reasons for Choice of Focus

The United States law has a worldwide reach in importance and influence. Being the most litigious nation on earth, the law of United States is most comprehensive, rich, detailed, and complex. Both for the ascertainment of binding intrinsic authority for practical purposes and/or for the identification of persuasive authority of reason for comparative study, the whole world is looking to the United State for leadership as well as lesson. This is true not only in the most controversial and technological areas but also in the field of trade, finance, commerce, and even other mundane concerns. American law provides a ready-made case law and legislative laboratory because of its scale and responsiveness to problems.[33] The much-feared phenomenon of Americanization in a wide-ranging area of international concerns is continuing to unfold before us, like it or not. The present economic meltdown and financial and banking crisis originate in the United States and quickly spread worldwide and it is the United States that has responded to deal with them through a host of legislative and regulatory measures in order to lead us all out of the mess. The decisions of the United States Supreme Court may have tremendously important impact worldwide. So are the actions and decisions of the United States President and its subordinate bodies. This is a universalistic as well as a polyjurial (多法) approach to law study. In essence, Americanization of the legal universe worldwide reflects the superior intellectual and material as well as the rich cultural conditions of the United States.

---

[33] D. F. Partlett, "The Common Law on Cricket: Book Review of Form and Substance in Anglo-American Law, 1987", 43 *Vanderbilt L R* 1401 (1990).

Section Three: Spirit and Fundamental Characteristics of American Law and Society

The people of every nation have certain unique nature, characteristics and aspirations. These immanent qualities, if not naturally endowed, are developed over time. And to a significant degree, history, tradition, geography, physical environment, cultural and economic developments play an important determinative role. What reflect and manifest these qualities are social structure, political arrangement, social and economic conditions, developments, as well as the cultural, spiritual, and financial life of the nation. But the fate of a people is never destined or preordained. The free will, wants, expectations, or aspirations of a people will over time flex its power, break context, and ultimately change the world for good or bad. This has been vividly witnessed in the endeavors, struggles, debates and conflicts of the people of the United States.

One cannot help but admires the farsightedness, statesmanship, and unselfishness that the founding fathers and her peoples had placed themselves in an "original position" and deliberated seemingly behind "a veil of ignorance"* on the fundamental values and principles that should guide the American nation. What they envisaged and crafted as a result has been called "The Original Vision."

The following visions are especially significant for the evolution and healthy development of its legal system and legal culture: liberty, individualism, distrust of government, tolerance, the rule of law, pragmatism, and optimism.

Following the presentation of these original visions, we mention certain newly developed and acquired aspirations and expectations that should be added to reflect the negative characteristics of the American people as well as certain critical observations and remarks to point out that the original visions, highly admirable as they are, do not always prevail in practice; they may very well be ignored, abused,

---

* 在罗尔斯的《正义论》中,有一个重要的理论:"无知之幕(Veil of ignorance)。"意思就是在人们商量给予一个社会或一个组织里的不同角色的成员的正当对待时,最理想的方式是把大家聚集到一个幕布下,约定好每一个人都不知道自己将会在走出这个幕布后将在社会/组织里处于什么样的角色,然后讨论针对某一个角色大家应该如何对待他,无论是市长还是清洁工。这样的好处是大家不会因为自己的既得利益而给出不公正的意见,即可以避免"屁股决定脑袋"的情况。因为每个人都不知道自己将来的位置,因此这一过程下的决策一般能保证将来最弱势的角色得到最好的保护,当然,他也不会得到过多的利益,因为在定规则时幕布下的人们会认同那是不必要的。

and even trumped over by those in high offices or power.

A. Liberty, Rights, and Government by Consent

The Declaration of Independence (1776) states that "we hold these truths to be self-evident that all men are created equal, that they are endowed by their Creator with certain unalienable rights, that among these are life, liberty and the pursuit of happiness, and that to secure these rights, governments are instituted among men, deriving their just powers from the consent of the governed."

Pursuit of happiness is not a guarantee of happiness. Nor it should be. After all, personal and subjective feeling has a lot to do it. The physical environment, material conditions, scientific and technological developments, and intellectual and cultural advancement of North America go a long way to facilitate and empower the exercise of this right.

B. Individualism, Competing Values, and Personal Choice

America is characterized as a republic of choice. The legal order is premised on each individual's capacity to freely choose among values without constraint by others or by the state. The American people recognize no hierarchy of values outside personal choice. All conceptions of the good are treated as equally legitimate. This is essentially what moral and value pluralism is all about.

Individualism comes hand-in-hand with personal responsibility and accountability. You learn, you act, and you take consequences. Ask not what your country can do for you. Ask what you can do for your country as President John F. Kennedy admonished. In times of hardship and financial crises, personal sacrifices and responsibility come to the fore.

C. Distrust of Government: Separation and Limitation of Powers, Checks and Balances(政府机关彼此之间的相互制衡), Political Accountability, and the Bill of Rights

Though not all government is bad, it has to be closely watched. Whenever any form of government becomes destructive of the ends and values as embodied in the Declaration, it is the right of the people to alter or to abolish it, and to institute a new government. The foundation of the new government will be laid on such principles and its powers organized in such a form as to them shall seem most likely to enhance their safety, prosperity, liberty, and happiness.

To achieve this end,

First, government was divided between a national government of restricted powers (certain <u>enumerated powers</u>[明示的权利]) and 13 original states, each with its own constitution and comprehensive and divided powers.

Second, separation of powers into three branches of government, each is specifically empowered, and any exercise of power beyond the reach allocated becomes ultra vires.

Third, there is an elaborate framework of checks and balances among and within the three branches of government: Congress has two chambers: Senate and House; hierarchical structure of the judiciary; relationships between Congress and the President in terms of spending, war, and the appointment of Supreme Court justices, for example.

Fourth, fixed elections to promote political accountability to people of the government's principal leaders.

Fifth, The Bill of Rights consisting of the first ten amendments to the Constitution was adopted by the first congress in 1789 and ratified by the requisite nine states in 1791, and Supreme Court enforces its provisions against all branches of government.

There is no doubt that these safeguards go a long way towards the prevention of abuse of power and the protection of rights and freedoms. But abuses of power and encroachments on rights have on occasion happened. The latest example is President Bush junior's executive order to imprison suspected terrorists at the Quantanamo Bay, Cuba indefinitely and without charge, and move, detain, and torture prisoners suspected of terrorist acts in foreign countries. And the Supreme Courts' denunciations of these abuses and ruling them as violations of the fundamental rights of citizens can only change the situation slowly if at all and can not undo the wrongs already committed.

A lawsuit against the United States Treasury Department filed recently by Shirin Ebadi for what they assert are regulations that cut off Americans from the work of scholars, dissidents and scientists in regions that we need to know more about. Ebadi is an Iranian human rights activist who received the Nobel Peace Prize last year but cannot publish her memoirs in the United States. The Treasury oversees the sanctions. Ebadi wants to write her memoirs for an American audience, but because she is not fully fluent in English, she would need the assistance of an American editor or even co-writer. There's the catch. United States trade sanctions against several countries, including Iran, prohibit providing services to anyone in those embargoed countries. Editorial, marketing and translation are among those prohibited services.

Ironically, if the book were issued in Iran, publishing a translation in the United States would be okay. It boggles the mind that sanctions put in place against dictatorships and terrorist threats should prevent someone—who, by the way, was once imprisoned by the Iranian regime because she was a proponent of women's and children's rights—from publishing a book in this country. It's a disgrace. And it's an example of how government can misuse its powers. Those rules need to be changed. If enough people raise loud and enough complaints, maybe they will be. Let's hope so. ㉞

D. Pragmatism in Law(法律的实用主义)

The dominant philosophy of law in America likely to command some consensus among lawyers and judges is the notion of Common Sense, in other words, pragmatism. Oliver Wendell Holmes, Jr. sums up this attitude: "The life of the law has not been logic; it has been experience." Grant Gilmore in his Storris Lectures on Jurisprudence at Yale reaffirms this view: "The principal lesson to be drawn from our study is that the part of wisdom is to keep our theories open-ended, our assumptions tentative, [and] reactions flexible..." There is no silver bullet in life. Don't easily trust anyone who claims he has found the best mousetrap.

Americans in general tend to have little interest in philosophy or metaphysical abstractions and even vulgarize it. They value what serves useful purpose; distrust intellectuals. Holmes' insight that "The prophecies of what the courts will do in fact, and nothing more pretentious, are what I mean by the law," best attests to this pragmatic truth.

Americans tend to avoid rule-like statements and eschew definition. For example, they would not rush out to define what is a table. They would say I know one when I see one.

The case method instruction de-emphasizes theory and doctrinal coherence and focuses on the facts of individual disputes. But such observations are not fully

---

㉞ Commentary by Myron Kandel. November 2, 2004, 10:37 AM EST CNN Money Website.

correct. Adjudicative theory(判决理论) and doctrinal exposition(学理上的阐述) go a long way to construct the needed coherence and consistence that underline all judicial decisions. It is legal scholars as well as judges who strive to discover these qualities through intensive analysis and comprehensive study of precedents. But such pragmatism with its elements of relativism and instrumental reason is buttressed by the original vision mentioned above.

Pragmatism in American must be take with a grain of salt(持怀疑态度). The deeply polarized partisan politics as evidenced in Presidential election and in the political and moral visions and agenda as advocated by the neo-conservatives in the Republic Party speak million for the anti-pragmatism stance.

Moreover, definition and statement serve important guidance and constraint values. Pragmatism is not devoid of weakness and immune of criticism. To an important extent, pragmatism lacks goals and objectives. Pragmatist knows what to do but not why it is done.

E. Government under the Rule of Law

Is the United States governed by the rule of law? That America is a society that is governed by the rule of law instead of man is certainly what the American people like to believe and the government works hard to project abroad. President George W. Bush in his nomination speech for the justices of the Supreme Court always stresses the importance of the rule of law. But to examine his records in upholding the rule of law is equally important. The rule of law concept is a loaded one. Both its theoretical and practical meanings are largely a matter of definition. Undoubtedly American's reification of pragmatism does appear sometimes to contradict the basic tenets of the rule of law.

The best time to test whether a government is ruled by law or by man who makes authoritative and effective decisions is when the very security and even survival of a nation is under attack.

The image of the United States as a country under constitution and rule of law has suffered heavily in the hands of Present Bush since the 911 terrorist attacks. For example, hundreds of people, citizens and aliens alike are suspected to be associated with or otherwise linked to terrorist groups, and who have not been charged of any crime yet, are held indefinitely at military bases in Guantanamo Bay, Cuba. without access to regular legal proceedings and legal counsel. This is all done in the name of fighting against terrorism and protecting the security and safety of the American homeland. It has been alleged that the rule of law, both nationally and internationally has been violated by such acts. In fact, both the courts and public opinions subsequently all have decided so.

If this state of affairs is truly representative of some kind of a systemic weakness or problem of the American political and legal structure, then the charge that the United States is somehow succumbed to the control of an arbitrary government, not law would seem not so incredible.

F. Tolerance

Americans are dissenters and nonconformists. The nation's fathers saw dissent as a positive force. The right of dissent in a political community requires tolerance of dissenters. The First Amendment mandates tolerance, at least by the government (governments at all levels): there would be no governmental ideology, no state newspaper, and no national religion. The separation of church and state is a fundamental constitutional value.

In certain sense, tolerance closely relates to the concept of individualism, competing values and personal choice, and even liberty and rights.

Religious tolerance touches the raw nerve of Americans. Religious tolerance closely relates to ethnic pluralism. The constitutional right of free expression could readily be invoked to support religious tolerance. That non-Christians may use their holy books other than the Bible in official oath ceremony is no doubt a giant step in the right direction. What remains disconcerting is the attitude and action of Americans in their daily lives and practices

If tolerance is understood as non-discrimination, then America is not that much better than many other countries. The U.S. republican system of governance, which granted residual powers to the states until the Civil War, made it impossible to put into full effect the U.S. Bill of Rights until well into the 20th century. It took the American Civil Rights Movement of the post World War II era, with the assistance of the U.S. Supreme Court, to bring African-American into the mainstream of U.S. politics and society. Barack Obama's election to the U.S. presidency is merely one more chapter in the U.S.' continuing struggle against overt and covert forms of discrimination, though some believe that President Obama symbolizes the achievement of a post-racial American democracy.

The best time to test vigorously for tolerance and non-discrimination is when the vital interests such as national security are at stake. It seems that the numerous testimonies to suffering from discrimination of all kinds against immigrants and minorities resulted from America's anti-terror policy after the September 11 attacks do not augur well for American on this account.

If tolerance is understood as non-discrimination, then America is not much better than many other countries. Countless examples can be provided to expose American intolerance. It has been recently reported that a United States town has long prohibited the broadcasting of Muslim prayer over a loud-speaker five times a day, while accepted as an integral part of Christian life the ringing of a church bell regularly. Intolerance of all kinds is frequently reported in the mass media.

On the question of whether or not the American secular society is a tolerant one, the jury is still out. Anecdote evidences direct toward both ways and remain inconclusive.

G. Optimism

The vast and bountiful virgin land and natural resources are the dream of pioneers and entrepreneurs. Empowered with the right to life, liberty, and of pursuit of happiness, Americans necessarily defy the notion of limited possibilities of human action and develop an optimistic character. What needs to be guarded against is not to let these conditions for optimism become the causes nourishing a feeling of moral superiority, a notion of manifest destiny, and feeding on excessive confidence and arrogance. Manifest destiny is the especially 19th century belief that the United States was intended by God to expand to the Pacific cost, and among some politicians eventually to cover all of North America. The present day manifestation of this manifest destiny is the neo-conservatism and the belief that the United States has a God-ordained mission to free the peoples of the world from all totalitarian regimes and to democratize their governments and political institutions; or the American Christian evangelists' faith to christianize the world. The unilateral actions steadfastly adopted by the US in many areas of international concern may very well have been made out of a sense of superiority or arrogance.

Another latest manifestation of American optimism is found in the common belief that the new administration of the Obama presidency will usher in the new and prosperous era for the United States and the world. There is no demise of American superpower status. The present financial crisis and economic woes may have tripped the American people. They may be down but not out. American will rise again and ready to lead. The slogan today is, yes, we can; Americans exhibit energy and hopefulness; Americans are walking tall and looking big.

H. Unity out of Diversity(差异带来的统一或联合)

To prevent the rich diversity and unfettered individualism from falling to chaos and conflicts, American was fortunately aided by a number of facilitating forces. Among these, we count the following:

English is the dominant language,

Common law tradition is widely accepted,

Federalism is the chosen dominant political structure for public matters or affairs affecting the nation as a whole,

Ever-expanding commerce clause of the Constitution further extends the reach of the federal government,

Bill of Rights goes a long way to expand the powers of the federal government and to restrain that of states,

Full faith and credit clause similarly serves a unifying function by requiring each state to recognize and in appropriate cases to enforce the public acts, records, and judicial proceedings of every other state. Congress by statute has made a similar requirement of federal courts towards states. The 13th, 14th, and 15th Amendments gave special importance to the equality principles and restrained state power to be divisive,

Emphasis on a common American law in legal education,

The promotion of legal unification through the National Conference(全国会议) of Commissioners on Uniform State Laws(统一州法委员会),

The establishment of the American Law Institute(美国法学会) and publication of Restatements of laws,

And even President Franklin Roosevelt's[*] New Deal can be all counted in the efforts.

---

* Franklin D. Roosevelt,富兰克林·德拉诺·罗斯福(1882—1945),他被视为美国历史上最伟大的总统之一,是美国历史上唯一连任4届总统的人,任职长达12年。他是身残志坚的代表人,也受到世界人民的尊敬。第二次世界大战中,1941年底,美国参战。罗斯福代表美国两次参加盟国"三巨头"会议。1933—1934年实行的罗斯福新政着重"复兴"。

I. Diversity as Divisiveness(差异引起的分歧): Disquieting Factors and Troubling Voices(不安定因素和声音)

Race and poverty combined have produced a social phenomenon that seems contradictory to, or incongruous with, the value of a republican aspiring to all the values orchestrated above. Accentuating on rights-oriented individualism loses sight of this ugly subculture. Liberty has become a broken promise; tolerance and optimism are in scarce supply. Excess in crime and violence committed by race or ethnic minorities signifies a breakdown in community and the failure of the legal system to maintain order and justice.

J. American Greed

Greed is said to be the DNA of capitalism. The United States no doubt best epitomizes both the good and the bad of capitalism. It comes as no surprise that greed is deeply ingrained in the corporate culture and practices in the United States

Greed is capitalism. Then, greed should not be decried and cursed, especially in good and prosperous times. No body would.

Lust and greed is a hot combination of fraud. CNBC TV has a show by the very name, American Greed which represents a series of continuing episodes of American greed imaginable as well as unimaginable in fields ranging from corporation, securities, currency, financial, charity, medicine, entertainment, art, and even religion and faith. People will do anything for money regardless of the untold devastation caused on people and society at large.

Another vice of free-market capitalism of the American unbridled version is risk-taking. Risk-taking is closely twined with greed. Risk-taking pure and simple is not bad and may under normal circumstances be regarded as virtuous and should be fairly rewarded. What is to be condemned are those specious undertakings and fraudulent schemes that are cleverly crafted by impetuous hothead—schemes and undertakings, such as "mortgage-backed securities(住房抵押证券)" and "credit default swaps(信用违约互换)" which are disguised in obscure, convoluted, and indecipherable language, and unscrupulously, wantonly, and even fraudulently marketed to unsuspected or equally greedy institutions and innocent investors for a quick and fat profit or commission. What is particularly evil is to lure charitable organizations without revealing the potential risks and downsides.

Securitization started as a good idea aiming at enabling banks to make more loans to good borrowers. It eventually had gone off the rails as the key-high fees drove bankers to lower lending standards to make more loans—a practice that unfortunately gave rise to the devastating subprime mortgage fiasco and the financial and banking crisis world wide.

The flip side of risk-taking is the imprudence. Had prudence and moderation been America's guide, the credit-card splurges, the bingo-capitalism, the Wall Street's greed, the executives' grotesquely inflated payments, the personal and national indebtedness, the fiscal deficits and all the other symptoms of a society living beyond its means that marked the Bush years of American politics would never have occurred. Cheap, borrowing, and printing money to feed on the insatiable greed would never realize the American dream.

In the largest Ponzi scheme in history perpetuated by Bernard Madoff, it has been reported that many investment funds funneled money to Madoff. Managers of investment "feeder" funds that relayed money to Madoff willfully turned a blind eye to his improprieties because they were paid generous fees.

Men in finance and business are the best epitomes of American greed. There are fewer place where the single-minded, avaricious, coarsely competitive, sharp-elbowed than the finance sector, where risk-taking is the modus operandi and greed, at least until recently when the American financial system virtually collapsed like a house of cards and the Madoff scheme exposed, was all good.

K. Corporate Bonuses, Compensations and Other Perks and Imprudence

People doing good works should be rewarded. Profits should be shared fairly by executives, employees, and shareholders and stakeholders alike. In good times, some reasonable privileges and special favors may also be granted to officers who are expected to render superior services or jobs.

However, in times of economic woes, financial crisis, credit tightening, and rising wide-spreading unemployment, family and household devastation, to award excessive bonuses and irresponsible compensations to already highly paid executives and upper-echelon employees must be exposed and condemned.

Unfortunately, the pay structure of the Wall Street, in which bonuses are based, overly emphasizes short-term profits and encourages employees to act like gamblers at a casino—and let them collect their winnings while the roulette wheel was still spinning. Compensation is flawed top to bottom. The whole organization is responding to distorted incentives. Traders ignore or plays down the risks they take until their bonuses are paid. Their bosses often turn a blind eye because it is in their interest as well. Investment banks like Merrill Lynch were brought to their knees because their employees chased after the rich rewards that executives promised them. In the case of Merrill Lynch, the game sadly ended with big bonuses for illusory profits.

L. A Nation of Excessive and Cheap Credit and Voracious Debtors

The root cause of greed is money and materialism. Americans are intoxicated with plastic money and borrowing heavily and irresponsibly to achieve material prosperity or hedonism. The pursuit of happiness is in fact a euphemism for property ownership and conspicuous consumption. The subprime mortgage fiasco amply testifies this truism. American is the most indebted nation in the world, with a $7.39 trillion and counting national deficit to fund, among other things, the most controversial, aggressive wars in Iraq and Afghanistan and the economic stimulus programs.

In order to expedite the realization of the American dream of liberty, equal opportunity, and happiness, legislation, policies and programs are purposefully crafted to provide credits(贷款) to people without collateral(所属担保物), down-payment(分期付款的首付), cash, and even job to acquire a house—this is the sub-prime mortgage(次贷抵押), so-called. It is this excess and irresponsibility that have eventually caused the most serve economic woes and financial crisis in the United States and the world at large. To achieve prosperity in America is by cheap money*, printing and borrowing.

As China is generally regarded as the only creditor(债权人) country able to continue funding these debts, it is said that the United States is soon becoming a financial colony of China.

Section Four: Basic Constitutional and Political Structure

The idea of American law is enshrined in Declaration of Independence (1776), the United States Constitution (1787), and the first ten amendments (the Bill of

---

* 经济学上用来描述旨在刺激投资加速经济发展而保持低利率的廉价货币制。

Rights of 1791). Conceived in hope and dedicated to opportunity, it has to an astounding degree accommodated different races, ethnic groups, and religions.

The transition from constitutional structure and system to legal and normative system is a logical and natural one. The Basic framework, structure, and institutions of the legal system constitute what H. L. A. Hart calls the "secondary rules," such as rules of recognition, adjudication, and change. These are also what Myres McDougal of Yale Law School·terms as the constitutive order decisions

As prescribed in the Constitution, the authoritative decision-makers, the power elite, or the major participants in the law-making process include:

The President, the various ministries and bodies of the executive and the ever-increasing number of administrative and regulatory agencies.

The Congress, its constituent parts, the House of representatives, and the Senate, and the numerous committees and subcommittees of both the House and the Senate as well as other authorized bodies, and

The Judiciary which includes all the courts in the judicial hierarchical structure.

The President is directly elected by the whole of the people (i. e. elected by special electors in each state who are in turn elected by the population at large), not secondarily by the legislative representatives. In fact, the presidential electors are invisible and irrelevant. The President serves a fixed term of four years and may serve only two such terms. He enjoys an independent and exclusive national political mandate and conducts the affairs of the state alone but cannot be assured of legislative support. Whether or not there is a clear national political mandate for the President depends largely on whether or not and to what extent he has the support of the American majority for certain clearly stated policies and agenda. He may have to confront a Congress in which one house is or both houses are, dominated by his sworn political adversaries. He proposes and may veto legislation. With a two-thirds majority, the House and the Senate can override his veto. There are circumstances in which the intersection of executive and legislative responsibility is more complex and the division of authority between these branches is often murky.

The Congress is composed of two houses: The Senate was intended to preserve the equality of the states and voters of each state. Regardless of population, each state elects two senators for a total of 100. Senators are elected for six year terms, which are so staggered that only about one third of the total number, at most one senator from any one state, is elected at each biennial election. The House of

Representatives is made up of 435 members, each of whom is elected for a two-year term by voters of one of the congressional districts. The number of districts in each state more or less corresponds to its population. Congressional districts are redrawn every ten years on the basis of the national census. It often happened that the gerrymandering, redistricting, reapportionment schemes made by either the Republican or the Democrat for partisan reasons ignored the change in population.

The twinned notions of separation of powers and checks and balances are designed to ensure each branch has sufficient power to blunt the possibility that another branch will abuse its authority. For an example, A U.S. president to get legislative action on his agenda has to do trade-offs with the agendas of powerful congressional leaders. Unless a party wins the 60-set majority in the Senate, his proposed legislation would be subject to devastating filibusters and other delaying tactics likely to be mounted by the other party. Areas of complexity and difficult include the conduct of foreign affairs, the regulatory state conundrum—the burdens of a sprawling and detailed regulatory authority have made the neat division impracticable—the birth of a neither-fish-nor-fowl legal animal, the administrative agency, and third, Congress' fiscal prudence led to inventive mechanisms of overseeing and assuring the legality of executive officials' behavior and conduct. A detailed, exemplary discussion of the interactive relationship between the three branches of government is given in Chapter six.

For discussion on the Judiciary, please refer to sections below on the judicial structure, jurisdiction, and power as well as judicial reason and the role of judges for the building of a good legal system.

Section Five: Division and Limits of Legal Authority of the United States

In a fundamental sense, the constitutive structure of a country—a constitutional democracy or parliamentary democracy—determines the division and the limits of legal authority and power. United States is a constitutional democracy and has a federal legal system. Each of the fifty states retains largely independent legal authority. The federal government in turn possesses a sprawling legal authority overlapping that of the states. And within each state, important legal authority is often delegated to a diverse structure of local governmental entities. There is almost as much overlapping authority across federal and state bounds as there is exclusively federal or exclusively state authority.

A. Originality of American Law

The triumph of the Common law in the United States was won with some difficulty. Nor was it complete. There are significant differences between English law and American law. Reasons for differences consist mainly in the difference in geography, population, political structure, a federal state, ethnic origin, religious affiliations, lifestyle, feelings and ambitions—the so-called American way of life.

1776, the year of American Independence is the watershed. There was never any question that statutes enacted in England after 1776 were not to be applied in the United States; nor were the English Common law developments after that year ever considered as inevitably having to form part of American law.

B. Place of Statute in American Law: the Abnormal or Excessive Attitude toward Statute

Belonging to the Common law family, the law of the United States likewise essentially judge-made. Thus, legislative rules, no matter how numerous, were viewed with some discomfort. They were not considered as the normal expression of the legal rule. They were only truly assimilated into the American legal system once they had been judicially interpreted and applied. When it is possible to refer to the court decisions applying legislative texts themselves, the preference is squarely in favor of court decisions. In honoring the Common law tradition, the attitude thus remains to be the anachronistic bent (bias) that when there are no precedents, there is no law on the point. This situation is not dissimilar to that prevalent among English lawyers.

Such proposition or observation as made above is highly questionable. All judicial interpretations are fact-based. As such, their scope of application is necessarily limited to the facts noticed. Unless a sufficient increase in the number of judicial decisions to have generated a coherent body of common law rules or principles, judicial decisions are not in the position to provide authoritative conduct guidance in every aspect of life. Besides, how was the very first interpretation and application of the statute made since there could not be any cases or precedents on the point at that moment? What could have been the base of authority for the every first judicial decision interpreting and applying statute? And what could possibly be the base or reason for according such overriding status to judicial decision in the face of the authority of statute? It may very well appear to be an over-blowing or extreme stance of the prediction theory of the American legal realism.

The prediction theory is in fact not realistic at all. It appears to have difficulty to square with the stance of the general public who routinely conduct their business and life in accordance with the formulaic rules found in legislation with or without the advice of lawyers. Moreover, the theory appears to contradict "the Supremacy Clause of the Constitution. Article VI, section 2 declares that the Constitution and laws of, and treaties made by the Unites States, shall be the supreme law of the land, and the judges in every state shall be bound thereby, any thing in the constitution or laws of any state to the contrary notwithstanding.

Section Six: Allocation of Legal Authority between Federal and State Governments

A. Inherent Legal Authority of the States

The states are fundamental building blocks of legal authority in the United States. Each state has its own constitution and laws. Municipalities such as cities, towns, counties are the delegates of state authority.

The federal government has only enumerated powers and enjoys only authority specifically granted by the various provisions of the Constitution; Article 1 deals with the legislative power. Article II executive power, and Article III judicial power.

B. Jurisdiction of Federal Law versus Jurisdiction of State Law

Due to this federal structure, for any given subject matter, the initial question is who has jurisdiction?

(1) **Principle of State Legislative Competence (州立法权能原则): Residual State Jurisdiction and Competence**

Amendment X to the American Constitution, enacted in 1791, is as specific and unambiguous as possible on the matter: "The powers not delegated to the United States by the Constitution, nor prohibited by it to the States, are reserved to the States respectively or to the people." On this basis, state legislative competence is the rule, while federal competence the exception. This principle was only natural; Until the War of Independence, the 13 colonies had been entirely independent of each other; they had nothing in common either in their origins, colonization, religious affiliations, political structures or economic interests. In a sense, they were sovereign within their respective political and geographical confines. Except their common link to the mother country, they had no political ties between them and no institutional framework bringing them together before the Revolution.

(2) Breadth and Diversity of State Law

Important differences arise under the respective statutory rules and judicial interpretations. Court and administrative structures vary from one state to another and so do civil and criminal procedure. Divorce is not granted everywhere upon the same grounds; matrimonial property(婚姻所得财产) may be community of property in one state and the principle of separation of property in another. The list of criminal offences(犯罪) and penalties is established by each state. As a matter of fact, with respect to most of the controversial social and moral issues, such as same-sex marriage, stem cell research, legality of marijuana, there is always a wide spectrum of diversity in state law.

Whatever importance federal law may have attained, it is nonetheless state law with which, in daily life, most citizens and lawyers have direct and regular contacts. In fact, this is true in any federal system to a varying degree.

(3) Residual State Jurisdiction: What States Can and Cannot Do

In exclusive federal competence, states are prohibited from passing measures that will conflict with the provisions of federal law. But they are not prevented for passing measures that complete the gaps left by the federal law or serve as additions thereto. Even in the field of international or inter-state commerce, an exclusive area of federal jurisdiction, there may be simply no federal legislative actions in certain subject areas, such as negotiable instruments, the contract of sale, commercial companies or the conflict of laws. The latter is governed by the Common law. An important caveat(警告): in the absence of relevant federal legislation, the states have not been allowed to legislate against the spirit of the Constitution by bringing restrictions to the concept of inter-state commerce. Any such actions would be considered unconstitutional, even though not incompatible with federal provisions.

(4) The Expansion of Federal Government's Limited Enumerated Powers Through Expansive Interpretation(扩张性解释) of the Constitution

In principle, all federal legislation is open to question on the ground that it exceeds the enumerated and narrow domain of authority. In reality, due to the liberal and expansive interpretation of the Constitution, most, if not all, of the legal barriers to the exercise of federal legislative authority has been removed. The realities of a national economy, and the overwhelming sense of national authority and responsibility that has come to dominate American constitutional law called for such expansion.

Inter-state and Foreign Commerce—This is particularly true in the commercial contexts. Article 1, section 8 of the Constitution grants Congress the power, inter alia, "to regulate commerce with foreign nations, and among the several states, and with the Indian tribes." This commonly known "the commerce clause(贸易条款)" has become a limitless source of power for the Congress to regulate commercial activity. Even federal regulation of local commercial activities has been sustained on this ground, while the obvious end of the regulation is social justice rather than economic efficiency.

C. Supremacy Clause

Article VI, section 2 of the Constitution reads: "This Constitution and the laws of the United States which shall be made in pursuance thereof, and all treaties made, or which shall be made, under the Authority of the United States, shall be the supreme law of the land; and the judges in every state shall be bound thereby, any thing in the constitution or laws of any state to the contrary notwithstanding."

The lowest federal legal stipulations are lexically prior to the highest state provisions. A valid discretionary act by a single federal administrative official will prevail over a conflicting provision enshrined in a state constitution. Federal law is said to preempt the conflicting state provisions.

While the principles underlying preemption are simple and absolute, their application in a particular case is often wrapped with interpretative difficulty.

D. Preemption Controversies(优先适用争议)

The primacy and preemption of federal law can be challenged on two grounds. First, is the federal action based on the limits of the enumerated powers of the federal government in the Constitution? Second, does a particular state legal provision actually conflict with federal authority?

One such controversy is Congress's cigarette warning label legislation. Could a smoker sue a cigarette manufacturer in a state court and invoke state liability law long after the effective date of the legislation? The question centers on whether a sensible Congress embarked on lawmaking in the area in question would have preferred exclusive authority in the area or would have welcomed the parallel regulatory efforts of state and local governments. Legislative intent is not always clear due to silence, inadvertence or political expedience. In interpretation, the Supreme Court was often divided. Consequently, what is the precise scope of preemption may change from one case to another. Uncertainty and indeterminacy rule.

E. Derivative Principle of Preemption Clause(优先适用条款的派生原则)

Two such principles further limit state competence.

First, unless Congress grants the states explicit permission to do so, they may neither tax nor regulate the federal government in any ways.

Second, in regulating or taxing persons or companies working for the federal government as employees or private contractors, states may not do so while impede the federal government in the pursuit of its diverse projects.

F. Continued Importance of State and Local Law

Regardless of the face that states are faced with an essentially unlimited authority and the unequivocal priority of national law, state and local law, to a surprising extent, continues to guide the basic components of modern life of residents. In area such as family, business relationships, civil and criminal liability for injurious conduct, control of the use of land, and the ownership and transmittal of property, it is the law of the state that dominates.

Section Seven: Judicial Organization

A. Organization of Courts

Federal Courts

At the base of the hierarchy there are the U.S. District Courts, and from these an appeal lies to the US Courts of Appeal; from these there is also a further appeal to the Supreme Court. There are about 100 of these district courts staffed with about 400 judges. Some of them are also divided into several divisions. In the most populous divisions, judges are sometimes assisted in their work by court officers known as "commissioners." These commissioners, in some instances may judge on their behalf. Each of the district judges has a young lawyer clerk assisting him in his research.

The US Courts of Appeal—formerly US Circuit Courts of Appeal(巡回上诉法院). There are 13 such circuits; 11 for geographical divisions, a 12th for the District of Columbia, and a 13th circuit to review cases from specialized federal courts. There are 80 judges serving in the Courts of appeal. The Federal District of Columbia is staffed with three judges hearing cases in all the principal cities of the court's jurisdiction.

The U.S. Supreme Court

Composed of a chief justice and 8 associate justices, all of them hear all cases. 90 per cent of cases seized require decision with reasons. Only 12 per cent of cases brought to it are adjudicated and 150 full written decisions are given annually. More information is give under E: Jurisdiction of the Supreme Court below.

Special courts(专门法院)

Established by federal statutes for fiscal or excise matters, patens, etc. There is the Court of Claims when the liability of the state is involved. There is also the Court of International Trade(国际贸易法院), and the Tax Court(税务法庭). Choice of either special court or district court could be had in some subjects; in tax matters, either in the district court or before the Court of Claims. There is also the Federal Circuit that deals with patent cases, certain claims against the United States, and most personnel matters.

B. Administrative Agencies and Tribunals(行政机关和行政法庭)

These and the important federal committees connected to the Congress are also attributed jurisdiction by virtue of federal statutes. From all these legislative courts and tribunals, an appeal is always possible to one of the traditional federal courts whether to a district court, directly to a court of appeal, or even directly to the Supreme Court.

Appeals from a district court are generally heard in the court of appeals for the circuit in which the district is located, though in rare instances appeal may be made directly to the Supreme Court. Because of the limitations on review by the Supreme Court, these circuit courts are in fact the courts of last resort for most federal cases. They also review decisions of certain federal administrative agencies.

Only the Supreme Court itself is created by the Constitution; all others are creatures of congressional enactment under the grant of power in the Constitution.

C. State Courts(州法院)

Most have three levels: a supreme court, a court of appeal and a court of first instance; some have only two degrees. The trial courts of general jurisdiction of states are variably called superior, district, or circuit courts. A single judge presides whether there is a jury or not, civil and criminal.

There are also special courts or divisions with limited jurisdiction, such as domestic relations, family, children's courts, probate courts or surrogate's courts for decedents' estates.

There are courts of inferior jurisdiction that handle petty matters, like the traditional justice of the peace courts. They have often been supplanted by county, municipal, small claims, or traffic courts.

State courts are local in their reach. Line between civil and criminal cases exists in many states. Many states have more than one level of appellate review, with a right to a single appeal, and review in the highest court only by permission of the court, a process known as Certiorari(诉讼文件移送命令).

A final warning: terminology varies widely, and so even courts with the same name do not necessarily perform the same function in very state.

In New York State, the court of general jurisdiction at first instance is the Supreme Court and division of it is situated in each county. Appeal may be had to one of four Supreme Court Appellate Divisions and from them appeal may lie to the Court of Appeals sitting in Albany. There is also a vast network of various inferior courts: Surrogate courts for matters involving wills and successions, Court of Claims for damages against the State itself, Family courts(家事法院), special courts for small claims or minor disputes.

D. Jury

The Seventh Amendment guarantees its retention. Any citizen may require that his dispute is to be decided by a jury when the sum involved is greater than twenty dollars—this may change over time—provided it is not a proceeding in Equity. There is no right to a trial by jury before the state courts. The option to have a trial by jury is nonetheless widely admitted in numerous states. Section K of Chapter nine give a more detailed discussion of jury trial and jury selection.

Section Eight: Allocation of Judicial Authority

A. General Allocation

The distribution of judicial authority between the state and the federal government parallels that of legal authority generally. Unless explicitly divested of their authority by federal legislation, state courts have subject matter jurisdiction (competence) to hear almost all legal controversies, state and federal, within the geographic sphere of their authority. In other words, whatever judicial jurisdiction has not been given exclusively to the federal courts remains in the state courts. In fact, the Congress has left this omnivorous state judicial authority intact in all but a few narrowly defined areas where it has made federal judicial jurisdiction exclusive.

In contrast, the subject matter jurisdiction of the federal courts is limited. Constitution confers on Congress discretion to create or not to create federal courts and to give them only part of the available federal jurisdiction. Therefore, the limit on federal jurisdiction is twofold: by Constitution and by Congress. Over the years, Congress has created a complex web of federal jurisdiction.

B. Two Primary Bases of Federal Jurisdiction

Diversity Jurisdiction involves controversies between the citizens of one state and those of another (citizens of two different states) or between the citizens of the United States and those of another (foreign) country where the <u>amount in controversy</u> (争议数额) exceeds $50,000. This may change also over time. This is designed to avoid the burden or inconvenience that a citizen of state A has to sue the citizen of state B in the court of state B. It is also believed that federal courts, their procedure, and court calendar are more favorable.

Federal Jurisdiction involves cases where issues of federal law are presented with no minimum amount required. This includes not only criminal actions, but also actions brought by the United States or by an agency or officer authorized to sue by an act of Congress. Controversies arising under the Constitution, laws, or treaties of the United States are all included in this category

In fact, most of the civil business of federal district courts is of three kinds:

First, cases in which the United States is a party;

Second, cases between private parties involving federal laws, under the so-called "federal question"; and

Third, cases between citizens of different states, under the so-called "diversity" jurisdiction.

In some cases, Congress has made the jurisdiction of the federal courts exclusive and in others it is concurrent.

C. Structure Parallel Systems of Adjudication: Judicial Dualism(司法二元主义)

As federal courts have only limited jurisdiction, very few state cases could ever be heard in a federal court. Ninety percent of the three types of cases specified above handled by state courts. But those concerning civil rights, racial integration(种族一体化), the application of anti-trust laws and the constitutionality of laws are generally judged by federal courts and eventually by the Supreme Court.

Cases that arise under federal law or satisfy the diversity of citizenship requirements can be elected to bring in either state or federal court. Federal legislation permits the defendant to remove to federal court a case first brought by the plaintiff in a state court. The party filing the case has the initial choice.

For a federal question case to originate in the federal courts, the case must actually arise under federal law. Once a case is in the federal system, it may be transferred to another federal trial court for the convenience of parties and witnesses. Rules respecting transferring case for convenience also apply within a state.

However, when a case involves a matter that could not, in first instance, be taken to a federal court, it necessarily follows that the decision of the highest state court is final and binding.

Added to the judicial dualism—federal courts and state courts operate together, there is also a double hierarchy of courts.

D. Foreign Sovereign Immunities Act(外国主权豁免法), 28 U.S.C, Para. 1330

The Act grants foreign governments immunity from suit in state or federal courts. The most important exception is "commercial activity(商务活动)" carried on in the United States by the foreign state. Sovereign immunity of foreign governments is a privilege that is granted mutually on a reciprocal basis through international agreement.

The Act provides for non-exclusive federal jurisdiction over any actions that satisfy one of the exceptions, whether the plaintiff is a citizen of the United States or a citizen of a foreign nation.

Thus, in cases falling in one of the exceptions, both the state and its citizen can sue in the federal courts. The Act has been interpreted to permit citizens of other countries to bring suit against foreign nations in the federal courts. Since every action against a foreign government must satisfy one of the exceptions to the general statutory grant of immunity, any qualifying action against a foreign government has been held to have arisen under federal law and fallen within the federal question jurisdiction.

New Exceptions—The protection enjoyed by foreign sovereigns from lawsuit in the U. S. may have already been compromised. For example, the Supreme Court recently ruled that United States citizens could sue foreign governments over looted art, stolen property and war crimes(战争罪) dating to the 1930s. Obviously, decisions of this nature are bound to inject great prospective uncertainty into the United States foreign relations.

Congress derives these powers by virtue of its authority over foreign commerce and foreign relations as well as the supremacy clause

A great proportion of cases are heard by state courts, though the average federal case tends to be much more complicated

E. Jurisdiction of the Supreme Court

Under the Constitution, the Supreme Court itself has original or trial jurisdiction. This includes disputes between states or between a state and the federal government. But such cases are not common.

The Court's jurisdiction is in the main appellate in nature as determined by the Constitution. It does not give advisory opinions(咨询意见), even on constitutional questions, at the request of the President or Congress. On this matter, the United States differs from Canada.

Limitations:

- Jurisdiction extends only to "cases and controversies," same as other federal courts in general. It will only decide lawsuits between adversary litigants whose interests in a ripened controversy are at stake.
- The federal questions must be "substantial."
- The Court will not review decisions of the state courts on questions of state

law. The state courts are themselves the final arbiters of state law and their decisions are conclusive on such matters.

For a case originating in state courts to be within the appellate jurisdiction of the Supreme Court, it need merely to present an issue of federal law.

The Supreme Court only reviews cases that raise an issue of federal statutory or constitutional law and only on the federal question presented.

Criminal cases were rarely granted for Supreme Court review, even though defendants often claimed violation of their constitutional rights.

The principal method of review is by writ of certiorari. This is a command issued from the Supreme Court to the lower federal court or to the state court of last resort. The issuance of such a writ is within the discretion of the Court. It is granted only for "special and important reasons" and the fact that the decision below is erroneous is not such a reason.

Cases to which a writ of certiorari will be issued include:

- A state statute has been held to be invalid under the Constitution or federal law.

- The existence of a conflict in decisions among federal courts of appeals for different circuits.

- A conflict between a decision by a state court on a federal question and the decisions of the Supreme Court itself.

The Court disposes of nearly seven thousand cases a year. Only 12 per cent of cases brought before it are adjudicated on merits and 150 full written decisions are given annually. (A reminder that all these are subject to change)

Section Nine: Reception of the Common Law in the United States

No legal system can be well understood without a good knowledge of its history. Many of the aspects of modern American private law, contract law included, are as much the product of history as they are the product of reason.

When the English colonized North America, the foremost practice and institution they imported was the Common law. It is important to point out at the outset that the Common law was used as an ideological weapon in the American struggle for independence, as it was looked upon as an embodiment of fundamental liberties and human rights. Even the United States Constitution and its seminal principle that no one can be deprived of life, liberty, or property without due process of law, can be traced back to Magna Carta and the general principles of the Common law.

A. Ignorance and Slight of the Common Law

In principle, the Common law of England was generally applicable according to the holding of the Calvin's case, 1608. Then, it suffered a restriction: the Common law was only applicable in the colonies so far as it was adapted to the local institutions and circumstances. The archaic and elaborated and complex procedural rules were totally unsuitable for the colonies, as there were no lawyers, no law books, and the substantive law had been made by and for a feudal society(封建社会). Moreover, the emigrants who escaped England largely looked upon the Common law not as the bastion of their personal liberties. The Common law itself was distasteful to the colonists who have been forced to emigrate to escape persecution. This attitude contrasts sharply with the stance of invoking the Common law as an ideological weapon in the American struggle for independence and as an embodiment of fundamental liberties and human rights. One can only explain this change of heart to the success of the independence—destroy the bridge after one has crossed it.

Roscoe Pound, the founder of the school of sociological jurisprudence, once aptly said: "a prime factor in shaping law... was ignorance." First there were special regulations issued by local authorities. Bible and judicial discretion were resorted to. In reaction to arbitrariness, primitive codes were drafted. So written law was favored.

B. Influence of the Codification Movement

Since Independence in 1776, republican ideals and an enthusiasm for natural law naturally encouraged the idea of codification. This trend led to the birth of the Constitution and the Bill of Rights. Louisiana after its being incorporated into the Union adopted codes of the French type and in particular a Civil Code 1803. Soon after independence, several states came out to prohibit the citation of English judicial decisions rendered after 1776. A number of territories even applied French or Spanish law. Moreover, the Common law was unknown to a host of new settlers; the Irish even disliked it. To codify American law was more and more advocated in all the states. The works of Pothier and Domat were translated into English. The movement best symbolized in New York by David Dudley Field and his efforts.

C. Triumph of the Common Law

While these Romano-Germanic codification movement and influences may help explain some of the peculiarities of American law, the United States ultimately remained within the Common law family, with Louisiana the only exception. Many important states adopted the Common law in principle. The triumph represents a victory of tradition.

Contributing factors for the triumph include:

a. It was difficult to break away from familiar concepts and techniques and from intellectual and sentimental reactions instinctively employed or experienced.

b. The use of the English language as a vehicle. The English influence was also strongly felt for quite some time during the early stages of the development of American universities and legal writing, American judges and lawyers looked to the English as a model for developing American law.

c. The influence of outstanding works of certain authors such as Columbia College law professor James Kent's commentaries on American law* (1826-1830), the works of Joseph Story, an Associated Justice of the United States Supreme Court, and the Commentaries of the law of England by Sir William Blackstone, a great systematizer and expounder of the Common Law. This single-handed work had gone a long way to ensure the continued reception of the Common law from the colonies into the constituent states of the new American Republic. Blackstone greatly enhanced the prestige and accessibility of common law doctrine. It makes in a single, compendious presentation what had been accessible only in thousands of cases found in the law reports and ancient institutional works.

d. The teaching of the Common law from the time of independence; the so-called "The taught tradition".

e. Improvement in living conditions and changes in economic and political ideas feel the need for a more developed law. Gradually the Common law was seen in a different light.

f. Used as a bulwark to protect civil liberties against royal absolutism—this is

---

* 《美国法释义》,詹姆斯·肯特著。1830 年之后,《美国法释义》的问世以及各种美国法专著的出现,标志着美国法对英国法的批判吸收并走上独立发展的道路。

more of a symbol than anything of practical relevance.

g. Seen as a strong link between all that was English in American in the face of the menace posted by Louisiana and French Canada.

Thus the United States has remained a Common law country in the sense that it retained the concepts, the methods of legal reasoning and the theory of sources, not in the sense that English Common law developed after Independence applies to United States.

In many states, the Common law was specified to be the basis of the law in force. In many instances, British statutes were favorably considered and applied by American courts. The English Statutes of Frauds of 1677 was one of such examples.

While state courts have inherited the law-making power of the Common law judicial tradition, this is not true of the US federal courts. Federal courts fortunately have always drawn upon ancient common law precedents in deciding maritime cases. When dealing with cases involving citizens of different states, they must apply, in a traditional common law manner, state law governing the dispute sitting as if they were courts of the state.

Section Ten: Is There a United States Common Law or a Distinct Common Law for Each State Individually

A. Different Social and Economic Conditions Produced Diverse Common Law

Before the Declaration of Independence, there were no political or institutional links among the colonies. They differed greatly in social and economic development and conditions. A conservative judiciary and political climate existed in some colonies. In others, a liberal one prevailed. Some had a largely agricultural economy. Some colonies were highly industrialized. All such differences contributed to and led to the development of different common law rules in different states. For example, courts in an agricultural state may have felt enough local pressure to develop a strong form of liability for nuisances that interfered with the exploitation of land for agricultural purposes. Courts in an industrial state may have countenanced weaker rules of liability in this area in order not to burden the emerging, infant industrial enterprises with heavy costs.

B. The Common Law Develops Along the Same Line and Way as Legislation: Federal and State

Could it be said that within the federal jurisdiction and competence, there is a United States common law? Could it also be said that a distinct common law of each state exists within the exclusive jurisdiction of state competence including residual state jurisdiction? In other words, the Common law develops along the same line and way as legislation. Due to the specific constitutional allocation of legislative powers between the federal and state governments, it is not unreasonable to say that a common law within the exclusive federal legislative competence exists along with as many state common laws as there are states. In applying statutory federal law, the federal courts over time have naturally built up a large body of precedent and thus tend to proceed in a traditional Common law manner.

It has been rightly said that no matter how much the substantive content of state laws may differ due to divergent applications and interpretations of the original stock of rules and principles, there is a continued uniformity of the Common law techniques of litigation and decision-making throughout all states.

C. Complicating Factors

(1) Even within Congress's legislative competence, states have a residual authority. It therefore follows that the judiciary of each state may very well create an individual state common law in the same way that legislative power falls to the legislature of each state.

(2) The dual court system(双轨制法院体系) (a sort of crisscross and overlapping jurisdiction), that is the organization of the American judicial system and the allocation of judicial jurisdiction between federal and state courts, may complicate the matter. State courts may hear disputes arising under federal law and federal courts may try cases bearing upon subjects with respect to which Congress cannot legislate, e. g., residents of different states and a sufficiently large sum of money involved. In other words, federal courts have diversity jurisdiction over subject matters with respect to which the Congress cannot legislate.

(3) The prevailing attitude of American people is that they consider themselves first and foremost belonging to the country as a whole rather than to any individual state. That is, they are American first, New Yorker or Californian second.

(4) The Judiciary Act 1789 (1789 年司法条例) requires federal courts to apply state statute. But not bound by State Common Law.

This Act required that federal courts, in subject matters not covered by federal statute, apply "the laws" of a specific state, the state as designated by the conflict of law rules that apply in the place where the federal court was located. In the absence of any law (i. e. statute), it seemed to some that the federal courts have an unfettered freedom that as an autonomous order of courts they were not bound by case law of any individual state. With respect to the question falling within their jurisdiction, federal courts may develop a federal Common law upon such topic, i. e. subject matter within state competence.

(5) Swift v. Tyson* (1842) affirmed the Application of General Common Law in Absence of Applicable State Statute:

Further on this matter, there was first the Doctrine in Swift v. Tyson (1842) which accepted the position of the duty of federal courts to decide according to general Common law rather that that of a specific state.

The critics of Swift alleged that in providing for the jurisdiction of federal courts in cases of diversity of citizenship, the doctrine had been intended to assure an equal justice to litigants of different states, and the doctrine had never been intended to authorize the creation of federal (common) law in matters with respect to which Congress was not able to legislate. The acceptance of this idea would result in the unintended supremacy of the federal judicial authorities in matters for which the Constitution had intended to create an exclusive state competence. This would also create an unjustifiable legal duality in practice: a dispute might be decided differently according to which court, federal or state, was seized.

(6) Erie Railroad Co. v. Tompkins (1938) and The Supremacy of State Law (statute or decision of the highest state court)

In this case, both the district judge and the Court of Appeals allowed the argument following the Judiciary Act 1789 that in the absence of state legislation the federal courts were to apply the general law and disregard the Common law rule of the State of Pennsylvania.

Justice Brandeis speaking for the majority of the Supreme Court: "except in matters governed by the Federal Constitution or by Acts of Congress, the law to be

---

* 1842 年斯威夫特诉泰森案,联邦法院私法管辖权扩大的里程碑。

applied to any case is the law of the State. And whether the law of the state shall be declared by its legislature in a statute or by its highest court is not a matter of federal concern." This decision has been reaffirmed on many occasions by the Supreme Court.

Can there be really no federal Common law? Could this lead to the catastrophic consequences of legal chaos and even political disintegration as the advocates of the unification of law feared? Was this an overestimated view of the real and practical meaning of Erie by certain observers and jurists of the Romano-Germanic family?

The holding of Erie does seem to conclude that there are as many common laws as there are individual states and that there is no federal Common law. Of course, there is no doubt that in matter governed by the Constitution and Federal statute, federal courts can still develop common law under them.

But the deep unity in American law was not negated by that case in any way.

Section Eleven: The Cohesion and Unity of American Law

A number of institutional factors including those mentioned earlier, and above all, the prevailing attitudes of Lawyers and peoples help greatly:

(1) The Bill of Rights (the first ten amendments) and the 13th, 14th, and 15th have made the federal courts the defenders of civil rights and freedoms of the ordinary citizen against federal authorities (1-10) and against state authorities (13, 14, 15th).

(2) The sharing of legislative jurisdiction has above all been changed by the Supreme Court in its liberal interpretation of certain provisions of the Constitution and its amendments. The net result has been the substantial increase in federal power and jurisdiction.

(3) General public loathes diverse interpretation and scholars advocate American law. While people in general and jurists may admit and tolerate the distinct nature of state law, especially statutory law, they are not willing to accept diverse interpretation given across the country to the Common law. Legal scholars rarely devote to the law of a single state. The law reports(判例汇编), encyclopedia(百科全书), legal treatises and law reviews generally embrace "American law". They are anxious to reconcile different holdings of state courts on matter of the Union and

Chapter Four: Legal System and Foundation of Law of the United States

attempt to enunciate the general principles flowing from them and, even in situation of conflict, consider the law of one state good law and that of the another bad law.

Some Critical Observations:

No doubt, all the above help greatly the achievement of certain harmonization, cohesion, or unity of American law in fields of federal jurisdiction more than in areas of exclusive state competence. The piecemeal approach of the Common law and the constraint and hold of the Constitution through judicial interpretation and application are too slow and inadequate to correct diversity and to achieve uniformity. Many examples could be cited to refute the unity thesis. Some of the most recent cases involve same-sex marriage and science curriculum of schools. In the former case, not only great diversity of position exists among states, within state, there is even no uniform view between the three branches of government. With respect to biological science, it has been reported that the radical Christian majority in the Kansas legislature attempts to rewrite the definition of science to include intelligent design in the evolution of man.

No doubt, to a significant extent, the federal courts, in their invocation, interpretation, and application function of the Constitution, do serve to achieve certain unity and cohesion in many important areas of nation-wide concerns. The following ruling is cited to illustrate this point by virtue of the doctrines of res judicata and stare decisis as well as the dynamic nature of authoritative and effective decision in terms of sources, process and outcome. To fully appreciate Judge's Jones' decision, one must analyze both the constitutional and the Common law authorities cited and those not cited but potentially applicable as well as the quality of his reasoning in supporting his decision. What has happened or is going to happen subsequently on appeal and other relevant cases, existing and future, must also be studied.

In one of the biggest courtroom clashes between faith and evolution since the 1925 Scopes Monkey Trial*, a federal judge barred a Pennsylvania public school district Tuesday from teaching "intelligent design" in biology class, saying the concept is creationism in disguise.

U. S. District Judge John E. Jones delivered a stinging attack on the Dover Area School Board, saying its first-in-the-nation decision in October 2004 to insert

---

* 斯科普猴子审判,又称"猴子审判",为20世纪20年代反进化论运动顶峰。

intelligent design into the science curriculum violated the constitutional separation of church and state.

The ruling was a major setback to the intelligent design movement, which is also waging battles in Georgia and Kansas. Intelligent design holds that living organisms are so complex that they must have been created by some kind of higher force.

Jones, a Republican and a churchgoer appointed to the federal bench three years ago, decried the "breathtaking inanity" of the Dover policy and accused several board members of lying to conceal their true motive, which he said was to promote religion.

A six-week trial over the issue yielded "overwhelming evidence" establishing that intelligent design "is a religious view, a mere re-labeling of creationism, and not a scientific theory," said Jones.

The school system said it will probably not appeal the ruling, because several members who backed intelligent design were ousted in November's elections and replaced with a new slate opposed to the policy.

During the trial, the board argued that it was trying to improve science education by exposing students to alternatives to Charles Darwin's theory of evolution (达尔文进化论) and natural selection.

The policy required students to hear a statement about intelligent design before ninth-grade lessons on evolution. The statement said Darwin's theory is "not a fact" and has inexplicable "gaps." It referred students to an intelligent-design textbook, "Of Pandas and People."

But the judge said: "We find that the secular purposes claimed by the board amount to a pretext for the board's real purpose, which was to promote religion in the public school classroom."

In 1987, the U. S. Supreme Court ruled that states could not require public schools to balance evolution lessons by teaching creationism.

Eric Rothschild, an attorney for the families who challenged the policy, called the ruling "a real vindication for the parents who had the courage to stand up and say there was something wrong in their school district."

Richard Thompson, president and chief counsel of the Thomas More Law Center in Ann Arbor, Mich., which represented the school district and describes its mission as defending the religious freedom of Christians, said the ruling appeared to be "an ad hominem attack on scientists who happen to believe in God."

It was the latest chapter in a debate over the teaching of evolution dating back to the Scopes trial, in which Tennessee biology teacher John T. Scopes was fined $100 for violating a state law against teaching evolution.

Earlier this month, a federal appeals court in Georgia heard arguments over whether a suburban Atlanta school district had the right to put stickers on biology textbooks describing evolution as a theory, not fact. A federal judge last January ordered the stickers removed.

In November, state education officials in Kansas adopted new classroom science standards that call the theory of evolution into question.

President Bush also weighed in on the issue of intelligent design recently, saying schools should present the concept when teaching about the origins of life.

In his ruling, Jones said that while intelligent design or ID arguments "may be true, a proposition on which the court takes no position, ID is not science." Among other things, the judge said intelligent design "violates the centuries-old ground rules of science by invoking and permitting supernatural causation"; it relies on "flawed and illogical" arguments; and its attacks on evolution "have been refuted by the scientific community."

"The students, parents, and teachers of the Dover Area School District deserved better than to be dragged into this legal maelstrom, with its resulting utter waste of monetary and personal resources," he wrote.

The judge also said: "It is ironic that several of these individuals, who so staunchly and proudly touted their religious convictions in public, would time and again lie to cover their tracks and disguise the real purpose behind the ID Policy."

Former school board member William Buckingham, who advanced the policy, said from his new home in Mount Airy, N.C., that he still feels the board did the right thing.

"I'm still waiting for a judge or anyone to show me anywhere in the Constitution where there's a separation of church and state," he said. "We didn't lose; we were robbed."

The controversy divided Dover and surrounding Dover Township, a rural area of nearly 20,000 residents about 20 miles south of Harrisburg. It galvanized voters in the Nov. 8 school board election to oust several members who supported the policy.

The new school board president, Bernadette Reinking, said the board intends to remove intelligent design from the science curriculum and place it in an elective social studies class. "As far as I can tell you, there is no intent to appeal," she said.㉟

Section Twelve: Unifying State Common Laws—Role of State and not Federal Courts

Therefore, it would be more correct to say that the 50 common laws of the 50 states, even though theoretically distinct, are considered to be, or ideally should be, identical. As a matter of fact, there is not much difference between 50 uniformly conceived laws and a single law that would be, in the breadth of its application, a federal law. On hindsight, one would be right to say that Erie R. R. v. Tompkins only decided that the judicial development necessary to reestablish the harmonious unity of American Common law had to be the work of state and not federal courts. The unity of American law has to be achieved by bringing together the law of 50 states; it is not to be accomplished by creating a federal Common law alongside the common laws of individual states—a legal dualism rejected by the Supreme Court.

It is for state courts to articulate and evolve American Common law in those areas where Congress has no power to legislate. In the operation of state courts, lawyers themselves tend to exert pressure to align the law of one state with the dominant current prevailing in other states.

So Justice Brandeis' expression that there is no federal Common law is more correct to be used in connection with the words "in the matter with respect to which Congress cannot legislate." It is equally correct to say that with respect to the matter to which Congress can legislate, there may be a federal Common law. With the continuing expansion of federal jurisdiction, a federal Common law is growing.

Interestingly, a recent observation on the dynamic and evolving nature of the Common law in the United States is entitled with the very term "The Supreme Common Law Court of the United States."㊱

Similarity of State <u>Conflict of Law(冲突法)</u> Rules Supports Unity: Identifying and Applying the Most Appropriate State Law (Common law and Statute).

One may also include the similarity of state conflict of law rules in supporting

---

㉟ Martha Raffaele, "Judge Rules against Pa. Biology Curriculum", *Yahoo News*, December 21, 2005.
㊱ Jack M. Bermann, "The Supreme Common Law Court of the United States", 18 *Boston Univ. Public Interest L J*, 110-170 (2008).

the unity. There is a new and widely followed method of interpretation that seeks out in each case that law which has the most meaningful connection or link with the case in question in light of the factual situation and the policies of the laws in conflict.

The "due process" clause has been interpreted to require that a case offer a sufficient connection with the state of the forum in order that its law is to be applied to the merits of the dispute.

The possibility is fast growing that the Common law of one state could be applied in another and even statutory law and content as provided by the party evoking it and upon reception by the presiding judge of its existence and applicability. An apt term for this phenomenon is Mutual Application and Recognition of State Law.

Section Thirteen: Codification of American Common Law

Jeremy Bentham's unsuccessful attempt (offer) to codify American Common law is well documented. His scathing attack was of no avail. He characterized the Common law as "shapeless mass of merely conjectural and essentially uncognizable matter, a confused, indeterminate, inadequate, ill-adapted and inconsistent, and a species of muck law." It was "some random decisions or string of frequently contradictory decisions, pronounced almost without any intelligible reason under the impulse of some private sinister interest."[37]

Much of the support for codification stemmed from dissatisfaction with the uncertainty and inaccessibility of the Common law arising from the multitude, diversity and frequent inconsistency of judicial decisions. Roscoe Pound argued that the great American legal treatises of the 19th century, by providing practical access to the Common law through the synthesis of the mass of decisions, were instrumental in defeating the codification movement. The West digest system provides another access tool. The success of the American Law Institute' restatement as well as the uniform law project all help ease the difficulty of access to the Common law corpus.

---

[37] Karl N. Llewellyn, *The Bramble Bush*, 1930, Oceana, 1975, pp. 42-43; Charles M. Cook, *The American Codification Movement: a Study of Antebellum Legal Reform*, Westport, Conn., Greenwood Press, 1981, p. 98.

Section Fourteen: A Systematic Statement of the Common Law

The Restatement of Law is a monumental undertaking by the American Law Institute, a private association. It attempts to explain in a systematic manner the rules of the American Common Law on many important subjects that fall within the legislative authority of the states in those branches of the law where legislative interventions have not been too numerous. And it then indicates which solutions are most in agreement with the American Common law system and should be accepted by American courts.

In addition, there are two other complementary series. One is the Restatement in the Court that indicates the judicial decisions of different courts in which an article of the Restatement has been cited by adopting, rejecting or distinguishing it. Another is entitled State Annotations showing to what extent and in actual fact the rules found in the Restatement are followed in different states.

As a precious tool providing a systemic exposition of American law, the authority of the various Restatements of law depends on and varies with, the status and prestige of its compilers or authors.

Section Fifteen: Protection from the Burdens of Multi-State Legal Authority

To the foreign lawyer or entrepreneur contemplating commercial activity in the United States, the decentralized structure of legal authority may seem daunting. Since each state has independent legal authority over matters within its legal boundaries, the possibility of inconsistent, unanticipated, and burdensome regulations, liabilities, and tax obligations, etc. immediately arises.

Elements and measures that are available to limit the scope of these hazards:

A. Tradition of Uniform Laws

The first of these protective shields that serves to avoid the inefficiencies and injustices of disparate regimes of state law is uniform laws. The <u>Uniform Commercial Code (UCC)</u>(美国统一商法典) is the most prominent example of such uniform lawmaking.

Model acts are drafted when there is no special need for uniformity but a demand for legislation in a number of states.

Benjamin N. Cardozo's call for a Ministry of Justice to watch the law in action led eventually to the creation of the Law Revision Commission by New York legislature in 1934. The terms of reference of the Commission are to discover defects and anachronisms and to recommend changes to bring the law into harmony with social changes and modern conditions.

The proliferation of enacted law poses a particular problem for the United States. The danger of states to enact statutory provisions to correct or supplement the Common law may destroy the uniformity of American law. Thus from a practical point of view, it is eminently desirable to propose uniform or model laws on certain subjects.

One of the American Bar Association's original objectives is to promote uniformity of legislation throughout the Union. This effort led to the establishment of the National Conference of Commissioners on Uniform State Law in 1892. Later in cooperation with the American Law Institute, the Uniform Commercial law was produced in 1952 that was subsequently revised many times. Uniform laws also exist in many other private law areas. However, even so, uniformity cannot always be guaranteed due to divergent interpretations in each of the enacting states.

Nevertheless, with the increasing authority of the Federal government and its intervention in areas having general national interest and trans-state implications, some success may finally be achieved in the realm of the uniformity of laws in the United States.

The proposed uniform law is proffered to the legislatures of the states for adoption as state law. States are free to adopt them as proposed or elect to adopt them with change or deletion of provisions. A search of any publication on uniform state laws in either printed form or websites would reveal the title of the uniform laws that have been adopted by states including the entity of the states, the title of those that have been drafted or in the process of being drafted.

In principle, uniform laws are open to divergent interpretations by various state courts. In practice, state courts tend in general to treat each other's judgments and opinions with the respect due to being members of a broader national legal community, and that uniform laws promote in state judges a particularly strong sense of being embarked on a common national endeavor.

B. Constitutional Limit on the Reach of State Court Jurisdiction and Choice of Law

Multi-state enterprises face two overlapping risks, first, to be exposed to divergent substantive responsibilities and liabilities from state to state (legislative, regulatory, and judicial) and second, to be subject to the adjudicative authority of the courts in a multiplicity of states.

In the latter case, a state court has to decide which state's law to apply. Normally states prefer their own law. In some cases there is a tendency to elect to apply the law of other states. Here the same unifying force is at work. The similarity of state conflict of law rules ensures the recognition and applicability by one state of the law of another state that has the most meaningful connection or link to the lawsuit in question.

Elementary concerns of fairness require that no one is to be subjected to the legal authority of a state where he has undertaken no activities of any sort, and where it would be difficult or impossible for him to anticipate that he would fall under the aegis of that state. Such concerns of fairness are further enforced by the tradition of due process as mentioned earlier under the unifying forces behind American common law.

The Supreme Court has imposed significant constitutional limitations on the authority of state courts to adjudicate controversies with which they have only attenuated connections. The exact scope of the authority to adjudicate remote controversies involving persons and entities not physically present in the state is not entirely clear.

Whether a non-resident state defendant has "purposefully directed" its activities towards the residents of the forum state, and thus has established the requisite "minimum contacts" with a state, can only be decided on a case-by-case basis. But what constitutes "purposefully directed" the Supreme Court appears divided on.

The second threshold question is: Would the extension of jurisdiction be consistent with the "fair play and substantial just?" This is more challenging due to the general and vague nature of test.

The choice of law decisions by state courts are generously accommodated by Supreme Court when the state whose law is chosen has any meaningful contact with the pertinent aspect of the controversy. But arbitrary and attenuated applications of a state's law will be struck down.

C. Negative Commerce Clause

Congress's authority to regulate commerce with foreign nations and among the several states does imply restrictions on state to some degree, though the restrictions are not explicit. Specifically, the doctrine bars states from:

1) Discriminating against interstate commerce

Two major exceptions to the discrimination restriction: ① Where the state acting as entrepreneur, instead of regulator, buying materials for its own purposes may prefer in-state sellers, or for manufacturing and selling commodities, prefer in-state buyers, ② Exemption may specifically granted by Congress, such as freely regulating the insurance industry.

2) Unduly burdening inter-state commerce

The unduly burden restriction could be a very strong constitutional medicine inviting the federal judiciary to review virtually every piece of state commercial regulation. Yet only in rather extreme circumstances, courts have been prompted to make such challenge, such as burden on the transportation of goods in interstate commerce, restriction inconsistent with national practice generally, and regulation unsupported by any significant regulatory concern.

3) Inappropriately taxing inter-state commerce

To satisfy proper taxation, the taxing state must have an appropriate nexus (contact) with the multi-state enterprise. Being a beneficiary of state facilities or services is one of such nexus. The taxing state must ensure that tax imposed is fairly apportioned to the enterprise's contact with the state. Examples of fairly apportioned tax include a road tax linked to miles traveled or to the number of days used in the state, and the corporate income tax is keyed to the percentage of total earnings, or total employee hours or compensation.

Two additional restrictions—when the tax that is imposed creates a substantial risk of international multiple taxation, and when the tax that is imposed is in violation or contravening obligations of treaties or conventions.

Review and Reflective Questions

1. Which one of the characteristics that inform American society and law is of particular significance in your view?

2. What are the factors that contribute to the building of a United States Common law instead of a common law for each state individually?

3. The U. S. government has seen its tentacles grow exponentially relative to those of the 50 states over the years and taken on more power and responsibilities than anyone at the time of the founding could have imagined. Is this happening compatible with many of the highly cherished values such as liberty and individualism of American law and society?

4. For foreign companies doing business in the U. S., one major concern is the costs and burdens of multi-state legal authority. For example, the complexity of the U. S. tax system with its 7,000-plus taxing jurisdictions could be a nightmarish spider web. A state might disallow deductions or refuses to recognize treaty-protected income. What measures have been taken to harmonize or ameliorate such costs or burdens?

复习及提问

1. 你认为哪一点对于今日美国社会及其法律制度的形成最为重要?
2. 哪些因素促成美国法的形成?
3. 与州政府相比,美国联邦政府日益扩张的权力和职责的触及范围是美建国之初任何人无法想象的。政府权力的扩张与美国社会及法律尊崇的自由和个人主义价值观是否相悖?
4. 对于在美国做生意的外国公司来说,需要考虑的重要的一点就是多个国家间的法律权限所带来的成本和负担。例如,美国复杂的税收制度包含7000多个税种,形成一张噩梦似的巨大蜘蛛网。某些国家可能不允许减少税额或拒绝认可条约保护性收入。可以采取哪些办法协调和改善这种成本或负担?

Chapter Five: Case Law: Form, Nature and Function of Judicial Decisions

Introductory Note

Case law is built on the bedrock of judicial decision. Judges play a determinative role in shaping the form and content of case law. We exam all the following: the overriding significance of the doctrine of Stare decisis (rule of precedent) in judicial decision, the meaning and content of the holding of a case as well as the question is there an ideal type of a holding. What are Ratio decidendi, Obiter dictum, and principle of law? Is there any difference between them? Should a judge overrule a prior decision as opposed to just distinguish it? What are the techniques judge uses to distinguish a case? Is the outcome of a case predictable basing on the principle of Stare decisis? Is the Common law a living law and thus continuing to keep abreast with the changing needs of a welfare and regulatory state? And how this is done?

简介

判例法是建立在司法判决的基石之上的。法官在判例法的形成和改进过程中起到了决定性的作用。我们来看一下以下内容:遵循先例原则在司法判决中的支配性地位,判决的意义和内容,何为理想的判决。什么是判决依据、法官的附带意见和法律原则? 它们之间是否有区别? 法官是应该推翻一个先例还是仅仅区分判例与正在审判中的案例间的不同? 法官是如何识别案例的? 基于遵循先例原则,案件的判决结果是否具有可预见性? 普通法是否是一个变化中的法,始终与福利和制度化国家的需要而与时俱进? 它是如何做到的?

Section One: Form and Content of Judicial Decisions

An English decision is no more than a single resolution or order making known the judgment in the dispute. English judge is not obliged to give reasons to justify his decision in the eyes of the parties. They do so primarily to instruct law students, the future barristers who traditionally received their legal education through an attendance at court and participating in the practical handling of cases. Often the judge's statements and comments are substantially broader than is strictly necessary for a decision in the instant case. This fact is what has prompted the technique of distinguishing cases.

Uniformity and Certainty of Judicial Decisions: The hierarchical structure of courts ensures to a great extent the uniformity and certainty of law. The Supreme Court watches the uniform application of legislation and judicial interpretation(司法解释). The concentration of the review power of the Supreme Court is the prerequisite for, and cause of, the development of the Common Law.

Only the decisions of the appellate courts carry authority. Appellate judges in common law systems are very conscious of their responsibility for providing lower courts with opinions that offer guidance in future cases. An important technique to fulfill this goal is to produce, whenever possible, an opinion of the court to which at least a majority of judges adheres. This authoritative view of the court would not unduly be compromised by dissenting* or concurrent opinions**.

Dissenting judicial opinions or minority judgments are peculiar to countries of the Common law. Published along with the majority opinion, these judgments and opinions are equally significant as a source of potential law. In fact, dissenting or minority judgments and opinions may very well become the dominant views of the law through re-imagination in the hands of the judges and legal scholars.

Section Two: The Judicial Function

First, the judicial function(司法职能), not peculiar to the common law, is to define and to dispose of the controversy before the court, for under the doctrine of res judicata*** the parties may not re-litigate issues that have been determined between them by a final and valid judgment. The doctrine of res judicata is well settled.

Second, unique to the Common law, it is the decision of the appellate court, especially the highest appellate court that establishes a precedent for the lower courts in the judicial hierarchy so that a like case arising in the future will probably be

---

* 少数意见。指案件判决中在论证、适用法律及判决结果上不同意多数法官意见的少数法官的意见。又称为"minority opinion"。

** concurring opinion, 指一名或少数法官的单独意见,同意多数法官作出的判决,但对判决依据提出不同的理由。

*** 既决事项、既判力、一事不再理。有合法管辖权的法院就案件作出终局判决后,在原当事人之间不得就同一事项、同一诉讼标的、同一请求再次提起诉讼,法院作出的发生法律效力的判决是最终的决定。

decided in the same way. This is the so-called rule of precedent that is often referred to by its Latin name: stare decisis.

Rule of precedent differs from res judicata. The latter refers mainly to the parties in a particular lawsuit, while in the case of the former, it is the legal issues in a lawsuit, any lawsuit for that matter that cannot be disturbed.

The decisions of the courts in the "countries of written law" are of secondary importance, not considered to contain rules of law, because quite independently of them there is a sufficient body of written law as codified.

In England, on the other hand, the role of judicial decisions has not only been to apply but also to define the legal rules. The rules set by decided cases must be followed or else the certainty of the Common law will be destroyed and its very existence compromised. The duty to observe the rules as stated by the judges (stare decisis—let the decision stand and not disturb settled points"—in other words, to respect judicial precedents is the logic of a judge-made legal system. It is only since the beginning of the first half of the 19th century that this was firmly established. Before this period there was concern for assuring uniformity in judicial decisions in order to maintain coherence in the law as a whole. The establishment by the Judicature Acts of a more systematic judicial hierarchy and the improvements in the quality of the judicial reporting were also important contributing factors.

The application of the rule of precedent in the Common law involves an analysis of these opinions or comments accompanying the decisions. The judge himself does not state what the ratio decidendi* or obiter dictum is in the case; it is for a judge in a later case to do so in order to decide whether the earlier decision applies in the matter he must decide.

Section Three: Meaning and Scope of the Rule of Precedent in British Law

The decisions rendered by the House of Lords are binding(有约束力的) precedents to be observed by all other courts including the House of Lords until 1966 when it announced otherwise in the interest of justice as dictated by new circumstances.

---

* (拉)判决依据。指法庭判决案件的法律依据。

The decisions of the Court of Appeal are binding precedents for all lower courts and the Court of Appeal itself except in criminal matters.

The decisions of a judge of the High Court of Justice(高等法院) must be observed by lower courts and have great persuasive value and are very generally followed by the different divisions of the High Court of Justice itself and by the Crown Court(英国刑事法庭).

At the present time, the principle remains largely intact in the face of increasing exceptions made.

The decisions rendered by other courts or quasi-judicial bodies and tribunals may indeed have some persuasive value but they are never binding precedents.

Section Four: Doctrine of Stare Decisis and its Justification

The justifications commonly given for the doctrine may be summarized in four words: equality, predictability, economy, and respect. Equality argues that the application of the same rule to successive similar cases results in equality of treatment for all coming before the courts. Consistent following of precedents contributes to predictability in future disputes. Economy requires the use of established criteria to settle new cases to save time and energy. Adherence to earlier decisions shows due respect for the wisdom and experience of prior generations of judges. Computer storage and retrieval of legal information provides a massive amount of relevant/applicable cases and arms lawyers with a rich base of sources of law in argument and persuasion, which judges must consider and taken into account in decision and stipulating ratio decidendi.

Section Five: The Doctrine of Stare Decisis and Ratio Decidendi or Holding of a Case

The doctrine of stare decisis rests mainly on the assumption that a "case in point (例证)" has "binding authority(有约束力的法律依据)" over the issues in a case to be decided. Binding authority, to which the doctrine of precedent does apply, includes decisions of higher courts of the same jurisdiction and decisions of the same court.

The doctrine of stare decisis closely relates to the concept of the holding of a case or ratio decidendi and whether or not a holding is narrowly or broadly cast in terms of the fact-situation involved in the case.

Section Six: Transforming Facts into Binding Legal Rules

The holding of a case or ratio decidendi can be further cast in the form of a legal rule.

Judges must in making decision take into account the facts of the case and then generalize from those facts as far as the statement of the court and the circumstances indicate is desirable.㊳ Facts permeate the structure of the Common law and often accede themselves to the rank of legal rules.

How could a general statement of facts by a judge become a legal rule? Doesn't this mean "what it is" amounts to or counts as "what ought to be?" What is the alchemy in the process of normative transformation? Is judge alchemist?

Not just judges transform facts into legal rules. Other branches of the government perform this trick too. One could also ask: Is the legislature e. g. , the United States Congress, a government ministry, or a federal official an alchemist of legislation essentially formulated on the basis of facts and happenings, past, present and projected? There is a simple answer to this question. Congress is authorized by the Constitution to enact legislation and the Department of Transportation is to make regulations respectively by delegated authority for example. H. L. A. Hart offers a theoretical answer by crafting an innovative idea that every legal system has rules of recognition that validate what the law is. In the United States, by virtue of the Supremacy clause of the Constitution*, a valid discretionary(自由裁量的) act by a single federal administrative official is not only recognized as law, it even prevails over a conflicting provision enshrined in a state constitution.

Other theories have been advanced to justify the transformation of an "is" as an "ought". According to the popular progressive view, any effective power holders

---

㊳ Llewellyn. Op Cit at 249, 250.

* 宪法最高条款。指美国《宪法》第 6 条第 2 项规定,宣布该宪法与依法所指定的合众国法律,以及根据合众国的权力已缔结或将缔结的条约,都是全国最高法律(supreme law of the land),对与之冲突的州宪法或法律享有优先权。

(socially allocated) can make law however it is based. Whether or not what is proposed or the "law" as projected is authoritative and effective is another question.

Section Seven: In Search of an Ideal Holding or Ratio Decidendi of a Case

The holding of a case must be determined from an analysis of the material facts, from the decisions, and from the reasoning(推理) of the opinion. Even this may be more difficult than would seem to be at least. It is often hard to know how far the process of abstraction should be continued.

There are some problems and difficulties in stating with precision the holding (ratio decidendi) of an appellate court—the core of the opinion that represents the propositions(论点) of law that will be binding on lower courts.

Factors compounding the formulation of ratio include:

First, each judge is free to enter a dissenting or different strand of reasoning for the decision.

Second, courts are not supposed to declare authoritative legal generalities in the abstract. Propositions of law must be connected and related to the facts of the dispute that judges are adjudicating, and the holding of a case can only be stated in terms of its essential facts. But what facts are essential or most important is neither preordained(预先规定的) nor obvious.

Third, what is more difficult is to decide how broad or how narrow are the propositions of law found in the opinion that can be thought of as necessary for the decision of the case on the basis of the facts found to be essential.

Fourth, The problem is further complicated by the tendency of American courts to write opinions at the considerable length, in which the main issues are revisited, with a variety of pronouncements and the proffering of different lines of reasoning, some of which may appear to be much broader than others.

A factual example of possibilities runs as follows:

In a case in which a woman companion had poured most the lemonade liquid into a glass, drunk some of it and discovered decomposed remains of a snail at the bottom of a bottle of lemonade offered by her host.

A fact-specific but intuitively ridiculous approach would formulates the proposition such: manufacturers of lemonade in opaque bottles are liable to people who become ill after drinking the beverage and then discovering a decomposed snail in the bottle.

At the highest level of generality, one may postulate that all manufacturers of goods are liable to any person who is injured by defects in the product.

The holding may be further modified to limit its application to food and drink products or to consumers as a class. So the proposition may be refined to read that manufacturers are liable to consumers who are exposed to traps or hidden dangers, and where they are entirely free of negligence in failing to discover the defect.

Ratio decidendi is a proposition of law that decides the case in the light and in the context of the material facts. The ratio is the central core of the meaning of a case. It is the sharpest cutting edge of the case that only is binding. The greater the number of facts in the ratio, the narrower its scope. Conversely the fewer or the higher the level of abstraction, the broader the reach of the ratio and the more fact situations it covers.[39] The inclusive nature of such broader statement of the ratio would come close to resemble the general rules found in codes of the civilian family.

Section Eight: Rule of Precedent and Statute Law

The rule of precedent is also applied in the interpretation of statutes. As a result, statutory provisions are soon burdened by a mass of precedents, the authority of which quickly replaces the text of the statute itself. Statutory precedents further obscure the general spirit and policy of the statute, and cause its object to be lost in a jungle of decisions, each of which in itself only decides some particular point of detail. This in turn has resulted in the laying down by the Congress in new legislation containing specific provisions to exclude judicial control and review.

The concept of binding, certainty and predictability of the law is much in the air when problems respecting interpretation and teleological application, etc become an issue. The 1966 Practice Statement (judicial precedent)[40] in Great Britain freed the High Court from the shackles and hold of discreditable doctrines. It is difficult to see how past precedent can play where the rule of law itself cannot be formulated with any precision. Doctrines formulated on the bases of common law cases and the principles derived therefrom can never replace the richness, diversity, and

---

[39] Id.
[40] [1966] 1 W L R 1234.

extensiveness of future cases yet to arise.

Section Nine: Obiter Dictum: Definition and Clarification

The narrow rule necessary to resolve the dispute that emerged from a specific fact situation is generally called ratio decidendi or the holding of the case. All the remaining language in the opinion is referred to as (mere) dicta, which carries less weight in legal argument. It is a well-established and respected maxim, not to be disregarded, that general expressions in every opinion, are to be taken in connection with the case in which those expressions are used. If they go beyond the case, they may be respected, but ought not be controlling the judgment in a subsequent suit when the very point is presented for decision.

Section Ten: Ratio, Obiter, and Principle: Distinction or Confluence (Conflation)

Ratio decidendi, obiter dictum, and legal principles are essential constituents of the Common law. They form the core of judicial reason. These elements though conceptually distinct are in fact and in operation closely related. And the boundaries between them are considerably tenuous, fluid, and changing unpredictably.

One may contrast a ratio decidendi with a legal principle that emerges from a line of decisions as a broader norm pregnant with reasons for those decisions; a legal principle therefore carries greater weight in legal argument. More often there is a line of decisions or perhaps several divergent lines, all of which might be regarded as cases in point. When confronted with such a complex situation, the operation of the doctrine of stare decisis would become highly complicated and contentious, as there are competing, if not conflicting, lines of decisions, legal principles or reasons. Facing with such a complex situation, it may very well be true that judges resort to discretion in hard cases as H. L. A. Hart advocates. And only R. Dworkin's Hercules judge could discern in such situations some kind of a super principle of law.

Identify and Cast Applicable Principle in Its Best Light—Would the manner and the style of opinion help in identifying the holding? Would it be better to simply abandon any notion that the holding in a case is a definite entity that can be discovered by applying some infallible formula? Wouldn't it be more profitable to regard the application of the doctrine of precedent as a process of arriving at what a court perceives as the best understanding of a flow of judicial activity over time? The correct statement of the doctrine of precedent is that it imposes an obligation to seek the best understanding of the most basic principles that a line of cases expresses. This view comes very closer to R. Dworkin's principled and integrative interpretation.

The dichotomy of holdings and principles is thus not free of difficulty. Unlike holdings that are inherently fact-based and constrained, principles extracted from a line of cases must be completely free of the constraint of facts informing the cases so based. Otherwise, the cumulated and combined effects of the aggregated facts would suffocate any strength of the principles so extracted.

To contrast holding with principle faces another challenge. At which point in the process, does a judge in formulating the holding of his adjudicating case leave the restricted zones and enters the wild West of free principle?

What is more problematic is that possibly both holding and orbiter are found in the same case. With the change of time and social conditions, holding and orbiter may easily change position through the distinguishing technique of either broadening or the narrowing of reasoning.

It has been insightfully observed that though extra-judicial comments do not carry the authority of precedent, however, in reality, they introduce doubt into the minds of lower court judges and practicing lawyers

Notwithstanding the constraint of the holding and the power to distinguish, what is the source or base of judicial re-imagination and creativity remains to be explained. The holding of a case doesn't offer choice whatever the manner or style. It seems the pliability of the holding is patently attributed to divergent interpretation. Ultimately, what is left to inform decision are one's value and belief system, moral view, political allegiance, etc. All these potentially are disguisted in the form of reason.

Does such progress from particular decisions towards a general set of principles mean Lord Mansfield's famous observation that "the common law works itself pure" from case to case? It may seem so pure to invite the criticism that general principles do not decide cases.

All such discussion sounds like Dworkin's advocacy for his Hercules judge to fit the case at hand with applicable past official decisions and to strive to cast the posited legal rule in the best light possible and make it the best it can be.

No wonder that in the non-judicial world of real life decisions, especially those in the economic and business fields, a principled approach to regulatory efforts or cost-efficient handling of constantly changing, complex, multifarious situation is highly favored as opposed to strict, formulaic rules.

Section Eleven: Doctrine of Stare Decisis in United States Law

The doctrine of stare decisis dictates that like cases should be decided today the same as they were decided in the past. However, the doctrine is not as vigorously applied in the United States as in England. In order to avoid an over-differentiation of the law between states, some suppleness in the rule of precedent is desirable when facing the need for security and stability.

The United States Supreme Court and the supreme courts of the different states are not bound to observe their own decisions and may in fact operate a reversal of previously established judicial practice. In the operation of state courts, lawyers themselves tend to exert pressure to align the law of one state with the dominant current prevailing in other states. At the federal level, the Supreme Court sees the compelling importance and need to adapt the Constitution to modern social thinking and economic necessities, as the Constitution can only be amended with very great difficulty. Many celebrated examples of how the United States Supreme Court had brought about fundamental changes to the law and about significant social and economic consequences and impacts were made through imaginative and novel interpretation of the Constitution and the technique of distinguishing previous decisions.[41] This is because the rule of precedent is a static and constraining factor instead of being an activist and liberating force. The mechanism of interstitial change in the Common law through a case-by-case manner simply is not suitable for the instrumentalist demands of the modern age.

In fact there may only be a slight difference between the juridical recognition of this rule and the voluntary adhesion by judges to some rules or doctrines stated by

---

[41] Some of the landmark cases in this respect are given in the notes on p. 436 of Major L egal Systems in the World Today, 1985.

their predecessors on account of arguments based on reason. The whole question is really much more a matter of legal psychology than of law. It may very much lie in the willingness or hesitation of judges to admit that distinctions may be drawn, whether or not they consider themselves bound by an aging principle, whether they are indeed aware of the need that the law evolves or, whether they are to be guided by progressive or conservative ideas. And the fact that every shade of opinion can find supporting precedents in the extreme mass of published judicial reports is another important factor.

No case has a meaning by itself. What counts and gives you lead and sureness is the background of the other cases in relation to which you must read the one at hand. The ratio is not fixed but a formula that is capable of adjustment according to the force of later development.[42]

Section Twelve: The Overriding Importance of the Opinions of the Appellate Courts

The doctrine of stare decisis is founded on the primacy of the opinions of the appellate courts. These form the main and primary focus of study and analysis of jurists, lawyers, and judges. The formation of legal education is based on these opinions. We study them just like we study the advocacy of star lawyers for the best form of strategy and techniques. Ditto for the most preeminent among jurists to ascertain the most comprehensive, extensive, and creative exposition and criticism of legal doctrines.

Section Thirteen: Factors Likely to Figure in Distinguishing Decisions

Many reasons work to scale down the mythical authority of judicial law. Judicial law developed on the basis of the rule of precedent is inherently distinguishable and may be weighted down in authority in subsequent cases. Factors involved in distinguishing a previous decision include the following:

The hierarchical(有统治权的) status of the court deciding the case.

---

[42] Karl N. Llewellyn, *The Bramble Bush*, 1930, Oceana, 1975, pp. 42-43, 256.

The reputation of the judges writing the opinion.

Is there a dissent or even a concurring opinion?

When was the case decided?

How does the precedent fit with the surrounding laws?

How has the decision been dealt with in later cases?

What authority does the precedent enjoy generally?

Conflicting precedents in different jurisdictions work to detract from the authority of individual decisions.

How does a decision fare in subsequent scholarly scrutiny (study and criticism)?

How does it fare in the hand of mass media? And what are the reactions of the general public?

Has it been affected or otherwise compromised by changes in social, political, or economic conditions?

What are the reactions of the legislative branch and/or the executive branch?

Is it generally followed in fact?

Has it fallen into desuetude?

Has the composition of the court changed?

Is it a memorandum decision, that is, a decision that sets forth no reasons while affirming a decision of a lower court that stated the facts and its reasons in an opinion?

Section Fourteen: Opposing Treatments of Precedents

The doctrine of stare decisis requires that cases with same fact-situation be treated the same way. But in actual fact, there are simply no two cases exactly alike. No two cases are on all four.

Essentially, methods are made possible that involve certain skillful manipulation of the nature, scope and significance of the holding of the earlier case(s) and the relevance and materiality of the facts in the case(s). Thus, the interchangeability between the holding of a case and its obiter dictum is very high and frequent.

To extend the principle of a prior decision to the present case is to profit from its wisdom and experience. Read the holding of the earlier decision more broadly; treat differences in the facts of the two cases as immaterial; regard as holding what might have been considered as dictum upon a narrow reading of the earlier case. In essence, this amounts to the formulation of broader legal principle to subsume under it both the facts of the earlier case and the case on hand.

If it seems undesirable to apply the rule of the earlier decision to the case at hand, just narrow the holding of an earlier case in order to distinguish it from the one before the court by treating differences in facts as material. What might have been considered as holding upon a broad reading of the earlier case will be regarded as dictum—as not necessary to the disposition of the dispute before the court.

The role of distinguishing cases is essential to the development of new laws or new rules. Judges distinguish cases either by limiting or broadening the extent and wording of a rule which inevitably seems to have originally been expressed in too general or too narrow terms in the face of new fact-situations. Even here the more conservative majority tends to use this technique to temper the daring, sometimes the extravagances of their more progressive colleagues.

Section Fifteen: To Distinguish or To Overrule(推翻先例) *

Even a binding authority is not absolute. When a decision would be patently wrong by following a precedent, the court may refuse to follow it.

The court may overrule a precedent when the precedent is so old and altered conditions or change of circumstance have made it inappropriate for the case at hand. The court is also inclined to overrule a precedent when the composition of the court may have changed so that what was formerly the view of a vehement minority is now that of the majority. This would be particularly needed on a constitutional issue where legislation is not an available remedial device. Please refer to the factors operative in opposing treatment of previous decisions mentioned above.

Distinguished decisions inevitably amount to overruled decisions. Tradition demands that where possible the doctrine of precedent be honored by careful distinguishing rather than by outright overruling of objectionable decisions. But in point of fact the decision that has been distinguished and expressly "limited to its particular facts" by a later opinion is often so whittled down as to be virtually overruled.

---

* 指在同一法律问题上,同一法院或上级法院作出的后判决与先判决相反时,就表示前一判决不再具有作为判例的效力。

When following precedent is a better option, such as in matter of commercial case or property law, the court may just go ahead in spite of the injustice in the particular case. When so doing, the court takes the view that any change to rectify the injustice should be left to the legislature to make.

Section Sixteen: Multi-legged Holding

This is another puzzle that adds to the complication of the doctrine of stare decisis. This concerns the weight to be given to a multi-legged holding—a decision that is based upon several grounds rather than a single-ground. For example, three distinct errors are cited as reasons for reversal by an appellate court. Could it be that either one without the other would have been sufficient for the reversal? Or neither one was necessary to the decision? Is there therefore no holding? And the entire opinion is a dictum? It is commonly accepted by prudent lawyer that precedents stay more firmly when they stand on only one leg and alternate grounds make a holding less reliable.

Section Seventeen: The Retroactive Effect(追溯力) of Application of Judicial Decisions

Tradition condemns the retrospective application of the law. Simple fairness requires that people have the opportunity to be informed of the requirements and application of the law and to conduct themselves accordingly. For this reason, legislation is generally enacted for prospective application only. And the ex post facto clause of the Constitution forbids retroactivity in criminal law.

With respect to legal issues of a civil matter, the question remains open. Here questions about legislature intent, judicial deference thereto, the requirements of fairness, and statutory construction are at issue. In many instances, retroactive application of law is rather desirable, fair, and just. One Canadian case involves the payment of retroactive benefits to survivors of same-sex relationships going back to the coming into effect(文件生效) of the Charter of Rights and Freedoms in 1985. The claims are based on a 1995 ruling of the Supreme Court of Canada that lesbians and gays are protected by the Equality guarantees in the Charter(宪章). The Canadian Government argued against such retroactive application alleging that "a finding which ignores the evolution of the issue through the courts would distort historical reality and the courts should not attempt to view events of the past through eyes of today. " Yet, it must be noted that in some instances, retroactive application of law and judicial decision are to the benefit of the class of people affected.

Judicial interpretation and application plays an important and even decisive role in the nature and reach of the retroactivity of statutes(成文法). A closely related problem concerns the retroactive effect of a decision that overrules a prior decision. The nagging question is how to treat cases occurred or decisions pending or rendered between the overruling decision and the overruled decision. What are their legal effects? How does a court escape this dilemma? Occasionally, a court, in an attempt to avoid the unsettling effect of retroactivity has refused to overrule an earlier decision but has expressed disapproval of the precedent and issued a warning that the old rule will not be followed as to facts arising after the new decision. In other instances, a court has overruled the earlier decision but has indicated that the new rule is not retroactive and is not to be followed as to facts arising before the new decision.

In the function of constituting the doctrine of Res judicata, judicial decisions are inherently retroactive because judicial decisions rule on the legal status of past conducts or decisions. Only when serving as a precedent in the spirit of ratio decidenti, the ruling of a court applies prospectively. As such, to simply announce that a decision applied prospectively does not eliminate the retroactivity for the conduct ruled upon.

There is another view. This is to treat the overruled decision as not just a spurious, incorrect, or deviant interpretation of the law, and not simply a bad law. The overruled law was not law at all since the very moment of its making. Such a view is not only destabilizing or disrupting but also potentially destructive of the entire system. It is destabilizing in the sense that it would put the legal status in serious doubt of all the pending cases(悬案) and cases that have been rendered between the time of the making of the overruled decision and that of the enunciation of the overruling decision. What is more serious and destructive is that the legal effect(法律效力) of all judicial decisions would be put in limbo as the danger of any decision being overruled in the future, near, immediate or far, can never be ruled out.

As noted above, it may be wiser to heed the demand of tradition that where possible the doctrine of precedent be honored by careful distinguishing rather than by outright overruling of objectionable decisions. This way the nagging issue over the retroactive application and effect of overruling decision would be eschewed(回避).

In a casebook entitled "An Introduction to Anglo-American Law" Professors Pan Weida and Liu Wenqi give an excellent exposition of the main issues involved on this point. Their exposition consists of a few actual cases given in English accompanied with an explanation in Chinese. Therefore, it would be most appropriate to refer to this work. for those who wish to study individual cases on the issues involved in the retroactive application of judicial decisions in Anglo-American law. To identify all other relevant cases on this matter, West's case digests and its key number system should be consulted or research databases online.

Even power, right, or benefit conferring statutes are not entirely devoid of potential harm or injustice. An adoption information disclosure statute empowering adopted children reaching maturity to track down their birth parents, and parents who want to track down now-adult children whom they gave up for adoption, can betray the expectations of parents and children who don't want to be identified. Another example of the destabilizing effect of judicial decisions that would not be easily eschewed by judicious distinguishing rather than outright overruling is the 2004 Supreme Court decision that declared that to ensure tax-free transfer upon death of one's financial assets in self-directed registered retirement savings plans or registered retirement income funds to a plan owned by your surviving spouse, common-law or not, or to a financially dependent child, one must specify so in a proper will rather than simply identify to the financial company the identity of your beneficiary.

In this connection, a recent editorial comment with respect to the American International Group's* bonus controversy is rather quite informative and insightful. The piece is quoted entirely as follows:

The bill that the U. S. House of Representatives(美国众议院) has passed to claw back 90 per cent of bonuses to employees of bailed-out corporations is based upon a well founded indignation, but it should not serve as a precedent to justify future retroactive legislation.

President Barack Obama, who is well-versed in constitutional law, knows that the U. S. Constitution contains clauses that might raise questions about the bonus bill: provisions forbidding ex-post-facto laws(有追溯力的法律), archaic,

---

* 美国国际集团,全球知名保险公司,2001 年度全球财富 500 强排名 65 名。

confiscatory "bill of attainder(剥夺公权法案)" and (though this one restricts only states) impairment of the obligations of contracts.

The case law that has grown up around these clauses is complex. Over two centuries, the U.S. federal courts have muddied them—as courts are apt to do—narrowing the ex-post-facto clauses that prohibit retroactive statutes, while greatly widening the bill-of-attainder clause, as if in compensation. The once-mighty contract clause(合同条款), for its part, waned long ago.

What matters, though, is the principles, well articulated in the Federalist Papers, the political-science classic by James Madison, Alexander Hamilton and John Jay, when they argued in 1788 for the ratification of the U.S. Constitution.

"Bills of attainder, ex post facto laws and laws impairing the obligations of contracts," wrote Madison "are contrary to the first principles of the social compact, and to every principle of sound legislation."

Madison warned against the propensity of legislatures to get overexcited, with "fluctuating policy... sudden changes and legislative interferences."

That was much finer hour for Madison than when as president he yielded to the clamour of "war hawks" in Congress, authorizing the invasion of Canada in 1812, which was fortunately repelled.

Later in the book, Hamilton likewise wrote against "the subjecting of men to punishments for things which, when they were done, were breaches of no law."

As for attainder, that was a confiscation(没收) of the property of the heirs of convicted and executed traitors in 16th—and 17th-century England, a favoured tool of the Tudors—higher stakes than million-dollar bonuses.

Even so, the principle against attainder has some bearing on the current controversy,. Statutes that target highly specific groups of people are likely to be unjust and oppressive.

The Canadian Constitution has little to say directly on these matters, though "the principles of fundamental justice" in the Charter of Rights and Freedoms(加拿大权利和自由宪章) surely include a bulwark against retroactivity. Cabinets and parliaments can get carried away here, too.[43]

---

[43] "Bonuses Clawback: Backdating the Laws", *The Globe and Mail*, March 20, 2009, p. A20.

Section Eighteen: Contradiction and Tension between Predictability and Hard Cases(疑难案件)

To insist on the certainty and predictability of judicial decisions by virtue of the application of the doctrine of precedent is to turn a blind eye to the criticism that American legal realism and the Critical legal study movement inflicted on the theory and teachings of legal formalism, mechanical jurisprudence. It is also to ignore the rationality of the proposition that in hard cases, the meaning and application of rules are always in dispute. All cases that have not been settled before trial and after the discovery process are hard cases.

Jeremy Bentham's unsuccessful attempt (offer) to codify(编纂) American Common law is well documented. His scathing attack was of no avail. But his characterization of the Common law would be hard to dispute. In his view, the Common law is "shapeless mass of merely conjectural and essentially un-cognizable matter, a confused, indeterminate, inadequate, ill-adapted and inconsistent, and a species of muck law." It is "some random decisions or string of frequently contradictory decisions, pronounced almost without any intelligible reason under the impulse of some private sinister interest."㊹

The fact that the parties in dispute are willing to go through the costly and time-consuming and painful process of litigation lends strong support to the indetermination and unpredictability of legal rules and judicial decisions.

Litigation(诉讼) and lawsuit(起诉) are caused by disagreement over facts, right and wrong or the meaning and applicability of relevant rules. In efficiently processed disputes, the available information and views on applicable rules predict a likely outcome. Any adjudication over disputes that could not be efficiently processed by the parties becomes a political choice and the decision is thus irrational.㊺

The flourishing of the interpretive scholarship, the heated debates between Lon

---

㊹ Karl N. Llewellyn. Ibid.

㊺ A good account of the efficiently processed dispute theory is found in Paul E. Campos. *Op cit*, *supra* note 14 at 58 et seq.

L. Fuller and H. L. A. Hart*, and Dworkin's** idea of the fictitious Hercules judge as the ultimate oracle of the legal enterprise, can all be considered derogatory of the applicability and soundness of the doctrine of stare decisis.

One of the latest examples of the weakness and vulnerability of the Common law relates to issue of the same-sex marriage. It has been aptly pointed out that the traditional definition of marriage between a man and a woman originates from the Common law, judge-made law. As such, it is destined to be "update", redefined, derogated from by judicial decisions of all lower courts in the country.

Uncertainty is simply a way of life. No rule or decision of elite powers, even of the highest legal authority, can do away with uncertainty. In a recent tax planning case, Lipson v. Canada, the Supreme Court of Canada, in ruling on the interpretation and application of the general anti-avoidance rule (GAAR)(一般反避税条款), appeared to have said that uncertainty was inherent in all situations in which the law had to be applied to unique facts.

Section Nineteen: More Characterizations of the Common Law

The Common law is originated from judges of the English royal courts on the foundation of the decisions and developed by courts of all jurisdictions following the Common law system. But as a set of rules, it misses the dynamic and shifting nature of law. As principles, and a system of legal thought, it is inherently incomplete, vague and fluid.㊻

It is a mode of treating legal problem (Note: Roscoe Pound is one the most prolific and influential legal theorists and the most preeminent advocate for the sociological school of law. His insights on the Common law can be found in most of

---

* 哈特(1907—),英国法学家,现代西方新分析法学的代表。他指出,法律不是以威胁为后盾的强制性命令,并从法律的内容、法律适用的范围,以及法律产生的方式三个方面论证了"命令说"的荒谬性。在此基础上,他提出了关于法律概念的重要性——法即第一性规则和第二性规则的结合。

** 罗纳德·德沃金,Ronald. Myles. Dworkin(1931—) 当代英美法学理论传统中最有影响的人物之一,在德沃金的法理学体系中,有四个主要的观点(它们构成了当代法学理论的重要组成部分):第一,批判并超越法律实证主义;第二,坚持认为法律理论依赖于政治与道德理论;第三,把法律理论根植于一种解释理论;第四,将平等的政治价值作为法律理论的核心部分。

㊻ A. W. B. Simpson, *Legal Theory and Legal History: Essays on the Common Law*, London: Ronceverte, W. Va.: Hambledon Press, 1987.

his writings.). It is a method of legal thinking. ㊼ It is consisted of a mass of custom, tradition or judge-made maxims㊽ which were the essential core of the Common law woven so closely into the fabric of life.

The unifying element of the Common law seems mystical; it is a kind of superhuman wisdom effected in the collective work of the Common law judges throughout the centuries but impossible for any simple person to posses. Judicial decisions do not make law but are depositories or evidences of the law. Judges are living oracles of the law. The legitimacy(合法性) and authority of the Common law should be grounded in community values and customs. As such, legal change goes hand in hand with social change. It develops with the growth, reinterpretation and restatement of precedents and the adjustment of legal doctrine(法律原理) to new circumstances reflected in the never-ending succession of cases brought before courts. The collective wisdom of judges captures the spirit of the value of the community as expressed in propositions and reasons. It is representative of an evolving collective legal consciousness, the charismatic authority of individual wise judges or the conception of delegated political power. It is the authority of a specific constitutional document providing the ultimate foundation of legal and judicial system.

The fact that easy and principled access to the mass of judicial decisions through publications such as digests of law, the Restatement of laws, or expository scholarship cannot cover up, let alone diminish or eliminate the conflicts, contradictions, confusion embodied in the decisions. Competing, conflicting, and contradictory decisions may be ignored, dismissed, or even distorted in some expository scholarship, but these same decisions may be resurrected, re-imagined, and revitalized in other legal scholarships.

The Restatements of the law that represent in one sense the most monumental intellectual understanding of the present time in scholarly exposition of the Common law in the United States are, in essence, the collective works of a group of like-minded legal scholars. In spite of these historical efforts, uncertainty and unpredictability of judicial decisions remain. This state of the Common law is amply illustrated by the two complementary publications; the Restatement in the Courts

---

㊼ Felix Cohen, *Ethical Systems and Legal Ideals; an Essay on the Foundations of Legal Criticism*, New York: Falcon Press, 1933, p.333.

㊽ Albert V. Dicey, *Introduction to the Study of the Law of Constitution*, 1819, V. 1; 57.

accounts the judicial decisions of different courts in which an article of the Restatement has been cited either adopting, rejecting or distinguishing it, and the State Annotations that indicates to what extent, in actual fact, the rules found in the Restatement are followed in different states.

In short, the Common law as a judicial law being facts-based and time and space tethered has only limited if not questionable precedent force. When generalized broadly enough to reach wider scope and application, it loses its material support in specificity and sharpening in underlying facts. After having suffered a strand of subsequent distinguishing and tested in the light of changes in circumstance and condition as well as further development, interpretation, and treatment, the Common law rules have to a significant extent lost their institutional authority and supported only by whatever reasons they may embody. At the point, it resembles juridical law.

Section Twenty: Is the Common Law a Living Law

Jurists are fond of saying that the Common law is a living law, and the Common law develops and purifies itself case by case continuously. And it grows infinitely like an ever-expanding seamless web. This observation, while interesting and significant may be both superficial and incomplete, if not irrationally exuberant. Beside the fact that there are conflicting precedents and opposing doctrines, uncertainty, indetermination, and unpredictability that emasculate the authority of the Common law, the corpus of the Common law itself is infested with gaps, misinterpretations and misapplications. For between cases, numerous critical reviews, comments, and evaluation may have been made. Recommendations and propositions for improvement and change may have been advanced. A renewed version of the law may have very well been recognized, put into practice, and operational. In many instances, when judicial elucidation and interpretation, become confusing, controversial, or simply unrealistic, legislation may be introduced to streamline, harmonize, prescribe the law by setting the record straight. As a consequence, the Common law is in fact living neither a complete nor a very healthy life.

Furthermore, the analogous reasoning method of the Common law through deducing rules from similar past decisions is an elaborate form of question begging.

Being a species of legal conceptualization, it is always fraught with ambiguities and dangers.⑭ This is due to the inescapable problems inherent in the task of determining which similarities and differences between cases are significant and trivial. Any thorough and comprehensive study of modern Anglo-American law will encounter a maze of conflicting formal rules, instrumental concerns and ethical norms. All legal concepts are socially constructed; their value and importance are relative and change with the policy and social trends. To choose any concept and doctrine as exclusively applicable and therefore dominant is to pit against or reject another of no less relevance and applicability.

Section Twenty-one: The Common Law—Vitality, Staying Power, and Continuing Relevance

Doctrines of absolute royal sovereignty were rejected by the Common law theory. The great Chief Justice Coke observed in 1611 that the King "hath no prerogative(总督委任组成的法庭) but that which thee law of the land allows him." Early declarations of the liberty of the subject and of restrictions on royal power such as the Magna Carta of 1215 came to be seen as part of the Common law tradition.

The English influence has been attributed to the fact that the judicial system and the administrative organizations and the laws of evidence and procedure, civil and criminal, have everywhere been established and set out along English lines.

The Common law, unlike that of the Romano-Germanic family, did not experience a renewal through Roman law, nor was it transformed by means of codification.

The important question is: How could a tradition determined by a few judges on an island thousands of miles away continue to maintain a strong hold on the juridical thinking in so many countries sharing the same tradition? How could rules with their roots in the 12th century have evolved enough to be relevant to the interests and needs of the high-technology world of today?

Even much of the statutory content of the Sale of Goods Act 1893(1893年货物买卖法) and the American Uniform Commercial Code represented a restatement of Common law principles developed on the basis the customs of the law merchant as

---

⑭ Paul F. Campos, *Jurismanias: The Madness of American Law*, Oxford Univ. Pr., 1998, p.83.

absorbed by the Common law courts.

The dialog and vigorous argument among the lawyers and the judges about the best way of understanding earlier decisions in the light of general considerations of efficiency, fairness, and justice have had a great deal to contribute to the development of the Common law. Through this process of ongoing argument and adjudication, the Common law became not merely a collection of individual authoritative decisions, but also a body of principles and concepts of public policy expressed and repeated by judges from one generation to another. In one sense, it has been hailed as the "Common heritage of the English speaking people worldwide." It is also in this sense that the Common law could be viewed as a living law.

But how did this body of principles and concepts of public policy come about? How could a collection of individual authoritative decisions give rise or lead to the emergence of a resultant body of principles and concepts of public policy which got invoked, applied, mentioned, considered or otherwise dealt with through generations? Seeds growing into grains need cultivation, nutrients, and cultivator. Who were the cultivators? What were the nutrients? How was the growing cultivated? Could it be that the constant stream of judicial decisions has fulfilled in the process all the three requirements in virtue of the doctrine of ratio decidendi, obiter dictum, and stare decisis? What are the nature, degree, and significance of the contribution of scholarly law in its various forms? What is the role of other lawmakers, authoritative decision-makers or sources of law?

Perhaps it may be summarized in this way: Customs and decisions work as seeds (authoritative and effective decisions). Principles and precepts of public policy are the grains (the law of authoritative and effective decisions). The on-going recognition and realization of justice, fairness, and other virtues work as the nutrient—authority and efficacy inform and sustain the life of the Common law. Lawyers, judges, jurists, and intelligentsia serve as the cultivators (expositors, critics, reformists, "rulifiers"). The healthy grow and continuous relevance of the Common law is an on-going process of shared and collaborated enterprise that is sustained and developed by power elites and public activists That the Common law works itself pure and perfect through times is best understood in this sense.

Section Twenty-two: Common Law in the Welfare State of the Twentieth Century—the Age of Statutes

A Common law for the age of statute is actually the title of a book written by Guido Calabresi* and delivered for the Oliver Wendell Holmes** lectures in 1982. The author was fully aware of the decrease in importance and influence, if not the demise, of the Common law in the modern time of welfare state when the supremacy of statutes instead of judicial decisions was in vogue.

In many liberal democracies(自由民主制), the liberalism that dominated until 1914 has ceded place to a socialist trend of creating a new social order of the welfare state. With the change, the Common law is undergoing a serious crisis: the judicial and case by case methods characteristic of its original development are no longer suited to the idea of bringing about rapid and extensive social change. Regulatory tribunals and administrative agencies have proven to be a more effective instrument to achieve the goals.

Among factors that contribute to this phenomenal surge in the importance of legislation include nationalization, regionalization as the European Union, globalization, Americanization of law, demise of the expository orthodoxy (doctrinal works), and the growing trends of theoretical approach to law.㊿ The Common law has become a footnote in history. As a tradition and a system, it has only limited impact. Systemic features such as process reasoning, doctrine of stare decisis, judge-made law, judicial review(司法审查) fare differently; some have survived and even are flourishing, while other considerably weakened.

Yet, the received wisdom that legislation is not law until it is interpreted, explained, or applied in a fact situation persists till today. And the legal realists' dictum that law is what the judge says finds many followers among lawyers. But whether or not and to what extent, a common law rule is authoritative can only be judged on a case-by-case(具体问题具体分析) basis.

It is nevertheless undeniable that facing the ever, fast changing social,

---

* 圭多·卡拉布雷西,美国著名法学家,经济分析法学的奠基人,美国联邦上诉法院法官,耶鲁法学院教授。

** 小奥利弗·温德尔·霍姆斯(1841—1935),美国著名法学家,美国最高法院大法官。

㊿ B. B. Cheffins, "Our Common Legal Heritage: Fragmentation and Renewal" 30(1) *Law Librarian* 3 (Mr 99).

economic, ethical, and environmental conditions and expectations, the slow, incremental pace of the Common law leaves much to be desired. This phenomenon of the Common law courts can be largely ascribable to the innate conservatism of the courts, the retarding influence of precedent, the relative antiquity of judges' education, the passive and reactive characteristics of judicial action, or the limitations on standing or remedy characteristic of judicial action(司法行为).[51]

Review and Reflective Questions

1. In the face of the Rule of precedent or doctrine of Stare decisis and a trend of past decisions in leading cases, how could a judge manage to decide in a new direction, that is, cast the case on hand in a new light?

2. How could judges continue to play a significant and meaningful role in the comprehensive decision making process of the law in the modern welfare states where legislative and regulatory decisions overwhelming every aspect of life?

3. Discuss in detail the pro and con of distinguishing versus overruling a case.

4. What are the techniques invoked by judges to distinguish a case?

复习及提问

1. 面对"遵循先例原则"和援引判例的情况,法官是如何对一个新的案件作出判决的?

2. 在现今几乎生活的每一个领域都已经覆盖了福利的国家体制下,法官是如何在复杂的判案过程中继续扮演者一个重要角色的呢?

3. 讨论:区别一个案例和推翻一个先例的利与弊。

4. 法官运用什么方法来区别案例?

---

[51] Cass Sunstein, "Statutes and the Common Law", 89 *Michigan L. R.* 907, 917 (1991).

Chapter Six: United States Law <u>in Action</u>(诉讼中的): the Operative and Interactive Dynamics

Introductory Note

The emphasis is on law in action as opposed to law in book. The focus is on process of law as opposed to sources or outcome of law. We prefer the concept of authoritative and effective decision process as opposed to the process of law. The former is a broader and more realistic conception of law.

Process is synonymous with participant and interactivity. In this chapter, we talk about the role and contribution of elite participants and their mutual informing and shaping. In the ever-continuing law-making process, the crucial question if what is the law and how to identify it. For this we offer some fresh, doubtless interesting insights.

One the downside of over-zealous regulators is over-regulation, what we call hypertrophying of law and legal reason. We talk about this with a critical eye.

简介

与法的运作概念相对应的是法律文本。本章是对法律产生过程的关注而非对于法律渊源本身。我们更喜欢用权威性的和有效的决定来取代法律过程的称谓。因为前者是对法律更为宽泛和现实的定义。

过程是参与者和互相交流代名词。在本章中,我们将讨论精英在整个过程中的角色和作用以及他们相互之间的影响。在持续的法律形成过程当中,最主要的问题是:什么是法及如何确认它。在这方面我们将提供一些全新的、有趣的视角。

过度热心的监管者的一个弊处是过度监管,我们称之为法律的臃肿化。我们将用批判的视角来进行分析。

Chapter Six: United States Law in Action(诉讼中的): the Operative and... 149

Section One: The Defining Character and Spirit of Anglo-American Law

One realistic and reliable way to ascertain the characteristics and spirit of Anglo-American law is to study the life of law in one of the most representative countries belonging to the Anglo-American legal system, the United States. The emphasis is on how the law and the legal system works and operates in practice and how elite participants in the comprehensive normative enterprise of the law act, react, and interact.

No doubt, there are many aspects and dimensions to a legal system and law in action. It is submitted that the most fundamental force or constitutive element that calls for special emphasis is interactivity. Interactivity ensures the mutual informing and shaping relationship between elite powers in government and society. Interactivity is the sine qua none(不可或缺的前提和条件) of law if law is to be regarded as a collective normative enterprise. The democratic spirit of the law and the legal system permeates and manifests itself vividly in the entire robust, interactive, dynamic process.

Section Two: The Contrast between Law in Action and Law in Book

To avoid turning the legal system into nothing more than ad hoc(特定的) commands, there must be congruence between the rules as announced and the rules as applied. This is the eighth way of Lon L. Fuller's eight ways of not to fail to make law. Fuller sees the possibility of compliance as a central feature of law. When law and social institutions fall into disrespect, they lose both authority and efficacy.

The concept of the law in action is viewed as a direct contrast to that of the law in book. One is dynamic and operational while another is static and formulaic. The rationale for the distinction is that often and in many important cases the law in fact operates in society differs to a significant extent from the law found in the established sources and materials. The focus of the dynamic and operational law in action is as much on the decision and the action of the decision-makers as on the interactivity between them. The rules, principles, policies, and precepts as posited and found in legislation, regulation, judicial decisions, and other established sources, if not invoked, applied or otherwise practiced, become the objects of analytic, interpretive, or similar academic study only. As such, they are not meaningful and relevant to the decisions and actions of the state, nor the life of the people. Discourses on the static, formulaic rules found in the law of book are engagements in irrelevance. Law in book focuses on the internal features, connectedness, structure, or other internal qualities of rules. As soon as the requirements or force of the law starts to impact on what happens in the real world as manifested in action and decision, law in book becomes law in action. The criticism that the law in countries including many liberal democracies that pay only lip service to the rule of law is a fungible(可替代的) phenomenon, highly elusive, and un-redeemably unpredictable, refers more likely to the jarring gaps between the law in book and that in action.

The concept of law in action maintains the distinction between validity, efficacy, and authority. Authority without efficacy is an empty shell. Efficacy without authority lacks legitimacy. Positivists' laboring on the meaning and significance of the validity of rules, while paying little or no attention to efficacy as Kelsen's distinction between validity and efficacy attests, only leads to confusing the law in action with the law in book.[52] Lon L. Fuller posits eight principles of morality that make law possible. Two directly relate to the efficacy of law. These are the failure to rules understandable and the making of rules that require conduct beyond the powers of the affected party.[53] Even H. L. A. Hart's rules of recognition must be effective in the practice of officials who perform the invocation, interpretive, and application functions. The emphasis on the law in action is especially important in jurisdictions where the law due to a number of reasons is not worth the paper it is written on.

In the real world of authoritative and effective decisions generating real law in action, the weaknesses and irrelevance of legal formalism is fully exposed and taken notice. In such a world, lawyers and jurists functioning in legal formalism are virtually engaging in normative irrelevance. The term "academic law" to a large degree signifies the insignificance to the real world of the works of jurists engaged in legal formalism or mechanical jurisprudence. This sad situation is perhaps more

---

[52] Hans Kelsen, *The Pure Theory of Law*, Translated by Max Knight, Berkeley, Los Angeles & London. University of California Press, 1970.

[53] Lon L. Fuller, *The Morality of Law*, New Haven and London, Yale University Press, 1964, p.39.

Chapter Six: United States Law in Action(诉讼中的): the Operative and... 151

evident on the international stage than on the national stage. On the international plane, what works and counts as law can be more readily appreciated. But in the domestic domain, the legal and political power of the state is so overpowering and overwhelming in impact that people and lawyers alike simply become enchanted, co-opted, and intoxicated by state law regardless of its efficacy. As a consequence, they completely become unconscious of the law that operates in decision and action of people in society.

Legal system can be viewed and analyzed in the same real and activist way. The crucial problem is how to capture the form and substance, and the essential features of the law including the legal system in action.

Legal system concerns primarily with the constitutive structure, institutions, what count as laws, decision-making process, decision-makers, and all other functions and operations in the comprehensive process of political morality.

Inquiry into the performance and operational process of the legal system does not concern much with the substance and rationality of decisions of any kind. In this sense, a legal system is in general morally neutral except for those moral principles that are constitutive of a legal system itself such as what Fuller advocates.

Law in action consists of both the operation of the legal system and the making, application and effectuation of the law in general and of individual laws in particular. The legal system and individual laws form in fact a unity; they work seamlessly as a fully integrated entity; they intrinsically inform and strengthen each other. Legal system is both the composite and the operation of the law.

To capture the law in action, one must explore the entire life history of the law. What is interesting and significant is not the nature, content, or purpose of any of the functional decisions in and of itself. What is crucial to the understanding of the law in action is to explore how elite participants interact with each other in its entire life span. The interaction of elite powers permeates in each and every function in the comprehensive authoritative and effective decision making process.

It must be submitted that due to a number of reasons, causes, factors, etc, the law in action or the law that is in practice operative in society can never be in full compliance with the law as prescribed in publications of legislation, judicial decisions, or other sources. Yet when the gap between the two versions becomes notoriously wide or when they point in sharply opposing or divergent directions, the very viability, if not the very existence, of the legal system is in jeopardy.

Law may be posited for reason of domestic politics, political expediency, international reputation, external pressure, etc. And commitment is either not taken seriously or never intended.

The authority of law fails because of under-reaching, over-reaching, non-enforcement, under-enforcement, adverse or unexpected or unforeseeable consequences, misinterpretation and misapplication, civil disobedience, deep divisive and intractable social or moral conflicts, as well as a host of other possible causes, factors, reasons. For example, to implement the Canadian Health Insurance Portability and Accountability Act (HIPPA) (加拿大健康保险便携与责任法案) would require training hundreds of thousands of medical workers. This has been easy and large gaps persist between what the law requires in principle and how medical providers interpret the law in the field.

The congruence between declared rule and authoritative and effective decision could also be destroyed due to an "inaccessibility of the law, lack of insight into what is required to maintain the integrity of a legal system, bribery, prejudice, indifference, stupidity, and the drive toward personal power."[54]

When rules or doctrines fail, we tend to fault application, implementation and other practices. What is easily overlooked is that the legal system and its political superstructures are the root-causes. To overcome the strict requirements of minimum internal morality of law as prescribed by Lon Fuller to build a good legal system[55], one may have first to critically study and reform the underlying political philosophy and superstructures at the root.

However, it must be pointed out that the phenomenon of incongruence does not truly or fully reflects the distinction or incongruence between law in book and law in action. The congruence or incongruence theory appears to take declared rule as the operative authority of the law and a standard for assessing the value and authority of consequent conduct, decision or action. In the same vein, to limit the compliance of a declared rule to "official action," as Fuller appears to do, paints only a partial picture of law.[56]

The problems and issues implicated in the evaluation of the law in book and law in action as well as the congruence or incongruence between declared rule and

---

[54] Lon L. Fuller, *The Morality of Law*, New Haven and London, Yale University Press, 1964, p.81.
[55] Please refer to the next chapter on good legal system for a detailed discussion.
[56] Ibid.

Chapter Six: United States Law in Action(诉讼中的): the Operative and... 153

authoritative and effective decision and action are much more complex, comprehensive, and challenging. The inquiry, analysis, and assessment required to have a realistic and true description in this respect must be equally inclusive, comprehensive, and in depth. What likely to require would include the identification and clarification of the type of source of law at issue, the nature and authority of the operative decision involved, and the outcome and efficacy of the decision. Official action and non-state or social or private action should be equally attended to. And the interactive relationship between all these elements is of no less importance for the task. It must be kept in mind that all the functions performed in the authoritative and effective decision-making process are potentially law-creating. When what counts as law is viewed as a collective normative enterprise participated by all elite powers in a polity, the problems and issues relating to the congruence between declared rule and elite power decision in reality and the distinction between law in book and law in action acquire suddenly a positive, activist perspective.

The law in book is in constant pursuit to catch up with the law in action as manifested in social change, material and cultural conditions and other normative expectations.

Law reform well attests both the existence of the law in action and necessity for bringing the law in book up-to-date in congruence with the law in action. Judges of the Supreme Court of Canada have openly expressed concern about their decisions being misread(误读), misapplied(误用), the public being mis-informed(误导), the adverse social impact of their decisions, and that their decisions are made prematurely. And it is not ideal to simply correct distortions and misunderstandings by subsequent decisions.

Benjamin N. Cardozo* is known to have called for the establishment of a Ministry of Justice to watch the law in action, to discover defects and anachronisms, and to recommend changes to bring the law into harmony with social changes and modern conditions. This eventually led to the creation of the Law Revision Commission by the New York Legislature in 1934. In fact, law reform has been widely recognized as an indispensable element of national law and a permanent feature of the legal institutions of all nation states, especially for those that aspire to

---

* 本杰明·内森·卡多佐, Benjamin Nathan Cardozo(1870—1938), 是美国著名法学家, 担任过美国最高法院大法官。

constitutional democracy*.

Section Three: Sites, Sources, and Manifestations of Law and Legal System in Action: State and Non-state

In its fundamental sense, the focus and concern here is the question: what counts as law? Law is authoritative and effective decisions. In keeping with the omnipresent nature of law in society, law and legal system in action finds its expression in each and every authoritative and effective decision-making. There is no prescribed form in which law and legal system expresses itself. Nor its substantive content is finite. The essential feature of the seminal works by M. McDougal and H. Lasswell on policy science** study of law is their insightful classification of the functions performed in the authoritative and effective decision-making process into intelligence, invocation, interpretation, application, prescription, appraisal, and termination. In each and every of these functions, the working and operation of the law and the legal system find their expression. Each time when an action is taken or decision is made in the performance of any of these functions, the law is set in action. In this conception, it seems undeniable that the most rich, multifarious, and meaningful sources displaying the law in action are the mass media, while keeping in mind of the fact that journalist's report of what transpires in fact is not always entirely objective. For example, we see the system and the law in action in every one of the actions taken by the New York Attorney General(纽约州司法部长) Eliot Spitzer to investigate the wrong doings of a corporation, an insurance business, or a financial institution.

Fuller in his seminal collected essays "The Principles of Social Order"(57) views the interactive process as the defining feature of law, any law. He identifies six sources or components that figure in the process. These include legislation, adjudication, administration, direction, mediation, contract, and customary law. In

---

* 宪政民主,用宪法和法律对政府权力加以限制,保障个人权利和自由。

** 政策科学,也称政策分析,指对政策的调研、制订、分析、筛选、实施和评价的全过程进行研究的方法。政策分析的核心问题是对备选政策的效果、本质及其产生原因进行分析。它是在运筹学和系统分析的基础上发展起来的。1951 年莱斯韦尔与勒恩纳合作,在美国出版《政策科学》一书,为政策分析奠定了基础。因此莱斯韦尔成为政策分析的奠基人。

(57) Lon L. Fuller, *The Principles of Social Order*, Ed. Kenneth I. Winston. Durham NC: Duke University Press, 1981.

Chapter Six: United States Law in Action(诉讼中的): the Operative and... 155

the same vein, Fuller conceives institutions in a broader sense. In his view, institution is not a simple static, directional, unilateral, multi-dimensional force. It is an active participatory interactive normative force in a complex and comprehensive context.

Sites and manifestations can be both state and non-state. Within the category of state sites, there are the various (three in the case of the Unites States) branches of government and their departments, committees, subcommittees, subordinate bodies, agencies, commissions, boards, etc. As to the legislative branch and the judiciary, ample discussions have been made in the various sections in Chapter Four. Sites in the non-state sectors or fields include all elite powers, entities and groups in society, such as corporations, interest groups, the mass media, churches, schools, and influential and prominent individuals. The idea to include non-state sites and manifestations of law and legal system in action is in conformity with the proposition that law in essence is authoritative and effective decisions, and that legal centralism and legal pluralism are not mutually exclusive but mutually informing, shaping, and reinforcing.

In many instances, the private sectors may assert an activist and leading role in the interactive process of government elites. For example, in response to the aggressive and ambitious implementation and enforcement functions of the Eliot Spitzer, the New York Attorney-General, in investigating and threatening to indict American business for wrong doing, and in shaking them down for multimillion-dollar settlements, Corporate America accused him for straying beyond the constitutional bound and encroaching on federal jurisdiction, and called upon the Congress to clip the wings of attorneys-general by passing a law that would make such multi-state settlements subject to congressional approval.[58]

Yet to fit the omnipresence of law in society, sources of authoritative and effective decisions should be even further extended to include all potential means and ways of communications in the public arena of political morality. Thus, we see the potential of words, movies, songs, etc in politics and law. Pictures speak a thousand words. The rhetoric and persuasive power of movies for example is hardly quantifiable. It has been opined that the leftist(左派) conspiracy freak Oliver Stone alone, had put more wrong ideas about United States history in Americans' heads

---

[58] Corporate American declares war on "Spitzerism" The Globe and Mail, Friday, May 27, 2005. p. B8.

than the whole school system could ever correct. Casual script rewrites have the potential to overthrow established fact and collectively threaten to destroy national identity. History and historical material facts are sources of bases and standards for political, moral action. From the perspective of jurisprudence, such social artifacts and their influences are not so much different from the eschewed portray of what counts as law as painted by the state apparatuses and its loyal legal positivists.

In the same vein, how could anyone taking an internal standpoint of law ignore the far-reaching impact and significance of the civil rights speeches of Dr. Martin Luther King Jr.* or the teachings and leadership of Mohandas K. Gandhi** in civil disobedience? Such political moral actions are the very seeds or manifestations of the law of authoritative and effective decisions. It is arguable that King and Gandhi have exerted more influence and impact on the life and action of people than any law, whether legislative or judicial in nature. The actions of both preeminent leaders are taken voluntarily and in full awareness of the consequences. ⑤⑨

For example, movie may very well be a political moral act and potentially represents a law in action. Fahrenheit 9/11 is crafted for the sole purpose to dethrone George W. Bush, Jr. The artistry is just a means to the end. Michael Moore, the author of the movie, is a self-crowned liberal crusader and the populist conscience of the United States. The movie was addressed to the sizable portion of the United States electorate whose political understanding has been forged exclusively by White House rhetoric and the compliant media. This documentary has been touted as the watershed event that may demonstrate for the first time whether the empire of poli-tainment(政治娱乐) can have a decisive influence on U.S. presidential campaign. Whether the potential of a mass medium, in this case, movie, can affect American politics in some new ways can also be tested. In other words, whether a political act will have a political result in reaching the target audience and changing their hearts and minds becomes a political moral issue. The fact that President Bush

---

* 马丁·路德·金(1929—1968)将"非暴力"(nonviolence)和"直接行动"(direct action)作为社会变革方法的最为突出的倡导者之一。1963 年 8 月 28 日在林肯纪念堂前发表《我有一个梦想》的演说。1964 年度诺贝尔和平奖获得者。

** Mohandas Karamchand Gandhi,莫罕达斯·卡拉姆昌德·甘地,尊称圣雄甘地,是印度民族主义运动和国大党领袖。他既是印度的国父,也是印度最伟大的政治领袖。他带领国家迈向独立,脱离英国的殖民统治。他的"非暴力反抗"的主张,影响了全世界的民族主义者和那些争取和平变革的国际运动。

⑤⑨ For a concise essay on civil disobedience in democracy, see Peter Suber, "Civil Disobedience". In: *The Philosophy of Law: An Encyclopedia*, Ed. Christopher Berry Gray, New York & London, Garland Publ., 1999, p.110.

was successfully reelected does not necessarily doom the potential of poli-tainment in influencing public conduct as an emerging genre of political moral action. Should any of such acts ever succeed and become authoritative and effective, it counts just as law as that made and posited by the state.

Due to the obvious influence of legal positivism, study of law in action tends to focus on the decisions and actions of state organs. And little attention is paid to non-state sectors, the so-called social fields, where autonomous self-defining orderings prevail. Among the state organs, even particular emphasis has been laid with the mass of appellate court opinions which is more than decisions and action of the legislature and regulatory bodies widely regarded by judges and lawyers alike as the very embodiments of the law.

Legal positivism has not securely anchored the concept of law. State power and forced or coercive implementation(强制性执行) of decision are not the defining and necessary elements of law. The act of State must be legitimate to be authoritative. Valid law (legislation or judicial decisions) may not be the law in reality.

But the phenomenon of law in action thus is not exclusively state-centered; it has its polyjural dimensions. Legal pluralism is not simply a matter of pluralism in morality but in fact more reflects the normative activities of a society.

This phenomenon of multi-level legal normativity(规范性) or polyjuriality has been most aptly and insightfully captured by the following observations on the insignificant role and status of the appellate court opinions in the total scheme of the law:

"[F]or every dispute that ripens into even the possibility of a lawsuit or an arrest, millions of frictionless legal transactions take place, most of them blissfully free of any conscious knowledge on the part of the participants that they are in any sense partaking in legal interaction. For every dispute involving some sort of formal legal action, there are dozens of conflicts where legal action was considered that were resolved without recourse to it. For every civil lawsuit resulting in a formal courtroom disposition, there are between thirty and fifty suits that are settled prior to this point. And for every lower court disposition of a case that results in an appellate court opinion, there are many more that do not."⑥⓪

One of the latest manifestations of the interactive dynamics of authoritative and effective decisions involving both the state sectors and a private participant is Chinese National Overseas Oil Corporation's (CNOOC)(中国海洋石油总公司) $18.5 billion offer to buy Unocal, a U.S. company with energy assets in both North America and Asia. As a result of intensive lobbying and pressure techniques mounted by U.S. lawmakers and other interests on reason of national security, CNOOC was forced to finally withdraw its purchase offer.

Yet, private ordering must not clashes with state law. When state law is silent or abstains, moral pluralism or polyjuriality prevails. On the other hand, any ethnic laws(民族法制), such as Sharia(伊斯兰教教法) in Muslim religious law(穆斯林宗教律法), may be recognized as valid by state law if not in violation of state law to be applicable in case of conflicts. In Canada, private tribunals(法庭) to solve civil disputes between individuals or businesses exist for many ethnic communities, such as Jewish, Ismaili Muslim and Mennonite. A pluralistic democracy can and should promote its core values and institutes without taking fright at the prospect of difference. Polygamists in Mormon group live in the United States just like all outlaws from the perspective of state law. When state law asserts its power, they either stop the practice or suffer consequences. In this case, reason eventually may fail; the majority rules and the law of the monogamists prevail. On the other hand, the debate over religious based arbitration is not about right or wrong; it is not an issue of religious tolerance and freedom. It is about the privatization of public institutions. The introduction of religious law as a substitute for state laws is detrimental to the well being of all citizens. The development of a civil society rests on universal(普世法) and secular laws(世俗法), which are inclusive and advance the values of human rights, equality and freedom of choice.

In some instances, state law and private normative ordering interact and inform each other. In a constitutional democracy, it is often the case that with respect to instances such as misconduct, dereliction of duties, abuses of office or power by

---

⑥⓪ Paul F. Campos, *Jurismanias: The Madness of American Law*, Oxford Univ. Pr., 1998, p.58.

Cause for Litigation—There is a number of reasons for formal legal action or official disposition of disputes to take place. It may be due to a disagreement about the facts of a social interaction, a fundamental conflict of moral views, or the ambiguous, contradictory, anachronistic, or otherwise controversial nature of relevant rules. And in many instances, people are simply willing to spend money to sublimate their emotions into public modes of expression, or to have their identity and status recognized in the legal arena.

public officials, the court of public opinions conducts investigation, charge, and conviction, and the state as the superior power holder executes the decision.

In other instances, they interact and fight for authority and control. Racial discrimination and its correlated issue of affirmative action(支持、鼓励聘用女性、少数族裔等受歧视者的积极行动或措施) have proven to the fertile ground for the interaction and the struggle for control between authoritative and effective decision-makers. In Brown v. Board of Education[*], the Court spoke unanimously to bring a historical end to segregation in the United States. In Richmond v. J. A. Croson, Co., the Court, justified by a set of sharply contradicting reasons, decided to emasculate or to erode the authority and application of Brown. The United States Congress in 1991 passed the Civil Rights Act to overrule the Supreme Court and instructed people to behavior yet in some other ways. Facing the instability of the legal system and the uncertainty of the law, the people of California resorted to put the issue to ballot(投票表决) via public initiative.

Section Four: The Life of Law in Common Law America: Selective Accounts of the Interactive Dynamics of Elite Power Decisions

Either by a comprehensive study of all levels of decision-making and subject areas or through selective sampling, the law and legal system of the United States can be cast either in a positive, favorable light, or in a negative and derogatory manner. In the process, both the beneficial and salubrious effects and their destructive and deleterious consequences are explored and discussed.

In any society of moral and value pluralism, competing values, visions and beliefs constantly clash and are in conflict. Personal choice is prominent. Consequently, different strands of authoritative and effective decisions struggle for primacy, recognition, and authority. This is especially true when deep divisive issues of a political and moral nature are involved and the struggle for primacy and control is fierce.

---

[*] 1954 年布朗控诉托皮卡教育局案,导致美国废除种族隔离法。

A. Check and Balance: The Overriding Principle of Interactivity(互动性原则)

Power corrupts. Authority can be abused. To ensure that authority and power are invoked and applied legitimately, judiciously and beneficially, control and necessary constraints must be designed and put into effect. Check and balance is not just a hallmark for countries of constitutional democracy but no less useful and needed for corporate governance in such entities as board of directors or trustees.

There is no doubt that the first and foremost institutional mechanism that sets the law and the legal system in action is the elaborate framework of checks and balances among and within the three branches of government as set out by the Constitution. Distrust of government is the pivotal reason for the establishment of this constitutional setup. Check and balance is designed to ensure that no action or decision from any one branch of government and a subordinate body thereof can become authoritative and effective without the bliss of the other two branches. Thus, there are two chambers within the Congress: one to satisfy small states that want equal representation (the Senate), and the other to accommodate the populous states with membership based on population (the House of Representative). Federal district courts(美国联邦地区法院) are checked in their power by the process of appeal and finally with respect to some of the most important cases to the Supreme Court. A bill only becomes law if both the Senate and the House of Representatives pass it by a majority vote and the President does not veto it. The Congress can control or terminate executive programs by denial of funds. The President as commander in chief may only initiate war upon its declaration by Congress. The President may make a treaty, but only if two thirds of the Senates provides its advice and consent. The President appoints justices to the Supreme Court, but they must be confirmed by a majority of the Senate.

B. Exemplary Interactive Relationships Between the President, the Congress, the Court and the States

Countless cases and incidences may be cited to illustrate the interaction and potential collision between the executive and legislative functions and the intervention of the judiciary. The following ones are particularly provided for reason of both their importance and their exemplary value.

(1) Treaties versus Legislation

There are two kinds of treaties, namely, self-executing(自动生效的) and non-self-executing. Self-executing treaties are those that directly effectuate domestic legal consequences. Non-self-executing treaties are those that would contemplate subsequent legislation to have domestic law effect. Self-executing treaties are preemptive of conflicting state laws and like other federal enactments displace earlier, inconsistent federal law. The President decides first the status of a treaty and whether to seek supporting legislation. In default(不履行职责) of such legislation, the judiciary determines whether a treaty is self-executing or not.

To place treaties on an equal footing as legislation is a two-edged sword. Just as self-executing treaties can displace prior federal legislation, so too can subsequent federal legislation displace the domestic law effects of extant treaties. The problem in this case is the effect of such subsequent legislation on the international obligation of the United States and the trustworthiness of the United States government in international relations.

What is more controversial is the status of "executive agreements." These are multi-national agreements entered into by the President without Senate approval. There are three groups of executive agreement. The first group includes those that subsequently are endorsed by a Joint Resolution* of the two houses of Congress. The second is those that concern matters within the exclusive competence and authority of the President. And the third group does not satisfy the narrow conditions of either of the two categories mentioned above. It is the domestic law status of this third group that is problematic.

There are many areas of authority that is concurrent and shared. In absence of either a Congressional grant or denial of authority, the President can only rely upon his own independent powers to effectuate changes in domestic law. Therefore, Congressional inertia, indifference or quiescence may result in enabling, if not inviting, measures on independent presidential responsibility. This is a sort of "zone of twilight(模糊区域)"—a conceptual area lying undefined in between two distinct fields (President's discretionary act and Congress's exclusive legislative power) having characteristics of both but belonging to neither.

---

* 上下两议院的共同决议案,经总统批准即成为法律。

(2) Legislative Veto(否决权) of Administrative and Regulatory Decisions

The Great Depression resulted in catastrophic consequences, social, economic, and psychological. To recover from its aftermath and to prevent its recurrence of similar catastrophes, a more nimble, expert, and ubiquitous governmental oversight is required. Consequently, substantial legislative authority is delegated to the executive branch itself or to quasi-independent administrative agencies to make rules or regulations. Over times, the Congress has inadvertently created a "fourth" branch of government, and an elaborate corpus(汇编) of law of its own has been spawned.

Along with legislative delegation of administrative authority, the Congress devised a mechanism called "legislative veto" to retain the capacity to revoke that authority in individual cases by some expedient way short of full legislative reconsideration.

In a case that involved the suspension by the Attorney General of deportation of individuals under certain limited circumstances of special hardship, the Supreme Court held unconstitutional such legislative veto and any comparable effort by Congress to retain summary authority over the delegatees of its authority. (The mechanism of legislative veto used in conjunction with the delegation of legislative authority is found in over two hundred different statutes.) The question of whether to suspend the deportation of a deportable alien was in its essence a legislative decision, the court ruled; Congress can make legislative decisions only under the full-dress circumstances of ordinary law making.

What is surprisingly asymmetrical of the ruling is that while a legislation delegatee can make legislative decision in an administrative fashion, the Congress that delegates the authority has to do it in a full-dress legislative way. Maybe due to the nature of administrative or regulatory decisions, such distinction is considered reasonable.

(3) Appointment and Removal of High Governmental Officials

The Constitution of the United States requires that high governmental officials of the federal government be appointed by the President and with the consent of the Senate. The Constitution is silent with regard to their removal.

The Court is distinctly uneasy about any arrangements for the removal of such officials that gives Congress exclusive control over their removal as this would raise the specter of a parliamentary government.

In mid-1980s, to impose more or less ironclad budgetary restraints on the entire federal government to the end of reducing the growth of the national debt, the Comptroller General(总审计长) was required to communicate relevant technical data concerning an excessive deficit to the President, along with detailed spending reductions proposals. And the President was required to issue an order mandating the specified reductions to congressionally authorized spending.

According to the legislation that established the Office of the Comptroller General, he can only be removed either by formal impeachment proceedings or by joint resolution of Congress. The latter avenue of removal can be on very general statutory grounds, including inefficiency and malfeasance.

The Court found that removing the Comptroller General from office on the basis of certain general policy grounds, such as inefficiency, would give to Congress far too much control over functions that belonged to the executive branch. And to allow this would violate the constitutional demand that executive authority remains separate from legislative control.

(4) Executive Power versus Civil Liberties

Another recent and notorious example is the attempt of the President to use executive order to declare obsolete and non-applicable the United Nations Convention Against Torture*, the Universal Declaration of Human Rights(世界人权宣言), and the International Covenant on Civil and Political Rights(公民权利和政治权利国际公约). The controversy involves the alleged systemic torture practices perpetrated by United States soldiers at the military bases around the world. This was done all in the name of the right of self-defense and the right to fight against terrorists. Possibly, Donald Rumsfeld, the US Defense Minister, is more than anyone else in the current administration, identified with the culture of extra-legal behavior in the waging of the "war on terrorism(反恐战争)" a war that he helped morph into the invasion of Iraq. This invasion, launched under the pretext that the world was in imminent danger from Saddam Hussein's non-existent weapons of mass destruction, was essentially a lawless operation. At least that is what by the critics believed.

In two separate decisions, though not directly speaking to the issue of torture, the United States Supreme Court attacked the President's executive order that mandates the indefinite detainment of suspected terrorists without access to legal process in Guantanamo Bay, Cuba. The Court ruled that President's decision could

---

* 全称为 United Nations Convention Against Torture and Other Cruel, Inhuman or Degrading Treatment or Punishment,《联合国禁止酷刑和其他残忍、不人道或有辱人格的待遇或处罚公约》。

not override civil liberties, in particular the right of the detainees to question their status before a neutral court. And "even a state of war is not a blank check for the President when it comes to the rights of the nation's citizens." "It is during our most challenging and uncertain moments that our nation's commitment to due process is most severely tested; and it is in those times that we must preserve our commitment at home to the principles for which we fight abroad." It has been rightly observed that this "decision marks the triumph of law over arbitrary rule(专制统治)."

What at issue concerns in the most basic, constitutive sense the wartime powers of the President, and the role of the courts and the role of Congress in reviewing the powers. Unfortunately, in a decision April 3, 2006, the U. S. Supreme Court rejected an appeal concerning the controversial designation of "enemy combatant." Coined by the administration. In other words, the justices sidestepped citizen's challenge to President Bush's war powers regardless of civil-rights activists' allegation that the designation of enemy combatants is a dangerous pretension that is unconstitutional and contrary to the international legal obligations of the United States.

Commenting publicly on the House of Lords' ruling on the Bemarsh prison case, Lord Steyn, one of the longest-serving law lords in Britain's top court accused the British and U. S. governments of whipping up public fear of terrorism, and of being determined to bend established international law to their will and to undermine its essential structures.

In fact, reactions with respect to the controversy and its related legal issues and implications go much beyond the governmental confine. Interaction can be transnational as well as sub-national. For example, the UN Committee against Torture rules in response to the petition of Houshang Bouzari, an Iranian-born businessman and a Canadian permanent resident and against the finding of Canadian courts that the duty under the United Nations Convention against Torture to provide a right to compensation trumps state immunity(国家豁免权). Amnesty International(国际特赦组织) in its 2005 annual report castigates the U. S. prison camp in Guantanamo Bay "the gulag of our time." On June 9, 2005, the Council of Europe Committee for the Prevention of Torture(欧洲反酷刑委员会) issued a damning report that concluded the handling of some detainees "could be considered as amounting to inhuman and degrading treatment." (61) Yet, the U. S. Government continues to move to, hold, and possibly torture, detainees on suspicion of terrorism in foreign jurisdictions in defiance of world opinion that such acts are in violation of international human rights conventions.

To implement policy mandate by executive order is the prerogative of the President. In the complex political system of the U. S. executive order can be employed by the President to bypass an often-fractious Congress to carry out the mandate and agenda of the Executive branch. On the other hand, some policies so made unilaterally by the President may turn out to be egregious. No doubt, this phenomenon constitutes great dangers for U. S. democracy and its sound system of checks and balances.

While to implement policy by means of executive order may manage to escape both legislative and judicial oversight some times, executive order remains vulnerable to the onslaught of an opposing new administration. In 2008, the President-elect, Barack Obama of the Democratic Party, has publicly expressed his intention to erase George W. Bush's legacy, especially those blatant and egregious legacies built on executive orders. As a matter of fact, that is exactly what Obama did after becoming the President using executive order as promised.

C. Life and Fate of Legislation

Legislation in its proper sense includes any codes, statutes, delegated legislation or other legislative acts coming from the legislative body or delegated legislative authority of a country. Civil code(民法典) being the most comprehensive legislative enactment of countries belonging to the civilian system continues to be modernized through legislation. Undoubtedly, in the modern age of regulatory and welfare state, legislation plays a pivotal role in the life and business of citizens. The slow and fragmentary resolution of individual disputes by appellate courts is simply not up to the task of undertaking a broad study of the whole field of problems and their complexity and nuance, and of structuring a unified comprehensive set of rules to meet the challenge. One of the most powerful legislative endeavors in history is the many sets of economic stimulus plans and financial and banking programs among other measures respecting housing, loans of various kinds launched by the Obama

(61) Clare Dyer, "British Judge Blasts U. S., U. K. for Fanning Terrorism Fears", *Guardian News Service*, June 10, 2005.

administration to ensure the stabilization, recovery, and growth of the economy. In countries of civilian legal system and common law alike, a set of elaborated procedural requirements for the enactment and publication of legislation is prescribed and generally followed. In this sense, therefore, the formal validity and procedural requirements of most laws so enacted are seldom in question. Unfortunately, overzealous regulators and legislatures are in abundance. Incidents or occurrences of egregious legislative abuses and administrative overreaching cannot be slighted and allowed to stand.

In the United States, the simple formulae, on the order of "the legislature makes law and the executive executes that law", are so far off target in many contexts to be all but useless. A proposed law made by the President may not pass successfully through the legislative process. To a considerable extent, this is due to the fact that his sworn political adversaries may dominate one house or both of the Congress. A number of proposed legislation are in fact dead in committees and never see the light of the day. Not unlike the vagary of regulatory process in terms of "agency capture" so-called, a proposed legislation may be very well torpedoed by lobbyists, if not in committees, in the Congress. It has been reveled during the hearings on the bankruptcy(破产听证会) and subsequently the nationalization of mortgage(抵押借款) giant Freddie Mac(美国弗雷迪马克公司) and Fannie Mae (美国房利美公司) that the government created mortgage entity waged a war of influence purporting to co-opted Congress by hiring former congressmen, former government officials, and lobbyists and consultants to kill any proposed law designed to tighten regulatory control and provide constraints.

On the other hand, a law passed by both houses may be rejected and vetoed by the President, except that the House and the Senate, in turn, can override the President's veto by two-third majorities.

All governments in power are transit and contingent; they come and go with the flow of public opinion and sentiment. Majorities are temporary and unstable. The life span of statutes is short and it may be quickly reversed at the next election.

One recent example of the temporary and unstable nature of executive orders is vividly illustrated by the pronouncement of the incoming administration of President-elect Barack Obama to completely obliterate the most egregious and notorious policy legacy of George W. Bush. As a matter of fact, that is exactly what Obama did after becoming the President using executive order as promised.

The Inherent General and Vague Nature of Statutes and the Issues of Executive Interpretation

Statutes since birth if not conception are subjected to diverse interpretations and implementations. This unfortunate state is not just due to the inherent weakness of statutes being general, vague, and often times self-contradictory because of not just difficulties in drafting but also the vary fact that legislation especially those enacted under a federal system tends to embody divergent and even competing interests of different states and constituencies—the elusive nature of legislative intent and purpose.

Moreover, facts evolve and conditions and circumstances change. Consequently, the implementation of a statute has to be kept abreast with new and emerging needs and objectives. In this sense, the life and fate of a piece of legislation virtually fall in the hand of the President and his ministers. The Troubled Assets Relief Program(不良资产求助计划) passed in 2008 in response to the most severe financial meltdown in recent memory provides a vivid example of this unfortunate situation. The shared intention of the Program between the President, George W. Bush and the Congress is for the Treasury Secretary Henry Paulson to buy illiquid assets to free the seize of credit markets, to spur or enable banks to lend, to stabilize the financial markets, to restore confidence, to stimulate consumer and business spending among other things. Mr. Paulson announced only two weeks later that he intended to abandon his original strategy, instead of focusing directly on banks and other financial institutions that fund consumer debt due to changed conditions, findings of new facts and a better appreciation of the problems and difficulties entailed in the programs as originally envisaged. The continued testimony by Henry Paulson* and Federal Reserve(联邦储备委员会) Chairman, Ben Bernanke before Congress signifies clearly the Program's evolving nature and that monitoring and oversight will be an on-going process.

D. Judicial Attitude toward Legislation: The Legal Standing or Status of Legislation in the Legal System

In the eyes of an English jurist, law which is legislative in origin has traditionally appeared as somewhat abnormal in character. Legislative provisions are

---

* Henry "Hank" Merritt Paulson,亨利·保尔森,是前任美国财政部长。他曾担任大型投资银行高盛集团的主席和首席执行官。

not fully assimilated into the English legal system until they have been taken up and affirmed and sometimes even distorted by the courts in the course of the normal working processes of the Common law. In ascertaining the meaning of statutory provisions, courts frequently seek out Common law analogies or doctrines. And statutes may simply reiterate key Common law terms for definition. In general, statutes must be read in the light of a historical development of relevant principles by the Common law courts.

In principle, a statute cannot be altered by judicial decisions. In practice it is within the power of the court through interpretation to give free rein to the statute or to hobble it. This phenomenon appears to be informed to some extent by the English court in treating the statute as an interloper upon the rounded majesty of the Common law, legislation only impinges upon and undercut the symmetry and the rational principles of the Common law, and makes its organic and unified system of rules difficult to maintain. Legislation was applied strictly and narrowly so that its application can be confined to cases that it expressly covered.

The above view, of course, is no longer tenable in the United States. The section immediately follows illustrates the modern day the general conception and view of statutes.

E. Place of Statute in American Law

Belonging to the Common law family, the law of the United States likewise essentially judge-made; legislative rules, no matter how numerous, are viewed with some discomfort. They are not the normal expression of the legal rule. They are only truly assimilated into the American legal system once they have been judicially interpreted and applied and when it is possible to refer to the court decisions applying them rather than to the legislative texts themselves. When there are no precedents, there is no law on the point.

To a considerable extent, this restrictive attitude fortunately no longer prevails in United States today. The propositions or observations mentioned above are highly questionable. It is to be admitted that legislation often tends to be general, vague, fuzzy, contradictory, full of gaps and loopholes, and may have unintended consequences. And as such, it is vulnerable to divergent and conflicting interpretations. Yet, it must be pointed out that all judicial interpretations are fact-based. As such, their scope of application is necessarily limited to the facts noticed.

Besides, how was the very first interpretation and application of the statute made since there could not be any cases or precedents on point at that moment then? What could be the base of authority for the every first judicial decision? And what could possibly be the base or reason for according such overriding status to judicial decision? This unhealthy attitude may very well be attributed to the prediction theory of the American legal realism(法律现实主义) and its excessive interpretation. It has been observed in ample places in this book that statutory law more than any other laws impacts the most on people and society at large.

F. Transforming Statutes into Common Law: The Life of Statute Takes on the Form of the Common Law

It has always been the duty of the Common law courts to perceive the impact of major legislative innovations and to interweave the new legislative policies with the inherited body of common law principles.

Moreover, with the passage of time, through interpretation, application, and other methods of judicial notice, an increasing body of case law has developed around the statutory provisions. The appellate decisions themselves become controlling authority under the doctrine of precedent, while the statute remains the original source of law. Consequently, a statutory issue at first has become over times purely a Common law subject. The policy of the statute and the principles that govern the application of the statute are, in the end, extracted from a body of case law that has attached itself to the statute, rather than from the text of the statute. And the court's opinion on the matter consists for the most part of a discussion of previous judicial decisions in the area. The text of the statute is relegated to the status of citation(卷宗号) or reference.

Even the principle of legislative supremacy(立法至上) is fed by judicial deference. Moreover, statutes may soon become middle-aged no longer serving current needs or represent current majority. Changed circumstances and conditions or new developments in the Common law may very well render some statutes inconsistent with the new social or legal topography. Statutes are relatively easier to enact and more difficult to be repealed. They thus remain on the book nevertheless. Furthermore, the same constitutional texts may be interpreted to achieve entirely opposing results by politically-value motivated judicial activism.[62]

---

[62] Guido Calabresi, *A Common Law for the Age of Statutes*, Harvard Univ. Pr., 1982.

G. Nature and Content of the United States Code

An important item of legal materials likely to cause confusion and misunderstanding to a civilian is the United States Code (USC)(美国法典). The United States Code differs markedly from the civil code of countries belonging to the civil law system. It differs not only in form and substance but also in nature and character. The United States Code resembles more or less the consolidated statutes found in countries, such as Canada and Great Britain. In essence, the USC is merely a consolidation of statutes: the statutes included are organized by subject matter and each statute consolidated forms an independent unity by and of itself rather than connects with other statutes in the Code in any organic and holistic way like a typical civil code. The USC is all-inclusive in content; it includes every legislative enactment made during a specific time period that remains in effect at the time of consolidation; a new edition or consolidation may be published after a lapse of certain years. And the new edition or consolidation supersedes all previous ones. In the case of the civil code, it is designed to be a one-time ever-lasting undertaking; Even though specific articles, parts or portions of the civil code may be replaced by later legislation as social changes dictate, the entity, form, and the integrity of the code remain intact.

H. Constitutional Activism of the Judiciary

Judges are the oracles of the law in the Common law system. Courts are believed to be the protector of the rights and freedoms of citizens against the encroachment and abuse of the power of government.

The eminent position of English superior court judges is really on the same level as the legislative and executive authorities. Responsible for the development of the Common law and Equity historically, superior courts created the law of England in its very foundations. Courts themselves were the champions in the struggle for the affirmation and protection of English rights and freedoms. Today, they continue to serve as a counter-balance to the consummated alliance that now exists between Parliament and government.

In the United States, this special feature of judicial review of the Common law system should not be attributed so much to the political system of checks and balances as to a mature notion of political morality and the requirements of justice.

The basic tenets of this view include the independence of the judiciary as a fundamental value and the belief that certain rights and freedoms of citizens are naturally endowed and inalienable and should not be subject to the vagary of the shifting and unstable ideology(意识形态) of political correctness or expediency.

The federal judiciary may be truly said to have neither force nor will but merely judgment. So it could be trusted to serve as an intermediate body between the people and the legislature and the government.

The heart of the role of the judiciary in the legal and political life of a nation is the institution of judicial review of the constitutionality of legislation and by declaring legislation in question ultra vires of an administrative action that is abusive of legislative authority. This state of affairs appears to be very alarming and incredible to a civilian where the supremacy of the legislature is unchallenged. The power of judicial review is not only vested in the highest court, such as the Supreme Court of the United States, but also all courts of general competence.

Under the leadership of the Supreme Court, courts are empowered to measure governmental conduct against the terms of the Constitution and to invalidate(使无效) that conduct if it is deemed inconsistent with the Constitution.

Chief Justice John Marshall* in Marbury v. Madison** provided the conceptual foundation for the power of judicial review. Marbury rested on three propositions:

First, the Constitution is law, not merely an enshrinement of a set of political ideals; second, the Constitution is the supreme law and overrides any conflicting source of law within the legal system; and third, judges have the same responsibility and authority with regard to the Constitution as they do with regard to other sources of law.

It therefore follows that all the rights, express as well as implicit, especially the rights to the integrity of the human person including the right of personality found in the Constitution are to be protected by judges directly by invoking the applicable provisions through the Common law process. To enact separate statutory provisions—a civil code is a special and comprehensive statutory enactment—for the implementation of these rights as espoused by many civilian jurists instead of relying on constitutional protection would be unnecessarily redundant, and possibly diminish

---

* 约翰·马歇尔,1801 年至 1835 年担任美国联邦最高法院第 4 任首席大法官,在任期内曾作为马伯利诉麦迪逊案的主审法官。

** 马伯利诉麦迪逊案,是美国宪法中最著名的案例之一,此案例确定了美国宪法中的司法审查先例。

the fundamental nature of such rights.

The Charter of Rights and Freedoms embodied in the Canadian Constitution has proved to be the most powerful instrument employed by judges to protect citizen from unjust encroachment(侵占行为) and abusive conduct(滥用行为), official or private, and to engage in social change and transformation.

A study of the origin, status, and protection of the rights of the integrity of the human person becomes even more interesting and challenging in a Common law country such as Great Britain which does not have a written constitution. In a way, one can say that in England, the fundamental rights and freedoms of citizens are recognized and written into an unwritten constitution by judges through judicial decisions. This is no difference from the situation in the United States where many of the fundamental principles, the structure of federalism, and separation of powers are the products not of the text or history of the Constitution per se but rather the products of well-established judicial decisions. The courts are in the position of both players and umpire in the allocation of power. They alone determine the extent of their own power and the limits of legislative power and that of the government. They are becoming a third legislative chamber. However, it must be pointed out that in many instances, such as those in the political, regulatory, and administrative fields, courts do prefer to defer to the government.

The right of the integrity of the human person including the right of personality is naturally endowed and a priori rights. They precede and are independent of law and institution, constitutional or civil. To trace the origin and protection of these rights to either the constitution or the civil law (code) is neither necessary nor logical. But political and institutional intervention and framework go a long way to affirm, facilitate and encourage their realization.

Civil law can be looked upon as a constitutional derivative enactment. It is formulated to implement these rights and freedoms, to wade off the abusive and tortuous conduct of private persons as well as the unjustified state encroachment and conduct acting in its private law capacity, and to prescribe necessary attributive and compensatory provisions. In this sense, it is reasonable and desirable to find that the relevant corrective and retributive provisions dealing with the integrity of the human person are found in the civil codes of the Romano-Germanic law family. As' judges in many countries belonging to the civil law system are yet to be empowered to directly apply constitutional provisions to right private wrongs, to incorporate such provisions

Chapter Six: United States Law in Action(诉讼中的): the Operative and... 173

in the civil code could serve as a necessary alternative.

If the legitimacy of judicial activism is in question, one can always argue that legislative inaction and abdication(责任的放弃) of responsibility presuppose the existence of wrongs and injustice demanding redress(补偿) and compensation. These are the very reasons that inform and support courts in taking an active and leading role. It is the constitutional duty of courts to enter aggressively where legislature is reluctant or afraid to tread. One recent example of judicial activism taking the place of legislature due to the latter's abdication of duty is a strand of court decisions legalizing same-sex marriage in Canada.

There is one significant limitation to the power of judicial review: it can only be engaged in where an actual legal case has appropriately engaged in the court's attention. Whenever the fundamental rights and freedoms of citizens are violated, trampled, or otherwise involved, judges will apply the test of reasonableness of the constitutionality of the decision or action in question. This is so regardless of nature, extent, scope, or social implications of the policy issue.

The impact of judicial review on the legal and political life of a nation is often quite durable and dramatic. Due to the terse, and often general and vague nature of the provisions of the Constitution, the court has wide-ranging judgment in interpretation.

One needs not to analyze cases on constitutional issues to affirm the tremendous impact of the decisions of the Supreme Court on American life. One of the latest metaphors in this respect is the allegation that President Bush Junior was chosen by the Supreme Court of United States rather than by popular and representative votes in democratic election.

The Supreme Court is not simply the oracle of the law but has taken increasingly a central role in social change. Many highly controversial constitutional decisions of the Supreme Court have helped shaped major features of social and political culture and trend of the United States. Important examples in this respect include rulings on the New Deal(罗斯福新政), the civil rights movements, the right to abortion in Roe v. Wade*, pronouncements on due process', equal protection, freedom of speech, and free exercise of religion, the abolition of prayer in schools, separation of church and state, etc. Judicial interpretation implicates not only the open-textured

---

* 1973年罗诉韦德一案中,最高法院根据第14条正当程序条款修正案,第一次认可妇女在怀孕起头3个月内有权选择终止妊娠。

and liberty-bearing provisions of the Constitution but also the commerce clause.

In truth, the constitution is by nature a creature of politics and political compromises.

Most if not all the constitutional provisions are atrociously written, general and ambiguous, and easily yield multiple interpretation of an often divergent, conflicting, or divisive nature. Judicial interpretation is in such cases simply utterance and imposition of a judge's personal political, moral view. In this sense, constitutive activism of the court is logically immanent in constitutional interpretation.

There are proponents and opponents of constitutional activism. The issues involved are multifaceted and very complex. In the final analysis, it is the original intent of the framers pits against the interpretive power of the judges, textualism against contextualism, constructionism against expansionism, and a dead constitution against a living one.

Such substantive reasoning more often than not is based on moral and ethic grounds and has great impact on political morality, and ineluctably embroils the court in political debates. Whether and to what extent this will erode the Court's institutional authority is an open question. Judicial instrumentalism* also finds strong express in tort law. Notable examples of such rulings include replacing negligence with strict liability, empowering private law to perform public law function, such as contingency fee rewards of attorneys and punitive damages. Thus, it is no surprise that in the United States, the selection and appointment of judges at the appellant levels, especially judges at the Supreme Court, is always given an extraordinary importance.

In Canada, Justice La Forest advocates judges taking on the responsibility of law reform where the legislature falls short. This is acceptable as long as the process is transparent and public. Judicial accountability to the public should be done through communication and feedback.

What is required is to achieve a fine and delicate balance between deference and activism in the same fashion as required by what Canada believed to be preferable in a constitutional, parliamentary democracy. It is not for judges to set the

---

* 司法工具主义,司法工具主义是法律工具主义的一个重要部分,是一种关于法律本质和法律功能的法学世界观和法学认识论。它强调在社会系统中,法律只是实现一定社会目标的工具性手段,强调法律的统治功能。在法律工具主义看来,法律是一种自身没有独立的价值和目标的东西,一旦有其他工具可以使社会控制在短期内效用最大化时,法律是可以替代或撤换的。所以,司法工具主义极易导致法律虚无主义,是极其有害的。

agendas for social change. Nor is it appropriate for judges to embrace over-zealously moral-loaded issues conveniently off-loaded by politicians. But it has been aptly put recently by someone that one person's brave court is another's usurper of political power. Likewise, one person's deferential court is another's cowardly one. What is recognized as a reasonable equilibrium of competing powers can only result from an active, dynamic interaction among all elite power participants in the enterprise of legal normativity.

I. Measures Taken to Counter Anti-democratic(反民主的) or Unpopular Judicial Review

What is both significant and disconcerting is that what has been declared unconstitutional cannot be simply displaced by the ordinary political process, such as by enacting a new, compliant or contrary legislation. Of course, governments often attempted to redraft the controversial provisions of a law and hope they would not be challenged or will pass the court's close scrutiny in the future. The United States Constitution guarantees judicial review of the constitutionality of statutes. And the independence of the judiciary from political influences helps guarantee this role. Some regard judges as robbed bureaucrats. Judges themselves are part of the political culture and are not immune in either theory or fact from the changes in political sensibilities that characterize their times. Should and how judges be held politically accountable? Anti-democratic or unpopular decisions cannot simply be rectified by the requirements and conditions associated with the office. The ultimate political response to an unpopular decision of the Supreme Court is the amendment of the Constitution.

Democracy is a delicate balance between majority rule and certain fundamental values of human dignity. Exclusive judicial control is antithetic to political accountability and would entail enormous vices and undermine the Constitution. Justice Powell in Goldwater v. Carter,[63] warned of the danger and vice of having the Supreme Court closely "oversee the very constitutional process used to reverse its decisions." It has been said that the resort to amendment (修正案), to constitutional politics as opposed to constitutional law, should be taken as a sign that the legal system has come to a point of discontinuity. Constitutional politics in the amendment process is a safeguard erected against the monopoly of the determination

---

[63] 444 U.S. 996 (1979).

of policy by judges. To undermine this safeguard would contradict the basic democratic principle according to which policy decisions in a constitutional democracy are to be determined by the people through their representatives.

The amendment process protects the representative system of government from arbitrary intrusions by the judicial supervision(司法监督) processes into the policy-making capacities that the Constitution confers on the executive and legislative branches of government as elected bodies. When faced with the challenges to ratification procedures approved by Congress, judicial deference to constitutional politics or judicial abstention from substantive review(实质审查) of constitutional amendment supervision would be necessary.

Judicial review of the constitutionality of legislation and administrative action raises a number of meta-law issues, among these, the following are offered for further reflection:

Being the interpreter of the Constitution, is the court (the Supreme Court) the oracle of the Constitution in the sense that the Constitution is what judges say it is? Judicial decision is just one of sources of law. As such, how could judicial decision set the priority among sources of law in conflict without being charged of judges being their own judges? Who judges the judges?

Are judicial decisions the first among equals? What happens to the constitutional imperative of "check and balance?" The Unites States is not a parliamentary government. Nor does it have a President with absolute and largely unrestrained power. What are the options both in and out of the Constitution to counter this judicial domination or even judicial absolutism?

In Canada, governments may resort to the "notwithstanding clause" enshrined in the Section 33 of the Canadian Charter of Rights and Freedoms to override judicial constitutional rulings that are considered wrong, anti-democracy, or unpopular. For Canada is a parliamentary constitutional democracy as well as a constitutional democracy. In the United States, the supremacy of the court prevails under its constitutionalism. When there is a conflict between the courts' and Parliament's interpretation of the Charter, the Parliament of Canada prevails. It is here relevant to point out that there is an opposing view that believes Canada is a constitutional democracy rather than a parliamentary one.

Since taking office on Jan. 20, President Obama has signed legislation extending government-financed health care to millions of lower-income children who lack it, a bill that President George W. Bush twice vetoed. Obama also has placed his signature on a measure making it easier for workers to sue their employers for alleged job discrimination, effectively overturning a ruling by the Supreme Court's conservative majority.

The above is offered to illustrate the dynamic nature of the law making and law application process, and how the three branches of government interact with each other. It is also intended to show how the concept of law would take on a much lively and realistic character when it is viewed as authoritative and effective decision rather than any formulaic statements. When the dynamic interaction is analyzed in terms of the makers of the decisions rather than the inanimate outcomes of the decision-making process, a fresh and highly enlightening perspective of what counts as law is suddenly shinning through.

J. Life and Fate of a Common Law Rule or a Common Law Case

Judicial decisions are accorded in the common law system a preeminent role in the normative life of people. Yet, even in the modern age of statutes, the Common law continues to govern important areas of litigation between private parties concerning the human person, property, or other related rights and obligation. The law of torts, for example, remains to a large extent untouched by legislation. Undoubtedly, the established stance of common law lawyers' suspicion of legislative enactment as law generating has gone a long way to fostering the supremacy of the judiciary. Oliver Wendell Holmes, Jr. and the American legal realism effectively capture the spirit of the overriding role of the court in the life of people. Law according to Holmes is what the judge says it is. At least as far as a practicing lawyer and his clients in litigation are concerned, there is nothing that is more relevant and significant than this so-called prediction theory of law.

Built on the Common law adjudication tradition and the doctrine of stare decisis, judge-made law has effectively extended their reach well beyond the private law concern to virtually all areas of public law. In deciding cases, courts resort directly to applicable precedents for reason and justification. The statutory provisions that govern the subject matter of the case have in fact been relegated to a source of citation and reference.

The doctrine of Res judicata and Stare decisis is designated to ensure the stable and predictable development of judicial law. Unfortunately, the Common law system has contained a systemic paradox. On the one hand, judges must have allegiance to the notion of the binding force of precedents in the sense that the legal system must protect settled expectations which would be dangerously disturbed if the highest courts were free to abandon position that they had earlier declared with authority. On the other hand, progress and development bring about new demands and new expectations. These sometimes require courts to act in a radical and sweeping way to see that the rights and freedoms of citizens are well and equally protected. Such paradox or opposition between legal conservatism committed to the status quo(维持现状) and judicial activism breaking with tradition becomes the crucial juridical challenge crying for resolution and guidance.

The unstable and indeterminate nature of judicial law is not simply a matter that a case may be reversed in the judicial hierarchical process, or that the Supreme Court is not bound by its own prior decision. Judicial decisions are informed by and based on the fact situation of cases. Common law rules are general and derivative statements of facts. Being fact-based and fact—limited, a Common law rule carries its own seed of destruction. A case may be distinguished (that is distinguishing the factual situations in the case at hand from that in a previous case in terms of their materiality as well as the technique of either narrowing or broadening the nature, scope, and reach of the holding or holdings of a cases) not followed, not applied, etc, in later cases due to this very reason. It is the potentially and highly destructive and manipulative technique of judicial treatment of prior cases that wreaks havoc to the integrity of the Common law. The fact that no two cases are on all four works to put the rule of precedent in a very precarious position. At its deepest theoretical level, the Common law has never regarded individual cases as representing a final expression of the law on a particular point.

The Common law works itself pure through a dynamic process of continuous and incremental adjustments and breakthroughs. But this purifying process, though forward-looking, is doomed to be open-ended, everlasting, and therefore never complete. This dictum is very much rhetoric and wishful thinking.

Dissents and concurrent opinions are integral parts of judicial decisions. Different strands of reasoning may appear in the opinions of different judges. These dissenting opinions or minority views of the court may very well become in future and with time a leading force precipitating a new trend of authoritative and effective decisions by reversing lines of precedents and at the same time ushering in a new era of legal policy and paradigm.

In conclusion, judicial law being fact-based and time and space tethered has only limited if not questionable precedent force. When generalized broadly enough to reach a wider scope and application, it loses its material support in specificity and sharpening in underlying facts. And having suffered its destiny of subsequent distinguishing and weighing and tested in the light of changes in circumstance and condition, it largely loses its authority and is supported only by whatever reasons it still embodies.

One innovative idea attempting at accommodating this seemingly intractable dilemma is Ronald Dworkin's integrative interpretation theory in adjudication. In his two closed twined tenets, he envisages both an omnipotent Hercules judge and compares adjudication to the writing of a chained novel. One must endeavor to fit one's finding and rationalization with extant applicable precedents and tradition and at the same time cast one's decision (i. e., law) in the best light it can be.

Long ago in England, Sir Edward Code and William Blackstone* complained bitterly of the ruination of the Common law by legislation. The proliferation of enacted law poses a particular problem for the United States. The danger of states to enact statutory provisions to correct or supplement the Common law may destroy the uniformity of American law. Thus from a practical point of view, it is eminently desirable to propose uniform or model laws on certain subjects.

K. Role of Lawyers in Shaping Judicial Law

Lawyers may be the officers of the court. But the adversarial system of litigation, argument, and decision-making throw the court into constant tension and contention. It is the lawyers, not the judge, who play a leading role in the making and re-making of the decision of the court. Lawyers almost completely control matter with respect to discovery of facts and documents, relevance of evidence, and questioning of witnesses, and generally the presentation of information and the record to be compiled. All these directly affect and shape the judge's deliberation and ruling. During the proceeding, the judge plays a neutral and somewhat detached role as an umpire. At the appellate level, the court cannot stray outside the record consisted of pleadings, exhibits, and transcript of the proceedings in the court

---

* 威廉·布莱克斯顿(1723—1780),是英国最富盛名的杰出法学家,表达了资产阶级对保护私有财产的要求。

below. And the appellate court can only review what are essentially framed by the actions of lawyers at both the trial and appellate levels.

In the face of vigorously argued contentious and conflicting views of the law, what is the judge to do? If there is a correct answer to the question at issue or an applicable precedent that controls the issues in dispute, it does not seem that it is available to the adversarial parties or recognized by them. Could the judge in such situations make a rational decision? Can it be really true as the Critical legal study scholars claim that judicial law is inherently contradictory and indeterminate. All cases are hard cases. Discretion, intuition, and even political consideration control all outcomes. Or as Pierce Schlag's efficient processed theory claims that all adjudications over deep, divisive conflicts of a political morality are irrational. [64]

L. Transforming Judicial Law by Legislative Decision or Executive Action

To transform judicial law by legislative measures may include the following: modification, replacement, exclusion, and authorization. In many fields of statutory authority as opposed to constitutional issues, judicial power may be given or taken away.

Many older statutes are often either simple codification of common law positions or restatements thereof with some reforming features. Present day examples of common law rules appropriated, codified and replaced by statute include Uniform commercial code, law of negotiable instruments, and law of security interest. Many statutes are informed or based on case law. Some may very well simply case law declared in statute form. One may be attempted to say that wherever a subject matter is infiltrated by legislation, possibly certain elements or aspects of the Common law have been transformed.

It has been argued that the growth of both statutory and constitutional law suggests that the scope of pure Common law has rapidly diminished. The Congress may use legislation to undermine common law rules. The Executive branch may also resort to certain innovative means to sabotage the rulings of courts. Tort law has substantially affected by legislative efforts in such field as no-fault(不追究责任的) insurance, medical malpractice and strict liability. The Children's Health Insurance Program(儿童健康保险计划) proposed by the Bush administration is the latest backdoor effort to undermine Roe v. Wade, the United States Supreme Court case

---

[64] Please refer to section on Legal reason for detailed discussion on this matter.

that established the right of women to abortion.

Tort reform is one of campaign platforms of the Bush administration in 2004. The tort system designed to compensate accident victims and deter negligence is considered expensive, economically distorting and hideously inefficient: The victims of negligence get a remarkably bad deal. Over half the compensation is eaten up by administrative costs in addition to court costs and lawyer's fees. President Bush wants to cap non-economic damages at $250000 and shift national class-action lawsuits from state to federal courts to stop plaintiffs shopping among the states for the highest pay-outs.

In the face of courts increasingly transforming statutory rules into common law rules and the danger of the latter working to replace the former in application, the Congress in new legislation formulates specific provisions to exclude judicial control and review.

Since taking office on Jan. 20, 2009, the President has signed legislation extending government-financed health care to millions of lower-income children who lack it, a bill that President George W. Bush twice vetoed. Obama also has placed his signature on a measure making it easier for workers to sue their employers for alleged job discrimination, effectively overturning a ruling by the Supreme Court's conservative majority.

One of the drastic measures that legislation is designed to transform judicial law is the decision by the Obama administration to authorize courts to re-write the loans terms of qualified bankrupted home-owners as an essential part of his housing stabilization program.

M. Judges and Judge-made Law versus Legislatures and Legislation

The judiciary is the least dangerous branch of government. The judgment of a court like poetry makes nothing happen, unless it ultimately persuades us that it is right. Judges are the oracles of the law, institutional custodians of constitution and justice. Judges rely on reason rather than will as its activating principle. Judges speak to us all at the deepest and fundamental level as a nation and society.[65]

A good and detailed comparison of courts and legislatures as lawmakers is

---

[65] A. Chayes, "How the Constitution Establishes Justice". In: *The Constitution, the Courts and the Quest for Justice*. Ed. R. A. Goldwin & W. A. Shambra. Wash, D. C., American Enterprise Institute for Public Policy Research (1989).

insightfully accounted by M. D. A. Freeman. (66)

Common law rules do not have canonical formulations because the scope of a rule may be cast in different ways. The ratio is not fixed but a formula that is capable of adjustment according to the force of later development. But the language of a statute or constitution is the language to which a court must refer. (67) English lawyers place the courts at the centre of their legal universe. But the jurisdiction and reach of courts are invariably constrained by the doctrine of "case and controversy".

Within constitutional limitations, it seems there are no areas exclusive of legislation. And court on the other hand should not go when what is involved are political questions, non-justiciable questions, poly-centric disputes, monstrously complex multipartite hearings, and questions affecting the public interest of the community as a whole. Even judicial activism must know the limit of its power.

The judicial process is one of constant interaction between judges, the legal profession, litigants, legislatures, and the general public and is best seen in this perspective to understand the judicial role.

Sir William Blackstone looked upon judges as the depositories of the laws—the living oracles of the law. When existing law is contrary to reason or divine law, or manifestly absurd or unjust, it should be declared as not law, not bad law; judges do not pretend to make a new law but to vindicate the old one from misrepresentation. This extreme view may lead to the potential logical end that all preexisting law (rules) may be declared as not law in the future or even what is the law won't be known until the base of vindication is announced.

Such iconoclastic statement is simply counter-factual(反事实的) because any rules being subsequently obliterated have heretofore been authoritative and consequential in value impact through acceptance and observance in conduct and decision.

In "What's so special about judges", Easterbrook justifies the deference to judicial decisions on the fact that judges decide on the basis of law while others (such as legislators and regulators) on moral and political considerations and grounds. (68)

---

(66) "Standards of Adjudication, Judicial Law-making and Prospective Overruling", 26 *Cur Leg Prob*, 166 (1973).

(67) Kent Greenawalt, "Determinate Law", 39 *UCLA L R*, 1 (1990).

(68) 61 Colorado L R 773 (1990).

It is important to point out that that fact the United States is a constitutional democracy as opposed to a parliamentary democracy essentially and systemically strengthens the position of the judiciary in the comprehensive process of authoritative and effective decision-making.

N. Scholarly Rendering and Exposition of Legislation

Unlike the practice in the civil law system, legislation is not a favored subject of legal scholarship. The main reason for this difference is that common law jurists do not consider legislation as an integral part of the law until it has been interpreted and applied by the courts. Legislation is posited in formulaic rule and is devoid of reason and justification. Legislative history, though readily accessible in Congressional Record(美国国会议事录), hearings and reports of committees and subcommittees (附属委员会), is mainly composed of policy statements. These are not suitable for vigorous scholarly analysis and exposition. When legislative issues do get chosen for analytical study, it is usually the case law interpreting and applying the legislation in question rather than the legislative provisions that becomes the center of attention.

The ascendancy in importance of statutory law in modern welfare states continues to overshadow the role played by the court in the practical decisions. The political and instrumentalist nature of statutes while seemingly defying the kind of systematic conceptualization and principled statements favored by traditional legal scholarship has been not surprisingly enthusiastically embraced by the New public law scholars. (69)

Most of the publications on legislation are in the regulated field. Even expository works of this nature are full of citation and analysis of judicial decisions. Remember that rules and issues of statutory origin have increasingly interpreted, applied or otherwise treated by courts and embroidered by a tightly woven web of judicial precedents.

As to the constitutionality of legislation in question, generally speaking, scholars tend to take attitude of deference and prefer to raise red flag over questionable provisions and leave the matter to the court to judge in an actual case as to the appropriateness and validity of the legislation in question.

---

(69) D. A. Farber & P. P. Frickey. "In the Shadow of the Legislature: the Common Law in the Age of the New Public Law." 89 *Mich L R* 875 (1991); Guido Calabresi, *A Common Law in the Age of Statute*, Harvard University Press, 1982.

O. Formation of Leading Cases(援引的判例): the Role and Contribution of Jurists

Leading cases refer to those judicial decisions that have well survived the test of time as well as the severe and critical scrutiny of legal scholars in exposition and criticism and judges in subsequent cases to acquire this authoritative status.

Scholars and judges receive the same training, speak the same language, and share a similar thinking and reasoning process. When scholars speak, judges listen. Prescriptive scholarship is particularly intended for judges.

Judges whenever deem necessary cite the works of legal scholars as supporting reasons for decisions. The expository works of legal scholarship shape not only the formation and re-formation of precedents but also the meaning of statutory laws interpreted and applied. Through legal education and vigorous analysis and criticism, the cogency and persuasiveness of judicial reasoning are affirmed and expounded. This directly shapes and influences the view of students, the aspiring judges in their selection of precedents and their formulation of reason and justification of decisions.

The expository orthodoxy is a highly cherished scholarly tradition. Through doctrinal works and juridifying essays, legal scholars enshrine their role and significance in the development of the judicial law. There is no doubt that the Restatement of law project epitomizes the normative enterprise of American jurists. The long-awaited, 125-page guidelines for spousal support in Canada result from a three-year painstaking effort of analyzing and distilling case law and systematic rendition of compelling patterns.

P. Scholars and Scholar's Law versus Judges and Judicial Law

Nobody would put jurisprudence anywhere near the sun—the centre of the legal universe—a pale moon reflecting the wisdom of the bench might be its appropriate place for scholars and their law in this cosmology. The fact that John Austin, the most influential positivist jurist of all time, was relegated to negligible position in contemporary England and his jurisprudence was denigrated as a work that stunk in the nostril of a practicing lawyer sadly reflects the serious misunderstanding of the true nature and contribution of jurisprudence. (70) The view that words in books and articles expressing tenable and arguable ideas rather than ultimate binding authority should be exposed to the testing and refining process of the adversary judicial process is only partially right. It is certainly correct to say that the words of scholars have the benefit of a broad and comprehensive study and extensive research and a lengthy period of gestation and even intermittent opportunities for reconsideration as a result of the feedback and criticism of fellow scholars. And it is equally sensible to observe that judge-made law has the advantage of that impact and sharpening of focus which the detailed facts of a particular case that necessitate and the aid of the purifying ordeal of skilled arguments on the specific facts of a contested case. (71)

The argument that it is the general principle underlying the cases or the obiter dictum rather than the ratio decidendi that constitutes the precedent value is simply self-contradictory. This is because dicta by nature are not facts-based. They are usually thrown into the body of decisions without in-depth investigation and analysis, without being subject to vigorous arguments during the adversarial proceeding, and without any supporting materials. As such dicta simply cannot be as vigorously and cogently reasoned as scholarly law. And consequently obiter dictum should be less persuasive in authority as compared to scholarly law.

The logic of this reasoning is that the more complex the facts informing the ratio are, the harder the discretionary manipulation is needed to fit the ratio or its precedent force with any later case bearing a different set of facts. These new facts can never be on all four with the cases decided earlier. The matching of cases in judicial decision is highly unreliable and uncertain due to the variations in cases in life not made to our hand. (72)

The positivist formulaic view of the Common law as an integrative corpus of rules systematically organized is simply no longer tenable today. (73) Instead of being compacted in a code that can be held in one hand, common law rules are spread out in haphazard order through thousands of volumes of law reports. (74) Of course, the

---

(70) See A. V. Dicay, "The Study of Jurisprudence". *Law Magazine and Review*, 4th series, 5 (August 1880) at 383.

(71) Megarry, "Argued Law is Tough Law", p. 375.

(72) Karl N. Llewellyn, *The Bramble Bush*, 1930, Ocean ed., 1975, p. 43.

(73) A. W. B. Simpson, "The Common Law and Legal Theory", *Oxford Essays in Jurisprudence*, 71,79 2nd series, 1973.

(74) Lon L. Fuller, Anatomy of the Law 105 (1968).

force of the bit of such criticism has been considerably dented due to the publication of the Restatement of law and other expository scholarship.

So, what and where is the authority of judicial law when stripped off its authoritative façade of institutional power and being exposed to its naked reasons free of the orthodoxy of the so-called intrinsic authority? It is especially enlightening to note that frequently in major shift in judicial paradigm in the so-called hard cases where supporting reasons were explicitly given, scholarly law often forms the bedrock of such decisions. For example, Justice Wilson writing for the majority of the court in Andrews [1989] 1 SCR 143 set out to extend the right to equal protection to non-citizens as a group of the disadvantaged and the vulnerable. For supporting reasons, he invoked not only John Rawls' principle of difference and Ronald Dworkin's rights to equal concern and respect but also statements made by J. H. Fly in Democracy and distrust (1980) and by J. S. Mill in Book III of the Considerations of Representative Government.

Thus scholarly writing becomes part and parcel of the essential constituents of judicial law through recognition and adoption. Moreover, scholarly law is law by and in itself without going through the judicial litmus test. For only reasons possess intrinsic value and immanent normativity. As such, the reasons underlying scholarly law need no political or institutional recognition or stamp of approval, state or non-state. Its process is directly social, moral and non-coercive. (75) Scholar's law is also argued law not unlike judicial law in this respect. The scholarly process of identifying and analyzing problems, the study and critique of past trends of decisions, the discussion of alternative solutions, and the projection of future impacts is no less presented in a sort of adversary fashion pitting one's own reason and argument against those of fellow scholars. Moreover, before its publication, scholarly law is usually read and commented by other experts in the field and subsequently improved and refined by incorporating to a maximum extent feasible all opposing and complimentary ideas and propositions. Legal scholars participate fully in almost every phase of the legal process through their role in training and influence of future lawyers and judges, etc. in legal education, in legal reform, and in expository and critical writings. In legal education, legal doctrines are ingrained and internalized during the formative stages of legal training.

---

(75) A detailed discussion on legal reason is founded in Chapter eight of this publication.

A. V. Dicey* was particularly frank about the role of jurists in creating and transforming major areas of the law. Frederick Pollock** was equally forthcoming and said that the influence of theorists on the judicial development of the English law is far greater than is generally supposed. Sir William R. Anson was more humble and stated only in unsettled matter: one feels the excitement of an explorer. Judicial law is heavily informed and swayed by the pressure of learned opinion. Busy magistrates take their principles from text writers. In 1914 when Lord Chancellor Viscount Haldane decided to further restrict the holdings of Derry v. Peel and its precedent consequences, he consulted with Pollock on the way this might be done.

In the United States as well as on the continent of Europe, for instance, no self-respecting practitioner would present an argument to the court without having paid due attention to the views of the leading academic commentators. The decisions of the Supreme Court of the United States as well as those of lower courts cite a mass of academic authority as a matter of course. (76)

Q. Inherent Self-contradiction and Internal Creative Destruction of Legislative, Executive and Judicial Authority

The following is rather a brief, convenient summary of what have been discussed in earlier parts of this book.

a. Legislative Authority:

Similar to the phenomenon that the Common law works itself pure through time, legislation may better and improve itself with each new legislative session or legislature. Legislation can be modified, amended, or even repealed and completely erased from the statute books. These creative destructive actions go much beyond the normal revision or consolidation of statutes.

b. Executive Authority:

With each new and change of government, the policies and programs of the previous administration most likely will be modified, changed or even eliminated. The most recent example of this development is the pronounced intention of

---

* 戴雪,英国法学家,他的《英宪精义》,在建构宪法学科和促成国人宪法智识方面,发挥了启蒙教本的作用。他主张议会主权,议会在其有权制定或者废除任何法律而不受法律限制这一意义上是至高无上的。

** 弗雷德里克·波洛克,英国法学家,主张法律面前人人平等。

(76) M. Zander. *The Law-making Process*. 3rd ed. Weidenfeld & Nicolson. 1989. p.371.

President-elect Barack Obama of the Democratic Party in November 2008 to erase the bad and egregious decisions and actions enacted by the Executive order of George W. Bush. That is precisely what Obama has done after inauguration.

c. Judicial Authority:

That the Common law built on judicial decisions works itself pure is a proud tradition. On the other hand, the Common law is said to be infested with inherent self-contradictions and famous for self creative destruction. Previous decisions, even so-called leading cases or precedents could be not followed, not applied, distinguished, among other deviating techniques, and even overruled by means of narrowing or broadening the scope and reach of a holding or the ratio decidendi of a case.

R. Some Anecdotal Observations of the United States Legal System in Action

The adversarial process and system of adjudication do necessarily ensure an approximation of, if not the emergence, of the ultimate truth. Yet, neither the system nor its process is satisfactorily structured to ensure justice

In the Tyco International Ltd. corporate(泰科国际有限公司) corruption trial, a high-profile case, the name of one of jurors was published in newspapers and was subsequently trashed and denigrated because he was the center of a potential implosion of the jury panel. The case was later declared as a mistrial(无效审判).

Criminal process(刑事程序) being one of the most important components of the legal system tells a lot about the working of a legal system. The fiasco and eventual acquittal of O. J. Simpson(欧·杰·辛普森) in his murder trial indicates beyond doubt the dysfunction and defects of American legal system, though some may praise the not guilt outcome for the very virtue of the system.

Police and investigation functions may be severely compromised and defeated by corruption. What has been exposed is more than some incidents of a few bad apples. Perjury(伪证罪), falsification(弄虚作假), blackmail(敲诈), torture(刑讯), and other improper and criminal practices may very well be systemic and structured. In one case, charges against three police officers were dropped when a key witness expressed extreme fear for his safety, recanted, intentionally injured himself, and even threatened further self-mutilation(自残) if forced to testify against the suspected police officers being investigated.

Children negligently were sent to institutions and war-houses or wrongly classified as feeble-minded for life, and used as cheap labor and in radiation experiment with the approval and compliance of the federal government.

In some cases, to criminalize certain conduct such as prostitution, or the use of marijuana and the delivery of heavy punishment thereto is equivalent to the practice of nailing garlic over the doorways to repel vampires.

Wording and language shift, and rhetoric tweak in the United States. Federal Reserve policy statement recently were designed to force financial markets to focus on economic conditions rather than on calendar. This was done to remove certain wrong impressions held in the financial and investment communities. The post-statement of the policy setting Federal Open Market Committee is traditionally one of the most dissected, scrutinized, and analyzed statements. This is done for no other reason than to predict the future trend of decisions in order to plan one's own course of action. It seems that the Federal Reserve's statements on interest rates policy are an ideal prototype for lawmaking. Its wording and language shift, e. g. , from "for a considerable time" to "patient" to at a "measured" pace are fully anticipated by the market and came as no surprise.

The insurance industry could look a lot different than it does today when New York Attorney General Eliot Spitzer is done with his investigation. His earlier probes into the financial services industry forced reforms in analyst research was found to be tainted by links to lucrative investment banking deals. And his probes into the practices of United States mutual funds, where select individuals were given trading privileges at the expense of the majority of investors, is expected to yield similar reform.

Now, he's clearly looking for changes in the way insurance is sold especially when it comes to how commissions and fees are assessed. And his disclosures of questionable sales practices could trigger new efforts in Washington to impose federal rules on an industry now largely regulated by the states, experts say. (77)

There are also certain international aspects of United States law in action. In Chapter one, section three, D as well as Chapter seven, section seven, the discussions of the implications of the globalization of law and the transnational components of the national legal system are of particular importance to the issues here. First, coordination and unification of private or regulatory law are still in the

---

(77) Eileen Alt Powell, "Spitzer Probe May Cause Insurance Change", *Yahoo Finance Website*, October 22, 6:49 pm ET.

infant stage. Second, with or without coordination or unification, the potential of conflict and crash between competing national laws remain very high. For example, on Friday, February 20, 2009, UBS AG said in a U. S. court filing that its employees would be forced to violate Swiss criminal law to comply with the U. S. government's demand for the identities of 52,000 private account holders as part of a massive tax-evasion inquiry. UBS also argued that the IRS's demand would require the rewriting of tax treaties between the two countries that dictate how and what information can be disclosed. To the extent that the one is not satisfied with treaties that the U. S. government has negotiated, that concern should be remedied through diplomacy. The legal fight does not only pit the U. S. Justice Department(司法部门) and the IRS* against UBS**, but also threatens to draw both governments deeper into the already acrimonious showdown between them.

R. The Democratic Process of United States Law in Action

The democratic foundation of the U. S. law is the overriding principle of checks and balances among the three branches of government. The kind of broader conception of what counts as law as espoused in the essays in this book includes elite power decisions and actions of the non-state sectors as well.

The democratic process of the U. S. law in action finds its express in each and every incident, event, decision, action, etc., of the elite participants, state or non-state, in the interactive dynamics of mutual informing and shaping in the authoritative and effective decision-making.

An explosive example of the democratic nature of the U. S. law in action is the Dubai Ports World of the United Arab Emirates' attempt to take ownership and control of six ports in the East coast. Dubai acquired the terminal leases in the fall 2005 when it agreed to purchase British ports operator Peninsular & Oriental Steam Navigation Co. In mid-January, The U. S. Committee on Foreign Investments, which examines foreign acquisitions with potential national security implications, cleared the deal after a routine, 30-day review.

The rationality behind the decision is that the majority of U. S. port operations are foreign-run, including more than 80 per cent of the largest port, Los Angeles. As well, although the terminals are leased, the ports remain publicly owned, with the

---

* Internal Revenue Service,美国国税局。

** United Bank of Switzerland,瑞士联合银行集团。

Chapter Six: United States Law in Action(诉讼中的): the Operative and... 191

U. S. Coast Guard in charge of overall security and U. S. Customs and Border Protection in charge of cargo checks.

The matter only came to public attention in early 2006. And the President was only informed after the approval of the transaction.

However, in the post 9/11 world national security consideration is the dominant, overriding force in the United States. Ports operations and management are regarded as an integral and important part of the security infrastructure of the United States. Dubai Ports World is a stat-owned and controlled entity of the United Arab Emirates, which is known to have served as an operational and financial base for hijackers in the attacks of Sept. 11, 2001. Public, adverse response and outcry are immediate and very strong accusing the Bush administration's insensitivity, trivialization, or disregard of the importance of the ownership, management, and operations of U. S. ports to national security and the Administration's sacrifice of national security to private, commercial interests. The President has gone public to support the inter-agency decision and justify the rationality of the transaction. More importantly, after the Congress vowed to pass legislation to block the transaction, the President even threatened to vote the legislation. In the process, the media played an important and arguably highly influential role in voicing the public's concern, in canvassing, analyzing, and reporting the views, stances, and comments of people, journalists, former public servants, representatives and senators, and in mobilizing public reaction.

Eventually, under mounting and withering pressure wide-spreading the entire country and the Congress's determination to override the President's veto by a 2/3 majority in conference, the President buckled and Dubai backed away in the face of unrelenting criticism from the deal and announced it would transfer the leases to those major East Coast port facilities to an unnamed U. S. entity. How and when this will pan out is still uncertain. The U. S. Congress will closely watch the matter. Meantime, the Committee on Foreign Investments(美国外资审查委员会) will continue with its 45-day review as required by law. But it is widely speculated that it would be difficult to find a U. S. company who is willing to pay the $700-million for the deal. But Dubai has yet to clarify its statement or the timing of any possible sale. Leading congressional critics threatened repeatedly to intervene if DP World's plans fell short of a full divestiture of its U. S. operations.

The saga is continuing to develop. Also proposed laws will be introduced to bar foreign ownership and control of U. S. ports and infrastructure security.

S. Conclusion—Some Tentative Ideas on What Count as Law in General and Anglo-American Law in Particular

The law of the Anglo-American world does not fit well with the command model. It is more an inter-subject or inter-decision-maker discourse or communication. There is a school of thought that regards law as communication. What prevails ultimately is a direct result of open, transparent, and fierce competition of ideas and reasons. Propriety of process (procedural justice) is valued more than substantive good. It is said that with a good legal system, good law naturally follows.

Law in its inclusive sense is an authoritative and effective decision. Political power is legal power. Law is politics moralized in public. Law is aptly viewed as a kind of collective and normative enterprise that is powerfully characterized by a dynamics of mutual shaping and mutual reinforcing. It results through a dynamic system of checks and balances. Participation in this dynamic process is inclusive and non-discriminatory. It is the outcome of continuing communication and dialogue between legislature, judges, officials, lawyers, legal scholars and all citizens who take an internal standpoint of the law.

Judges are the oracles of the law. The legislature is the patriarchy and enforcer. Legal scholars are the cultivators. Reason and its authority is legal scholar's only weapon. We take our responsibility seriously and zealously guide our mission in the dynamic process of authoritative and effective decision-making. We analyze, expound, criticize, and recommend. In education, publication, and vigorous advocacy, legal scholars take their stand in politicizing public morality. Therefore, scholar's law ought to be law, will be law and is law. Legal scholars are at the center of the legal universe.

As such, to limit one's inquiry and study to only state powers, especially the established branches of government, is to take an exclusive and excessive positivist view of law and consequently to paint an incomplete and defective picture of the life of law. The appreciation of this truth would cause us to realize suddenly that the static and formulaic existence of law in rules and principles is nothing but the so-called law in the book, and they may or may not represent realistically the law as it is. They are sources of law. To be thorough and realistic in presenting the true picture of law, one must include in one's inquiry and analysis, when engaging in any exposition function of the law, the input and contribution of all the non-state sectors

Chapter Six: United States Law in Action(诉讼中的): the Operative and... 193

as hopefully epitomized by the normative statements and propositions of scholars in non-legal field. As the cultivator of the law, legal scholars should take very seriously their task and never shirk their responsibility in making their efforts and impact felt.

Holmes's prediction theory of law should no longer be limited to the judicial realm but be expanded to the entire process of decision-making at all level, state and non-state.

Section Five: Some Critical Observations on the Law of the United States in Action: Phenomenon of Idealization of Law(法律的理想化), Juridification Saturation(法律的饱和) of Society and Hypertrophying of Law and Legal Reason

One glaring fact or aspect of the American law in action is the hypertrophying or excessive growth of the law and legal reason. Critical observations and pointed criticism of this unfortunate fact can be found in both legal text and media literature. It seems that the American has a near fetishistic faith that social, political, moral issues and problems can be rationally solved by legislation, regulation or judicial fiat. Even the most intractable issues and problems of such nature are amendable to more extensive rationalist inquiry and solution. The more the law and the more elaborate and sophisticated the reason underlying the law, the better. Legal modes of vocabulary and behavior pervade even the most quotidian (commonplace or trivial) social interactions: the working place, the school, and even the home mimic the language of the law. The high court of the country even sees it fit to pronounce spanking law. It seems that no part of the public as well private life has not been or cannot be "juridified." The political and the moral dictate that the state has no business in the country's bedrooms may be soon eroding.

As a result, such excessive pursuit of legal instrumentalism and rationalization necessarily results in the hypertrophying of the law and legal reason. This regrettable state occurs whenever further deployment of reasons and continuous engagement in rationalist inquiry and assertions become superfluous, futile and indeed unreasonable. Notorious artifacts of such rationalist excess manifest themselves in the three-day deposition, the six month trial, the decade-long appeal, the 100-page appellate court opinion, the 200-page law review article, the 1000 page statute, and

16000 page set of administrative regulations and so on. The excessive, jurismaniacal character of these monuments is aptly understood as the product of an obsessive-compulsive reaction to the neurotic structure of American legal thought. (78)

What is disturbing is that judges, jurists, and lawyers are all well aware of the blunt truth that the law is a naked emperor and legal reasons are fake, axiomatic assertions, circular propositions. And yet, they continue to engage in such excess and futility. For example, with respect to the calculation of damages for lost of future earnings, there is always multiple variables that affect the Herculean task of discounting to present value a hypothesized stream of future earnings. To demand for reasoned decisions in hard task like this amounts to an invitation to indulge in analytically pointless and yet ideologically potent forms of juridical rationalization.

It is generally reputed that the United States is the most litigious country on Earth. In the 2004 November 2 Presidential election, it was reported that teams of lawyers for both candidates were said to have been ready to jump in when the slightest irregularity in the election process was found.

There is a remarkable romanticism that surrounds the cultural ideal of law in American society. "The Solomonic judge, the passionate defense attorney, the stout-hearted juror: these are the figures that dominate the American idealization of law: these are the cultural representations of legality that help produce that profound fascination with law so characteristic of both elite and popular American culture. American courts are a gigantic organization of bureaucracies that process more than thirty million lawsuits per year." (79) There is "juridification" saturation of American society and life. There is an obsessive proceduralism that often seems to amount to a belief in the process for its own sake. The system ceaselessly produces a divergent interpretation and application of an almost unlimited quantity of massive, procrustean legal documents. Legal decision-making is essentially ad hoc in nature. There is an irrational worship of reason in general and technocratic rationality in particular and a faith in the moral perspicacity of that small group of career bureaucrats called judges. (80)

"The hypertrophied rationalism of American law is a product of trying too hard to be good." "Americans insist on subjecting themselves to a dictatorship of the

---

(78) Paul E. Çampos, *Jurismania: the Madness of American Law*, Oxford Univ. Pr., 1998, at 101.

(79) Id., at 178.

(80) Id., at 179.

bureaucratic" and are obsessive toward legal perfectionism; "toward getting it 'right'; toward 'solving' through juridical intervention all moral, political, and cultural problems, no matter how insoluble those problems may actually be." As a consequence, in the process of attempting to provide answer to every important social conflict, Americans produce more rules and procedures, more rights and obligations, more "reasons" and "principled justifications", that is more law.[81]

Given the current cultural dominance of the American rule of law ideology, the idea that much of the basic structure of American law might be a pointless or even pathological outgrowth of various rationalist delusions is likely to be dismissed out of hand as nothing less than bizarre. The sacrosanct status of law in American culture may well ensure that, for the orthodox legal mind, a sincere engagement with any fundamental criticism of the legal system is simply not an option."[82]

In the eye of the some critics of law, the constitutional theory is an incoherent mess made up of conclusory and muddled doctrines enunciated in methodologically useless multi-factor tests that decide nothing and that no one even pretends to take seriously.[83]

Section Six: Modes and Levels of Dispute Resolution

Dispute resolution is known to be a major proponent of the law in action. Resolution of disputes and conflicts represent the negative display of legal normativity, a sort of necessary evil.

One way to view and describe how disputes in the United States law are processed, for that matter in almost all countries of the world, is to divide the process and its manifestation into three levels as follows:

First, at the individual, unilateral level, legal normativity or obligation is internalized. We act or plan our conduct and make decision in accordance, or in compliance, with the requirements of the law on a total voluntary and consensual basis. There is no reason or cause of any sort for an individual to take deviate or derogatory political, moral action. The law in such a state is hardly noticed, recognized, or acted upon in any conscious way. The law is invisible and works

---

[81] Id., at 183.
[82] Id., at 184.
[83] Id., at 73.

splendidly in silence. At this level, disputes or conflicts of any sort that emerge will be settled to the extent that the available information predicts a likely outcome. This is a legal system that is efficiently processed.[84] One would not hesitant to add that such a system is rational.

Second, at the bipartite interactive level, two opposing interpretations, visions, views of the law are presented at the initial stage and consequently come to convergence by mutual concessions and compromises. As a result, the disputes or conflicts are eventually settled out of the court or other official adjudicative mechanism to the satisfaction of both parties.

Third, this is the most evident and noticeable manifestation of the law, though in the negative sense—third party intervention and resolution. At this level, the parties that hold sharply opposing views, interpretations, and visions of the law, insist on the correctness and justice of his or her own claim, rights, view, interpretation, and vision. And each at the end of the deadlock is willing to refer the conflict or dispute to a third party for resolution. This third party may be an administrative body, a regulatory agency, or some other mechanism, governmental or non-governmental. Ultimately, the disputes would be referred to the judicial system of the state for final disposition. When a dispute reaches in such a state, it is said to be in "a legal equilibrium zone." A legal equilibrium zone is defined as a distinct state of affairs in which the state of all materials such as rules, principles, policies, and social power that are considered as relevant by the parties to the processing of the dispute remains in equilibrium. And this state of affairs makes it difficult or impossible to predict how the dispute will be resolved. The critics of law, legal reason in general and judicial reason in particular, believe that "in an efficient dispute processing system, the terminal decision making structures of the system will resolve disputes arationally."[85]

Yet, in some instances, scenario two and three above may operate together, in tandem. The parties ultimately willingly settled their disputes by themselves may very well be due to the likelihood that when the hand of a judge seized of the case is forced, his judgment may satisfy neither party. This is what Judge Spencer said in the case between NYP and Research in Motion concerning certain patents infringement issues that the case was really a business decision, not a legal decision.

---

[84] Id., at 62.
[85] Id., at 64.

The judge was absolutely surprised that the parties had left this incredibly important decision to the court. In the landmark antitrust ruling against Microsoft Corp, the European Union (EU)(欧洲联盟) declared it guilty of abusing its dominant position with Windows. On appeal to the European Court of First Instance(欧洲一审法院), the Court which has the option to suspend the EU order either in total or in part but can not rewrite it, chose to play rather the role of a facilitator, mediator than an adjudicator. In its role as a facilitator, the Court nudged the parties to move closer together, making nitty-gritty suggestions to them to find a common ground.

Section Seven: Critique of the Efficiently Processed Dispute Theory and its Notorious Conclusions

The celebrated political philosopher John Rawls insightfully observed that in a constitutional regime with judicial review, public reason is the reason of its highest court. The above argument of the critics sharply contrasts with this insight since they believe the reason given by the appellate courts is arational.

The entire legal community, the bar, the bench, and the academic is "a community united by faith in the power of reason." The critics' argument also severely undermines the faith and value of the legal community in their attack on reason.

There are more criticisms that follow:

First, the theory, as it is presented, is pure academic, if not fictitious. No factual and credible evidences have been submitted to support the claim. What materials are considered as relevant? How does one establish that the state of all relevant materials is in equilibrium? Who is to judge? These and many other closely related questions make the theory too complex and too difficult to be certain and reliable.

Second, what is rational, arational, or irrational is a matter of competing subjectivity claiming for paradigmatic status and control. Competing claims for authority in legal and moral pluralism are the very nature and essence of public discourse through which we continue to search for the optimal rationality. Such competing claims manifest particularly vigorously with respect to deep controversial social or moral issue, such as abortion, same-sex marriage, etc. Critics of reason dismiss the joint opinion of the Supreme Court in Planned Parenthood v. Casey as nothing but rhetorical tricks phrased in abstract, oracular and question-begging language. Critics pointed out that as a general practice, opinions of appellate courts are most often drafted by junior law clerks. For this reason, they accuse an eminent professor who penned en encomium edifying the opinion lost his mind. Who is right, more persuasive, and to be trusted, the critics or the mainstreamed scholars?

To brand judicial decisions as arational or irrational is simply anti-intuitive and unrealistic. Some may appraise a decision for its rationality, while other may just attack its reason as arational or irrational. Critics of reason would rather praise the "puke" test for the rationality of judicial reason as wholesome, though short of advocating for its precedent value. (86)

Third, it is reasonable to suggest that all the cases that have been referred to the appellate court for disposition are hard cases. In cases of this nature, H. L. A. Hart believes that judges resort to discretion, while Ronald Dworkin suggests the judges should strive to discover principles of law. Only Critical legal studies movement protagonists claim that political considerations loom large in the process. Whatever the base or justification a judge invokes for his decision, be it may a discretion, a principle, or a political consideration, the material base invoked for justification is reason nonetheless.

Fourth, It appears that the efficient processed dispute theory is in fact a fatal exercise in self-contradiction, if not self-destruction. According to the theory, disputes before reaching the terminal dispute processing point are justly and harmoniously settled on the basis of all relevant materials including law, principle, politics, or social power. As "law" is the first factor mentioned that is relevant, it would be natural and right to accord the consideration of "law" the most significant and weighty role in the process. What is most important to be pointed out in this respect is that what is considered as the "law" by the critics is made to a significant degree by judicial decisions, particularly by the opinions of the appellate courts. What is fatal and self-contradictory is that these very opinions are regarded by the proponents of the theory as arational, irrational, or exercise of rationalist frivolity. (87)

Fifth, frivolous cases in the eye of the efficient process theory are inefficiently processed disputes before they approach the terminal point in the formal dispute processing system. An important question is why a dispute that can not processed

(86) Id., at 67-68.

(87) Id., at 69.

efficiently by the parties armed with the applicable law, principle, and other relevant materials and is referred to the court of law for disposition is to be branded as frivolous? Is it because "[t]he lawyers who pursue such disputes further to the formal dispute processing system do so because they, unlike the lawyers, namely judges, who decide the disputes, lack the requisite cognitive skills to subject the disputes in question to successful rational analysis?" In this case, it would not seem that outrageous but in fact reasonable to claim that judges in general do possess superior knowledge of the law and higher analytical skills than the lawyers who present frivolous cases for judicial disposition otherwise amendable to further extensive rational analysis. Or perhaps, the judicial process by virtue of its disciplinary procedural requirements, the adversarial mode of argument, and the judge's judicious intervention does provide an ideal environment for settling a dispute in a more rational way.

Or it might very well be the case that judges and law professors do possess superior knowledge of the law and analytical skills than most lawyers that they are in a much better position to analyze rationally these seemingly intractable social, moral disputes. Considering the fact that judges are chosen from among the best of the legal community and law professors are experts in their specialized areas of the law, one would find the claim for superior knowledge of the law and higher analytical skills not unreasonable.

What is incredible is how could the court brand as frivolous disputes that do not involve intractable social or moral issues. And how could the court throw such disputes back to the parties for more extensive or efficient analysis, since such disputes are supposed to having been already processed inefficiently under the theory, and presumably the parties did not know how to process them efficiently? What is mind-boggling is why the proponents of the efficient process theory do not find irrational the court order demanding for more extensive rational analysis by the parties in such cases? On the other hand, when further rational analysis of disputes is to be done by the court, the proponents of the theory would cry foul. What a double standard!

Why critics such as Schlag would not include in the efficient processing theory they advocate all formal dispute processes, including the adjudicative process of the court? Schlag's efficient processed dispute theory appears to rest on a distinction between state dispute settlement mechanism and private resolution of conflicts and ordering. Surely, it seems always the case that in hard cases, in which seemingly intractable social or moral issues are involved, a host of interest parties, governmental as well as many in the social, economic, and other fields are called upon to participate in the disposition and resolution process. Deep divisive labor disputes certainly involve potentially intractable social, economic, or moral issues. Labor mediators or arbitrators play essentially a similar role as judges in deciding hard cases of this kind calling upon the disputing parties to come to their sense in accepting a common mandate or ground, a compromise, in the name of some basic normative text, justice, fairness, what have you.

In the landmark antitrust(反垄断的) ruling against Microsoft Corp, the European Union (EU) declared it guilty of abusing its dominant position with Windows. On appeal to the European Court of First Instance, the Court which has the option to suspend the EU order either in total or in part but can not rewrite it, chose to play rather the role of a facilitator, mediator than an adjudicator. In its role as a facilitator, the Court nudged the parties to move closer together, making nitty-gritty suggestions to them to find a common ground. (88)The critics of judicial reason attack not just the reason of law, specifically judicial reasoning. They have no hesitation to mount a frontal assault(人身侵权) on the very foundation of constitutional democracy and its institutions as well as the truth that rational public discourse and reasoned decisions are the very essence of democratic institutions.

The voting booth and the jury trial are two most basic institutions of the American legal process. Paul E. Campos is one of the most eminent protagonists in the critics of the reason camp. He sees a similarity between making a decision on the political and moral question as to whether a fetus has a right to life by consulting scientists, moral philosophers, judges, and other experts and making a decision on the scientific question whether a meteorite in Antarctica holds evidence of life on Mars by a general show of hands. And he criticizes both decision-making methods as a ridiculous post-hoc rationalization. He thinks decisions of this nature are in fact made not as a result of any analytical or reflective thinking process but on the basis of what Holmes, the great skeptic judge, called "can't helps."(89)

---

(88) In fact, judges in Denmark have since March 1, 2003 been authorized to offer mediation to parties in civil case as a quicker and cheaper way to resolve difference. This has turned out to be a big success and been followed by a number of countries in the region.

(89) Campos, op cit at 70.

Campos attacks the jury trial as another evidence of American's willingness to tolerate irrationality in its dispute processing system. He claims that the extraordinary technical and complex hours-long instructions given at the end of the pleading process to the jury are often barely comprehensible to the lawyers in the court. And it would rather be irrational to expect that the decision finally reached by the lay jury who takes away no more than the most rudimentary understanding of the law on the issues at hand is any better than coin-flipping.[90] What figures large in the decision-making is nothing but axioms, intuitions, and beliefs.

Section Eight: In Search of an Emerging Law

Whenever and wherever competing or conflicting decisions and actions exist, the authority and efficacy of decisions are in question and must be ascertained. The task here involved is not a simple ascertainment of binding or persuasive authority. The task has spatial, temporal, as well as personal and material aspects. Due to a number of reasons, such as in the case of deep intractable social issues and conflicts, new, emerging, or novel technology and subject matter, there may be simply no legal authority that commands general acceptance. There may be competing authorities regarding the issue in question. What one faces are rather continuous, strong elite power interaction, discourse, persuasion, action, threat of action, claims and counter-claims, etc. In such cases, searching for legal authority within the existing body of the law sources will not do, especially by resorting to the established positivist methodologies or approaches. What is called for is a re-imagination of existing legal text and materials, a jettison of the positive law mindset, and to craft certain innovative, integrative approaches that would comfortably embrace all the existing legal schools and thoughts and at the same time make legal sense of them all.

A practical and timely example of difficulties and problems likely to be involved in ascertaining the authority of law is the heated debates and divisive positions regarding the question whether or not gays and lesbians have a legal right to get married. There is a significant amount of uncertainty and predictability before the Supreme Court as the ultimate oracle of the law speaks. Divergent and opposing

---

[90] Id., at 71.

interpretations and views come from many sectors, state as well as non-state. Facing such an uncertain and evolving situation, the crucial question is how does one plan one's life and conduct. It may take years for the judicial branch to communicate its view and decision. And even this will not unify the divisive views and positions and put the matter to rest.

It is fairly popular and often submitted that with respect to many new, emerging issues and problems, there is simply no law. This is a question-begging(诉诸问题), specious view. Does this mean that with respecting to such issues, problems, people just stop taking stance, making decision or entering into personal or business relations? The answer must be definitely negative. Such a view is only valid and makes sense when referring to a lack of normative prescription of the state, such as legislation or judicial decision. But there is much more to law than normative sources of an official nature.

Another example of the dynamic process of authoritative and effective decisions and of what counts as law in an area of universal concern is international trade law. The Byrd Amendment(伯德修正案) of the United States enacted ostentatiously to discourage and punish antidumping(反倾销) practices has unfortunately become an abusive, bullying protectionist policy. It is a thorny point in the trade relations of the U.S. with a number of other countries. It has been vehemently criticized as a flagrant violation of international trade law. It is an embarrassment to the proclaimed free-trade principles of the United States. Canada and many other countries have successfully challenged its legality before the World Trade Organization since 2003. Promise of eventual reform from the United States administration has been given. Yet, no action to bring about its reform or repeal has been taken by the Congress, ever mindful of the domestic political ramifications. Canada, the European Union and many other countries have been authorized by the WTO to retaliate. Out of frustration and other alternatives, some of these countries have proceeded to do just that. The situation remains uncertain as to how the U.S. will respond, and what will be the final outcome.

In the softwood lumber disputes between Canada and the U.S, the interactive relationship has gone on for years. In August 2005, the NAFTA* dispute panel firmly dismissed claims by the United States that Canadian softwood exports are

---

* 北美自由贸易协定,全称为 North American Free Trade Agreement。

unfairly subsidized and damage the U. S. lumber industry. Yet, the U. S. government continues to refuse to comply with the ruling alleging that the ruling fails to deal with a 2004 decision from the U. S-based International Trade Commission that supports the U. S. position, although it is believed the said decision and other earlier decisions have all been trumped by the NAFTA conclusion. Consequently, Canada was talking about the need of resorting to litigation or trade sanctions to have her position validated. Other strategic leverages at the disposal of Canada include its rich natural resources especially oil that can be employed to effect decision. Other view the NAFTA deal is a dud as the very foundation of the trade deal-secure market access and binding dispute settlement—has been destroyed by the U. S. action. Unfortunately, the WTO dispute settlement panel subsequently came out with an interim ruling in favor of the U. S. position. Although, the WTO and NAFTA rulings aren't so much contradictory as mutually exclusive as NAFTA panels determine whether a country is complying with its own laws, while WTO panels check adherence to international trade laws, any retaliatory measures or duties to be taken by Canada must be pre-approved by WTO. Trade courts give and trade courts take away. Politics rules above all. Even WTO adjudications can be trumped by domestic politics. It is said that the U. S. lumber industry controls enough politicians in Congress, and contributes enough to the Republican Party, that its voice is more powerful than that of any tribunal. There are about two dozen of cases pending at the WTO, under NAFTA and before the U. S. Court of International Trade. What one faces is stalemate, uncertainty, long drawn—out standoffs. Should Canada continue to pursue the litigation route or return to the negotiation table as the U. S. prefers?

The transnational aspects of the United States law in action have many interesting dimensions. The following statements quoted entirely are of particular significance both the United States perspective and that of China as well as their international impacts.

Move over Ben Bernanke[*]. Step aside Tim Geithner[**]. There's a new power in international finance: Zhou Xiaochuan, governor of the People's Bank of China, the $2 trillion central bank of China. It has the tools and the financial interests to be the new power player on the global financial stage.

Zhou Xiaochuan—better learn how to spell it and pronounce it—threw down the

---

[*] 本·伯南克,美联储主席。
[**] 蒂姆·盖特纳,财政部长。

gauntlet this week at the Obama-Geithner-Bernanke financial regime. His remarks can only be interpreted as a slap in the face of U. S. policy during the severe financial crisis that has swept the world. His prescriptions are bound to be debated in London next week at the G-20 parley and for years to come.

Boldly stated, Zhou—backed by Russia, Brazil and India—wants to break the dollar's hegemony in global finance. In a paper grandly called "Reform the International Monetary System(国际货币体系)," Zhou has called for the creation of an international currency unit that he admits will require "extraordinary political vision and courage." He suggests that we start with a blend of the dollar, pound, yen and euro—the so-called Special Drawing Rights*(SDR) created by the IMF** in 1969 that borrowed a concept first recommended by famed economist John Maynard Keynes.

Zhou's provocative remarks come only days after Premier Wen Jiabao demanded U. S. action to safeguard China's holdings of U. S. bonds—some $740 billion of Treasuries and $600 billion of other debt.

"We have lent huge amounts of money to the U. S. [and] we are concerned about the safety of our assets," said Premier Wen. Indeed, China has bought $200 billion of Treasuries while selling agency securities over the past six months. But it also lost about a third of its equity holdings, including $5 billion in the Lehman bankruptcy.

Zhou's rationale appears reasonable. "A super-sovereign reserve currency not only eliminates the inherent risks of credit-based sovereign currency, but also makes it possible to manage global liquidity(流动资金)," writes Zhou. "This will significantly reduce the risks of a future crisis and enhance crisis management capability."

By the way, don't dismiss Zhou as just a voice in the wilderness. His plan for a global reserve currency is backed by multibillionaire trader and economic wise man

---

* 特别提款权(SDR)是国际货币基金组织创设的一种储备资产和记账单位,亦称"纸黄金(Paper Gold)"。它是国际货币基金组织分配给会员国的一种使用资金的权利。会员国在发生国际收支逆差时,可用它向基金组织指定的其他会员国换取外汇,以偿付国际收支逆差或偿还基金组织的贷款,还可与黄金、自由兑换货币一样充当国际储备。但由于其只是一种记账单位,不是真正货币,使用时必须先换成其他货币,不能直接用于贸易或非贸易的支付。因为它是国际货币基金组织原有的普通提款权以外的一种补充,所以称为特别提款权(SDR)。

** 国际货币基金组织,全称为 International Monetary Fund。

George Soros*, as well as Martin Wolf, an influential columnist for the Financial Times(金融时报). Geithner, queried at the Council on Foreign Relations(美国对外关系委员会) on Wednesday, said he hadn't read Zhou's proposal, but praised his counterpart as "a very thoughtful, very careful, distinguished central banker." Geithner added that he was "quite open" to the suggestion of expanding the SDR's role.

Zhou has surprised the experts by suggesting that international financial institutions such as the International Monetary Fund should manage some nations' currency reserves. The IMF uses its funds to prop up nations in financial crisis. Expanding the SDR would give the IMF the potential to "act as a super-sovereign reserve currency" and to increase the IMF's resources, Zhou emphasized. "The scope of using the SDR should be broadened so as to enable it to fully satisfy the member countries' demand for a reserve currency," adds Zhou.

This would be a shocking change in a system where central banks maintain control over their reserves and many keep their operations entirely secret and non-transparent. Zhou makes a telling point when he insists that "the centralized management of part of the global reserve by a trustworthy international institution will be more effective in deterring speculation and stabilizing financial markets." In other words, Zhou is saying that the recent vicious meltdown might have been avoided if the world's financial system was not tied solely to the American dollar, the currency at the focal point of the global economy.

"For a country like China that prizes its sovereignty and to date hasn't even been willing to report the currency composition of its reserves to the IMF [something most other countries do], this would be a big step," says Brad Setser, a fellow of the Council on Foreign Relations and former Treasury official in the Clinton administration.

In a second address Thursday, Zhou took an even tougher whack at some American institutions and financial concepts. He blasted the way "the global financial system relies heavily on the external credit ratings(信用等级) for investment decisions and risk management." Having three U. S. ratings agencies dominate the world results in "a massive herd behavior at the institutional level. Moreover, the rating models for mortgage-related structured products are

---

* 乔治·索罗斯,著名的货币投机家、股票投资者、慈善家和政治行动主义分子。核心投资理论就是"反射理论"。

fundamentally flawed." All true. The massive write-downs across the globe were the result of these flaws in the American way of doing things.

Then, Zhou goes on to blame the American fair-value accounting system and especially the mark-to-market model for the intense market fluctuations and disorderly trading. Take that America. China described the "negative feedback loop (负反馈环)" as the most toxic American export ever. Zhou also crowed about how China's "macroeconomic (微观经济) measures," including a massive stimulus program, have produced "some leading indicators pointing to recovery of economic growth, indicating that rapid decline in growth had been curbed."

Then, Zhou really stuck it to Obama-Geithner-Bernanke, as well as to Europe and Japan. "Facts speak volumes and demonstrate that compared with other major economies, the Chinese government has taken prompt, decisive and effective policy measures, demonstrating its superior system advantage when it comes to making vital policy decisions." Talk about gauntlet dropping. (91)

In short, the Washington consensus(华盛顿共识), the Anglo-Saxon paradigm (盎格鲁一撒克逊模式), the European Model, and the market fundamentalism* are all out. In their place, we have a more democratic, more leveled place field, universal, and stricter regulatory oversight and constraints.

In the Terri Schiavo right to death case, the debates and struggles finally came to an end: The attempted intervention by Congress and the President has been resoundingly rejected—not just by the courts but by the large majority of Americans and even conservative commentators.

In a recent case challenging the constitutionality of the Canada Health Act which prescribes an universal, single-paying, free and equal access to health care for all citizens in Canada, the Supreme Court ruled in June 2005 that the constitutional right of Canadians in seeking private health care especially when potential harm caused by unreasonable delay is involved can not be denied. However, judicial decisions that involve broad social, economic, financial, or political matters are seldom self-executing and require implementing actions by the government. In this case, whether or not Quebec, the province directly impacted by the decision, will resort to the notwithstanding clause in the Constitution to neutralize the ruling or will

(91) Robert Lenzner, "Dollar Slams Up Against a (Great) Wall: The People's Bank of China Flexes Its Muscle in Call for a New Reserve Currency", *Yahoo Finance*, March 27, 2009.

* 市场原教旨主义是指市场可以自动恢复平衡,不需政府以任何方式进行干预。

eventually enact necessary rules to govern the provision of private health care and private health insurance figures more significantly in shaping the form and content of the health care law in Canada.

In the NTP versus RIM (the Blackberry smart phone maker) patents infringement case, Judge Spencer made it very clear the case is really a business decision, not a legal decision. The judge was absolutely surprised that the parties had left this incredibly important decision to the court. He also warned that if he was forced by the parties to make a decision, it would not satisfy neither party.

Economic life is arguably the most important part of the vitality of a nation and the lives of citizens. It often takes precedent over everything else. Yet, when two economists are put in the same room, there will never be an agreement emerging respecting the issue in question. In time of crisis, such as the economic woes and the collapse of the financial systems worldwide that we are presently witnessing, there is only fear and no certainty. Predictions by economic pundits and leaders are all over the place. There are optimists and soothsayers as well as pessimists and doomsayers.

Not even those, who profess to be realists, can tell us what's going to happen next. The universe is a lot messier and more unpredictable than we think it is. You could never get a model that would give you predictive certainty. It isn't a clockwork universe. Instead of trying hard to predict, the most realistic economic insight teaches the value of probabilities. We submit that in law, we would do much better by following the teachings of the probability theory. Of course, the crucial question is: What are the bases, factors, or considerations that one should use to identify, analyze, and assess probabilities?

And there doesn't seem to be any law to guide you. The economic stimulus (stabilization and recovery) plan as enacted the U. S. Congress at the request of the Obama administration has so far failed to restore any confidence in people. The financial, housing, and stocks markets continue to stumble. You are on yourself.

The crucial question arising from the above is what in the most realistic and mundane sense counts as the law. Is it the political decisions of the elite powers or the ruling of the court, the decision of jury, or the decision and action of the companies involved, or those of the investors that count as law? Unless one steadfastly adheres to the traditional, practically and largely irrelevant concept of law, predominately of a positive law nature, one must look to these events to guide one's decision and action. It is both interesting and significant that Justice Spencer proclaims from the bench that the dispute in thr RIM patent infringement case(专利侵权案件) mentioned earlier is an important business matter that should be settled between the disputes, not by the court. By the same logic, it would be reasonable to argue that family disputes should be decided by the family members concerned, labor disputes by the union and the employer, etc. One is wondering loudly just what kinds of disputes and issues should be left to the court? Certainly, most if not all of the disputes of a commercial, family, labor nature involves important issues of rights, obligation, justice, corrective or distributive. No wonder, there are no lack of lawyers, jurists, scholars, who seriously doubt the importance and role of the court in the enterprise of the law. It looks, upon further analysis, quite clear that the land of the law is very much non-judicial.

In this respect, it seems that the most comprehensive and detailed framework and propositions for finding in any uncertain situation a politically appropriate and morally compelling legal authority is offered by the configurative jurisprudence of Myres McDougal of the Yale Law School. Based on a powerful and realistic analysis of Harold Lasswell's policy science study, McDougal and Lasswell lay down in a series of seminal works an unprecedented and interesting framework for authoritative and effective decision-making. In their view, law is the pivotal and most representative form of authoritative and effective decisions. In essence, they suggest that to capture the true nature and spirit of the law, one must pay close attention to participants, objectives, conditioning factors, strategies, and effects or outcomes in terms of human dignity values. Closely related to this configurative way of looking at the decision—or law-making or—remaking process, a functional approach to decision-making must also be employed. Among the most important functions, there are intelligence, recommendation, prescription, appraisal, and termination.

It is submitted that to undertake such a comprehensive and detailed study of the law is extremely challenging and daunting. Superior scholarship by nature challenges the most serious and creative mind. To this end, we would perhaps obtain the best result by following the approach and technique that McDougal and Lasswell advocate.

The law in effect must be captured at the every moment when a political moral action or decision takes place. Political moral action is a personal choice and decision. When mobilizing all necessary base powers to effect decision, one must be resorted to make one's view and stance stick. Reason is the most compelling force among base powers behind the efficacy of any decision and authority. At the global and macro level, it is definitely enlightening to learn that Hillary Clinton, the Secretary of the State of the new Barack Obama government prefers diplomacy to military forces to effect decisions. The action that was initiated by China quoted above for the purpose of establishing a new, super-national currency in the form of a Special Drawing Rights (SDR) to replace the dominant sovereign dollar of the United States is of particular significance. Even the lawsuit filed by Freedom Watch in the U.S. District Court in Los Angeles against AIG seeking the return of bonuses and other perks should be counted as law-generating. In fact, countless other decisions and actions taken by states, groups of states, international organizations, governmental or non-governmental, corporate entities(公司实体), public or private, activist individuals are all legitimate normative forces in the comprehensive process of authority and effective decisin-making.

Keeping in mind that any law or authoritative and effective decision—a term we prefer—once enacted, pronounced, juridified, formalized—a sort of abstraction, of not ossification—becomes law in book. Principles and doctrines are the conceptual superstructure of the normative enterprise of the law. Theories and paradigms are the conceptual superstructure of economic policy and orthodoxy. Principles, doctrines, theories and paradigms are inherently general, vague, and manipulative in nature, and thus subject to competing, conflicting, and divisive interpretation and application. Therefore, to capture or predict the form and content of the continuous evolving constituents of political, moral normativity for conduct-guidance is quite difficult and risky. In section four above on the life of law in America, the interactive dynamics in the relations of the decisions of power elites has been illustrated in details.

Economist John Maynard Keynes* emphasized the flimsiness of the expectations on which economic activity in decentralized markets is based: the future is inherently uncertain; investor psychology is fickle. If this is true, how could one plan and conduct in this most important field of life? Authoritative and effective decisions made in the economic fields impact the most every aspect of peoples' lives and the

---

* 约翰·梅纳德·凯恩斯(1883—1946),现代西方经济学最有影响的经济学家之一,他创立的宏观经济学与弗洛伊德所创的精神分析法和爱因斯坦发现的相对论一起并称为20世纪人类知识界的三大革命。

welfare of the country. The enacted as well as planned financial stimuli, if not well thought out, may become the worst mistakes of the Obama presidency and could lead the country into a recession(经济衰退) far more devastating than people expect; to eliminate President Bush's tax cuts whereas to cut taxes for the middle-class in order to achieve fairness and to increase taxes for the rich in the same breath if not handled judiciously would only constitute a form of "capital punishment(死刑)" for those adversely affected; and to heighten further the corporate tax rates, already the highest in the world, will risk a flight of capital of historic proportions, and could decapitate prosperity for years to come.

Moreover, authority and effectiveness are not always mutually reinforcing. Whereas there are leading cases of precedent-setting, there are also leading cases of uncertainty, unpredictability, and questionable compliance, non or weak implementation and hence under shoot of goal-achievement. With respect to the Troubled Asset Relief Program or TARP, the Government Accountability Office(美国国家审计总署), the investigative arm of Congress, reported that the Treasury Department(财政部) had no way of ensuring that firms receiving federal funds are complying with limits on dividends or executive compensation, had little ability to monitor potential conflicts of interest among independent contractors helping to implement the program, and that the Treasury was reluctant to use the TARP funds to aid homeowners due to alleged complexity in designing an efficient and effective mechanism for such a program. What further complicates the difficulties in implementation are continuing weakening of the economic conditions, rising unemployment and declines in consumer spending and manufacturing.

The quest for the emerging law in the interactive and dynamic process of elite power decisions is rather a fairly complex and involved enterprise. The task involved goes much beyond a simple identification, ascertainment, distinction, elucidation of recognized forms of established sources of law, such as legislation, judicial decisions, order and action of the executive branch, political moral actions of non-state entities. Nor it is determinative just to cast the inquiry in the distinction between the legal, the political, and the moral. At the international level, ditto the distinction between so-called soft law* and hard law**, resolution, declaration,

---

* 软法,一般是指在严格意义上不具有法律拘束力但又具有一定法律效果的国际文件,包括国际组织或国际会议通过的不具有法律拘束力的决议、决定等。

** 硬法,指正式的法律规范体系。

treaties, customs, etc. Sources of law are nothing more than recognized forms of manifestation of political moral prescription. As such, they are in and of themselves do not equate with authoritative and effective decisions. What counts as law is found in nothing other than the authority as recognized and expected and efficacy, in real life, of a given political moral decision or action. Furthermore, authority and efficacy have their spatial, temporal, personal, and material dimension. They have general as well as particular implications. These no doubt further complicate the task and effort in ascertaining the law emerging. In the final analysis, law is what one chooses for action and decision at a particular time and space. This is what we advocate as one of the themes in this book the jurisprudential paradigm "I am the law."

Review and Reflective Questions

1. There are a number of elite participants in the comprehensive process of the making, unmaking and remaking of the law. What are the role and contribution of each of these elite participants?

2. Over-regulation means juridification saturation and hypertrophying of law and legal reason. Is there really such a phenomenon in American society?

3. How is a leading case so-called formed? What is its significance?

复习及提问

1. 在法律的制定、拆解和重新制定过程当中有众多的精英之士参与,请分别论述他们各自的角色与作用。

2. 过度管制意味着司法的饱和和法律的臃肿不堪。在美国社会是否存在这种现象?

3. 作为先例援引的案例是如何形成的?它有什么作用?

Chapter Seven: Good Legal System, Good Laws, and Good Decision-makers Lawyers

Introductory Note

We believe in good legal system. We discuss both the formal and substantive requirements for a good system. We think the concept of legal simplicity or legal complexity is false and their distinction unnecessary. We also believe that to have good law and a good legal system, there must be good men. We discuss in detail the qualities and requirements for a good judge, a good politician, a good regulator, a good lawyer, a good scholar, a good corporate citizen, and a good citizen.

简 介

良性的法律制度是值得人们信赖的。本章讨论了一个良性的法律制度形式和实质上的必要条件。我们认为,法律简单性及法律复杂性的概念是错误的,而且两者的区分也是无谓的。我们同时也认为为了获得良法和良性的法律制度,就必须要有良好的人。我们具体讨论了一个优秀的法官、优秀的政客、优秀的调控者、优秀的律师、优秀的学者、优秀的法人以及优秀的公民所分别应当具有的品质和条件。

Section One: Legal System and System of Law Distinguished

Literature on legal system is abundant. Little attention is paid to system of law. Often one is confused with the other. Other times the two concepts are treated as one and the same thing. If the distinction between them is taken for granted, this is not evident from the literature. It seems the confusion is further compounded rather than clarified by jurists who discussed and advanced criteria for discussion that appears to be applicable to both the construction of a legal system and the making of a system of law. The Austin's* view that a legal system is something more than a series of patternless exercises of political power applies to both notions.

A system of law signifies the laws as enacted, posited, accepted, and prevail （优先适用）in a country are an integrative, systemic, or organic normative unity. There is close interrelationship, interconnectedness, consistence, coherence, or other similar qualities between laws in terms of form, substance, and policy goal. In short, the laws belonging to and making up the system form a seamless web-like entity. Thus when one talks about the features, qualities, aspects, etc that are immanent in the laws themselves, one talks about the system of law, not the legal system, if confusion is to be avoided between them. For example, the Internal Revenue Code, the Tax code, the labor code all may be regarded as systems of law. Whereas, the Civil code of countries belonging to the civil law system may be considered as a system of law as well as consisted of many systems of law.

Legal system, on the other hand, must be defined differently, if confusion or collapse with system of law is to be avoided. The concept of legal system can be used to refer to the much broad, inclusive phenomenon of the entire normative enterprise of authoritative and effective decision-making of a society or can be employed to point to a particular component of the enterprise, such as the judicial system or the regulatory system or regulatory process. When the special characteristics of the Common law such as reasoning and decision-making process, fact-based rule-making versus conceptual application, and the relative importance of the role of judge and lawyer in the adjudication（裁决,裁定）process are at attention, it is to consider the Common law as a distinct legal system. Though, in this case, the concept of the legal system is focused on a specific component of the entire legal system.

Approaching a legal system from possibly the broadest and most inclusive perspective, one would count in its reach the constitutive and structural elements and characteristics, the formal and procedural concerns and requirements as well as the role, status, and qualifications of elite power participants—the human factors and considerations. Weaving together these three parties to form an integrative unity there is a vital operational element: it is the interactive dynamics between and among elite power decision-makers.

The legal system and the law of a country have another important component:

---

* 约翰·奥斯丁,英国法学家,现代法理学之父,法律实证主义创始人之一。

that is the philosophical ideas of political morality. The idea of legal philosophy defines the moral quality of the legal system of a country and its law.

It is important to point out at the outset that any attempt to study the law and legal system of a country in a complete and realistic manner must take a broader and inclusive view of what constitutes a legal system.

Law and legal system is best defined to include more than the official, state law, whatever importance one may wish to accord it. The term national law(国内法) or national legal system must be broadened to incorporate the law and the legal system of the international community to which a country is a member in good standing as well as the submerged landmass of legal normativity prevalent in a society. Understood this way, law and legal system of any sovereign state must be defined to include its national, transnational, and its sub-national components. The sub-national variations should count in the provincial or state, municipal and local portions as well as the non-state or unofficial sectors—that is, law of the social fields. In other words, whatever is law generating is legitimate(合法的) concern of the legal system.

Fuller in his seminal work The Morality of Law(《论法律的道德性》) discusses eight ways or canons to (fail to) make law. Among these, generality, non-contradiction, publication, possibility of performance of rules and congruence of rules as announced, and rules applied and practiced are of particular relevance. These canons appear to apply to both a system of law and a legal system though some are more important to the legal system than to the system of law. (92)

The relationship between a system of law and a legal system is comparable to the bonding between chicken and egg. Questions respecting the validity(合法性) of distinguishing system of law from legal system are fundamental interesting. Nonetheless, it seems rather declarative to say that in the United State alone, thousands of systems of law co-exist. What is unclear: Could more than one legal systems co-exist in a society at the very same time with respect to a given conflict, issue, subject matter, or question.

Section Two: Good Legal System Produces Good Laws

That good legal system tends to result in producing good laws is one of the

(92) Lon L. Fuller, *The Morality of Law*, New Haven and London: Yale University Press, 1964.

central themes of Fuller's "internal morality of law." In his view, a proper respect for the internal morality of law would limit the kinds of substantive aims that may be achieved through legal rules. It is to be expected that through negative elimination of objectionable policies and aims, good laws would result.

A. The Formal and Procedural Requirements for a Good Legal System

A legal system is a highly elaborated intellectual and political moral art of social organization. It is normally quite comprehensive, extensive, and complex. Being political, it is normative. Being an intellectual pursuit and endeavor, it extends and represents the possibility of human knowledge, aspiration, and achievement. The study of a good legal system does not directly concern itself with the question of what is the highest human good or what is the ultimate aim of human life. A good legal system explores the ways that are open to human persons to arrange their mutual relations so as to achieve their individual and collective ends whatever these ends may be.[93]

Discussion about good legal system does not concern so much with the intrinsic worth of either the Common law system or the Civil law system and for that matter of any other legal system. Nor does it deal the comparative merits of any one system. The discussion primarily attempts to explore and clarify the intrinsic nature and immanent features and characteristics of a legal system properly conceived. This is not a relentless pursuit for an ideal type of the legal system, but the identification and clarification of the true nature and properties of any system aspiring to be so-called.

What counts as a good legal system? How to define "good"? A good system is not the same as an effective system, though a system must also be by and large effective to be viable. This is what Hans Kelsen* has in mind in writing his Pure Theory of Law(纯粹的法学理论). A good legal system presumes the existence of a legal system, good or bad. Therefore, Fuller's "internal morality of law" and its eight cannons or any other principles of procedural justice should not and can not be invoked to determine whether or not a particular legal system exist. A good legal system is just a normative exertion of morality of aspiration. Even an evil system may be quite effective in achieving its outrageous aims and objectives at least for a short

---

[93] Fuller, op cit at 49.
* 汉斯·凯尔森,20 世纪美国法学家、法哲学家。

period of time. However, it has been consistently proven beyond any doubt that such evil system by flagrantly violating the principles of legality(合法性), would have sooner that later compromised its own legitimacy and the integrity of its law, erodes its bases of authority, and eventually destroyed itself.

A good legal system must meet the stringent requirements of principles of legality, what are also referred to as procedural justice and what Lon L. Fuller calls the "internal morality of law." These principles are considered the pre-conditions or sine qua none of law and a legal system. In his most acclaimed work, the Morality of Law, he pronounced the eight ways to fail to make law. These are:

1) A failure to achieve rules at all, so that every issue must be decided on an ad hoc basis;

2) A failure to publicize or at least to make available to the affected party, the rules he is expected to observe;

3) Abuse of retroactive legislation;

4) Failure to make rules understandable;

5) Enactment of contradictory rules;

6) Rules that require conduct beyond the powers of the affected party;

7) Introducing such frequent changes in the rules that the subject cannot orient his action by them, and finally; and

8) Failure of congruence between the rules as announced and their actual administration.

Law is the pre-condition for good law. This is the central theme of Fuller's philosophy. These eight canons equally apply to judicial and legislative power and are designed to fulfill the essential requirements of procedural justice that go a long way to produce good laws. In American legal history, these canons have been regularly invoked as grounds for the judicial invalidation of legislative acts.[94]

B. Legal Proceduralism

A good legal system requires a good set of rules that detail specifically the requirements for how decisions and actions of a public moral nature should be made. These stringent requirements must be both cost-efficient and reasonable for the tasks at hand. The emphasis on the legal process and formal and procedure

---

[94] Lon L. Fuller, *The Principles of Social Order: Selected Essays*, Ed. Kenneth I. Winston, Durham NC: Duke University Press, 1981, p. 40.

appropriateness is a long Common law tradition. The concept of adjective law is one of the most important features of the Common law system. It is rested on the belief that good legal procedure ensures good legal end. Good outcome logically results from a democratic, equal, fair, or just legal procedure.

Legal proceduralism in celebrated cases such as the O. J. Simpson trial epitomizes the rule of law ideology of the United States in full bloom. Some of the most extreme forms of the various characteristic features of the American legal system include the following:

"[T]he attempt to rationalize every aspect of the decision-making process, the distrust of spontaneous action, the demand for something approaching perfection in the handling of the relevant legal materials, the urge to maintain a continuous and pervasive managerial control over every participant, and above all, the daunting complexity of the rules that such a system requires."[95] The elaborated and detailed requirements and strenuous efforts for the jury selection process that seemingly is designed to achieve a rough balance of partisan prejudices unfortunately result in a deliberated manipulation by lawyers of the rich and the famous. The application of the English system of selecting jurors at random would deprive wealthy defendants of the advantages to be gotten from the hiring of high-priced jury selection consultants, who tend to defeat comparatively overworked and understaffed prosecutors in the playing of this particular psychological and demographic game.

This will to process—the urge to rationalize, codify, administrate, proceduralize, and otherwise complicate a system of social coordination and dispute processing—increasingly makes that system available only to the social elite who have the resources to manipulate it.[96] As a result, the excesses of American legal ideology tend to transform the system into a kind of luxury good functioning as a complex cultural mechanism for the protection of privileged class. Justice in America becomes a quantifiable commodity that increases or decreases in value in direct proportion to a party's wealth.

Unfortunately, even a set of well-designed and well-intended rules to ensure process efficiency and procedural appropriateness may be hijacked, compromised, abused, or otherwise caused it to fail in achieving its goals and expectations. In other words, the rule of law is no absolute guarantee. Other constitutive and institutional

---

[95] Paul F. Çampos, *Jurismania: the Madness of American Law*, Oxford Univ. Pr., 1998, p. 22.
[96] Id., at 24.

arrangements as well as conscientious, good human intervention are also required.

Habermas'*Proceduralism(程序主义) or Procedural Republic

There is no strict dichotomy of procedural justice and substantive justice. They are intractably interrelated and mutually reinforcing. One cannot cancel or displace the other. Procedural justice is amply permeated and infested with substantive law assumptions. Surely, communicative action cannot obtain rationality without pre-dialogical or extra-dialogical assumptions, even though discursive proceduralism is neutral as to perspective and conception of the good. On the other hand, procedural justice works to prompt the approximation of substantive justice. Good legal system produces good law. Habermas' procedural paradigm of communicative action, dialogical reciprocity and transformation is certainly not an end onto itself captivated in a ceaseless, endless perpetual enfolding process always in the working and going nowhere.

Section Three: Good Law Informs Good Legal System

It is no denying that good law would entail a good, healthy, vigorous legal system. Yet, the existence of morally repugnant laws cannot be invoked to fault the existence of a healthy, vigorous legal system in terms of structural soundness and operational efficacy. In this sense, it would be irrational to deny that the Aparthead South Africa, the criminal Nazi Germany regime, and for that matter, the U. S. before the Civil War, the franchise of women in the 1920s and the enactment of the Civil rights(民权法案) legislation, all enjoyed a functional and valid legal system. To hold a contrary view, one has to resort to criteria other than of, say, a formal, or procedural nature, such as Fuller's internal morality.

A. Substantive Moral Requirements for a Good Legal System

Good laws and good legal system are not the same but are intractably linked. While it may be true that by and large a good legal system tends to produce more good laws, it would be hardly expectable that a corrupt and unjust system would produce many good laws. A good legal system is necessarily resulted from a corpus of good laws, laws that are in full compliance with the principles of legality as well as

---

* 尤尔根·哈贝马斯,德国哲学家。

fulfill the minimum moral requirements of a substantive, constitutive nature. As the laws that are constitutive of a good legal system are part and parcel of a corpus of good laws, it therefore follows that good laws almost necessarily result in a good legal system.

Fuller's internal morality of law, in addition to ensure the quality of a good legal system, is designed to achieve certain desirable, indispensable policy goals and aims to assure the system's very existence as well as its healthy development.

There are many virtues and values that can be said to inform the basic, constitutive structure of a good legal system. At the general level, a good system aims to be rights and power conferring; it improves and enables individual zones of choice and control rather than becomes more prohibitory and intrusive. This is not the same as the extreme claims of the small government proponents.

Van Caenegem advances eight criteria of good law, many of which are of a substantive moral nature. These are:

1) Incorruptible and impartial judges;

2) Participation of citizens in the law making process together with a open court and free press;

3) Democratic recruitment of judges;

4) Competent and professional judges;

5) Comprehensible and cognoscible (recognizable) law;

6) (Timely) accessible justice;

7) Humane justice—inquisitive system, torture, etc. flout human rights; and

8) Legal system based on broad public consent—no groups or sections of people excluded or oppressed. [97]

Other moral qualities and virtues can be readily added to the list above to include the following: the presumption of innocence until proven guilt, the right to remain silent, equal and timely access to counsel, rules against self-incrimination, free of unreasonable delay (justice delayed is justice denied), protection against unreasonable search and seizure, Rawls' principles of justice, Dworkin's rules of fairness and equal treatment, the moral autonomy and integrity of the physical person, a regime of private ownership, and protection of private property. And the list goes on. It all depends on the comprehensiveness of one's conception of the

---

[97] *Judges, Legislators and Professors*, Cambridge Univ. Pr., 1987.

minimum content of a morality of aspiration.

No doubt, the constitution of countries of the civilized world, especially in the part dealing with rights and freedoms, such as the Bill of Rights or Canadian Charter of Rights and Freedoms is designed to satisfy the requirements of the minimum moral content of a good system of law. Many of the rules and principles of this nature are developed by courts through liberal and expansive interpretation of the constitution. This is the case in the United States, Canada, and the Great Britain for example.

No doubt, the various United Nations conventions on human rights and other human dignity values are attempts to enshrine the minimum moral requirements of a substantive nature and posit as standards for civilized nations to adopt. In recent years, the outlaw of capital punishment as barbarian and inhuman punishment has captured worldwide attention. Reactions to any practice perpetuating such punishment are swift, strong, and highly condemning. The following quote illustrates this very well: California's execution of Stanley Tookie Williams on Tuesday outraged many in Europe who regard the practice as barbaric, and politicians in Governor Arnold Schwarzenegger's native Austria called for his name to be removed from a sports stadium in his hometown. At the Vatican, Pope Benedict XVI's top official for justice matters denounced the death penalty for going against redemption and human dignity. "We know the death penalty doesn't resolve anything," Cardinal Renato Martino told AP Television News. "Even a criminal is worthy of respect because he is a human being. The death penalty is a negation of human dignity."[98]

It is reasonable to say that neither Fuller's nor Van Caenegem's* list is exhaustive of the desirable, if not defining, element(s) or determinants of a system of good law. But the ideas they have advanced have gone a long way towards producing both a good legal system and a corpus of good laws.

Are there other virtues and requirements that must be fulfilled for a country to claim the envied status of a good system and good law? Is there any particular form of government that is more desirable or conducive to the promotion of a good legal system? Should there be a separation of government powers? How about a basic welfare system that would include unemployment insurance, public medical care, public housing, legal aid, etc. The list of desirable characteristics is long and

---

[98] "Europeans Outraged at Schwarzengger", AP-Tuesday, Dec 13, 2005, 9:54 AM ET. Vienna, Austria Yahoo News.

* 凡·卡内刚,比利时根特大学教授。

possibly infinite. The search for the optimal moral content of a good legal system and good law like civilization itself is a continuous process of human aspiration.

However, it is important to point out in this connection that whether or not there is the minimum content of a substantive natural law that informs a good legal system and to what extent this is so is highly controversial. Fuller questions Hart's search for a "central indisputable element" in human striving can be successful. Fuller ventures to discern only one central indisputable principle of substantive natural law: "Open up, maintain, and preserve the integrity of the channels of communication by which men convey to one another what they perceive, fell, and desire."[99] This is all very nice except that one still has to ask what kind of political and legal system has to be established first in order to make Fuller's principle possible.

It may be argued that legal system, namely, its very existence is a powerful historical manifestation of human strive. Legal system may be regarded as a symbol of the moral development of a society. And as such, it in and of itself represents the good. In this sense, to speak of a good legal system appears somewhat self-contradictory. In the same sense, the notion that a system can be either good or bad is a misconception. For a legal system represents at least the minimum duty of morality of a society. On the other hand, to develop a good legal system through pursuit of the optimal moral content of the legal system can be considered a moral aspiration of a society.

B. Democratic Foundation and Spirit of Law and Legal System

It is submitted that one of the most fundamental, desirable features of a good legal system is the democratic foundation of the law in the sense of an equal, inclusive, non-discriminatory participation in the authoritative and effective decision-making process.

Democracy is one of the first principles of justice prescribed by John Rawls for social and political organization. Democracy like proceduralism figures most prominently in the means and ends relationship. Social ends can be identified and clarified, but not prioritized in advance. Infinite variables and extents get involved in the choice of one end at the sacrifice of another. For example, the preservation of life is paramount and overriding. But what happens when two lives require equal

---

[99] Lon L. Fuller, *The Morality of Law*. New Haven and London: Yale Univ. Pr., 1964, pp. 184-186.

protection as in the case where childbirth threatens the life of the mother?

Any society that cherishes and aspires to the equal worth of the human person would choose to decide in a democratic way matters concerning values of human dignity, such as those mentioned above respecting to the building of a good legal system and the making of good law.

But concepts of democracy, like justice, liberty, and freedom, are not attainable directly. They need facilitating and enabling institution, rules and procedures to be obtained. Nor democracy like the concept of justice itself is easily to be ascertained or defined in isolation. John S. Mills defines freedom as absence of constraints. Thus freedom is not an absolute value. When, where and how to impose what constraint on freedom cannot be conceived in vacuum or in advance. Constraint must be determined in context democratically. Democracy is the best and the most equitable way to make decision on constraints.

Micheal Oskeshott conceives freedom as an object of social policy that depends on formal arrangements for its realization. And the best formal political arrangement is the institution of democracy. [00] Freedom and democracy go hand-in-hand.

With respect to law, legal power must be democratically distributed, checked, and balanced. An active and healthy relationship of interactivity among participants in the authoritative and effective decision-making process strengthens the democratic foundation of the law and promotes its democratic spirit.

Democracy and legitimacy are the foundation of law and the legal system. Election and popular vote for power elites in both government and certain fields of public concerns in society are the most basic and effective method of manifesting the wishes and expectations of citizens in democracy. Democracy is a living organism that can be easily weaken, emasculated, and wounded fatally. It must be revitalized, continuously re-defined, and reconstituted. For a healthy development of the political and legal structure, serious weakness, problem, and issue of the democratic institution must be exposed, recognized, and corrected. The democratic idea and institutions must be continuously nurtured. Political power is legal power.

Election is the most meaningful instrument for the general public to the exercise of political and legal power in democracy. Unfortunately, it appears that marching to the polls at election time has become more a hallowed ritual of democracy than a

---

[00] M. Oskeshott, "Political Education" In: *Philosophy, Politics and Society*, Ed. Peter Laslett, Oxford: Blackwell, 1956, p. 10.

meaningful exercise of the political right of citizens to make a difference.

The scandalous system for funding campaigns, a throwback to the buy-a-vote days of yore, could stand another massive dose of reform. Of course, asking lawmakers to curb new soft-money groups, to fix the near-broke Presidential campaign fund, and to help challengers have a shot at dug-in incumbents, is like asking them to saw off an arm. Reform requires recognizing that there exists something called the national interest, and demands a rare moment of vision by Capitol Hill's(美国国会) shameless partisans.

Unless the United States wants to continue on the path—declining participation, permanent incumbency, less competition for ideas, increased balkanization, and more big-money politics—reform isn't an option. It is perhaps the most urgent priority facing the republic as it lurches into the harsh light of a new century burdened by a political system that seems less democratic by the day.⑩

For example, it has been held by court that it is a good thing to put certain spending limits on political campaign in partisan politics. Unrestricted political advertisements could manipulate or oppress the voter.

Democracy can be easily hijacked and rendered outdated or emasculated. The irony that we vote and they rule is one of such misfortunes. In order to gain more representative seats to control the congressional process and outcome, both the Republican(共和党人) and the Democrat(民主党人) resort to gerrymandering(不公正地划分选区), redistricting, and reapportionment schemes, while ignoring population change and running afoul of one-man, one-vote requirements. In the past, the Supreme Court often signaled that they would not intervene in any cases involving such maneuvers done for partisan reasons. And when they do intervene, often it would be too late and the damages have been done. There is a sort of malaise in the democratic process in many modern liberal democracies. There are weaves of citizen indifference and cynicism*. To give the true meaning to participatory democracy, the political process must be reinvigorated and strengthened by empowering and making citizens the master not only at the ballot boxes but also at every stage of the public decision-making process.

Decisions and actions of government and political institutions are not just the

---

⑩ "Does Your Vote Matter?" *Yahoo Finance webpage* (6/6/04 10:03 AM).

* 犬儒主义,又称新柏拉图学派,古希腊四大学派之一,基本思想是:人要摆脱世俗的利益而追求唯一值得拥有的善。

direct sources of the law; they are laws. When the legitimacy of government and basic political institutions are in question and when massive non-or ineffective participation of citizens in the political process becomes rampant, the system is weakened or severely restricted, the authority of law is in danger.

C. Democratizing Law-making (Authoritative and Effective Decision) Process

To set law on the foundation of democracy, the authoritative and effective decision-making process at all levels of government as well as that in the private sectors must also be democratized. This basic requirement goes well beyond the demand that the head of the state and the representatives in legislature are elected by popular vote. It demands that the decision-making of every piece of law be democratically informed and shaped. Fortunately, in countries of constitutional democracy, the democratic spirit does permeate to a considerable extent every stage of the law-making process. In the United States a bill or proposed law can be introduced by the constituency(选举团体); public hearings(公开听证) and expert testimony(专家证言) are routinely held at both the committee and subcommittee levels; a bill must be passed in both houses; assent or signature of the head of state must be obtained.

With respect to the making of delegated legislation, namely regulation, public input and feedback should be solicited at both the decision phase and post-decision stage. As it is observed that a valid discretionary act of a federal official takes precedence over even an article of the constitution of a state, the significance of delegated legislative act needs no special emphasis. The following anecdotal evidence amply illustrates the working in general of the decision-making process of administrative and regulatory bodies in the United States.

Democratizing Rule-Making at the United States Securities and Exchange Commission (SEC)(美国证券交易委员会)—In order to modernize corporate governance to protect investors' interest, the SEC solicits input and comment from all concerned upon its proposed draft rules and regulation. Facing opposition from corporations, business groups and some of its own commissioners, the SEC routinely considers altering part of its proposal to give disgruntled shareholders more clout. Through reworking the most heavily criticized aspects of the proposal, the SEC holds roundtable discussions, deliberates on the wide ranging and divergent views, balances concerns that have been raised from all sides, and tries to coalescing them into a rule so as to accomplish the objectives of the Commission's rule-making. With respect to the regulation of the mutual fund industry, good governance requires, among other things, independent monitoring and oversight by a group acting as a proxy for investors. From the perspective of the fund companies, a reasonable <u>quid pro quo(合同对价)</u> for submitting to governance requirements should be the removal of prohibitions on late trading, market timing, self-dealing, and related-party transactions. Critics may brand regulatory compromise of this nature as agency capture or cop-out. Nothing could be further to the truth.

Only the decision and action made at the executive level appear to be incompatible with the democratic spirit of the law. One should not be overly concerned with the democratic foundation of the office of either the President or high officials as the former is democratically elected and the latter subjected to strenuous, democratic scrutiny and confirmation by elected representatives. It must be added that the eye of the public is sharp and fierce when informed and enlightened by independent media. It is the decisions and actions made at the lower administrative and regulatory levels that must be attended to. Here, it is submitted we are concerned mainly a question of the legitimacy and validity of elite power decision in democracy in general.[102]

Judicial lawmaking is a paramount and unique issue in democracy. The role, function, and authority of judicial decisions in the Common law America along with constitutional <u>activism(能动主义)</u> of the judiciary have already been amply discussed in other parts of the essays in this book. Suffice it to say that the democratic foundation and spirit of judicial lawmaking that inform the entire adversarial process of argument; the relative retiring role of the judge, and the inclusive participation of all interests affected, either claimed or requested, all testify to this truism. When judges are struggling with a monumental task of developing badly needed rules, criteria, or tests they appeal to the lawyers before them for assistance. Accusation of judicial activism and <u>usurpation(侵犯)</u> of the legislative power of representatives of democracy and the lack of political accountability of judges direct primarily at the substantive content of decisions rather than the appropriateness of the process.

Democracy is a powerful, loaded, and elusive notion. The meaning and content

---

[102] Please refer to "Elite Powers and Democracy" in "E" below for more information.

of democracy vary greatly among countries, even among liberal democracies. It seems that democracy is more a process of decision-making than an embodiment of certain a priori prescribed values. The true meaning and content of democracy can only be established in special context taking into all relevant factors, circumstances as conditions.

Under constitutional democracy, law is a collective normative enterprise. Public participation(公众参与) in the making of authoritative and effective decisions should be inclusive, non-discriminatory, and transparent. It has been critically pointed out that election campaigns in Canada Toronto's municipalities(地方自治政体) are overwhelmingly bankrolled by corporate money, most of it from the same developers responsible for cascading sprawl in the region. The sheer amount of cash flowing from developers to incumbents as opposed to coming from citizens who believe in a candidate's platform erodes the concept of democratic representation of equal voice and participation in the law-making process.

The concept of the supremacy of the legislature and judge as the oracle of the law, even though holding up unchallenged under the light of legal positivism are only partially true. For all such seemingly preemptory concepts of legal absolutism(专政主义) must hold up under the gauntlet of certain concomitant principles such as transparency, accountability, regulating the regulatory and judging the judge, etc. Only the normative dynamics of mutual informing and shaping between all authoritative and effective decision-makers or elite powers in both the state and non-state sectors may be able to truly capture the essence and spirit of the democratic nature of the law. Over and above all the authoritative elite, people undoubtedly hold the ultimate power. This not only is true at the voting station but also should be honored at every operating stages of the law.

The interactive and mutual shaping dynamics rests on the universal truth that law as politics of public morality is a fundamental concern of all citizens. What constitutes the good and moral righteousness is to be decided democratically. No individual, group of individuals or organization is allowed to claim superior knowledge and insight to use political power to achieve partisan ends. This also serves to defuse the danger of totalitarian(极权主义者) impulse and moral absolutism and imperialism(帝国主义). It is derived from one of the old standbys of liberal theory—the distinction between force and persuasion.

D. Open and Transparent Decision-making

As a general principle, all decision of any nature, at any level, and whatever the subject matter, should be open and transparent. This open and transparent requirement applies far beyond the concept of an open court. The system of public hearings held during the legislative process and similar sessions for public input set up before regulatory hearings are all designed to meet this requirement.

A correlate requirement for open and transparent decision-making is open and transparent public reason. In the public arena of political morality, decision and action must be reasoned. Open and transparent public discourse on all social, economic, moral issues and matters is a sine qua non(不可或缺的前提条件) of a good legal system. Pluralism is a fact of social life everywhere. Political and moral pluralism is recognized and encouraged in all liberal democracies. Only an open and transparent decision-making and public discourse would enable peoples holding opposing views and opinions to sit down together to engage in the building of a collective normative system of the law and to ensure an effective system of law and an effective legal system supported by legitimacy and authority. Only through an open and transparent public discourse and persuasion and non-discriminatory participation therein, all the other good things will follow.

If democracy is more a process than a substantive political morality, then the open, transparent, and participatory mode of lawmaking or the making of authoritative and effective decision in the Anglo-American world appears to have captured well the democratic spirit of the law.

Open and transparent decision-making is the essence of the democratic process. Democratic principles require that the people be informed of the activities of their government. Yet, the Bush Administration has precluded the public—and often members of the Congress—from knowing about some of the most significant decisions and acts of the White House. They base their need for confidentiality not simply on the imperative of protecting national security at a time of war. Their proclivity for privacy was well demonstrated before 9/11. The Bush administration did this by creating a broad new category of sensitive information and toughening the standards for what the public can obtain under the Freedom of Information Act. What should be matter for public debate has become the prerogative of a closed circle of elite decision-makers. Information so withheld includes the inner workings of the White

House energy task force and the President's secret authorization surveillance of without warrant of people inside the US suspected of communicating with terrorists abroad. What is even more unfortunate if the federal court is to dismiss any suits involving such acts as struggles between the executive and Congress. Such flagrant and excessive unilateral assertions of presidential powers if unchecked would ultimately threaten the constitutional principles of separation of powers and check and balance.

Fortunately, the new Obama administration has already started, within just one day after being inaugurated, the process to reverse the Bush administration's legacy of secrecy, opaque decision-making, and oligarchical style of governance. With the signing of five executive orders, he spelt out sweeping new rules on lobbying, government ethics, and transparency. The new rules of the road provide a fresh reinterpretation of the Freedom of Information Act with the presumption: "In the face of doubt, openness prevails."

For most of its history, the Federal Reserve's Open Market Committee that sets interest rates has worked in secret, perpetuating the belief that operating like a Sphinx was the most effective way to carry out monetary policy.

Certainly the view years ago was that the Federal Reserve ought to try not to communicate its objectives to the market, but keep them as undercover as possible. The current theory, however, is that clearer signal from the Federal Reserve about economic conditions and interest rates can help shape public perception and assist the Federal Reserve in attaining its goals.

To influence economic activity, the Federal Reserve adjusts the target for the federal funds rate. "Monetary policy works largely through indirect channels—in particular—by influencing private-sector expectations and thus long-term interest rates." "Consequently, failing to communicate with the public ... only reduces the potency and predictability of the effects of given policy actions."

For a long time, private economists had to monitor the Federal Reserve's daily buying and selling of Treasury securities to figure out whether the central bank was changing the funds rate. For years, Federal Reserve officials argued that immediate release of policy decisions would make markets more unstable and policy implementation more costly and difficult. Federal Reserve's communications policy in the 1970s and the 1980s was described as a black box. It could take a couple of days before we knew what the funds rate target was.

A breakthrough came in 1994 when the Federal Reserve began to state when it was changing the federal funds rate. Eventually the Federal Reserve began to release statements after each of its eight regularly scheduled meetings a year and did so even when rates held steady. Over time, the Fed began to give a reason for its actions and a brief assessment of economic conditions. Since early 2002, these statements also include how members voted. "We have achieved a far better balance, in my judgment, between transparency and effective monetary policy implementation than we thought appropriate in the past," Greenspan said in 2001.

When Greenspan wants to send a signal to investors, he does. Other times, he is deliberately oblique. Once pressed about the course of interest rates, Greenspan's stock response is that he was scrupulously open to extraordinary ambiguity on that very subject. Openness is important, but is hard to accomplish because miscommunication is so easy.

Some Federal Reserve watchers have suggested that the Committee conducts its deliberations on interest rate policy in public, possibly televised on C-SPAN, rather than in private, as is now the case. But Greenspan, Poole and other Federal Reserve policy-makers have suggested that such openness probably would curtail a free-flowing discussion, send confusing signals and roil financial markets. "Making effective monetary policy(货币政策) is no Sunday drive in the park."[103]

What is particularly gratifying to note in this respect is that China appears to have taken a giant step toward a new era of openness and transparency in government. It has been widely reported in the mass media that China's Auditor General's 2004 report exposes to the widest expectation and satisfaction of the nation countless incidences of bribe, corruption, embezzlement, criminal wrongdoing, or simply dereliction of duty at the various levels of government. Other incidences of this nature include the high praise levied upon a number of the Chinese intelligentsia who dared to expose the true rampant situation of AIDS in China despite of all the potential risk and adverse consequences. What is extremely significant is that both men are being nominated among other candidates to the most newsworthy man of 2004.

In Canada, to require the nominees of the Prime Minister of Canada to appear before an ad hoc committee of the Parliament was regarded as an important step

---

[103] Jeannine Aversa, "Greenspan Has Created More Transparent Federal Reserve, after Years of Working in Secret", *Yahoo Finance Website*, December 12, 2008, 9:36 pm ET.

toward great transparency and accountability in the appointment process. On the other hand, to vest an un-reviewable power in the hands of the Prime Minister alone for appointment of judges, especially of the highest court, in the Charter of Rights era, would be widely seen as being inconsistent with basic democratic norms.

The major concern in this respect is to ensure both the independence of the court and the transparency and accountability of the appointment process. Once these twine concerns are taken care of, it would be more likely than not that a candidate would be appointed with a superior personal qualification, highest level of proficiency in the law, superior analytical and written skills, proven ability to listen and open-mindedness and soundness of judgment. To help obtain these goals, certain safeguards are needed. The thrust of the safeguards should attend to three aspects: who, how, and what. It has been suggested that the review or vetting committee should include not just members of the legislature but also experts and knowledgeable individuals of integrity and commitment to the independence of the judiciary; there should be review or vetting protocol to govern the proceedings and smooth working of the committee; and limitation and constraint should be established as to the nature and content of questions that could be asked of the nominee.[104]

In the case of the inter-agency decision of the U.S. to outsource the management and operations of six ports on the Eastern seashore to Dubai Port World, a state controlled company in the United Arab Emirates, both Republicans and Democrats of Congress for national security reason came public in joint force to decry the lack of public input and open consultation and transparency, and threatened to pass legislation to block the deal, and in case that the President lives up to his publicized intention to veto any such legislation, to pass a joint resolution of both houses to overrule the veto.

Whether or not the governing and decision-making process is open and transparent could be discerned in places that are the least suspected. For example, under the Bush-Cheney administration, the residence of the Vice-president in Washington is a pixilated blurry mess. Coinciding with the Obama-Biden assuming power, the satellite images of the ornate 19th-century home suddenly become clearly visible. This is hailed by many as emblematic of a new era of openness and transparency in Washington.

---

[104] Patrick Monahan, "A Very Judicious Process", *The Globe and Mail*, Feb. 22, 2005, p. A15.

E. Right to Know and Freedom of Access to Information

Correlated closely to openness and transparency is the right to know and the right of access to information about both the action and decision, of the government and about oneself.

In Canada, freedom of information is a quasi-constitutional right(准宪法权利). Yet, almost everywhere, governments are trying to roll back obligations of openness, by claiming concerns about security or privacy, or by under-funding the commissioners who oversee right to know laws. They use delays to frustrate inquiry, release tampered records, refuse to keep written records to ensure paper trails (duty to document) and resort to what is known as the "oral culture, to thwart media scrutiny by concealing, altering or destroying records. Statutory exemptions are severely employed to limit transparency. In many instances, it requires the power of an auditor-general or judicial inquiry(司法调查) to get at information beyond the anodyne contents of annual reports.

In Ontario, two decades after the freedom of information legislation was enacted, there are still far too many civil servants remain oblivious of the fact that the information kept in filing cabinets and computers is not their to guard and protect, and that it is the information of Canadians. Citizens have a right to know what their governments are doing.

Unfortunately, the right of access to information of a public nature is not absolute, but limited. In the Dominic Racco case that is presently before the Supreme Court of Canada, the pro and con are argued by the opposing and interested parties. On the one side, it was forcefully maintained that access to information was not a constitutional right, but a privilege bestowed on the citizenry. It was a revocable gift. Governments were fully justified if they were to eliminate all freedoms of information provisions in one fell swoop. The judges were urged not to impose any obligation on governments to provide information upon request. To do so would set a precedent that would run roughshod over the court's gradual, careful approach to developing the Charter right to free expression.

On the other side, it was submitted that the images of documents flying out of government files is distorted and false. The sky is not falling. In fact, what is argued is only the right for provincial and federal information commissioners to release any document with a "compelling public interest" component that clearly outweighs government confidentiality views. It was further argued that taken to its logical conclusion, an overly protective government could twist the opponents' argument to justify imposing absolute secrecy over its activities. History has shown that one of the first things that anti-democratic leaderships do is to pull a curtain of secrecy around their activities.

The opponents cautioned that opening confidential files to the public could chill debate within government institutions and caused police investigators to pull their punches when they report on cases or decide whether to lay criminal charges.

Lawyers for the Federation of Law Societies of Canada(加拿大法律协会联盟) and the Canadian Bar Association(加拿大律师公会) also warned the court not to compromise the free flow of advice between solicitor and client.

Justice Ian Binnie interjected at one point during the proceeding and said that both sides of the case have resorted to "apocalyptic" visions of what would happen if their advices were not taken. Several other judges also expressed reservations about hampering the institutions of government by making the confidentiality within which they operate open to prying by individuals seeking documents. It was said that Supreme Court judges created private notes and held case conferences, and that the court would be unable to function if these things could be made public.

The opponents also argued that police would become wary of committing their thoughts and observations to paper and civilians could become reluctant to speak to police in case their statements would later become public.

The proponents on the other hand emphasized that few documents would make it through the filter of the need to establish a compelling public interest that outweighs claims of confidentiality based on solicitor-client privilege or the needs of law enforcement.

The administration of justice thrives on exposure to light—and withers under a cloud of secrecy, Justice Morris Fish of the Supreme Court of Canada wrote in a 2005 ruling upholding the media's Charter-guaranteed right to gather and report the news.

Yet, since 2006, clerks at court-houses across Ontario have cast a cloud of secrecy over sexual assaults(性侵犯), extortions(勒索罪) and a host of other serious crimes. They refused to allow journalists to see the court file—documents clearly on the public record—if there was a ban on publishing information that could identify the victim or a witness.

The reason? A policy of the provincial Ministry of the Attorney General that deemed such files not accessible to the public without judicial direction." That was the practice until the week of April 6, 2009, when Attorney General Chris Bentley lifted the restriction and acknowledged that "the administration of justice is strengthened by being open."

The court file is the institutional memory of a case. It contains details of the allegations(主张) and the alleged offender, and records every hearing held and decision made during a prosecution. Journalists use the file to check facts, dates and the spellings of names, and to find additional information about the case. Without it, complete and accurate reporting is difficult.

The policy change is also important to the general public who rely on the media to know what is happening in the courtroom and whether justice is being done.

Publication bans to protect the privacy of crime victims and witnesses are an exception to the open-court rule but were never intended to hinder media coverage. Ontario's policy transformed a defensible ban on specific information into an outrageous order sealing the entire file.

Freedom of speech and freedom of the press "depend for their vitality on public access to information of public interest," Justice Fish noted in his ruling. "What goes on in the courts ought therefore to be, and manifestly is, of central concern to Canadian."

Those should be words of caution to anyone who tinkers with a principle as vital as the openness of the courts. [105]

F. Elite Powers and Democracy

Democracy does not signify absolute equality. Equality like democracy is a value that is being defined and redefined on a continuous basis. The form and substance of equality will never attain their final or purest manifestation. It is essentially a morality of aspiration. The most progressive modern illustration of equality in liberal democracies include, at the most minimum level, one man one vote, equality before the law, equal treatment, and equal opportunity.

Power is never equally distributed in society just like the difference found in the intelligence, knowledge, efforts, personal quality, and wealth of people. There are leaders and there are followers. Elite power is simply a fact of life in any society.

---

[105] Dean Jobb, "Rolling Back Secrecy on Court Files", *Toronto Star*, April 9, 2009, p. A25.

Elite power decision prevails in both national law and international law. And examples are abundant. (106)

The most crucial issue concerning elite power is whether or not its coming into being and its continuous exercise are legitimate and with the bliss of the governed. What that means is whether or not it is in compliance with the law or other unusual but generally accepted forms or practices of legitimatization, whether it has accountability, commands trust, recognition, consensus of those concerned. When and only all such requirements have been met, elite power and its decision can be said not anti-democracy.

G. Equality before the Law: Equal Protection of the Law

Equality before the law is solidly anchored on the foundation of the first principle of democracy that no one is above the law, and fair and equal treatment by the law is the sine qua non of any constitutional democracy.

Equality before the law means that participation in the comprehensive process of the authoritative and effective decisions of the law is free of discrimination of any kind, regardless of sex, race, age, color, position, status, or wealth. Everyone is to be treated by the law in an equal manner. Heads of the state, such as president and prime minister can be summoned for jury duty or to testimony before the court or other adjudicative or investigating bodies. Bill Clinton was almost impeached(弹劾) for improper conducts in the White House during his presidency. Tom Delay, the House chairman, has been indicted and arraigned through the regular criminal proceedings for illegal campaign financing and money laundering. A House committee investigating the government's response to Hurricane Katrina issued a subpoena(传票) Wednesday to force Defense Secretary Donald H. Rumsfeld to turn over documents. When asked about alleged abuses under Bush, Barack Obama unequivocally said that no one "is above the law". Human rights and civil liberties groups have called for senior Bush administration officials to be prosecuted for a series of alleged abuses, from mishandling the conflict in Iraq to the illegal detention

(106) For example, what constitutes genocide and are the people Darfur victims of genocide are questions essentially decided by international elite powers. Top diplomats such as U. S. Secretary of State Colin Powell and Allan Rock, Canada's ambassador to the United Nations, have described the crisis in stark and urgent tones while deliberately avoiding use of the word genocide. UN Secretary-General Kofi Annan openly shared the same view. As a result, no action to stop the conflict has been taken by the world's major powers under the Genocide Convention.

and torture of terrorist suspects and domestic spying. On April 21, 2009, President Obama said that American lost its moral compass during the Bush years and left open the possibility that senior officials might be prosecuted for devising a flawed legal cover for torture.

Of course, there are in law many attenuated factors and circumstances that may be considered in the application of the law, for example, as in the case where benefits are granted to certain class of people in need of special help. Yet, any differences, deviations from the principle of equality must be within the reasonable limits of the law and judiciously(审慎地) applied.

Unfortunately, in actual fact, inequality before the law becomes a fact of life in many countries, even in liberal democracies. Celebrities, famous politicians, and even the super rich often easily got off or simply being given special treatment. For example, Svend Robinson, a well-known former NDP member of the Canadian Parliament, who pleaded guilty for stealing an expensive diamond ring, was only asked to do 100 hours community service instead of a jail term. The reason given by the judge is that Mr. Robinson has faced public humiliation, been vilified and embarrassed, lost his hob and the opportunity to do what he does so well. Mr. Robinson's lawyer calls his theft "a cry for help."

On the other hand, Martha Steward, the United States style guru, began serving a five-month prison sentence in West Virginia on October 9, 2004. She was convicted in March for obstructing justice and making false statements to federal agents investigating her sale of nearly 4,000 shares in ImClone Systems, a biotechnology company. There was no special or preferential treatment for her because of wealth and celebrate status. She was treated just like other prisoners.

The notion of equality should be appreciated in the same way as democracy. Unless and until we find some means by which equality can be defined and administered, we do not know the meaning of equality itself.[107]

This principle has led to many spectacular judicial developments in a variety of fields. For example, to artificially delimit electoral districts in order to derogate from equal representation of all citizens was prohibited. Legislation allowing unjustifiable discrimination based on sex was struck down. The equal legal status of legitimate and out-of-marriage children was required. More importantly, the "separate but equal"

---

[107] Lon L. Fuller, *The Principles of Social Ordering*, Durham. N.C., Duke Univ. Pr., 1981, p.62.

principle in education in segregated schools in many southern states has been rejected. It now requires the law to be color and race blind. One wonders how to rectify the inequality in the 2004 November Presidential election in the United States in that the country was even more split among politically polarized regions and millions of disenfranchised voters resided in the already decided areas? If that is the way democracy works, then that is a skewed democracy.

One recent outstanding example in this respect that is worth of special mention concerns religious arbitration for ethnic minorities in Canada. Justified by the fundamental principle of equality under the law and under the banner of one law for all Ontarians, Premier Dalton McGuinty solemnly announced that Ontario will ban all religious arbitrations including those long been practiced by Christians and Jews while disallowing the demands for Sharia—Muslim religious law—to decide family-law matters.

Equality of the law has it positive, empowering requirements as well as its negative, protective aspects. The notion that nature is just is faulty. Both Hart's conception of justice as fairness in the sense of equal concern and respect and Rawls' structure of a system of justice from the original position and behind the veil of ignorance and his equality of opportunity strongly speak the positive, empowering requirements.

Genuine equality requires taking into account of relevant differences as well as relevant similarities. Justice that is based solely on similarities and communalities at the exclusion or sacrifice of differences is a kind of truncated justice. In this respect, good lession can be learned from for example, Rawls's counterfactual contractarian conception of justice reached at the original position and behind a veil of ignorance, Hobbes's imaginary state of nature contractarianism, Kant's universal moral imperatives—a sort of solipsism(唯我论), and Habermas' dialogical (dialective) communicative action that both establishes and validates consensus. *

The crucial question is to have all men, given the necessary resources and opportunity, to excel in life, preferably on a continuing basis. Lincoln said: the civil war is a struggle for maintaining in the world that form and substance of government whose leading object is to elevate the conditions of means, by lifting artificial weights from all shoulders, to clean the paths of a laudable pursuit for all, to afford all an

---

* 在这方面,我们可以从以下范例中学到很多,例如罗尔斯的反事实契约性正义观念,霍布斯的自然状态契约论,康德的普遍道德要求理论和哈贝马斯的已经建立并得到验证的对话沟通行动概念。

unfettered start and a fair chance in the race of life. If justice of this positive nature requires redistribution of assets, rights, etc., so be it.

What needs to be zealously guarded is Tocqueville's "soft dspotism(温和专政主义)," an immense protective power that secures enjoyment, is thoughtful of detail, order, and watches over every aspect of men's fate, and to keep them in perpetual childhood. [108]

Everyone may be equal before the law, but justice comes only if you have money. In Canada, while everyone enjoys a basic medicare under a universal system, justice is still just an aspiration for most of Canadians. There are only two groups of people who can enjoy justice: the rich because they have money and the very poor because they have legal aid. For most Canadians, justice is like a Ferrari: You can have it if they sell the house. In Ontario, for example, to charge an elected official, such as a city councilor, a school trustee, or the major, with a breach of the municipal conflict of interest law would be a daunting process that is too expensive, and with a system too stacked in favor of the elected official.

However, politics and pragmatism(实用主义) do play a significant role in the political life. Even a fundamental principle, such as the equality before the law, may, on occasion, be compromised by the politics of authoritative and effective decision. It has been critically observed that Barack Obama;s administration appears to have been blindsided by the torture furor, which threatens to overwhelm his ambitious political agenda. The President is being assailed from the left and the right for his handling of memos of detailing the Bush administration's authorization of waterboarding and other extreme techniques on terrorist suspects. He subsequently appears to regret his willingness to accept a so-called truth commission to investigate the issue, fearing it will suck up the political oxygen in the capital. As Obama tries to navigate between ideological polar opposites, the question is whether he can keep his health-care, environment and other priorities on track, even as Congress becomes increasingly obsessed with the who authorized what, and who's to blame. Now, Obama can only hope that the torture issue eventually blows itself out, allowing Congress and the administration to move ahead with his agenda. Past experience, however, suggests that nothing incites ideologues of all stripes like a knock'em-down

---

[108] *Democracy in America*, Vol. 2, pt. 4, Ch. 6, p. 692; Walter Berns, "Justice as the Securing of Rights." In: *The Constitution, the Courts and the Quest for Justice*, Ed. Robert. A. Goldwin & William. A. Schambra, editors, Washington, D. C. American Enterprise Institute for Public Policy Research, p. 40.

fight over who did what in the war on terror.[109]

H. Timely Access to the Court

Access to justice, manly the court, is a fundamental right. In countries of constitutional democracy, it is constitutionally protected. Nobody should be denied the right to defend oneself. The right to have one's day in the court is deeply entrenched in the American popular culture. So is the right to sue, the right to <u>due process(正当程序)</u>, to go to the courts for redress for wrong, injustice, or other reasonable <u>grievance(申诉)</u>. Any scheme that purports to shield wrongdoers form potential lawsuits should be highly questioned. A recent test case on this very issue in Canada is the constitutionality of a restructuring plan for the $32 billion worth of non-bank, asset-backed commercial paper that grants <u>immunity(豁免权)</u> against third parties. Leave to appeal a decision of the Ontario Court of Appeal will be requested of the Supreme Court of Canada to contest the ruling that upheld the retooling plan by backing a lower court's finding that it was both fair and reasonable.

The right to a trial within a reasonable time protests the innocent because there can be no greater frustration imaginable for innocent persons charged with an offence than to be denied the opportunity of demonstrating their innocence for an unconscionable time as a result of unreasonable delays in their trial.

The war power of the United States President to classify suspected terrorists as enemy combatants to be held indefinitely without being charged and without access to counsel and the court of justice to defend themselves, is the most egregious attack on the constitutional principles of due process. It assaults frontally the most basic values of human dignity.

Justice delayed is justice denied. Timely access to the court and counsel is one of the fundamental rights of citizen in constitutional democracy. This requirement applies equally to <u>bail hearing(保释听证会)</u>. An excessive delay caused by unreasonable backlog for example in bail hearing amounts to a denial of fundamental justice. This is also one of the requirements of procedural justice. A case may unreasonably mired in legal molasses due to institutional causes such as shortage of courts, judges or physical resources as well as judicial over-caution, defense tactics.

---

[109] John Ibbison, "Obama Can Only Hope the Torture Flap Blows Over before It Blows Up His Agenda", *The Globe and Mail*, April 24, 2009, pp. A1, A12.

What eats up the clock may be the preliminary hearing(预审) or pretrial motions (审前动议). Adding to the problem is that judges go to extraordinary efforts to cover every base in order to protect their own integrity and reputation. There may also be instances in which an accused is not interested in exercising the right to a trial within a reasonable time. Such procedural molasses work to push the virtuous British adjective law(英国程序法) to an unreasonable extreme. At any rate, unreasonable delay in the delivery of justice may have serious consequences on the justice system and its participants, police, prosecutors, defense lawyers, judges, those accused, victims and their families and witnesses. For example, as a consequence of a ruling by the Supreme Court of Canada in the 1991 Askov case, 50,000 plus criminal charges in the Province of Ontario were dismissed on the basis of unacceptable delays.

Timely access can be severely hampered by ineffective and inefficient operation and function of the judicial system in terms of collection and dissemination of judicial data and information. Justice James Farley, retired, scathingly pointed out that Canadian courts are technology starving. They are not able to electronically process the ever-growing mountains of data that are introduced as evidence in most civil lawsuits facing the exploding volume of complex data communicated via e-mail as evidence. Instead, they continue to rely on traditional means of printing and shipping services.

The recommendations of a recent report by a former top judge, Patrick LeSage and University of Toronto law professor, Michael Code aiming at reining sprawling cases decries the fact that criminal courts in Canada are reeling under the weight of timid judges who fail to enforce order in their courts, inexperienced lawyers and Byzantine legal procedure(拜占庭[东罗马帝国]法律程序). The cause for this unfortunate state is what it is called a "complacent culture," which permeated the court system. As a result, judges and lawyers simply subscribe to a belief that marginal legal motions, endless cross-examination, and repeated adjournments are perfectly permissible. Their proposed answers to the problems identified are particularly enlightening. To deal with obstreperous prosecutors or defense lawyers who disrupt, obstruct, and refuse to make concessions, their solutions include: having strict judges who rein them in; enforcing misconduct charges by the Law Society of Upper Canada; to solve the problem caused by inexperienced or incompetent defense counsel being paid by Legal Aid(法律援助), who unduly string out and complicate cases, they suggest we provide financial incentives to attract senior layers to these cases; tight control by Legal Aid of who gets these cases, and how they conduct the defense; Their solution for ill-advised charges laid by police is to locate prosecutors in police stations to provide advice as a case develops; For prosecutors who are close-minded or overly antagonistic toward the defence, the solution is to better prosecutorial hiring practices; To counter late disclosure of evidence to the defense by police and Crowns, they suggest strict deadlines, and embracing new technology and judicial intervention. (One remedy suggested among others is to entice senior lawyers back to the legal aid plan by creating a special category of counsel who would qualify for considerably higher hourly fees. ⑩

In the case of Maher Arar suspected but not yet accused of terrorism, his lawyer repeatedly told a panel of 12 judges that Mr. Arar was a victim of an intentional conspiracy, one that reached to the highest levels of the U. S. Justice Department (美国司法部) and the Federal Bureau of Investigation(联邦调查局), the end run around the law as made specifically to outsource torture, and that the U. S. officials intentionally attempted to keep Mr. Arar from the courts by scheduling a lengthy removal interview and made only the most perfunctory attempt to contact a defense lawyer.

Equal and timely access to the court of justice is very much a morality of aspiration. Here the principle of fairness, equal concern and respect has to be strictly applied. One of the requirements in this respect is to level the playing field in order to accord all parties in a dispute a reasonably comparable opportunity as well as ability to have a fair trial in terms of representation as well as persuasion. In this sense, the concept that the rich and powerful can buy more justice in the sense of quicker and favored access is a troubling one. The concept of a fair trial, though closely relates to the issues discussed here, is another important constituent conducive to the building of a good legal system. The admission and exclusion of evidence play a crucial role in this respect. Generally speaking, any evidence that is obtained by a contrived and brazen breach of the defendant's constitutional rights should be inadmissible. In Canada, three cases, R v. Harrison, R v. Grant, and R v. Shephard among others are presently before the Supreme Court of Canada that are

---

⑩ "What Ails Criminal Courts", *The Globe and Mail*, Nov 29, 2008, p. A10.

seen as a springboard to modernize the all-important section of the Charter of Rights and Freedoms that applies to excluding evidence. The existing tests require judges to balance such factors as the severity of the police misconduct, the important of the tainted evidence to the Crown's case, the way a search and seizure is conducted, and the expectation of privacy an individual would have in the location where the search takes place.

For discussion on the independence of the judiciary and political interference in the administration of justice—Please Refer to Status and Role of Judges in Good Legal System in a later section of this Chapter.

I. Non-retroactive Application of Legislation

As a general, introductory piece, the following is sufficiently informational.

The bill that the U. S. House of Representatives has passed to claw back 90 per cent of bonuses to employees of bailed-out corporations is based upon well-founded indignation, but it should not serve as a precedent to justify future retroactive legislation.

President Barack Obama, who is well-versed in constitutional law, knows that the U. S. Constitution contains clauses that might raise questions about the bonus bill: provisions forbidding ex-post-facto laws, archaic, confiscatory " bills of attainder(剥夺公民权法案)" and impairment of the obligations of contracts(损害合同义务).

The case law that has grown up around these clauses is complex. Over two centuries, the U. S. federal courts have muddled them—as courts are apt to do—narrowing the ex-post-facto clauses that prohibit retroactive statutes, while greatly widening the bill-of-attainder clause, as if in compensation. The once-mighty contract clause, for its part, waned long ago.

What matters, though, is the principle, well articulated in the Federalist Papers, the political-science classic by James Madison, Alexander Hamilton and John Lay, when they argued in 1788 for the ratification of the U. S. Constitution.

"Bills of attainder, ex post facto laws and laws impairing the obligations of contract," wrote Madison "are contrary to the first principles on the social compact, and to every principle of sound legislation."

Madison warned against the propensity of legislatures to get overexcited, with "fluctuating policy..., sudden changes and legislative interference."

That was a much finer hour for Madison than when as president he yielded to the clamor of "war hawks" in Congress, authorizing the invasion of Canada in 1812, which was fortunately repelled.

Later in the book, Hamilton likewise wrote against "the subjecting of men to punishments for things which, when they were done, were breaches of no law."

As for attainder, that was a confiscation of the property of the heirs of convicted and executed traitors in 16th—and 17th-century England, a favoured tool of the Tudors—higher stakes than million-dollar bonuses.

Even so, the principle against attainder has some bearing on the current controversy. Statutes that target highly specific groups of people are likely to be unjust and oppressive.

The Canadian Constitution has little to say directly on these matters, though "the principles of fundamental justice" in the Charter of Rights and Freedoms surely include a bulwark against retroactivity. Cabinets and parliaments can get carried away here, too.⑪

Section Four: The Virtue of Legal Simplicity

A. General

The concept, form, and content of a legal system can be approached from many different standpoints and perspectives. At the most fundamental, constitutive level, there is also debate between legal simplicity and legal complexity.

Richard A. Epstein(理查德 · A. 爱泼斯坦) in his Simple Rules for a Complex World mounts a vigorous advocacy for legal simplicity. He opines that it would be self-defeating or a disservice to a good legal system if there are too many lawyers and too much law. Law can be viewed as antithetical to a good society. Law flourishes whenever and wherever families, schools, churches and other social institutions fail. And the rise of law signifies and leads to a decline in morality. This is exactly the bit of the criticism of Confucianism(儒家思想) inflicted on the legalism(法家学说) of Han Fei Tzu in China.

Law necessitates lawyer. A large number of laws feed on a large number of lawyers. Working together, they constrain incentive and suck creative energy. When

---

⑪ "Backdating the Laws", *The Globe and Mail: Comment*, March 21, 2009, p. A20.

their number is excessive, lawyers tend to stimulate the <u>torrent of litigation</u>(民事诉讼) that, far from encouraging production, perpetuates an endless cycle of wasteful and expensive transfer payments through litigation and regulation.⑫

We would never let any opportunity of a significance slip away from under our critical eye. No doubt, Epstein's position and Confucius' criticism both adhere to a particular concept of law, that of the legal positivism. From the perspective of law as authoritative and effective decision, there is neither too much nor too little law. The law of authoritative and effective decisions manifests itself exactly in the normative relationships of a polite among people and between state and citizens in their infinite nature and varieties.

Legal simplicity goes hand in hand with limited government. In contrast with a government that overtaxes and overreaches, a limited government enables, empowers, confers people, rather than dictates to or pre-empts them; a government that, except on rare occasions, leads from behind rather than always has to be out front and centre; a government that does a few things well rather than attempts everything and succeeds in little.

In the economic and financial field, the so-called "Chicago School" of neo-liberal economics as represented by Nobel Prize winners Milton Friedman, George Stigler followed by Allan Greenspan, the former Federal Reserve Chairman, vigorously advocates the view that markets are best left to regulate themselves and require no oversight or transparency. And the libertarian think-tank, the Cato Institution advocates individual liberty above all else and decries most forms of government intervention.

Unfortunately, the 2008 financial and stocks markets' crash and the financial and banking markets' meltdown, necessitate, as a result, massive urgent governmental interventions and rescues plans. That these measures have to be made have strongly proven the falsity and fallacy of such theory bragged as the truth and infallible virtue. It is particularly significant that many financial institutions eventually had to be nationalized—a desperate measure that smacks of the practice of a central-controlled economy. It is rather ironical that John Kenneth Galbraith, the protagonist of "Progressive economists" passionately argues in writings that ignorance and stupidity most often decide great affairs of state and those in charge have no deep

---

⑫ Richard Å. Epstein, *Simple Rules for a Complex World*, Harvard Univ. Pr., 1995, p.14.

understanding of the economy. On the other hand, the libertarians, particularly of the American breed even argue that it was too much state intervention and regulation that brought about the present crisis.

Regulatory Failures: Regulatory failures are often cited as a forceful argument against big government and its excessive and invasive regulatory attempts. To encounter and deal with the historical economic woes, financial crisis, credit freezing, and other misfortunes, all originated from, and caused by, the burst of the housing bubbles due to wanton and explosive sub-prime mortgages lending(次贷危机), the Congress enacted in 2008 the so-called Troubled Assets Relief Programs (TARP)(不良资产救助计划).

The Congress-appointed panel overseeing the TARP program released a stinging report of the regulatory failures that led to the current financial crisis.

"The regulatory system not only failed to manage risk, but also failed to require disclosure of risk through sufficient transparency," the report concludes.

Among the report's recommendations are that future regulation include better oversight of systemic risk, reducing the potential impact of "too-big-to-fail" institutions; improved transparency through "better, more accurate credit ratings" and better regulation of consumer products, which would "curb excesses in mortgage lending." *

The panel's report also calls for the creation of executive pay structures "that discourage excessive risk taking."

The panel was created under the Economic Emergency Stabilization Act, which was signed into law in October and authorized the Treasury to spend up to $700 billion in propping up the financial system. The panel is known as the Congressional Oversight Panel(美国国会监督小组) or COP, and is headed by Harvard University professor Elizabeth Warren, who has been consistently critical of the TARP program's administration under former Treasury Secretary Henry Paulson.

The 78-page report includes so-called "alternate views" from one panel member, which include making the Federal Reserve the "systemic regulator."

The COP report also identifies three "highly technical issues" that have had a key role in the regulatory structure that need serious review by the agencies with

---

* 该报告的建议是:未来的监管应当包括对系统性风险更好的监督,减少由于巨型企业存在带来的潜在冲击,通过更好、更准确的信用评级和对消费产品更好的监管来提高透明性,从而达到遏制过度按揭贷款的目的。

oversight: accounting rules, securitization of debt and short selling. The report says COP also plans to "address financial architecture" in a future report.

CNBC.com has also obtained a copy of the joint dissenting views of Hensarling and Sununu. Though there is considerable overlap in the findings, their report places great emphasis on the failure to "consolidate, strengthen and increase regulatory oversight of Fannie [Mae] and Freddie [Mac], the two government supported mortgage companies that were taken over by federal regulators late 2008.

Their recommendations include reforming the mortgage financing system, through less government intervention in the housing market by entities like Fannie and Freddie, as well as improved origination and disclosure standards

Hensarling and Sununu also call for the merger of the Securities and Exchange Commission and the Committee Futures Trading Commission.[13]

The economic woes and financial crisis worldwide caused by regulatory failures have brought to the fore the debate over the virtues and vices of regulated capitalism (资本主义) versus the U.S. style of laissez-faire capitalism. In the 2009 Davos Economics Forum, this very topic has been heatedly debated. Both Russia and China pointedly attacked the regulatory failures of the U.S. Europeans prefer their kinder, gentler version of capitalism blessed by a universal health care, a more generous system of social security and a general principle of almost free university education.

Mired in indecision and uncertainty, the world's foremost gathering of the best and brightest in government and business failed to come up with any new plan to stem, much less reverse, the global financial meltdown. The five-day World Economic Forum in the Swiss alpine resort wrapped up Sunday in the same atmosphere of doom and gloom that it began, with a realization that the depth of the crisis is still unknown and the solution remains elusive.

To some, there is a need to do a fundamental reexamination of the whole global system. Yet, nobody at the Forum is yet ready to ask these kinds of fundamental questions such as a redesign of the global systems of banking, financial regulation and corporate governance. The idea of a "Global Redesign Initiative" was supported almost by every world leader who attended forum, from China's Premier Wen Jiabao to U.N. Secretary-General Ban Ki-moon.

---

[13] "TARP Panel Report Cites Regulatory Failures In Crisis", *Yahoo Finance*, January 29, 2009, 1:32 pm EST; A copy of the draft report, which will be presented to Congress, was obtained by CNBC.com.

"Wall Street made mistakes. Regulators made mistakes. Rating agencies made mistakes. Central banks made mistakes. Politicians made mistakes—we all did it. The blame game can go only so far. In the final analysis what is badly needed is to think through what is the proper role of the state and how the private, free markets system would provide the best path to prosperity without the devastating consequences of the boom and bust cycle.

In the Bernard Madoff $5-billion Ponzi scandal, a former fund manager who brew the whistle on Mardoff, first took his concerns and reports to the SEC in 2000 and was ignored and treated with scorn, refusing to return his calls. The senior editors of the Wall Street Journal declined to pursue his story. In his testimonies in the Congress, he ridicules all those, the regulators, the Wall Street Journal and some accountants involved in the scheme. With regard to the complex financial products, he said that "if you flew the entire SEC staff to Boston, sat them in Fenway Park, they would not be able to find first base." The SEC "is a group of 3,500 chickens tasked to chase down and catch foxes which are faster, stronger and smarter than they are." Feeling so frustrated with SEC's operations and conducts of its senior officers, one Congress committee member called the agency useless. Representative Gary Ackerman told SEC enforcement director Linda Thomsen that "we thought the enemy was Mr. Madoff. I think it's you."[14]

Yet, in defending the integrity and efficacy of the SEC, Donald Hoerl, director of the SEC's Denver office, said the agency has filed about 70 Ponzi cases in the last two years and has filed four cases since Madoff was charged in early December 2008.[15]

Only a few weeks later after the unravel of the Madoff Ponzi scheme, the 8-billion Stanford International scandal of greed and fraud was also exposed. This is another major blow to the SEC.

There is also the debate over rule-based versus principle-based regulation. While a strict precise rule-based regulation tends to suffocate or discourage initiative, innovation or creation, a principle-based regulation may be vulnerable to subjective interpretation, manipulation, or speculation. With regard to the economic stimulus

---

[14] Paul Waldie, "The Blew the Whistle and No One Listened", *The Globe and Mail*, February 5, 2009, pp. B1, B6.

[15] Karey Wutkowski, "SEC Says Magnitude of Ponzi Schemes Growing", *Yahoo Finance*, February 6, 2009, 12:17 pm EST.

plan, it is widely observed that Treasury Secretary Timothy Geithner did a great job in painting the broad strokes of the problem and laying out general principles, but it was a dig disappointment not to have more details. As a result, the markets plunged.

A crucial question is: would a modest government be politically marketable in the long run, particularly when its opponents offer more visible and activist government as a superior alternative? Difficult times necessitate extraordinary measures. The issue is not over-regulation but right and reasonable regulation. It must be admitted that it would be a Hercules task to strike a proper balance between private and public, state and markets, and the visible hand and the invisible hand. Here the intractable relationship between the notion of rule of law and that of rule of man appears to bring on an added dimension to the challenge.

Sensing the urgent need for a strong and timely regulatory action in response to the global financial meltdown and banking crisis, the International Money Fund(国际货币基金组织) or IMF urged a new system of government oversight of big hedge funds, private-equity firms and other financial firms whose failure poses a major or systemic risk to the global economy, along with other moves to dramatically widen the scope of international financial regulation. Specifically, IMF suggested that governments adopt a "binding code of conduct across nation" to coordinate how and when they would intercede in troubled firms, and how to share losses from major financial institutions that operate across borders. The IMF proposals are aimed at influencing the April 2, 2009 summit in London of the so-called Group of 20 members. The IMF plays a huge role in the international co-ordination of regulatory policy only. Each of the G-20 nations would have to enact its own rules comparable to the others for any enhanced regulations to operate effectively across borders. The White House and the U.S. Congressional leaders also want to reach a "conceptual agreement" on how to regulate systemic risks in time for the G-20 session. The IMF is endorsing a previous G-20 idea to have the regulation of major financial firms overseen by "colleges of supervisors"—essentially regulators from a financial firm's home country and other countries where it does business. Surely, regardless of the merits of an idea, there is always some dissenting voice. A former official of the Bush Administration alleged that such restrictions could backfire by limiting growth of innovative companies, and could reduce the flow of capital to higher-risk developing nations. ⑯

The test of legal simplicity is the great trade-off between social incentives and administrative costs. These could be understood to include all costs, waste, destruction, and other deprivation of values, human dignity, physical, material, or other intangible incurred during the entire process of law-making, application and implementation. ⑰

The other constituent of the foundation of legal simplicity is the improvement of incentives to human action. The goal of a good legal system must be the maximization of social improvements and wealth. The costs for the creation of some administrative structure must be smaller than the gains obtained from the improvement for desirable human incentives, individual and organized. The limitations imposed by the legal rules must be smaller than the freedom generated. In this respect, the school of law and economics, especially its thesis on transaction costs, may throw more light on the discussion.

Legal simplicity is not a movement back toward the state of nature. While the goal of a society without government may rightly be dismissed as utopian, the goal of a society with less government should be paramount. In the same vein, L. Fuller advocates the virtue of autonomous ordering of society. The discussion on non-state sources of law in the second chapter of this book should be examined for more insight.

Legal simplicity necessarily means less government and less law of a positivist nature as imposed by the state. Legal simplicity does not directly entail a normative deficiency in society. In any market-based economy, there are complex, sophisticated, and carefully deliberated networks of rules, principles, standards, either explicitly or implicitly regulating the conducts and decisions of persons, physical and corporate. These normative or customary rules and practices remain unwritten until they are stated or juridified in rule-like, formulaic forms by members of legal community, such as robbed bureaucrats(官僚), the judges, who have the insight to foresee the needs. The unwritten or customary rules and principles constitute the massive submerged normativity of the legal iceberg.

---

⑯ Bob Davis, "IMF Seeks 'Binding Code of Conduct' to Oversee Global Financial Players", *The Wall Street Journal*, later reported in The Global and Mail, March 6, 2009, p. B7.

⑰ For a detailed and exemplary account of such costs, see Epstein, op cit at 30 et seq.

B. Some Defining Elements of Legal Simplicity

Epstein advances six simple rules for a good legal system and argues quite persuasively for them. These are self-ownership or autonomy; first possession, voluntary exchange, protection against aggression; limited privilege for cases of necessity; and takings of property for public use on payment of just compensation.

The simple rules insight starts with well-defined rights to individual labor and talents. A strong system of property rights permits the intelligent use of natural resources and facilitates gains from trade in competitive markets. The rules of contract organize and promote free and beneficial exchange. The rule of protection ensures that the ownership of property does not become a club with which individuals beat, pollute, or defame their neighbors. The necessity principles and the just compensation principles allow a sensible social response to the coordination problem without running rough-shod over the rights of those persons whose resources are needed for social purposes but whose consent is not forthcoming.[19] When taking (appropriation) officially sanctioned for commercial or housing projects works to enrich excessively private project sponsors, it is either compensation unfair or system corrupted.

Under the taking rule, all forms of regulation should be subject to scrutiny of the rule of law. It is designed to subject every form of government restriction not only to judicial review of its constitutionality but also to the civil court for its reasonableness and fairness or adequacy(适当性) of the compensation. For example, relaxing by government the rules of trespass(侵权) may result in compromise or may damage the use or value of land. So are land tax and rental control.

These rules may be regarded as some of the first principles of legal conservatism (保守主义). They may also be treated as the basic rights of citizens in society.

Section Five: The Falsity of Legal Complexity

Conversely, legal complexity inexorably results from the pressure of innumerable special-interest groups and over-confident government and the view of legal instrumentalism. The fatal impulse in pursuing perfect justice is another contributive

---

[19] Richard A. Epstein, *Simple Rules for a Complex World*, Harv. Univ. Pr., 1995, p.139.

factor. Another cause is the false belief that the complex forms of regulation that work within small, voluntary groups can be duplicated in larger, impersonal social settings. Society with its plurality in interest, belief, value system and morality is not and can not be a family or group writ large as this operates by nature on the basis of benevolent and reciprocal interactions and sharing.

To advocate for complex rules that purport to obtain perfect justice is a grossly arrogant proposition. For the stance rests on a false, impractical belief that adequate and relevant factors, data, and information can be cost-efficiently marshaled and taken into consideration in a reasonable and appropriate manner to fashion just decision. The gains from seeking perfection are an illusion, for with complexity comes the opportunities for gamesmanship. Gamesmanship is part and parcel of social life so long as resources are scarce and individuals are motivated by self-interest. [19] All comprehensive legal systems due to their infinite rationalization and juridification lead to necessary paradoxical outcomes of simultaneous prohibition and requirement. This is because there are evidentiary problems and conceptual incommensurable factors that must inescapably plague any social coordination and dispute processing system. [20]

It may also be submitted that the rise of the modern welfare states has naturally led to the explosion and primacy of statutes. The multitude of the law is a direct response to the demand and expectation of people.

Whether one believes that the best society, economically and politically, would be a society mostly governed by a few wise men or the teaching of the classical liberalism(自由主义) of decentralized decision-making or not—the best systems maximize the freedom of the individual, subject only the constraints of others in the system—the human element is crucial.

Could it be that legal simplicity and legal complexity are in fact the two sides of the same coin? Small government ultimately leads to irrational laissez-fire capitalism and all its accompanied vices. The gist and beauty of capitalism is its inherent power of "creative destruction." A market economy will incessantly revitalize itself from within by scraping old and failing businesses and then reallocating resources to newer, more productive ones. This pattern of progress and obsolescence repeats over

---

[19] Id., at 38.
[20] Daniel E. Campos, *Jurismania: the Madness of American Law*, New York, Oxford Univ. Pr. 1998, p. 35.

and over again. Unfortunately, this continuous gale of creative destruction always takes place in the context of boom and bust, accompanied by untold sufferings and misfortunes.

Cycles of economic fashion are as old as business cycles. Liberal cycles are followed by conservative cycles, which give way to new liberal ones, and so on. Each cycle is triggered by crisis. The last liberal cycle of the New Deal associated with economist John Maynard Keynes was triggered by the Great Depression(经济大萧条).* The New conservative cycle was triggered by 1970 inflation with Milton Friedman serving as the economic guru. The new classical economics taught that governments should concentrate on keeping money sound and in the absence of egregious government interference, economies would gravitate naturally to full employment, greater innovation and higher growth rates. Economic moderates have criticized the lack of regulation and the failure of oversight on risky investments and careless mortgage lending, and called for even more bailouts. In response, libertarians argued that it was too much state intervention and regulation that brought about the crisis. The Cato Institute, libertarian think-tank argued that if it was cheap money that caused the housing bubble, then making money even cheaper is not the right way to go. In any way, throw good money to bad and reward risk-takers amount to encourage bad behavior that creates a moral hazard.

At issue is the oldest unresolved dilemma in economics: Are market economies naturally stable or do they need to be stabilized by policy? Keynes emphasized the flimsiness of expectations on which economic activity in decentralized markets is based. The future is inherently uncertain; investor psychology is fickle. The neo-classical revolution held that markets were much more cyclically stable than Keynes believed, that the risks in all market transaction could be known in advance, that prices will therefore always reflect objective probabilities. Such optimism led to deregulation of financial markets in the 1980s and 1990s, and the subsequent explosion of financial innovation that made it "safe" to borrow larger and larger sums on the back of predictably rising assets. The just-collapsed credit bubble, fuelled by so-called special investment vehicles, derivatives, collateralized debt obligations and phony triple-A ratings, was built on the illusions of mathematical modeling. Both

---

* 指20世纪第二次世界大战前持续近10年的全球性经济大衰退,它是20世纪持续时间最长、波及面最广、衰退最深的经济危机。该次经济衰退首先源于美国,其标志性事件是1929年10月29日的股市大崩盘(这一天被称为"黑色星期二"),但很快波及于其他国家。

have their characteristic benefits and costs. Liberal cycles, historian Arthur Schlesinger believed, succumb to the corruption of power, conservative cycles to the corruption of money.

The cycles in economic fashion show how far economics is from being a science. One cannot think of any natural science in which orthodoxy swings between two poles. A few geniuses aside, economists frame their assumptions to suit existing states of affairs, then invest them with an aura of permanent truth. They are intellectual butlers, serving the interests of those in power, not vigilant observers of shifting reality. Their systems trap them in orthodoxy. When events coincide with their theorems, the orthodoxy they espouse enjoys its moment of glory. Whey events shift, it becomes obsolete. As Charles Morris wrote: "Intellectuals are reliable lagging indicators, near infallible guides to what used to be true. "[22]

Big government even in constitutional democracies with a well-established system of checks and balances produces blind-folded "bailout-nation," such as what is being witnessed in the United States and many other countries in 2008/2009 in the aftermath of the U.S. sub-prime-mortgage collapses leading to world economic woes and financial crisis. No government arguably could be as big and aggressive as what is presently being practiced in the Unite States, when wholesale nationalization of some of the financial institutes and measured nationalization has already been or is being completed as well as strict and restrictive regulations clamped upon the Wall Street which symbols the most free market capitalism.

Perhaps, what is needed is a reasonable, strategic and effective balanced mixture of both systems pragmatically oriented to the needs of the time. To give one example, regulations for corporate governance should aim at both constraint and facilitation. Instead of the one-size-fits-all strict rules-based, check-boxes approach, regulators could resort to the flexibility of principles-based guidance in order to minimize regulatory, compliance costs and to free and enhance the power of corporations for positive and profitable contribution to shareholders and society at large. After years of pushing for smaller government and market deregulation, Mr. Harper, the Prime Minister of Canada, now presides over one of the most rapid government expansions in modern Canadian history on welfare-state entitlements, on training and on the bailout of the auto industries. The rise and fall of either big

---

[22] Robert Skidelsky, "The King is Dead. Long Live the King", *The Globe and Mail*. Tuesday, Sept. 16, 2008, p. A19.

government or small government intractably links with the conditions and needs of a society at a particular time.

One of the crucial issues that closely relate to regulation is the nature, suitability, and content of regulation. Economics by nature is dynamic and volatile and the issues are complex and fast moving—exactly the kind of situation the regulatory system has proven ill-suited to address. Therefore, the issues is really not state imposed regulatory guidance, discipline, and control versus markets self-generating spontaneous patterns of decisions and actions. Each has its proper role and function in the normative enterprise of the law. What is always and should be happening is mutual informing and mutual shaping. In many instances, regulation at best serves the role of confirmation, consolation, and declaration—a sort of official juridification.

Another latest example is the proposed public and private partnership to buy troubled assets of banks. The official plan would use government money to support private sector purchases of bad assets that are weighing on banks' balance sheets and keeping them from resuming more normal lending.[12]

Yet, It is important to note that even a good and timely balance of big government and free markets, public funds and private equities may not guarantee success. Right after the highly anticipated public announcement of the Obama's economic stimulus plan and the financial stabilization programs, the markets sell-off sharply. Whether or not such knee-jerk reaction will auger an uncertain and devastating future cannot be predicted at the moment. This is the dilemma of the law in terms of authoritative and effective decisions when prediction is beyond the horizon and conduct-guidance becomes difficult to come by.

Regulated Capitalism(调控下的资本主义)—Isn't this what China has been doing with her open-door policy in since 1978? Any mix and balance of state funds and role and private equities may become strictly controlled or highly regulated financial markets. When this is handled badly, fiascos happen as we are witnessing in the United States and many other capitalist countries. The situations much resemble a casino with a house rule saying if you win, you take the money, and when you loss, you don't pay.

Speaking on February 20, 2009 at a conference featuring Nobel laureates,

---

[12] Martin Crutsinger, "Official: Bailout Overhaul Likely to Include Private-Public Partnership to Buy Bank Assets", *Yahoo Finance*, February 9, 2009, 2:58 pm EST.

economists and investors at Columbia University in New York, Paul Volcker, a top economic adviser to President Barack Obama and a former chairman of the Federal Reserve, cited not only the lack of understanding of the global financial meltdown but the "shocking" speed with which it had spread across the world.

Volcker didn't offer specifics on how long he thinks the recession will last or what will help start a recovery. But he predicted that there would be some lasting lessons from the experience. While he assured his audience of his confidence that capitalism will survive, Volcker said stronger regulations are needed to protect the world economy from such future shocks. [123]

It is particularly relevant to point out that the distinction between legal simplicity and legal complexity is a fallacy and a misconception. The concept of legal simplicity and legal complexity are misnomers and irrelevant to the establishment of a good legal system. This disparagement of the distinction between them holds true unless one stubbornly subscribes to the positivist view that law comes exclusively from the state and that the comprehensive, complex, opaque interactions, relations, networks, and transactions, etc. that are crafted, forged, engaged and propagated by corporations, individuals, and other commercial and business entities are not law-generating.

The most crucial and essential point of the debate over the virtues and vices of big government versus small government is no doubt nationalization(国有化) versus private ownership and management. The unprecedented economic meltdown since the Great Depression and the accompanying collapse of the financial system worldwide that has been brought about by the unraveling of the sub-prime mortgages fiasco in the United States has brought the debate to the fore. Is nationalization of the banks the ultimate tool of the government to stop the continuing downward spiral of the meltdown of the economy and to rescue banks from collapse? In the face of increasingly mounting uncertainty, lack of confidence, and anxiety of investors and institutions alike, the Obama administration continues to believe that banks should remain in the private hands and the Federal government has no intention to nationalize any institutions. On the other hand, Nouriel Roubini, economics professor of NYU and chairman at RGE Monitor told CNBC Tuesday, February 23, 2009 that nationalizing insolvent US banks is the best solution to avoid a Japan-like

---

[123] Eileen Aj Connelly, "Volcker Sees Crisis Leading to Global Regulation: Volcker Sees Greater International Cooperation on Regulations Growing from Economic Crisis", *Yahoo Finance*, February 20, 2009, 6:29 pm EST.

scenario in which "zombie" financial institutions would eat up public resources while the US economy would teeter on the brink of depression. A growing list of prominent experts say at least partial and temporary nationalization may be necessary, including former Fed chief Alan Greenspan, Nobel Prize-winning economists Joseph Stiglitz and Paul Krugman, and former Fed vice-chair Alan Blinder. Senate banking committee chairman Chris Dodd has also acknowledged a seizure of one or more banks may be unavoidable.

Some believe that whether or not some of the U. S. banks have in fact been nationalized has become a matter of semantic. After having obtained a 36 percent of CitiGroup through a conversion into common stocks of the money used by the U. S. Government to bailout the Company, the board of directors and the operations of CitiGroup are virtually under the effective domination and control of the Federal Reserve.

What is most inspirational is that in launching the unprecedented, most comprehensive, stringent, and effective economic stabilization and recovery plan, President Obama said "the choice we face is not between some oppressive government-run economy or a chaotic and unforgiving capitalism." It is imperative is to create a new regulatory structure for 21st-century markets. Strong financial markets require clear rules of the road, not to hinder financial institutions, but to protect consumers and investors and ultimately to keep those financial institutions strong. The new structure of oversight will almost certainly insert the federal government more deeply into the economy. To help assure that taxpayers' money will not be wasted, the Federal Reserve as the lender of last resort in many cases must fully understand the institutions it insures and actively monitors them to keep their risk-taking in check. The overhauled regulatory structure must be strong enough to withstand both system-wide stress and the failure of one or more large institutions. President Obama also called for greater transparency, more uniform supervision of financial products, and strict accountability for market players who engage in risky behavior. Executives who violate the public trust must be held responsible. Other items tackled by the Congress include expanding regulation to hedge funds and exotic financial instruments, such as credit-default swaps, beefing up consumer-protection laws. The Obama administration is seeking a delicate balance between responding to populist anger against big Wall Street banks and knowing that a properly functioning financial system is vital to any economic recovery.

Section Six: Private Ordering versus State Law

The contrast between legal simplicity and legal complexity can be best appreciated when placed under the light of the distinction between private or individual decisions on the one hand and official and state decisions on the other. The factual assumptions underlying state legal rules or decisions are manifestly at odds with social reality. Only decisions or rule making at the individual or private level can best take into consideration of the different distinct features, characteristics or factors involved in the particular contexts, circumstances, and situations.

It is highly questionable to view only law posited by state as a formal means of social guidance and control, while looking upon social norms, moral principles, and religious precepts, etc as informal and at best supplementary. What is problematic is that such dichotomy seems to imply that written rules of any kind that are emanated from non-state sectors are not laws at all. Such a positivist view leaves much unsaid.

This is the insight upon which the superiority of private ordering or dispute settlement institutions, mechanisms and services is founded as compared to those at the state levels. When comparing private legal system to the state one, it has been submitted that the private dispute settlement and ordering is accommodative rather than confrontational in nature. In a private system, benefits and costs are largely internalized, procedural fault, if there is any, is more willingly to be ignored, and parties engaging in such ordering and dispute resolution have strong incentives to minimize future conflicts. On the other hand, state judicial or regulatory mechanism for dispute settlement or ordering is highly adversarial in nature in which benefits and costs are externalized with the most of them go to special interests. The state system is not hesitant to dismiss cases on procedural ground. Moreover, in the state system, abuses in all kinds and discrimination of different nature could be a major problem; the market favors the rich.

These advantages of the private ordering and dispute settlement mechanism can be easily incorporated into the state system, if the various decision-making authorities of the state only recognize these advantages and take proper action to implement the normative trends and expectations of the community.

To a significant extent, the common law tradition flourishes on this very truism. Judges make law by recognizing and transforming the material facts in cases into legal rules. And in some degree, legislation, delegated legislation and the quasi-judicial ruling by administrative and regulatory bodies can succeed in a similar fashion by making their decision openly and transparently to reflect social trends and expectations.

In some instances, private autonomous law preempts official state law. For example, prenuptial agreements unless blatantly unfair would be respected by courts even when they conflict with state or provincial law requiring an equal division of assets when a marriage relationship ends.

Law work best in silence. State law and especially the opinions of the appellate courts represent merely the tip of submerged iceberg, and indeed can only claim an insignificant part of the normative universe of the law. [124]

"Lawless" from the perspective of state law signifies only the non-application of state law. Lawless is not lacking of normative order. Lawless in the sense of non-applicability of state law is not chaos. Anthropologist Renato Rosaldo claims that chaos appear more as a trope for use in debate, an only half-revealed threat of what would happen if proper means of communications for mutual informing and shaping are available. [125] When government law is unavailable or undesirable, private options fill the void. [126]

Civil disobedience is not lawless; on the contrary, it is law generating. Civil disobedience when organized by elite powers in society constitutes public political moral action. Neither the authority nor the efficacy of such actions should be casually questioned and dismissed. In Canada, church often grants sanctuary(避难所) from deportation(驱逐出境) orders to people who have been treated unjustly or have had their lives put at risk by Canada's refugee adjudication system. In granting sanctuary, the churches are not calling attention to sanctuary itself but the flaws in the system, specially the lack of a merit-based appeals process. If as an outcome of such disobedience, the state changes its law accordingly, so much the better. If not, the political moral action of the church stands as the law on the issue.

The interactive relationship between state law and private ordering is much rich, comprehensive, and complex. The interaction is a constant, continuous, dynamic

---

[124] Paul E. Campos, *Jurismania: the Madness of American Law*, Oxford Univ. Pr., 1998.
[125] R. Rosaldo, Culture and Truth (1989) p.100.
[126] Bruce L. Benson, *The Enterprise of Law: Justice without the State*, San Francisco, Cal., Pacific Research Institute for Public Policy, 1990, p.321.

process. Sometimes, it is due to this interactive relationship of mutual informing and shaping that a final resolution of a dispute is reached. For example, in the Oracle-PeopleSoft merger case, the agreement ends an 18-month feud between the two that featured courtroom intrigue and pithy public statements, and cheered investors who feared the battle would distract the companies from their core businesses.

The private sectors may avoid, lessen, attenuate, or neutralize the force and constraints of state law. Even the lawmaking of a dictator commonly undergoes some accommodations to demands tacitly expressed in rumbling discontent. [127]

The truism that the state has no business in the nation's bedrooms " only partially and insignificantly describe the issues involved. The state has its own proper domain of regulatory normative concern, and competence. So does the society. A proper and judicious division of power between the private sectors and the state domain requires an extensive and serious study. A limited and small government may not be a bad thing.

It has even been suggested that state law has started to decline. State increasingly contracts out their services, functions, and other activities. With this trend, what used to be formalized in state law has begun to be taken over by private normative rules. State law in many instances is not only anti-democracy; it is anti-market. The smaller the role the state plays in our life, the bigger the private autonomous self-ordering. The function of the state power operates in inverse proportion to the working of the private ordering; the more is the growth of the market economy, the less is the role of state and state law.

On the other hand, it must be recognized that market failure does occur. History has proven amply so. When this happens, legislative regulation and intervention should be able to correct. And that is exactly what is being tried by governments all over the world in order to deal with the devastating damages brought upon the economy and financial and banking industry by the sub-prime mortgage originated in the United States due partially to regulatory failures. Of course, whether or not the "right and correct" regulatory measures would succeed this time around, only the future can tell.

It has been reported that John Trinkhaus, an emeritus business professor at Baruch College in New York, has spent more than a quarter of a century recording

---

[127] Lon L. Fuller, *The Principles of Social Order*, Ed. Kenneth I. Winston. Durham, NC, Duke Univ. Pr., p. 172.

the little decisions that people made in the course of a day. What he is interested in includes whether it was to stop at the stop sign, cut through a parking lot to avoid a traffic light, or bother with bottle-and-can recycling. Professor Trinkhaus, a professor of Trivia, believes that his compilation of weird facts and statistics may shed some light on contemporary values and normative expectation of authority. From the perspective of the law, the question is what legal (political moral) implications these facts and data may entail. As parts of the submerged landmass of the legal iceberg, such little decisions may very well cause a normative social reaction and set a new normative direction.

From the perspective of competing powers and authorities, it must be submitted that ultimately, the overwhelming power and authority of the state must be reckoned with. This is especially true in cases where the value of private ordering comes in direct conflict with the requirements of state law. For example, under mounting pressure from many concerns that the Sharia system of arbitration for family-law matters discriminates against women, both Ontario and Quebec in Canada have decided to outlaw such private ordering along with the ban of other religious arbitration that have enjoyed by Christians and Jews. Of course, such high-handed measure from the state can never rule out the certain disobedient practices on the part of hard-core religious believers to continue such arbitration while fully aware of the depriving consequences.

Yet, for private ordering to flourish, certain fundamental conditions and constitutive structures must exist and be fully recognized. Constitution decisions, such as the Bill of Rights or the Canadian Charter of Rights and Freedoms as well as a enlightened recognition of the proper role of public, government powers in an increasingly growing ethnic and ethical pluralism in society are essential conditions and requirements to prevent harmful state encroachment and private aggression.

Fuller distinguishes legal morality into morality of duty and morality of aspiration. The relationship between state law and that of the social sectors resembles in a way the relationship between duty and aspiration. Invoking the analogy of a kind of scale, Fuller sees starting at the bottom of the scale duties that are most obviously necessary to social existence and basic security and ending at the top with the highest and most difficult achievements of which human beings are capable. The crucial task is where to place the invisible pointer of divide. If the pointer is set too high, the rigidities of duty may reach up to smother the urge toward excellence and personal dream and substitute for truly effective moral action a routine of obligatory acts.[128]

Section Seven: Transnational Components of the National Legal System

There is an important transnational component in every national legal system. Every time when a decision or action taken by an international organization or by a foreign country that has a material impact or implication on another country's sovereign rights, values, interests, the transnational dimension of the national legal system comes to play. Treaties and other international agreements are also the law of the land according to the United States Constitution.

In the same vein, every time when the decision or action taken by the power elite of the United States that has transnational impacts, beneficially or deleteriously, the law of the United States kicks into action on the international plane.

In an increasingly globalized world of increasing interdependence and of mutual informing and shaping, the law of authoritative and effective decisions of the United States is bound to interact with those of the rest of the world. This is especially true in the field of trade and commerce. But interaction may also be political, military, diplomatic or in many other fields of transnational concern. Interaction may take many forms: unilateral, bilateral, regional, institutional as well as customary.

Nowhere is this interactive relationship more evident and significant than that found within the framework of the United Nations and the World Trade Organization, among other international governmental or non-governmental entities.

One recent example is the decision of the European Union to slap Microsoft Corporation with a fine of unprecedented size along with the toughest set of regulatory demands to weaken its anti-competition actions. Strong reactions have quickly emerged from a sympathetic United States government that may take trade or other retaliatory measures against the European Union.

The <u>International Court of Justice（国际法院）</u> ruled in a case involving 51 Mexicans on death row held in American prisons. The Court said that the United States had repeatedly violated the 1963 <u>Vienna Convention on Consular Relations（维也纳领事关系公约）</u>, which requires police to tell foreigners under arrest that they

---

[128] Lon L. Fuller, *The Morality of Law*, New Haven and London: Yale University Press, 1964, p.170.

have a right to contact their country's diplomats without delay. The Court ordered American courts to take an effective review of the convictions and the sentences. The Court has no power to enforce its rulings. But world public opinions and shame count. It was unclear whether American courts would heed the ruling and whether and to what extent the American government would go about implementing the ruling.

In the softwood lumber disputes between Canada and the U.S, the interactive relationship has gone on for years. In August 2005, the NAFTA dispute panel firmly dismissed claims by the United States that Canadian softwood exports are unfairly subsidized and damage the U.S. lumber industry. Yet, the U.S. government continues to refuse to comply with the ruling alleging that the ruling fails to deal with a 2004 decision from the U.S-based International Trade Commission(国际贸易委员会) that supports the U.S. position, although it is believed the said decision and other earlier decisions have all been trumped by the NAFTA conclusion. Consequently, Canada was talking about the need of resorting to litigation or trade sanctions to have her position validated. Other strategic leverages at the disposal of Canada include its rich natural resources especially oil that can be employed to effect decision. Other view the NAFTA deal is a dud as the very foundation of the trade deal-secure market access and binding dispute settlement has been destroyed by the U.S. action. Unfortunately, the WTO dispute settlement panels(WTO争端解决专家组) subsequently came out with an interim ruling in favor of the U.S. position. Although, the WTO and NAFTA rulings aren't so much contradictory as mutually exclusive as NAFTA panels determine whether a country is complying with its own laws, while WTO panels check adherence(加入) to international trade laws, any retaliatory measures taken by Canada must be pre-approved by WTO. Trade courts give and trade courts take away. Politics underlying the authoritative and effective decisions in question rules above all. Even WTO adjudications can be trumped by domestic politics. It is said that the U.S. lumber industry controls enough politicians in Congress, and contributes enough to the Republican Party, that its voice is more powerful than that of any tribunal.

One of the most important happenings presently evolving is the G-20 or G-2 (U.S. and China) summit economic meeting. In order to influent the agenda and the outcome of the meeting, many countries come out to forcefully advocate their ideas and propositions. For example, Prime Minister Stephen Harper says the G20 should see Canada as one of the healthiest economies in the world—where citizens won't face higher taxes to make up for profligate spending, where markets still function freely and where the banking system offers an example to the world. He positioned Canada as a model for fiscal policy, banking regulation and financial stability. China in the same vein suggested that her political and economic system has proven that she can deal with the economic meltdown and financial and banking crises more effectively and promptly.

On the question of whether economic stimulus should take precedent over effective regulation of the financial, banking and other sub-banking entities and what would be the best combination of both, basically three propositions have been advanced, that of the U. S. Great Britain and Canada for massive economic stimulus, that of the European Union for tough regulatory oversight, and that of the emerging powers, China, India, and Russia for reforming the International Monetary Fund and the World Bank in order to have a greater voice in running them along with help for the poor countries.

The outcome was finally out on Wednesday, April 2, 2009.

Leaders at the G-20 summit in London declared: "a global crisis requires a global solution." But that doesn't mean they are in agreement on just what the solution should be.

"We are undertaking an unprecedented and concerted fiscal expansion, which will save or create millions of jobs which would otherwise have been destroyed, and that will, by the end of next year, amount to $5 trillion, raise output by 4 percent and accelerate the transition to a green economy."

The words in the communique were strong but in reality the major countries did not pledge any additional efforts on government spending or tax cuts to boost their own economies.

Because of strong opposition from France and Germany, President Barack Obama was not able to achieve his goal of getting the other G-20 countries to commit to spending the equivalent of 2 percent of their domestic economy on stimulus efforts to boost jobs. That is a goal the United States has reached with the $787 billion two-year stimulus program Obama pushed through Congress.

The European countries argued that they had already made major commitments and did not want to risk exploding their own deficits the way the United States was doing. One European leader, Czech Prime Minister Mirek Topolanek, called U. S.

deficit spending a "road to hell."

"Confidence will not be restored until we can rebuild trust in our financial system."

Obama successfully deflected a push by France and Germany to create a "global regulator," something that the administration believed would represent an unwelcome foreign intrusion（非法侵入）into U.S. financial markets. However, the G-20 communique did call for tougher regulation in an effort to fill the gaps exposed by the current financial crisis, the worst to strike the global economy in decades. Many of the proposals track suggestions put forward by Treasury Secretary Timothy Geithner a week ago when he unveiled the administration's financial regulatory overhaul proposals.

"The era of banking secrecy is over." So is the Washington consensus, the Anglo-Saxon paradigm, the European model, and the market fundamentalism. The new era ushers in instead the Beijing consensus and the regulated capitalism.

The G-20 agreed to work together to shut down global tax havens where investors hide their assets, depriving their home countries of billions of dollars in tax revenues. However, it remains to be seen whether small countries that have benefited for years by operating such havens will respond to the increased pressure for more transparency.

"We are determined to reform and modernize the international financial institutions to ensure they can assist members and shareholders effectively in the new challenges they face."

The G-20 leaders pledged a significant expansion of resources for the International Monetary Fund and other international lending institutions—a boost of more than $1 trillion. They're not just writing a trillion-dollar check, though—much of the support would be in the form of credit lines from the United States and other wealthy countries that the IMF could draw upon if the global crisis becomes more severe and greater resources are needed to prop up emerging economies. The harder part of the G-20 pledge may come in reforming the IMF and World Bank, where growing economic powers such as China have sought more of a say in running the institutions for more than a decade. Such reform has been elusive given strong resistance from European nations that would likely lose some of the voting strength they now wield.

"We will not repeat the historic mistakes of protectionism(贸易保护制度) of previous eras."

The G-20 leaders repeated a pledge they made at their first summit last November in Washington to refrain from erecting new protectionist barriers during the current economic crisis. Economists see this commitment as critical to avoiding the mistakes that turned the downturn of 1929 into the Great Depression. Back then, country after country imposed trade barriers in an effort to protect domestic industries, only to see global trade plummet—which left all nations harmed. The problem with this repeated pledge: By one estimate, 17 of the nations at the Washington meeting, including the United States, have already acted to protect domestic industries during the current downturn.[29]

What is significant from the perspective of mutual informing and mutual shaping is how national law interacts with international negotiations and the ideas and propositions of other countries at the international levels.

When both the international component and the non-state component are equally considered as integral parts of the national legal system, the questions, issues, problems, requirements, considerations become much more involved, complex, and challenging.

Section Eight: Human Elements of a Good Legal System and Good Law

A. Rule of Law versus Rule of Man

The rule of man is the antithesis to rule of law. Both notions seem to have a well-established meaning. The rule of man signifies that the whim and wish of the man in power count as law. In such a system, there is no procedural justice, no systemic control, and no minimum moral requirements of the law and the legal system. This is at least the stereotype understanding of the notion. One wonders could such a polity have any normative system at all. Such a polity is usually found in a dictatorship(独裁政治), totalitarianism, oligarchy(寡头政治), and their modern variants. Such a polity requires the total loyalty and subservience of all

---

[29] Martin Crutsinger, "Meltdown 101: What G-20 Leaders Said—and Meant: Meltdown 101", *Yahoo Finance*, April 3, 2009, 9:36 am EDT.

mortal souls found themselves in it. Under such a regime, there is no legal obligation so-called; citizens are constantly under the gun of naked power, violence, and coercion. H. L. A. Hart ridicules such a regime as a gunman writ large.

The rule of law signifies the supremacy of law; all decisions and acts are subjected to the normative requirements and conditions of what is recognized as law in the form of legal rules, principles, standards, precepts, etc which are internalized by citizens willingly. Decisions and acts here are generally referred to those made by the state. Yet, when the concept of the rule of law is conceived broadly, whatever counts as legal decisions or acts should equally be subjected to the constraint of the rule of law. It therefore follows that not only decisions and actions made by the three branches of government, legislative, administrative, and judicial are regulated and constrained by the rule of law, but also all those made in the non-state or private sectors are similarly constrained.

Within the government, when applied to adjudication, the rule of law requires impartial and publicly established tribunals following established procedures that reasonably ensure, among other things, fairness, the right to a hearing before such tribunals, the independence of the judiciary, and minimal reliance upon subjective interpretation and discretion. In this respect, the overriding principle of habeas corpus and due process of law are paramount. In the same vein, it is submitted that the entire corpus of the rules or code of civil procedure are designed to ensure the requirements of the rule of law are satisfied and the constraints thereof obtained. Of course, the constitutive principles such as those enshrined in the constitution of a country go a long way to secure the legitimacy and validity of authoritative and effective decisions under the rule of law.

It can never be overemphasized that when and where the court cannot adjudicate independently, the law is often whatever the most powerful official within earshot says it is. In situations like this, individuals and companies must constant wrangle and second-guess. Certainty and predictability that are essential for conduct-guiding and planning are in short supply.

With respect to the decisions and acts of quasi-legislative and quasi-judicial bodies, it may be argued that as long as the rules and procedures governing the decision-making of such bodies are honored, rule of law prevails. The same may be said with respect to the legislative process.

The requirements mentioned above are all of a procedural nature. These are not concerned with the substantive quality or moral content of the rules. Hardly there is no country in the world that does not have a set of procedural rules governing government decision-making. In this sense, it is reasonably assumed that all governments operate under the rule of law. Even when measured against the requirements of procedural justice, such as Lon L. Fuller's "internal morality of law", hardly any state would fare badly.

Professor Friedmann offers a neutral concept of law by simply defining the rule of law to mean "the existence of public order. It means organized government, operating through the various instruments and channels of legal command. In this sense, all modern societies live under the rule of law, fascist(法西斯主义) as well as socialist(社会主义者) and liberal states."[129]

Thus, one author opines that in law-making, the rule of law implies some sort of constitutive structure to regulate and legitimize the process: rules and principles must exist to determine whether a law has been duly enacted or has passed some other test of validity.* Arguably, no substantive constitutional constraints are implied by the rule of law itself, except that law must aim for the characteristics that allow subjects to guide their conduct by it.[130]

Is it reasonable to assume that the concept of rule of law has no substantive connotations? Could the concept be devoid of certain minimum requirements or content of what is considered as constitutive of a good legal system? Is the concept moral neutral like a vessel through which anything passes? Are the rules embodied in Fuller's internal morality of law and other rules of a similar nature sufficient to satisfy the requirements of a good rule of law? Could the rule of law be bad as well?

The rule of law does not automatically prevent tyranny and oppression. For example, the bicentennial celebration of the U. S. Constitution was notably silent about the fact that the original document legitimated the enslavement of an entire race of people.[131] The idea that law binds the politically powerful and the governors as well as the governed is an unquestionable improvement over the abuses of whimsical and

---

[129] W. Friedmann. Law and Social Change (1951). p. 281.

* 因此,作者认为,在立法中,法治原则意味着某种规范调整立法过程的组织结构,存在某些规范和原则,从而保障一部法律得以适当的制定并符合其他有效的标准。

[130] Kenneth Henley, "Rule of Law", *The Philosophy of Law: an Encyclopedia*, Ed. Christopher Berry Gray, New York & London: Garland Publ., 1999, p. 765.

[131] See Marshall, "Commentary: Reflections on the Bicentennial of the United States Constitution", 101 *Harv. L Rev.* 1 (1987).

arbitrary tyrants. But that does not alone ensure that the rule of law is the rule of good law.[13]

Is it reasonable to submit that the moral conditions and content given at the beginning of this chapter form the minimum requirements of a good rule of law? Many of these questions are of a constitutive nature. Judges are the oracles of the rule of law and guardians of the constitutionality of law as well as administrative and regulatory action. Then should a polity trust judges with the responsibility of sustaining and promoting the rule of law? And even to the judiciary alone?

The rule of law is an idealistic, ambitious, loaded and convoluted concept. All governments in the civilized world aspire if not claim to be a state governed by the rule of law. And yet, many a state may be said to have failed to achieve the much-coveted status of a state ruled by law, not by man here and there. Unless the concept is completely devoid of moral content, a bar of moral requirement must be set. The higher this bar, the more states will fail in more instances.

Moreover, both the meaning and the application of law, that is, the very sets of rules and principles that are the material bases of the rule of law, are always subject to interpretation, distinguished or hijacked. There are a number of causes for this. The problem of uncertainty, unpredictability, indeterminacy, internal-contradiction of legal rules and competing or conflicting principles all work to cut deep into the vitality of the notion of rule of law.

Thus, the integrity of the law is not beyond question. The tenuous nature of the rule of law is unfortunately much illustrated by the heated debates, strategic communications, manipulations, and struggles among the opposing special, and lobbying interests and parties active in the nomination process of Supreme Court judges in the United States. This is so for no other reason than the belief that the rule of law that has so far been well established on certain social, political, and moral issues can be eroded to a significant extent by the voice and act of one single, new judge chosen. For example, in the nomination debates and struggles to replace Sandra Day O'Connor, special interest and lobbying party joining in the fray include, among others, the Alliance for Justice, the Coalition for a Fair and Independent Judiciary, the White House, big business, and battalions of grassroots groups, worried about everything from abortion to women's rights to religious freedom.

---

[13] Joseph Raz. Authority. pp. 211, 227 as quoted in Lynne Henderson "Authoritarianism and the Rule of Law", 66 *Indiana L J* 379, 399 (1991).

And it seems that the very institutional structure of constitutional democracy built in the foundation of the rule of law may work to erode the very integrity of the rule of law. Lawyers are engaged in law talk through both sides of their mouths. This is required by partisan advocacy in adversarial proceedings. In hard cases, the discretionary judgments made by judges sitting alone are most likely based on personal political conviction. Sitting in panel, judges decide by majority vote. This democratic decision-making method and the ex post facto justificatory nature of the supporting reason for decision speak volume to the tenuous nature of the rule of law and its intractable relationship with the rule of man.

Anecdotal evidences speaking to the significance of the rule of man in shaping the rule of law are abundant. In selecting Judge John Roberts, Jr. as the administration's candidate to replace retiring Judge Sandra Day O'Connor in the Supreme Court, President George W. Bush in his nomination speech said that in doing so, he put the majesty of the law in the human hand of a man. In the same breath, he reiterated his position and belief that judges should uphold and be faithful to the integrity of the constitutional law and should not legislate from the bench. What is left unsaid is rather the hurting truth that judges are the oracles of the law and he who holds the swinging vote in the court may impact the life of Americans for generations to come. The answer many are anxious to know is the question will Judge Roberts decide to overrule Roe v. Wade, the trend setting decision upholding women's right to abortion or work to erode the effect of the decision case-by-case overtime?

A latest illustration of the impact of legal politics on the tenuous nature of the concept of the rule of law is the Chrysler LLC's filing for bankruptcy. Deploring deeply the unfortunate event, President Obama castigated the more than 20 investment firms and hedge funds who demanded more money than Washington was willing to pay in last-minute negotiations. On the other hand, the fund managers who all own Chrysler debt, retured fire by accusing the U.S. President of flouting decades of bankrutcy law in his failed bid to force through a restructuring that would have avoided bankruptcy. And they issued a stark warning that by trying to bend these rules, the government has risked overturning the rule of law that has made the United States' economy stable and successful.

Another closely related issue is the validity of the dichotomy of law and politics. Three legal realist themes have been advanced in this respect: One strand believes there is a radical indeterminacy in law; another stresses the ideological foundation of law; the third group comes outright to claim that law is politics and legal decisions are political decisions. Should such claims be proven to be true, the notion of rule of law goes right out through the window. Could the rule of law idea still be redeemed? If yes, how? If the job could not be done by the rule of law itself, could we put our hope on the rule of man?

Man of law signifies completely the opposite. Law is not pre-ordained. Law in society is man-made. This is not a throwback to the rule of man. It is simply to recognize the truth that the rule of good man informs and shapes good law and good legal system. All participants in the normative enterprise of the law or all authoritative and effective decision-makers in the domain of political morality informs and shapes the law and the system. Thus, what does man of law, such as lawyers, judges, legal scholars, legislators, regulators, and all non-state elite power groups, entities, and individuals do, act or decide is a matter of significant concern.

In a way, the dichotomy of rule of law and rule of man is analogous to Fuller's distinction of morality of duty and morality of aspiration. He gives the following example to advocate the need for morality of aspiration. The President of the United States conducts with the advice and consent of the Senate relations with foreign countries, relations that obviously cannot be set by fixed rules of duty, because foreign relations involve decisions made by powers beyond the reach of our law. [134]

It has been said that the rule of law is most likely to flourish in a society where men may meet today to legislate their duties not knowing tomorrow whether they will owe these duties or be their beneficiaries. What is startling is the conclusion that the notion of the moral and legal duty can reach its full development only under capitalism and the rule of law would collapse in any society that abandons the market principle. [135]

President Obama in rejecting such "false choice" of safety or ideal, and with a strike of the pen, he completely erases the destructive legacy of George W. Bush. In a series of commands, President Obama ordered Guantanamo closed within a year, banned harsh interrogation—widely assumed to be torture—by Central Intelligence Agency operatives, outlawed secret overseas prisons and banned "rendering," the practice of sending suspects to third countries for interrogations that might be illegal

---

[134] Fuller, *The Morality of Law*, New Haven & London: Yale Univ. Pr., p. 170.
[135] Id., at 24.

in the United States.

Mr. Greenspan of the Federal Reserve of the United States is another example. He said in a recent speech, "during his 16 years running the United States central bank, he and his colleagues have no road map for dealing with their biggest challenges, such as the 1987 stock-market crash, the early 1990s credit crunch and the 1998 debt-markets crisis." Mr. Greenspan attributes the Federal Reserve's recent success to setting monetary policy according to "risk management" rather than rules. [39] Risk of management emphasizes the role and judgement of man.

The above statements are rather more of a premature, bloating nature than a considered rational reflection. The 2008 housing debacle as triggered by the irrational exuberance in sub-prime lending and the subsequent credit crunch (freezing) and banking and financial crisis worldwide have powerfully revealed the potential, inherent weaknesses and problems caused by imprudence and even criminal wrongdoings of man. Many view this chain of events as likely to signal the demise of the American brand of capitalism and free-market and call for the reconstitution of the world's financial institutions.

The theory of reflexivity by George Soros, the hedge fund legend, is based on a two-way relationship between the markets and market participants. In sum:

Instead of accurately reflecting underlying reality, the markets typically distort reality. This "mispricing" of the markets affects the decision-making of investors and policymakers. That, in turn, can impact the markets, further distorting reality and reinforcing how those same participants view it.

Unfortunately, where to locate this pointer of divide between the rule of law and the rule of man can only be determined on a case-by-case way.

In the most notorious and biggest 50 billions Ponzi (fraud) scheme in history as perpetuated by Bernard Madoff, it is generally agreed that the failures of regulation and private-sector due diligence are obvious; yet to embark on some broad new legislative or regulatory mandates on the rest of the securities industry may not be a right course of action. What we may have in the Madoff case is not necessarily a lack of enforcement and oversight tools, but a failure to use them. This clearly and squarely places the blame on the human element involved—the failures of career officials, commissioners, and their supervisors in the Securities and Exchanges

---

[39] "Greenspan sees economic recovery as vindication for Fed" Dow Jones Business News, *Yahoo Finance Website*, January 4, 2008, 11:10 pm ET.

Commission. Extensive investigations are focused on why e-mail warnings from dozens of current and former SEC officials were ignored; why a number of "red flags" missed; the relationship between Mr. Madoff's niece, Shana, who worked at her uncle's firm, and her husband, Eric Swanson, a former SEC compliance lawyer; and whether SEC staff were awed by Mr. Madoff and failed to scrutinize his operations.

B. Good Lawyer, Good Legal System and Good Laws

(1) The Legal Profession (Check sections on Philosophy of AAL study)

The "law job" or the legal enterprise or simply lawyering is basically a political moral act or undertaking. It is much more than a trade or a soulless unsatisfying handicraft.

The legal education and training that the law is formal, neutral, impersonal, and universal would not make all lawyers think alike like robots. Nor would initiation and association empty lawyers of their bias, passion, or personal commitment. To think like a lawyer should not unduly limit your normative horizon or truncate (diminish) your personal or professional aspiration. This contrasts with the observation that to think like a lawyer is to engage in a purely legal rationalization process. Rationalism necessarily separates the legal self from its contexts thus emancipating the self from all forces and influences other than the law itself.

Lawyer-politicians even as hired hands belong to opposing political camps or parties and have different agenda and hold divergent political and moral views.

Judges do not always agree with each other. Dissenting opinions are a rampant phenomenon in judicial decisions.

Jurists are free souls. They set their own research goals, belong to different schools of thoughts, freely select, from a jurisprudential(法学的) smorgasbord of normativity, orientations of their choice: formalism, contextualism, conventionalism (传统主义), pragmatism, or legal positivism, the natural law school and what have you, and live in their own worlds of law.

Lawyers are regulated by the states and are subject to the supervision of the Supreme Court of the respective state. Law professors and salaried legal counselors are not so. Lawyers generally can only practice in the state admitted professionally as well as before the Supreme Court upon payment of a small sum. All states normally permit a lawyer from another state to appear in individual cases in their courts. Most states admit to the legal profession of their states a lawyer who has practiced in another state for a given period usually five years and even to practice full-time. To allow non-state lawyers to provide legal advice within their borders has been tolerated—important for clients whose legal problems are national or across state lines.

About two dozen states permit graduates of foreign law schools to take the bar examinations. American Bar Association (ABA)(美国律师协会) publishes an annual guide to the bar admission requirements for all jurisdictions.

Notary Public in America is a person who has merely been confided the right to authenticate signatures of those requiring this service for some reason. He is not a lawyer. This is similar to "the commissioner of oath(宣誓)" called in some other jurisdic tions.

As a matter of general practice, it is admitted that lawyers may be remunerated in proportion to what has been earned for the client. This "contingent fee" practice is anathema in England.

ABA is open to any lawyer in good standing in his or her own state. It is a federation of state and local bar associations and other important legal organizations, such as the American Law Institute. It promulgates a model ethics code that influences rules of individual states, but has no disciplinary power. The Rules of Professional Conduct is the latest version of the model ethics code. And so far it has been adopted by three-fourths of American jurisdictions. Of course, the latest status of code should be always checked.

Lawyer's confidentiality obligations largely duplicate the substantive law of fiduciary duty(信托人义务). They address such issues as lawyer advertising, the organization of law firms, and conflicts of interests.

A lawyer charged with wrongdoing has a right to a hearing, entitled to notice of the charges, to be represented by counsel, to subpoena witnesses and evidence, to cross-examine(交叉询问) opposing witness, and to testify in his own defense. Disciplinary(惩戒权) authorities are empowered to impose minor discipline, such as private reprimand, while major discipline (disbarment[取消律师执业资格], suspension, public censure) is the responsibility of judges. Disbarred lawyer can reapply for admission after 6-7 years. Those convicted of criminal conduct will automatically be disbarred. The disciplinary process may be open to public after probable cause is identified.

There are state bars, and even city and county bar associations.

Judicial authority to regulate and discipline lawyers is inherent in the Constitution. This includes practice of law, advice or representation, appearances in courts, drafting, and counseling.

Law graduates hired by a law firm are allowed to choose which associates they will retain and promote to partner after a six-year or so probationary period. Those not chosen leave to pursuit career in government, corporate, teaching, or judicial fields. Many young law graduates begin their employment as an appointed state trial court judge or as an assistant district attorney. Solo practitioners are in decline.

(2) **Malpractice and Related Claims**

Lawyers could be suited for breach of contract, tort, and breach of fiduciary duty. Tort claims can result in remedies unavailable for breach of contract actions, including punitive damages(惩罚性损害赔偿) and damages for emotional distress (精神损害赔偿). Lawyers may also be liable to third parties injured by their clients if the lawyer helped the client cause the injury (e.g., to commit fraud)—an exception to the privity requirement. Not every mistake by a lawyer amounts to professional malpractice(渎职行为) or negligence, as long as reasonable degree of care, skill, and judgment has been taken.

(3) **Court Sanctions**

In addition to the risk of being disciplined and the risk of civil liability, any lawyer who acts improperly in litigation may be sanctioned by the court. Rule 11 of the Federal Rules of Civil Procedure(联邦民事诉讼规则) states that "a lawyer who signs, files, submits, and advocates based on a pleading or other document submitted to the court thereby certifies the following to the court: 1)...not presented for an improper purpose; 2)...non-frivolous argument for the extension, modification, or reversal of existing law or the establishment of new law; and 3)... allegations have evidentiary support..."

(4) **Effective Counseling and Advocacy**(辩护)

Criminal defendants have a constitutional right to effective assistance of counsel. The Supreme Court has held that counsel becomes ineffective if his or her advice is not within the range of competence demanded of attorneys in criminal cases. The test is an objective standard of reasonableness. The requirements include vigorously advocating the defendant's cause, consulting with him or her on important decisions, keeping him or her informed of important developments, etc. However, an ineffective lawyer acting in advocacy was rarely found by the court. Malpractice is another issue entirely. Once established and shown that there is a reasonable probability that, but for counsel's unprofessional errors, the result of the proceeding would have been different, the defendant will be entitled to a new trial.

(5) **Conflicts of Interest**

This rule has two specific aims: first, to ensure that lawyers will not act disloyally to a current or former client; and second, to ensure that a current or former client's confidential information will not be misused. Furthermore, a tax lawyer's conflict is imputed to all other lawyers in his firm.

There is also a rule that ensures that lawyers will not be tempted to exercise their dominance over clients to persuade them to make gifts to the lawyer or his relatives. Similarly, business transactions entered with a client must be fair and reasonable with terms fully disclosed to him in writing and in a manner reasonably understood, afford the client a chance to obtain the advice of independent counsel, and have the client's consent in writing.

(6) **Revolving Door Conflicts**

The revolving door is a metaphor for the common practice of lawyers who move between government service and private practice. Ethical rules and statutory law limit the ability of government lawyers to exploit their governmental connection and knowledge once they enter or reenter private practice. It also ensures that government lawyers do not choose the targets of their investigation because they anticipate being able to use their accumulated knowledge about those targets on behalf of private interests once they leave the government. American rules generally do not impute the conflicts of former government lawyers to other lawyers in their firms so long as the former government lawyers are screened from participation in the particular matter. Otherwise, private firms would be discouraged from hiring potentially promising former government lawyers and vice versa.

(7) **Confidentiality**

Protection of client confidence is one of the major goals. The communications between lawyers and clients or agents of client are privileged. All states recognize this. Exceptions include client waiver and communication in furtherance of a crime or fraud. The confidence rule also includes information that lawyer obtains about clients.

Three broad categories of exceptions can be defined:

American Bar Association model rules permit, but do not require, a lawyer to reveal confidential information "to prevent the client from committing a criminal act that the lawyer believes is likely to result the imminent death or substantial bodily harm". Some states even extend this exception to financial or property crimes as well.

Model rules permit revelation of confidential information when a lawyer for self-defense in disciplinary violation, in civil claims malpractice, is charged with criminal conduct, and for legal fee.

In a situation where a client lied on a material point during a deposition or during a trial, most states view lawyer's obligation to correct the lie is superior to the confidentiality obligation. Or when withdrawal from representation is not possible, a lawyer should take pains not to do anything in the representation that will help the client take advantage of the lie.

(8) **Adversary Justice**

Parties largely conduct their own investigations and determine the issues to be decided. The judge and jury are relatively passive, hearing the evidence and making a decision according to the applicable law. Judges superintend the progress of the litigation and ensure that the procedural rules are followed, believing that the right result or justice would more likely emerge. Also, the autonomy(自治) of clients must be respected. In criminal cases, prosecutors are required to provide the defense with any information that tends to exculpate the accused. When perjury is known to have committed by the client, the lawyer may not seek to exploit the false evidence. Though cannot lie himself, a lawyer is free to encourage the fact-finder (judge or jury) to reach a wrong conclusion or to discredit the witness even if the lawyer knows the witness is telling the truth.

(9) **Legal Fees**

Lawyers are free to negotiate fees with the client. Ethic rules require a lawyer to charge fees that are reasonable. Contingent fees are common in personal injury actions, but generally forbidden for public policy reasons in criminal cases and in matrimonial cases. In personal injury cases, the maximum is one-third of the total of the recovery. Contingent fee(律师的胜诉酬金) agreements must be in writing and filed with the court. The lawyer is also required to clarify what expenses, if any, will be deducted from the recovery before the contingent percentage is applied. After withdrawal with client's consent, a lawyer may charge fees for services done (retainer

［聘用律师费］ agreement).

(10) Lawyers Employed by Corporations

In-house lawyer, such as a law firm lawyer working on retainer to a corporation, works through and must take direction from, and provide advice to, its officers and directors. Lawyer also has responsibility to protect the corporation's interests from improper conduct of its officers and directors. Measures include reconsideration of the matter, report to the Board, and seeking outside legal opinion, etc.

(11) Marketing Legal Services

Until the mid-1970s, virtually all efforts by lawyers to bring themselves to the attention of the public through paid advertisements were prohibited except being listed in lawyers' directories and phone books. Since then, the Supreme Court ruling allowing legal clinic's newspaper advertisement has been extended to radio and television. Dramatizations are prohibited. Mail solicitation is allowed. False and misleading messages or assertions of fact that cannot be verified, such as the "best firm," are prohibited. Also prohibited is in-person solicitation like visiting the homes of accident victims uninvited (such as coffin chasing) except when solicitation is addressed to corporate bodies.

Although protected under the First Amendment's free speech guarantee, lawyers' advertising is deemed commercial rather than political. As such, it is not immune from state regulation. Using group purchasing power to obtain legal representation and services is similarly protected.

(12) Future Competition

Competition in the provision of legal services may come from the increase in the number of lawyers; paraprofessional handling routine, largely non-discretionary tasks; banks and accounting firms providing legal advice as part of a broader package; foreign law firms operating and having office in United States. And last, computers and advances in electronic communications, such as the Internet, coupled with the increasing globalization of the law industry may erode many of those rules. Outsourcing legal practice-relating services overseas is a growing trend in order to cut costs.

C. American Law Schools and Legal Education

(1) Objectives and Ideologies of Legal Education

Generally speaking, the following are the possible models:

Guild(同业行会) Training—It consists of socialization into a group professing a particular practical skill and the inculcation of this skill. This is an exclusive community.

Learned Profession—A model of black letter law learning for the tasks of lawyering—lawyers serve as the hired gun—the model of a legal technician.

Academia—As an academic community of jurists concerned with relevant knowledge derived from humanities and social sciences as well as that generated internally from legal doctrines—as law teachers or legal scholars.

Legal social engineering—work as civil servants. [139]

Legal Education in Broad University Intellectual Context versus Legal Study in Trade School

The legitimacy or the ratio d'etre for legal education to be taught in the university as opposed to be learned in a trade or professional school is the understanding that law should not be simply learned in a narrow, pedantic and scholastic manner. To be learned in law is not primarily a means of achieving certain required professional and technical capability and proficiency. Training in a trade or professional school is the very anti-thesis of the spirit of liberal education. In the broader perspective of a university, law should not only be taught as it is in the so-called expository tradition. In addition to the techniques and knowledge of lawyering, law is best learned in a broader university context of intellectual, philosophical and juridical pursuit of truth, justice, fairness, equality, freedom and other human dignity values.

More than training legal technicians or lawyers in the narrow sense as a profession, legal education should emphasize more importantly the philosophical, juridical, and critical faculty of learning. It performs more than the simple service tasks.

One of the fundamental questions in this respect is how comprehensive and inclusive should legal education be? Is it desirable, appropriate, or reasonable to adopt a universalist, polyjural approach to legal study as opposed to a national, monojural one? The normative nomos of polyjural approach includes search for authority and reason. It compasses official, positive sanction-based sources as well as private, unofficial, unwritten materials. Its geopolitical reach is national,

---

[139] B. S. Jackson, "British Legal Education", 81 *L L J* 667 (1989).

international, and transnational.

(2) Case Method

The first law school evolved out of law office that took in apprentice clerks for a fee. This practical education was supplemented with lectures roughly following Sir William Blanckstone's Commentaries and with periodic examinations. In 1871, a lasting transformation by institutionalizing legal education within the university tradition as the European did was initiated at the Harvard Law School. The case method education was introduced with the publication by Professor Christopher Columbus Langdell* of his casebook on contracts, an ordered collection of cases consisted of appellate court opinions. Langdell believed that the shortest and best way of mastering the few basic principles on which the law is based was by studying the opinions in which they were embodied. With this method, the traditional lecture method was abandoned. As the cases the student was required to read may come from different jurisdictions and contain inconsistent or divergent findings and holdings, the student should take a comparative approach and evaluate conflicting rules in the context of an actual situation.

Of course, to believe that all the law could be learned from cases is a bad mistake. Legislation has increasingly been assuming a central role in the life of people. This Socratic dialogue form of teaching method soon was to be supplemented by the lecture method.

And the so-called casebooks have been supplemented by text of legislation, extracts of legal writings, legal forms, and even materials from other disciplines such as economics, philosophy, sociology and history, etc. The stress remains on reading case analysis, identify problems, issues, questions, synthesis, legal reasoning, and the application of legal principles. Active class participation in discussion is favored. This casebook instructional method is justified as a scientific process to elaborate the general, organic principles of the Common law. Today, more and more clinical method is adopted for real life experience within a legal aid organization and under the supervision of a lawyer who also serves as a professor.

In tune with the limitations of the case method of teaching and the increasing importance of legislation as well as the transnational dimensions of <u>domestic law(国内法)</u>, the content of the curriculum has been considerably enriched. Now it is a

---

* 克里斯托弗·哥伦布·郎德尔,哈佛大学前法学院院长,于 1870 年任院长期间最早将案例教学法应用于法学教育中。

common practice for law schools to include in their instruction major subjects such as constitutional law, administrative law, family law, labor law, etc and even subjects in the fields of business and commerce, in the international domain, public and private, as well as post-modern theories of law.

Among the philosophical ideas and insights that inform legal education, the so-called "law and" or interdisciplinary approach and research seems to have drawn particular attention. A quick glance at the handbook published each year by law schools which details the courses offered and the outline thereof, one would see a great variety of lectures in the "law and" variety offered as elective to interested students.

The establishment of the American Bar Association (ABA) (1900) and Association of American Law Schools (1970) brought a substantial degree of uniformity by setting national standards and in the case of the ABA by achieving accrediting power. There are detailed standards for student admission (the LSAT), duration of the J. D. programs, faculty and student body diversity, faculty qualifications, school governance, curriculum, library, physical facilities, and financial resources.

Beneath the façade of uniformity implicit in a successful effort to raise the nationwide standards lies a rich diversity. Most has been striven by private law schools in terms of programs and subjects specialization as well as promising career opportunities.

(3) **Appraisal and Criticism of American Legal Education**

It is safe to say that from Langdell to the present, legal education has never seriously attempted to incorporate moral principles into instruction. This may be attributed to the heavy influence of the positivist paradigm that law is essentially moral-neutral. The ordinary religion of the classroom consists of:

a) A skeptical attitude toward generalizations;

b) An instrumental approach to law and lawyering;

c) A tough-minded and analytical attitude toward legal tasks and professional role; and

d) A faith that man by the application of his reason and the use of democratic processes can make the world a better place. [38]

---

[38] J. Cranton, "The Ordinary Religion of the Law School Classroom", 29 *J Leg Edu* 247, 248 (1978).

Law teachers stress cognitive rationality along with hard facts and cold logic and concrete realities. ⑬ Law is taught in an objective, conceptualistic fashion, tempered with socio-economic commentary. The law primarily based on the Western moral tradition of Judeo-Christian values is regarded as fundamentally fair and right regardless of the immorality in individual laws. ⑭ Context and interdisciplinary approach is notoriously lacking in instruction—too much is presented with little or no context, abstracted from history, economics, philosophy—from life as it is. An interdisciplinary approach to enhance a student's understanding of how and what is learning fits into the larger picture of the world around us is advocated to broaden the scope and dimension of legal education. ⑭

(4) The Conditions, Qualifications, and Requirements of a Good Lawyer

When law is viewed as the display and expectation of authoritative and effective decisions, a good legal thinker and actor taking on the role of an elite participant in the decision-making process become indispensable.

Whether at the original stage of constituting and establishing a good legal system or for its healthy development, the role of good lawyers is indispensable. Lawyers are much more than the officers of the court. This is essentially the conception of the legal positivists who unduly emphasize the importance of the judicial branch of the government in ordering human conduct to the governance of law. Lawyers who aspire to play an influential role in the health of the legal normative enterprise of society actively participate in very stage of the comprehensive process of the authoritative and effective decision-making. Lawyers who conceive their role in this way would play conscientiously and forcefully their role in legislation, regulation, policy-making, administrative direction and guidance, negotiations for autonomous ordering arrangements of individuals, corporate entities, organized efforts including mediation, contracting, and the simple planning of an orderly life.

To competently take on the challenges associated with such a comprehensive role, a good lawyer must equip with certain specific knowledge, skills, and personal quality. The following may serve as a starter:

- Adequate knowledge of the basic legal rules and principles;
- Good research skills and competence to ascertain legal authorities;

---

⑬ Id., at 1027.
⑭ P. G. Haskelf, "Teaching Moral Analysis in Law School", 66 *Notre Dame L R* 1025 (1991).
⑭ Haywood Burns, "Legal Education in the Next Century", *New York Bar J* 54, 56 (My/Jun 1991).

- Good investigative ability to discover and analyze facts and factual situations;
- Superior interpersonal skills necessary to communicate effectively; and
- Superior analytic skills and reasoning faculty.

It goes without saying that professional education is the very basic requirement for being a good lawyer. But the possession of such basic education and knowledge does not necessarily elevate one to the status of a good lawyer. Then, the question naturally follows is what are the additional requirements that are needed to launch one up the trajectory to the status of a good lawyer?

Doubters of law and legal reason believe that the American law school is a professional cartel, "a seiminary for the production of a mystifying priestcraft, whose obscurantist incantations help legitimate the power of the social and cultural elite. In academic terms it is a mostly fraudulent operation that teaches neither theory nor practice."[42]

Perhaps, what is needed is for lawyers and legal education to take a broader and more inclusive view of what counts as law. The contextual, sociological policy approaches to law and the "law and" insights all go a long way to broaden the scope and dimension of law and to bring the received formalist concept of law in conformity with the actual law operating in a society.

How to Measure the Success of Legal Practice:

There are at least six criteria that are often used to grade the success of legal practice. These are: understanding the client's goals; expertise; efficiency; responsiveness; predictive accuracy and effectiveness. While each of these criteria can be further elaborated, suffice it to say that the ordinary and plain meaning of these terms would serve well most practical purposes. No doubt, satisfactorily fulfillment of the requirements, qualities, and conditions discussed above would go a long way to ensure one's successful passage to being a good lawyer.

(5) Personal Qualification and Experience

In tune with the broader perspective of what makes a good lawyer, does personal experience or qualification in a particular field or area elevate one to the rank of a good lawyer? Or in the final analysis, personal experience or qualification in any of special area is no substitute for the disciplined study essential to achieving expertise.

But training and knowledge is a progressive endeavor. Could any lawyer do as

---

[42] Paul E. Campos, *Jurismania: the Madness of American Law*. Oxford Univ. Pr., 1998, p.175.

good a law job as one who is more experience in law, possesses superior knowledge of a particular field, or has gained an extensive understanding of the issues, subjects, problems that are involved? It appears utterly counter-intuitive to argue affirmatively.

The discussion on trial delayed is justice denied under Section three H earlier in this Chapter should throw more light on this matter.

(6) Impartiality (公正), Strong Sense of Responsibility, Empathy, Open-minded (开放式思维)

In a heterogeneous world of moral pluralism and value diversity, and different knowledge bases and life experience, the demand on a good lawyer is much more stringent. A good lawyer must be open-minded, non-partisan, help disputants or parties in negotiation with recognizing and understanding one another's truth claim, appreciating one another's values, and accommodating as far as possible the legitimate projects of one another's wills. One must try to jettison the limitations and constraints of history, conditions, and their pre-conceptions. The value and meaning of others must be understood as the others do in their own conceptual and normative system.

We need to abandon the idea that the trial is an inductive inquiry into the facts of a past event and to adopt a theory of the trial as a reasoned inquiry into ongoing social dynamics. It is much more than a win-or-lose or zero sum battle but an accommodating and mutually benefiting collaborative normative enterprise.

Political institutions and legal rules have to function best when times are worst and moods are ugliest. It is not enough for the system to work well when in the hands of an enlightened statesman. It is also necessary to ask how it will operate in the hands of the quintessential villain. A legal system is not a complete social system. Legal remedies should be reflexively invoked to enforce whatever conduct thought to be socially desirable. The uncritical reliance on coercion drives out informal sanctions and curtails possibilities for displaying the personal virtues we all prize. No legal system should become too inclusive and intrusive to destroy all informal systems of social ordering. The concept of legal rule and legal freedom recognizes the proper limits to law and its authority.[48]

However, doubters of law and reason attempt to make believe that "properly

---

[48] Richard A. Epstein, *Simple Rules for a Complex World*, Harv. Univ. Pr., p.316.

socialized lawyers are in a sense required to inhabit a cognitive universe that features profoundly untenable assumptions concerning the relationship between legal imperatives and the social reality these imperatives are attempting to regulate. Such legal actors are thus to some extent impelled to adopt irrational beliefs regarding the legal reason's power to determine rationally what those imperatives should be."[147]

It must be admitted that this is one of the sections that could need more research and reflection to it fuller and useful.

(7) Philosophical Outlook of Lawyers

Lawyers are known not interested in philosophy. That claim is either a false or a scam. To claim to be legal theory neutral is actually to accept legal positivism as a given jurisprudence. For example, the values a lawyer hopes to call into play in a litigation shape how he develops the fact of the case, and good fact-handling skills are of critical importance to the present reality of the political struggle in a courtroom.[148] All theories and philosophies of law may enrich and strengthen the reason and argument of a lawyer and consequently his or her persuasive power. In this respect, the ideas and propositions of many of the postmodern schools of law such as "law and literature and popular culture," "law and economics," law and policy science, and the sociological school of law, etc should not be overlooked.[149] Should we hesitate to add that the philosophical ideas and insight informing this book throughout would much extend a lawyer's normative horizon and enable his or her to reimagine the law job in a new way.

(8) Jurisprudential Horizon of Legal Materials

Closely related to the general philosophical outlook, lawyers must broaden their jurisprudential horizon of what counts as legal materials that directly and significantly inform and influence their stance on what counts as law. Lawyers must expand their horizon of the materials and sources of legal information and knowledge beyond the traditional categories as notoriously typified by those of a positive law nature, and break with the so-called received wisdom that primacy is given to "primary" over "secondary" sources. The unrepresentative nature of judicial decisions in the total scheme of dispute resolution and lawmaking together with the disproportionate weight

---

[147] Paul E. Campos, *Jurismania: the Madness of American Law*, Oxford Univ. Pr., 1998, p.168.
[148] N. E. Bourke, *A Difference of Reason*, University Press of America 1997. p.162.
[149] Kuo-Lee Li, "Information on Philosophy of Law: Study, Research, and Materials", *The Philosophy of Law: an Encyclopedia*. Edited by Christopher Berry Gray. New York & London: Garland Publishing, 1999, p. 402.

in authority accorded them has been widely criticized. That legislation is contingent, partisan, and unduly influenced by special interests is common knowledge. The rationality of legislation must be critically evaluated. For this, there are Fuller's unwritten rules as well as other yet-to-be fully articulated principles, including Dworkin;s principles of political morality. William Twining insightfully pointed out the importance of the records of institutions specialized to law, be they governmental, "para-statal(半国有的)," or private as well as the factum of appellate courts and lawyers' documents. A. W. B. Simpson's historiographical works and others in the same genre are important counterparts to law reports.

In this connection, the section on the sources of law as well as the sections dealing with the significance of autonomous ordering and dispute settlement of the non-state spheres should all help broaden lawyers' jurisprudential horizon of legal materials.

(9) Impact of Professional Training and Indoctrination (Solipsism) and a Good Lawyer

Are lawyers professionally solipsistic? Is it possible not to be infatuated and enchanted by established or received texts, materials, sources, notions, doctrines, rules, principles, standards, precepts, etc. to be critical, original, reformist, or context-breaking?

According to Karl Llewellyn, the hardest job for the first year students is to lop off their common sense, to knock their ethics into temporary anesthesia as well as their view of social policy, sense of justice along with woozy thinking, and ideas all fuzzed along their edges.[447]

It has been further critically noted that a successful legal education sharpens and desensitizes the adept's sense of analytic complexity, sharpens it so that the advocate can identify various plausible arguments, and then deadening it for the purpose of making and (especially) deciding between such arguments.

As a result, an aspiring lawyer being brilliant and simpletonist at the same time understands and exploits and at appropriate times forgets the evidentiary problems, conceptual incommensurability, and ethical dilemmas that always characterize difficult legal issues. "To be trained to think like a lawyer is to be taught how to evoke all the chaotic complexity of law, and then how to repress the intolerable doubt

---

[447] Quoted in Paul E. Campos, *Jurismania: the Madness of American Law*, Oxford Univ. Pr., 1998. p. 120.

that same evocation can produce by going on to achieve the "luminous certainty" required of the advocate or judge.[148]

As a hired gun, to be trained to think like lawyers is to hold various unambivalent yet rationally unjustified beliefs, necessary for the vigorous deployment of social power, that nevertheless remain highly role specific, and are therefore subject to change at a moment's—or a client's—notice

On the other hand, professional training and legal education can well equipped lawyers as committed advocates. To be a committed advocate can be understood to be professionally committed, ethically, and jurisprudentially. More importantly, an ethically and professionally committed lawyer must not be afraid of representing the most notorious, evil, malicious, and even murderous accused or defendant. The responsibility goes much beyond a commitment to the noble constitutional principle of presumed innocent until prove guilt or without proof. To challenge the government's evidence at every turn can work to keep prosecutors and police honest. Just imagine a world or a country without such lawyers would look like.

In Chapters three of his book "The Principles of Social Order", Professor Fuller discusses lawyer as an Architect of Social Structures. This has much to do with what is meant to be a good lawyer serving as a activist, transforming social agent.[149]

Redeeming the Legal Professionalism(法律职业特性)

Lawyers are officers of the court. Lawyers are also hired guns operating in a work world that measures worth in 15-minute increments. Lawyers, especially young lawyers, have to work very hard to survive under the pressure of having to achieve the goal of 2,200 billing hours a year. Thus, they often have to sacrifice any change for necessary learning and experience enhancement, and neglect ethical standards to do so. A worrisome trend develops that erodes professional standards as billings take precedence over the long-term development of proficient, ethical well-rounded lawyers.

Legal professionalism is generally meant to include civility, mentoring, continuing education, maintaining client confidentiality, avoidance of conflicts, and maintaining independence. It is about being a part of a professional that is given a stature and a certain prestige and, in return, includes a significant service

---

[148] Id., at 121.
[149] Lon L. Fuller, *The Principles of Social Order: Selected Essays*. Edited with an introduction by Kenneth I. Winston, Durham, N.C., Duke Univ. Pr., 1981.

component. Are lawyers expected to volunteer their services in legal aid or community counseling? How many lawyers or law firms have taken on the initiative to do so?

The answer to this malaise or unhealthy situation is to shore up ethical standards and mitigate the billable-hours mentality. It is gratifying to learn that a number of law schools and law societies or simply bars have started to introduce compulsory ethical training course. No doubt, the legal profession must struggle to maintain a sense of realism about life in the legal trenches, while working hard to abate the various trashing or derogatory remarks of its business and services as typified in a Maclean's magazine cover story that characterized lawyers as "dirty rats."

D. The Conditions and Requirements of A Good Judge

(1) Methods of Selection of Judges

There are three general selection methods in the United States:

• Appointment—applies to principal judges in the federal system. They are named for life by the President upon the ratification of the Senate, usually from among lawyers who have had considerable practical experience and gained a high reputation. Judges are often drawn from the practicing bar and less frequently from government or the law teachers. A certain number of the Justices of the Supreme Court have been appointed from among law professors of great American universities. This may indicate the special relationship between the work of the courts and the role of legal writing. Nevertheless, the U.S. style confirmation hearings(人事任命听证会) and elaborated process do not necessarily guarantee that the strongest, most qualified candidates will be appointed to the Supreme Court. In Canada, even though a selection panel of experts and a set of public hearings are in place, the power to appoint Supreme Court judges remains solely in the hands of the Prime Minister. When politically motivated, the Prime Minister has often brashly ignored the selection panel and public hearings.

Judges in the U.S. Tax Court, Court of Federal Claims and those in specialized functions (bankruptcy) are also appointed by the President, but no life tenure, but usually 15 years.

The United States has no career judiciary. Judges need not serve any apprenticeship or other prescribed service, such as law clerkship. Many of the outstanding judges of the highest courts have had no prior judicial experience.

Some states also use the appointment method. This is done either by the governor or by local officials for terms of various lengths.

- Election—most on a nonpartisan basis, some run with the support of their political party. Terms vary from 4 to 15 years. In many states, in keeping with their preoccupation with democracy, judges are selected by universal suffrage. Later reform in this respect includes the prolongation of the period of elected office, a procedure of simple ratification by the electorate of appointments made first of all by the state governor, and the preliminary approval of the candidates for office by the state bar association.
- Appoint combined with Election—first appointed and then run a "retention election" voted by citizens.

The American Bar Association Code of Judicial Conduct (1990) addresses many facets of a judge's work and life and instructs to avoid impropriety and the appearance of impropriety in all of the judge's activities, such as impartiality, demeaning office and integrity. Full-time judges may not practice law. Nor joint clubs practicing invidious discrimination on the basis of race, sex, religion, or national origin.

There is a range of punishments for unethical conduct by judges ranging from private reprimand, reproval, public censure, removal, and suspension. Judges with life tenure (federal judges) can only be removed or suspended from office by impeachment by Congress.

(2) Independence of the Judiciary

The manner by which judges are chosen and removed, their salary and remuneration, the tenure(占有) or term and condition of their service all potentially relate in one way or another to the independence of the judiciary.

None of the methods for choosing judges is immune from political influence. In fact, there is a loud cry for politicizing the judiciary for reason of accountability. Doubters of law and legal reason allege that judges are no better than a special species of robbed bureaucrats. And due to the very fact that law is essentially indeterminate and legal meaning is vulnerable to divergent interpretation, judges in reality dispose of cases basing on personal preference and political orientation.

It has even been pointed out that extra-judicial interpretations or public defense of a judgment by judges are always troubling, because they implicate both judicial independence and impartiality. They also threaten the integrity of the rule of law, which places great emphasis on precedent and on letting judgments speak for themselves. Of course, this does not mean that judges cannot make public speech. Nor write essays, books out of experience and learning to express their own philosophical ideas of law, or to educate the public.

The central justification for an independent judiciary is its ability to operate at a remove from the passions of politics; It is to decide individual cases on the merits; and in constitutional cases, to take a longer view than is possible for those who are under pressure from an aroused public or from politically powerful groups.

An independent judiciary is indispensable to the rule of law. This is stated unequivocally by the Supreme Court of Canada in defining judicial independence in terms of financial security, security of tenure and administrative independence. Its reasoning applies to appointments as well. Requiring judges to defend their past decisions to a legislative committee, and offer their views on the court's constitutional cases could create the perception that judges who pass through it would not be independent of legislature. Constitutional guarantees for judicial independence should not be limited to those mentioned in the constitutional text. The principle of judiciary independence is an unwritten yet binding constitutional constraint on governments that supplements existent constitutional provisions. This constitutional principle applies to all levels of court, including the Supreme Court itself.

The independence of the judiciary is a collective politico-social morality of aspiration. Neither constitutional prescription nor sufficient monetary or other materialistic rewards would guarantee its existence and viability. No one factor can be sufficient. Nor a combination of some of the factors discussed in the news media of countries that lack independence of the judiciary will do.

To bring into being the institution of the independence of the judiciary and to nurture its healthy development, a country must have a proper combination of all necessary social, political, legal, economic, and cultural conditions. How is one to identify these conditions? One relatively simple and sure way is to identify and study such conditions in a country that has the independence of the judiciary. At a fundamental level, the establishment of a democratic government based on constitutionalism, separation of power, checks and balances, and individual human rights along with a free press would constitute a giant step in the right direction.

(3) De-politicizing or Politicizing the Courts

Judicial independence means that neither the legislature nor the executive, nor other power elite can, and should appear to, exert political pressure on the judiciary, and that the relationship between the courts and the other branches of government and social elite must be de-politicized.

On way to ensure judicial independence is the mandate that all changes to judicial compensation be made only after review by an independent, effective and objective compensation commission. And governments can only depart from the recommendations of the commission with compelling reason.

There are many possible ways by means of which the court, judge, judging, and judging the judge can be politicized. First of all, the nomination and appointment process can be politicized; Judges themselves are no different from you and me having political orientation and moral view; legal issues so called entangled in cases, especially hard cases, those of a constitutional nature, are politically and morally infested.

In a constitutional democracy as the United States or Canada since the repatriation of the Constitution from Great Britain and the usher-in of the Charter of Rights and Freedoms, the political-legal power is shared among the branches of government, if not dominated by the courts. Certainly, in Canada, the shifting of power to the courts is especially dramatic and significant.

In addition to financial security, security of tenure（房屋使用权保护）, and administrative independence, the appointment process must also be free of political manipulation and influence. Requiring nominees to the court, especially the Supreme Court as in the United States to defend their past decisions to a parliamentary or congressional committee, and to offer their views on the Supreme Court's constitutional cases and legal and judicial principles as well as whether or not an existent decision of a controversial nature should be overruled could create the perception that judges who pass through it would not be independent of Congress. On the other hand, judicial philosophy matters greatly. Judge's judicial philosophy is about when and why it is beneficial for judges to impose their own controversial judgments about constitutional meaning on legislators and other elected officials. Judicial philosophy describes what kinds of problems should lead courts to intervene in policy disputes, not just legal disputes.

To recognize the need for some form of prior parliamentary review of appointments to the Supreme Court of Canada does not necessarily entails politicization. Given the enormous power wielded by members of the court in the

Charter of Rights era, the traditional appointment process, which essentially vested un-reviewable power in the hands of a single individual, the prime minister of Canada, is widely seen as being inconsistent with basic democratic norms.⑲ What is particularly deplorable is that at times, this power could be readily abused for political expediency and gains.

A non-partisan appointment commission to make non-binding recommendations may be a reasonable compromise. The deliberation and determination of the commission must also be free of influence and control of any one branch of the government. Government, in reality, the head of the state, can only depart from the commission's recommendations by justifying its decisions publicly, subject to judicial review. There are suggestions that the decision of the commission should be final. There is no need for approval by the head of the state, the President or the Prime Minister.

As the courts, especially the highest court, play an increasingly potent role in the politics of the country, to seriously commit to democracy requires the democratization of the courts through the appointment of judges. Judicial appointments are always political, whether they masquerade under the dubious label of merit or not. The question is whose politics should prevail—the politics of the judiciary, the government, the legislature, or the public at large as expressed by its elected representatives. Judges are known to hold certain political and moral stance. John Roberts, the new Chief Justice(首席大法官) of the U. S. Supreme Court of and Samuel A. Alito, yet to be confirmed at the time of this writing, are both viewed to be allies of manufacturers and businesses. Lewis Powell, retired, built a reputation as business friend. The post-New Deal court favored regulation and the 1970s court feared too much regulation. The Supreme Court can be conservative as well as liberal. A conservative court will likely turn the tide on the civil rights movement and achievements making it easier to challenge affirmative action programs and more difficult to establish claims of employment discrimination. The Court can quickly respond to a conservative shift in majoritarian attitude about race discrimination, and exhibit a proper sensitivity to the evolving content of fundamental social values in its decisions. The most apt explanation for such observations is that judges track social change and trend, they are politically sensitive, and the

---

⑲ Patrick Monahan, "A Very Judicious Process", *The Globe and Mail*, Feb. 22, 2006, p. A15.

judgements reflect their political views and biases. And hence all these preclude the existence of any qualitative differences between the Supreme Court adjudication and ordinary politics. [50]

Therefore, to appraise any nominee to the Supreme Court as to his or her loyalty to the rule of law is nothing more than political demagoguery, an instrument of strategic communication.

The Americans know very well that court decisions are inherently, necessarily and unavoidably political. For example, in the 1857 Dred Scott decision, the U.S. Supreme Court in upholding slavery ruled that the abolition of slavery violates the property rights of white men. Those who think that judges are more enlightened than elected representatives should consider the words of the then chief justice Roger B. Teney, who described blacks as "beings of an inferior order and altogether unfit to associate with the white race, either in social or political relations; and so far inferior that they have no rights which the white men is bound to respect."

In recognizing the courts' power to shape public policy, Americans have also created numerous legal foundations that advocate philosophies from across the political spectrum. For example, the Institute for Justice in Washington, D.C. represents individuals in their fight for private property rights, economic liberty, freedom of the speech, commercial freedom, racial equality and the right of parents to raise their children free from state interference. In Canada, it has been submitted that the taxpayer-funded left-wing groups like the radical feminist Legal and Education Action has successfully persuaded the court to adopt the view that Section 15 of the Canadian Charter on equality rights should mean equality of condition, or equal outcomes, to the detriment of individual freedom and true equality before the law.

What is important is to bring judicial politics into public view and scrutiny. Ensuring judicial independence does not require us to abandon efforts at political accountability. It is a trade-off. If judicial independence is to mean that judges are left almost unregulated in their activities and behavior, then their appointment must be as democratic as possible. The tenure of judges should be fixed for a reasonable period. The commission should be empowered to receive complaints and to discipline judge. The dismissal of judges should only be done after a formal approval by the

---

[50] G. A. Spann, "Pure Politics", 88 *Michigan L R* 1971 (1990).

legislature, such as impeachment.

The appointment commission should also administer a code of judicial conduct incorporating a public register of judicial interests and a tougher set of conflicts rules.

Judges are the oracles of the law. The court is accorded with the supreme status by virtue of this truism. Moral and political issues of the most intractable nature that the normal political process cannot digest have been dumped onto the court for solution and guidance. Partially emboldened by the increasing demand from citizens for justice and the protection of their fundamental rights and freedoms from state encroachments and partially indulged in self-aggrandizement, the court willingly and aggressively plunges itself into the debates and conflicts on the most divisive social and moral issues. *

Judicial activism** is the worst possible charge that can be leveled against a judge. Judges are traditionally bestowed with a fairly restrictive role in interpreting the law to flash out the true meaning, if not the original intention of the lawmaker according to the language of the text, the context, and if necessarily by resort to legislative history. In applying law, they should <u>follow precedents（遵循先例）</u>. Policy analysis, instrumental goals, or social sciences inquiry are off the limit. According to this restrictive view, making law from the bench is illegitimate and amounts to usurpation of the power and prerogative of the legislature.

But such view is both wrong and anachronistic. That judges are oracles of the law goes hand in hand with that judges are the guardians of the Constitution. Unless you like your constitution dead, judges must keep its meaning and requirements abreast with the needs and aspirations of the society. If you call this making law from the bench, then judicial activism is very much inherent in the judicial function itself.

Does judicial activism politicize the court? If making law from the bench is a political act, then judges in virtue of judicial activism have politicized the court and themselves.

---

* 部分由于公民对自由公正和免受政府侵害的需求日益高涨，部分由于法院沉迷于自我膨胀，法院干劲十足地投入广泛多样的社会及道德问题的争论中。

** 司法能动主义，一种司法理论，它鼓励法官摆脱对于司法判例的严格遵从，允许法官在制作判决时考虑其个人对于公共政策的观点，以及以其他因素作为指导，通过判决来保护或扩展与先例或立法意图不符的个人权利。遵循该理论，会造成某些判决侵犯立法权和行政权的结果。

(4) Politicizing the Court is a Necessary Evil

Politicizing the court refers to the political action or decision that influences or determines the composition of the court, its function, and its conditions of service with the aim to influence how the court as an institution or individual judges decides cases. Specifically, to politicize the court targets at the appointment of judges. Ironically, the attempt to politicize the court in this sense does not purport to nor has it been proven, to compromise the independence of the judiciary(司法独立).

The United States Supreme Court is perhaps the most politicized adjudicative body. The process of nomination by the President, Senate ratification(批准) hearings(审讯), the input of the general public, especially the pressure exerted by elite powers, amply attests(宣誓) it. For example, in the fight to replace retiring judge Sandra Day O'Connor, it is said that the great political battle is about to consume the City of Washington for the rest of the summer. Around the Supreme Court now, everything is political and nothing is law. So galvanized are the partisans about the coming contest, a congressional(国会的) "war" has been predicted over the matter even though no candidate has yet been named. Joining in the fray are battalions of grassroots groups worried about everything from abortion to women's rights to religious freedom in addition to the host of special, lobbying advocacy groups. Thus it is no surprise concerning the nomination of Robert H. Bork to be Associate Justice of the Supreme Court*, a hard core neo-conservative(新保守主义) know to hold adverse views on women's rights, the Planned Parenthood declared that "the Senate vote on Bork may be more important than the next presidential election." Laurence Tribe wrote that the "fundamental choices about what sort of society we wish to become turn on who sits on the Court." Hamilton's least dangerous branch in the sense that the court would have "no influence over either the sword or the purse, no direction either of the strength or the wealth of the society, and can take no active resolution whatever" has come to occupy so important a place in the nation's political life that the question of its future course is capable of generating a controversy more intense and more divisive than all but a very few contests for political office.⑬

The Supreme Court is so highly polarized that Mr. Obama, in choosing the candidate to replace retiring judge David Souter, will be under intense pressure from

---

* 最高法院大法官。美国联邦最高法院由9位大法官组成,其中一位为首席大法官,其他为大法官。

⑬ Terrance Sandalow, "The Supreme Court in Politics", 88 *Michigan L R* 1300, 1301 (1990).

the left wing of his party to pick a judge who doesn't wander very often off the ideological reservation. And Mr. Obama will almost certainly oblige regardless of whom he will be choosing, a woman, a Latino, an Asian, or someone who is openly gay. Political considerations will most likely prevail in this case, even though Mr. Obama has made it clear that he will search for a judge who embodies the qualities of empathy, of understanding and identifying with people's hopes and struggles. In other words, strict constructionists need not apply. Should we say that in doing so, the rule of law concept is virtually got thrown out of the window?

In Canada, federal judges have frequently been individuals who were cronies, soul-mates, buddies or political friends of political ministers. Thus, to reform how judges at the Supreme Court are chosen is long overdue.

The court is the guardian of the Constitution and the arbiter of democratic principles. The Constitution is the most fundamental, political, moral document of a country. Every constitutional question or conflict is a political, moral one. Every interpretation and application of the Constitution is a political, moral act. The politicization of the court comes with its role as the guardian of the Constitution. Democracy is a political, moral principle. It has been said that it was OK for a judge, or a panel of judges(合议庭) to intervene in the political process and make sure things work as they are intended. Some mainstream legal thinkers characterize such intervention by the court in the political process as a dialogue among the branches of government, not a coup d'etat(政变) by the judges.

Politicization of the judiciary feeds on judicial activism. And vice versa. It has been suggested that public debate and participation mediated by a complex set of institutions over Supreme Court nominations may well be unavoidable if the Court remains in the vanguard of social reform, imposing constitutional solutions for controversial political issues even when those solutions lack a foundation in constitutional traditions. Politicization of the judiciary may very well be an necessary evil as the public and its leaders increasingly come to see the justices as political actors, whose function is not markedly different from that of other political actors, both the processes and bases of selection are likely to approximate, more and more closely, those for the selection of other political actors.[153]

In truth, the constitution is by nature a creature of politics and political

---

[153] Id., at 1325.

compromises.

Most if not all the constitutional provisions are atrociously written, general and ambiguous, and easily yield multiple interpretation of an often divergent, conflicting, or divisive nature. Judicial interpretation are in such cases simply utterance and imposition of a judge's personal political view.

Thus, it comes as no surprise in the insightful observation that the Canadian Charter of Rights and Freedoms revolutionized the work of the Supreme Court in an unimaginably profound way. It means the judicialization of politics and the politicization of the judiciary. The court is neither the least dangerous branch nor the most dangerous one.

(5) **No Political Interference in the Administration of Justice(公平的裁决)**

As a fundamental collateral condition for the independence of the judiciary as well as a logical extension of the concept, there should be no political interference in the administration of justice in any circumstance, under any condition, and at any time. Administration of justice can be understood as a much broader conception than the adjudication process of the court, civil or criminal. The logical reach of the administration of justice includes the pre-adjudication phases, such as police investigations, the prosecutorial works, discovery tasks, the entire proceeding of adjudication, and the post-adjudication enforcement, and execution of judgment. Political decisions with regard to the constitution of the court, appointment of judges, terms of remuneration, terms of tenure or service, working conditions, budgetary or other administrative or management matters do not constitute as political interference. No doubt, all of these have the potential to seriously impact or compromise the independence of the court.

Power corrupts. Those who hold political power tend to abuse it. To use overt or covert coercion, threat, or other means of force or violence, power holders purport to influence the outcome of investigations, prosecution, adjudication, and enforcement. This is one of the worst evils that can happen to the healthy administration of justice. Political interference in the administration of justice is particularly rampant where ironically the health of the legal system itself is in serious question. Wherever power is centralized, the independence of the adjudicative and regulatory process is either lacking or non-existent. It is a sort of vicious circle. Should such abuse be left unchecked and the disease not cured, it would sooner or later lead to the destruction of the government itself and erode the authority of the law, and severely damage the health and integrity of the legal system.

There is a "sub-judicial" rule, a long-standing, self-imposed convention that requires members of a legislative body to refrain from commenting and debating on cases before the courts. Public discussion by politicians about difficult issues, such as the question of bail(保释金) in murder cases is both necessary and desirable. But it is an overarching concern when politicization of the criminal process is entailed. Micro-management of individual cases is to be made by the Crown Law Office(律政事务处) (Criminal) on the basis of legal principles and requirements, not political considerations or partisan interests.

One recent example of political interference in administration of justice is that British Home Secretary David Blunkett resigned after allegations that he abused the position for personal reasons. Blunkett, 57, stepped down Wednesday, December 16, 2004 after weeks of questions whether he helped speed up a residence visa for the nanny of a former lover, a U.S.-born magazine publisher Kimberley Quinn.

To prevent political interference in the administration of justice requires that not only political and legal systems have to be reformed or strengthened but also conducive social and cultural conditions have to be provided and constantly nourished.

(6) Judging the Judge

This is an issue that relates closely to judicial independence and politicization of the court. Primarily due to the increasing awareness of judicial activism and its broader social and police impact and implication, who judges the judge and how have become the topic of front page debates among all concerned. The concept of judicial accountability differs from the civil or criminal responsibility of judges in their position as citizens. Increasing awareness of judicial activism has led some to call the court the most dangerous branch. The allegation is that the court has undermined the law and democracy. Judicial accountability refers to what a judge is required by law to do and not to do during the judicial decision-making process(司法决策过程). The hierarchical structure of the court is expected to ensure that mistakes, neglects, mis-application, wrong application, etc will be corrected internally. The contention is whether or not judges should be held accountable in cases where the judicial process fails or falls short of expectation of justice. And as a consequence, miscarriage of justice is resulted. Judicial error has been alleged to be the ultimate cause of a wrongful conviction. In such cases, should judges be required to testify and answer questions at a public inquiry. It has been argued that as long as public inquiry is measured, civil, focused on the alleged miscarriage of justice, and devoid of aspersion, public scrutiny can be an earmark of a healthy, democratically mature society.[154]

(7) Code of Judicial Ethics and Discipline

To ensure that judges adhere to certain basic moral and ethical requirements in their professional conduct, a code of judicial conduct is enacted as an integral component of the judicial institution. The code purports to avoid in a reasonable manner all potential conflicts of a personal and ethical nature to ensure impartiality. What results to this effect is disqualification and recusal(不合格). Personal interests and conflicts not only include oneself but also one's family, former employers, associates, and clients. One of the examples of ethical conflict is the unseemly conduct of attempt to judge one's own opinions or cases made at a lower court level.

Freedom of speech is not absolute. For judges, free speech has its limitations. Not only extra-judicial comments or interpretations of a judgment do not carry the authority of precedent, they introduce, in reality, doubt into the minds of lower court judges and practicing lawyers. Moreover, they may implicate both judicial independence and impartiality as well as threaten the integrity of the rule of law.

Moreover, judges must conduct themselves within the confines of the law and morality. both in and out of the court. For example, discriminatory remarks against lawyers of the disputants, vicious personal attacks on colleagues backed up by bullying and intimidation may lead to disciplinary sanction(批准). Yet, any discipline hearing of such nature must be public as the very integrity of the administration of justice is at issue.

The Ontario Superior Court justice Paul Cosgrove's misbehavior during a runaway murder trial tarnished his credibility so severely that a Canadian Judicial Council inquiry panel has recommended for his removal from the bench. He was accused of a failure in the due exercise of his office by abusing his power as a judge by insulting witnesses and maligning state officials. Ontario Attorney-General Michael Bryant complained about his displaying apparent bias against authorities by making 150 findings of Charter breaches by the Crown and police. His misconducts

---

[154] Kirk Makin, "Judicial Accountability Urged in Wrongful-Conviction Cases", *The Globe and Mail*, June 13, 2005. p. A5.

include everything from rude, abusive or intemperate language up to misuse of the contempt power or threats to do so, making defamatory statements of persons who had done no wrong, ceding control of the trial to defense counsel and failing to rein in scurrilous allegations and grossly unprofessional conduct. The entire Canadian Judicial Council of approximately 20 top judges from every federally appointed court has to consider whether to endorse(背书) the inquiry panel's recommendation. Should they agree that Judge Cosgrove can no longer function as a judge, it would then take a vote of Parliament to complete his removal.

A very interesting and seemingly controversial development in this respect is the federally funded study in Canada asking 3,000 lawyers across the country to comment on the competency and biases of more than 1,000 judges, specially their temperament, abilities, legal knowledge, and fairness, as well their leanings toward categories of litigant(诉讼当事人), male or female in family law, and motions, findings of guilt, sentencing recommendations and so on. Apprehension is running high that the results could be used to discipline or discredit judges whose leanings on controversial criminal law issues or the Charter of Rights run counter to the conservative philosophy of the conservative Harper government. Asking people to evaluate judges seems to have hit a nerve. The Attorney-General of Ontario instructed prosecutors that it would be inappropriate to participate in the survey. Some provincial law societies have also expressed concern that it could violate their codes of professional conduct for a lawyer to critique judges. Researchers undertaking the study alleged that they purported to report overall statistical trends, not the results for individual judges; it would identify weaknesses in the system, how to fix them, and to shed light on whether judicial appointment practices adopted since 1988 have improved or harmed the quality of the judiciary. The identities of responding lawyers are to be kept confidential.

(8) Judicial virtue, humility and deference

What is judicial virtue? Opinion differs. Like judicial activism, judicial virtue is in the eye of the beholder. Certainly, republicans and democrats have different, often sharply opposing definition and anticipation from a partisan perspective. Judicial virtue is demonstrated with each decision by judges both collectively and individually. What constitute judicial virtues comes to the forefront in glaringly display during the nomination and confirmation process. In the case of John Roberts being nominated first as an associate judge to replace Justice Sandra Day O'Çonnor and shortly after as the Chief Justice after the death of Chief Justice William Rehnquist, President Bush vehemently reiterated the importance of the rule of law in his nomination speech and praised all there justices for their virtue in upholding the rule of law.

In this respect, John Roberts himself hoists the values of modesty and humility seven times in an eight-paragraph response in his responses to a Judiciary Committee. Modesty and humility, though normally related to personal virtue, equally apply to one's view toward fellow judges, precedents, and the judicial branch as a whole. In the deliberating and gestating discourse with fellow judges respecting a case, is one committed to one's stance as well as open to be persuaded, regardless of one's initial position, majority, minority, concurring or dissenting? Should judges sublimate their personal preferences to judicial precedent and philosophy? How would a judge treat past efforts by the court to right social wrongs? Would he or she humbly respect those earlier decisions or overturn them as examples of judicial excess? When John Roberts talked about the lump in his throat as he walks up the Supreme Court's marble steps, it has been said that he was not interested in burning the place down. Should judges ardently oppose judicial meddling in divisive issues and prefer leaving them to lawmakers? Unfortunately, questions of this nature bring us back to the same perennial debate relating to the need of judicial activism and virtue of judicial deference.

(9) Role of Good Judges

Humility is a virtue of judges. The concept that the law grows best in an incremental way finds its expression in the virtue of humility of judges. For group solidarity of judges, it is far better to have cases decided on a narrow point, and not to make too express any new rule. This approach affords all judges greater flexibility in deciding the case before them. Surely, such advocacy against outright or presumptuous assertion or creation of new legal rule and principle through judicial pronouncement contrasts with the increasing phenomena of judicial activism nowadays.

E. Condition and Requirements of A Good Politician

Morality of Duty—The minimum moral requirements prescribed for the development and nurture of a good legal system are equally applicable to a good politician. This is because the decisions and actions of the state elite powers entail important, sometime long-term consequences for society at large and individuals of all walks of life.

The term "politician" is generally understood to include elected members or other high level officers serving in both the legislative and the executive branches of the government.

Most politicians are well known to be the least trustworthy class of people in society. Under the dictate of politics and political expediency, they tend to notoriously promise more than they can deliver. Politicians' notorious reputation is comparable to the reputation of a used car salesman, real estate agents in Western societies. Politicians are often accused of lying in public. Thus, the principle of an open and transparent decision-making process, the moral imperative of political accountability, and many other requirements are of particular significance.

An Ontario Superior judge absolved in January 2005 Ontario Premier Dalton McGuinty of breaking an elaborately signed contract promising not to raise or create new taxes, saying anyone who believes a campaign promise is naïve about the democratic system. Concepts of law such as the duty of care or negligent representation do not apply in the political process. Breaking campaign promises cannot be invoked as a ground to invalidate legislation. Even in applying the two-part test of the "duty of care(注意义务)" standard, it has been consistently invoked to absolve government or public agencies of any liability in law for pure policy decisions made in the broader public interest. This is the judicial view in lawsuits respecting the SARS epidemic for which responsible governmental bodies issued "directives" to hospitals, nursing homes and local public health officials—on everything from visitor restrictions, isolation wards, disinfection procedures and patient discharges and transfer. The reasons are twofold: policy decisions of government or public agencies should not be second-guessed; To allow claims for negligent representation for decisions of this nature would raise the spectre of unlimited liability to an indeterminate class."

The overriding importance of the role and responsibility of a politician in the authoritative process of decision-making is beyond any doubt. Under the primacy clause of the Constitution of the United States, it is understood that the lowest federal legal stipulations are lexically prior to the highest state provisions. A valid discretionary act by a single federal administrative official will prevail over a conflicting provision enshrined in a state constitution. Federal law is said to preempt the conflicting state provisions.

In the context of making public decisions, the requirements for a good politician match closely those prescribed for a good legal system. Among those requirements, special emphasis should be laid on openness and transparency, accountability, free and equal communications to and from constituency. In Canada, the following leaders' traits are prescribed: honest and trustworthy, vision, understanding the problems of Canadians, can manage the economy effectively, strong and decisive, ability to understand complex issues, care about concerns of Canadians, inspiring confidence, cares about the environment.

It goes without saying that to identify and clarify the conditions, qualities, and requirements for a good politician would necessarily call for a comprehensive and systematic study and analysis. Short of this, insightful anecdotal observations, comments, and analyses should be sufficiently illustrative.

In the Presidential election 2008, President-elect, Barack Obama was praised as the "better angels" of the American character. It is highly questionable that such general, admirable characterization can be easily translated into his ability to successfully discharge the duty and responsibility of the "most powerful person on Earth," the President of the U.S.

Judgment has been widely hoisted as the most cherished of the leader's attributes. Barack Obama is highly praised for having rooted principles and a curious mind, reflective intelligence, natural empathy, a strong moral compass, the ability to question those presenting him with ideas, not running around with instant solutions when crisis hit, not acting impetuously, dividing people, and understanding complexity as the antithesis of the ideological mind and the hallmark of a pragmatist, deploying oratory to galvanize, uplift and inspire in the very best tradition of American presidential rhetoric, having a sense of detachment about self and circumstance, rediscovering the common weal, renewing America's faith in itself, inspiring an alienated electorate back into the political process, fundamentally realigning American politics, and electrifying the world with his promise to end American unilateralism(单边主义) and overt militarism(军国主义). Even experience was twisted to mean not so much professional years in the halls of power but personal, life experience by background, upbringing, race, community involvement and demonstrated knowledge in understanding the complexities of problems. To cast a negative light on the persona of Barack Obama, it has been said that his elusive personality hides behind a mask of cool detachment that has been called the Rorschach blot politician, because everyone sees in him what he or she want to see. Which may come to haunt him.

Leadership Power includes both soft power and hard power. A proper and strategic balance of them is smart power that is what the Obama administration orchestrates. Soft power is the ability to attract others. And the three key soft-power skills are emotional intelligence, vision and communications. A successful leader needs the hard-power skills of organizational and Machiavellian political capacity. Equally important is the contextual intelligence that allows a leader to vary the mix of these skills in different situations to produce the successful combinations that is smart power. Obama sounded the themes of smart power in his inaugural address, a willingness "to extend an open hand to those who unclench their fists." Contextual intelligence is the intuitive diagnostic skill that helps a leader align tactics with objectives to produce smart strategies in different situations.

A decade ago, the conventional wisdom was that the world was a unipolar American hegemony. Neo-conservative pundits drew the conclusion that the United States was so powerful that it could do whatever it wanted, and that others had no choice but to follow. This new unilateralism was based on a profound misunderstanding of the nature of power—that is, the ability to affect others to get the outcomes one wants—in world politics. That United States may be the only superpower, but preponderance is not empire. The United States can influence but not control other parts of the worlds.[155]

Oratory was always an element of great leader. We judge leaders not only by the effectiveness of their actions, but also by the meanings that they create and teach. Simply to be "the decider" as claimed by George W. Bush has done is not only inadequate enough but often exceedingly destructive. Successful vision is one that combines feasibility with inspiration. Barack Obama's ascendance to power is his oratory ability to tap into a powerful human emotion called "elevation." Powerful moments of elevation push a mental reset button, wiping out feelings of cynicism and replace them with hope, optimism and moral inspiration. Oratory is always an element of great leadership. In classical times, in Greece and Rome, battles turned on one man's ability to inspire his troops. The effect of elevated language upon an

---

[155] Excerpts from Joseph S. Nyes' The Power to Lead. Oxford; New York. Oxford Univ. Pr. 2008.

audience is not persuasion but transport. People feel like they are being called to their higher, better selves.

Political Correctness, Intelligence and Judgment

Political correctness is a gale force of populous trends. As such, it comes and goes with time and the change of social conditions and needs. A good politician may refuse to succumb to the battle cry of political correctness and stick to his reflective judgment. Paul Martin, the former Prime Minister of Canada was saluted as the man of 2008 by many on account of his judicious balance between prudence on fiscal matters, especially for his stance on the banking industry and the integrity of banking operations in Canada, and enlightened compassion on social policy. Through his intelligence and foresight, the Canadian banking system is hailed as a model of good financial and banking regulation of the world in the midst of the historical, devastating crisis.

Senator John McCain, a highly respected public servant in the United States who lost the race to the White House in the 2008 presidential election made an insightful admonition on leadership courage, character, honor, and dignity that is particularly relevant to the virtues of a good politician. Some excerpts of the article are quoted as follows:

To a significant extent, courage to admit and answer to mistake goes a long way toward the institution of political accountability. The virtue of courage applies to politicians both individually and collectively. A most recent example of collective expression of regret for inaction, acquiescence, or mistake by politicians is the U.S. Senate's apology for failing to enact anti-lynching legislation until now despite the fact that nearly 200 anti-lynching bills had been introduced in Congress during the first half of the 20th century, seven presidents appealed unsuccessfully for the Senate to end the practice between 1920 and 1952, and the House of Representatives three times passed anti-lynching bills. Admission of mistake or wrongdoing must be public and sincere, and not strategically calculated. Colin Powell, the former secretary of state said in a taped television interview broadcast on September 9, 2005 that his 2003 speech to the United Nations, in which he gave a detailed description of Iraqi weapons programs that turned out not to exist was "painful" for him personally and would be a permanent "blot" on his record.

A negative and pitiful example in this respect is the evasive regret expressed by George W. Bush when asked about his decision to invade Irag on the false pretense of existence of Weapon of mass destruction in Irag and the imminent danger to world peace. In his reply, he reverted to annoying equivocation: "That's an interesting question. That is a do-over that I can't do."⑭

Good Senators—In the normative enterprise of the U.S. law, the senate plays a prominent and pivotal role. James Madison called the Senate a fence against the fickleness and passion of public opinion. The rules of the place ensure that it is as cumbersome and restrictive as that sounds. Any of the 100 members can try to change, or completely hijack, another member's bill as it comes up for a vote. And any one of them can bring the place to a halt with a filibuster(阻挠议事的议员), as long as the minority party can marshal enough votes to prevent the majority party from riding roughshod over the legislative process. Mastering a powerful institution as the Senate that relies on comity but requires confrontation, takes a special kind of talent.

There is no fixed journey to greatness in the Senate. Instead there is a whole variety of skills that American senators have developed over 218 years to help them raise and spend tax dollars, oversee the operation of government and, in the case of the best among them, pass laws that benefit their constituents, their country and the world.

Time Magazine recently identified ten best senators and classified them into ten distinctive categories of desirable quality and skill. These are the contrarians, the mainstreamers, the debaters, the wise men, the bird-doggers, the operators, the dealmakers, the providers, the statisticians, and the persuaders.⑮

Alas, the prescriptive nature of morality of aspiration must be distinguished from political realities. American as a republic is a hard-won virtue and cannot be taken for granted. For example, the Senate houses lots of inexperienced rookies—wealthy businessmen, sports starts, even the occasional actor. Courtesy to a skewed, crazed campaign-finance laws, if you are rich in the United States, you can virtually buy your Senate seat. Though the Founders of the Republic believed in aristocracy, but their idea was government by natural—not inherited—aristocracy, an aristocracy of " virtue and talent," as Jefferson put it. Of course, American does have her own history of dynastic succession in the name of Adamses, Harrisons, Roosevelts, Kennedys, and Bushes.

---

⑭ "In Search of Courage: Finding the Courage Within You", Yahoo Webpage, Sep 11, 2008.
⑮ *Time*, Canadian edition, April 23, 2006, pp.15-26.

Political accountability does not just happen at the ballot boxes during election time. Politicians even a sitting Prime Minister in Canada have to face the discomfort of subjecting to piercing scrutiny and answer under oath intensive questions at a commission of inquiry into alleged crimes or wrong doings. Paul Martin stood at the Gomery Commission. Sir John Å. Macdonald was in the hot seat in the Pacific Scandal in 1872. No matter of his favored tactic of delay, denial, and defending for a considerable period, Macdonald had to resign finally. Japanese politicians and high-ranking officials like to be faithful to the highly honored tradition of self-criticism and humiliation of making apology in public. Richard Nixon was forced to follow a similar path instead of risking the possibility of impeachment.

Normative prescriptions for a good politician and his or her conduct usually are proposed in the wake of political scandal or wrongdoing. In Canada, in the aftermath of the sponsorship scandal under the Liberal government and Justice John Gomery;s inquiry into wrongdoing, coming to the fore is the doctrine of ministerial accountability and the roles and responsibilities of politicians, ministers, political staff and bureaucrats.

To ensure accountability sticks, tough and viable rules have to be introduced. The Gomery Commission has made a total of eighteen specific recommendations. For example, it proposes that bureaucrats must create a clear paper trail, and top civil servants must answer to Members of Parliament (Mps); Parliament's watchdog committee on spending must get more money and act in a less partisan way; Political staff must be prevented from telling bureaucrats what to do; and A Prime minister's special reserve funds must follow rules and be reported to Mps.

The essential and overriding goal of the recommendations is to define as clearly as possible the line between politics and administration. Deputy ministers, the public servants accountable for the administration of their departments, should answer on that score to the House of Commons' public accounts committee, whose job is to hold the executive responsible for how it spends the public's money. Ministers, politically responsible for the way their departments operate, should be held politically accountable in the Commons itself. Parliament's traditional role of watchdog of the public purse must be restored. The reforms are aimed to shifting from the "culture of entitlement" and operational opaqueness to a "culture of integrity" and service.

Critics see the problem with ministerial accountability is that no one understands what the hell it is because the doctrine says ministers are accountable for everything but responsible for nothing. Besides, who are political staffers if not adjuncts of the ministers? There cannot be a watertight compartmentalization between civil servant-as-administrator and civil servant-as-taker-of-directions. Otherwise, civil service becomes a machine without direction—or worse, like all bureaucracy, it becomes a machine with its own rhythms and direction, accountable primarily to itself.

In fact, the qualities and requirements for a good politician can be analyzed on the basis of Lon Fuller's morality of duty and morality of aspiration in both the positive and negative senses. No doubt, the recommendations of the Gomery Commission and the Conservative government's proposed Accountability Act are only structural constraints and operational requirements. These alone are not sufficient to prevent wrongdoing and malfeasance of politicians.

Political ethics and accountability as well as lobbying issues are never simple and easy matters. This is especially true in modern liberal democracies where partisan politics predominates. In Canada, there is an Ethics Commission at the federal level. The Ethics commissioner is appointed by the Prime Minister with the consent of the Canadian Parliament. The ethics rules and the investigation and finding of the Commissioner are designed to help ensure the proper conduct of politicians. The mandate of the Commission is extremely complex; there are two codes and hundreds of rules. Under the Conflict of Interest Code for Public Office Holders, like cabinet ministers or the prime minister, the Commissioner has the power to summon witnesses and compel them to testify. However, such power does not apply to inquiries of complaints filed under the code off conduct for Mps (members of Parliament.) When overstepping the boundaries of its mandate and crossing the boundary between arbitration and advocacy, such as the act of adjudication could be branded as dead commissioner walking.

It is <u>terra incognita</u>(未知领域). The commissioner, a highly respectable position, is subject to be labeled and accused as a "lapdog" or "partisan appointee" of the government who exercises bad faith, negligence and misuse of office. The commissioner himself was once found in contempt of the Parliament for violation of the MP's code of conduct. All these work to vilify and undermine the Ethics commissioner.

The United States Senate ethics rules prohibit senators and their staffers from using their positions to further their personal financial interests. Taking official action in return for money or other benefits is illegal. Ethical issues arise more frequently than issues of a criminal nature. Usually these types of situations are political and not legal issues.

Behavior constraints are needed for politicians even after they have left office. Similar to the revolving door restrictions for lawyers moving from government position to private practice, a comparable constraint should be established for politicians lobbying for private interests after they leave office using their inside knowledge, expertise, and connections.

The Government of Canada under the Conservative Party has a proposed Federal Accountability Act shortly after coming to power in 2006. The Act is designed to stop, among other things, high-level government officials with party connections from getting rich by going back and forth between government and the world of lobbying. Under the proposed law (bill), cabinet ministers, their senior staff and senior public servants are prohibited from becoming registered lobbyists for five yeas after leaving government. But there would be only a one-year ban on the common practice in which political staff leave to advise those who do the actual lobbying. Because of this weakness and other exemptions, ethics critics allege that these weaknesses and exemptions leave enough and significant loopholes that you could drive a truck through them. The revolving door seems to be alive and well with a bit of creativity. It's an architectural façade.

Politicians are required by law before assuming office to disclose all personal and business interests, holdings of securities, or other similar connections in commercial establishments. In order to prevent the appearance of a conflict of interest situation from arising, a politician should in the exercise of duties abstain from any participation in discussion or decision-making process involving direct dealings with such establishments.

Politicians often switch parties or "floor-crossing" for one reason or another. When a politician switches to assume a cabinet position, an investigation by the Ethics commissioner may be conducted to find out if an unlawful "inducement(诱因)" is offered. But "considerable increase in salary, augmented potential pension, staff and assorted perks enjoyed that go along with the position" do not constitute an illegal inducement.

The U. S. executive branch's vetting process for appointment of high-rank officials is the significant step for ensuring at the outset the professional and moral quality of a good politician.

The extensive vetting process that President-elect, Barack Obama put in place is specifically designed to make sure he is fully armed with information that could hold up nominations in the Senate confirmation hearings(参议院的同意权听证会). The Senate confirmation process applies to cabinet(内阁) appointees, Supreme Court judges, ambassadors, and other officials as prescribed by the Constitution. The majority of the nominees(被提名者) are approved by unanimous consent rather than a contentious roll call vote. The vetting process is designed to avoid wasting time and to avoid embarrassment later. After the honeymoon, a period traditionally enjoys by the president, fades, any missteps by the appointees will be exploited and jumped on.

The process entails reviews by the Office of Government Ethics of candidates' financial interests for possible conflict of interest. Its queries include disclosing insurance policies, stock holdings, equity interests, tax irregularities and speech royalties. A White House personal data questionnaire quizzes nominees on finances, foreign travel, in-laws, mental health history, brushes with the law, drug and alcohol use and issues of potential embarrassment to themselves, their family or the President. They are also subject to full FBI background investigations.

United States President's nominees for high office must be completely honest, forthcoming, and untainted by the slightest of wrongdoings. Four of these nominees withdrew from consideration without going through the vigorous Senate confirmation hearings process due to exactly a failure in meeting the minimum requirements for a good politician.

The latest imbroglios (debacles) involve two high-profile nominees. Tom Daschle withdrew on February 3, 2009 his nomination as the U. S. secretary of health and human services after weathering four days of scrutiny over unpaid taxes. This incident promoted President Barack Obama to concede having "screwed up" in undermining his own ethical standards by pushing the appointment. Mr. Daschle was at least honest and courageously forthcoming in saying that he would not have been able to lead a reform of the nation's health-care system with the full faith of the Congress and the American people. Mr. Obama's nominee to be the chief White House performance officer, Nancy Killefer, pulled her name from consideration because of unpaid payroll taxes for a household employee.[158]

---

[158] Jennifer Loven, "Tax Controversy Forces Daschle to Pull Nomination for Key Heath-Reform Post", *The Globe and Mail*, Feb. 4, 2009, A15.

New Mexico Gov. Bill Richardson was Obama's first choice as commerce secretary. He withdrew in early January following disclosure that a grand jury is investigating allegations of wrongdoing in the awarding of contracts in his state. Richardson has not been implicated personally. [59]

A good politician however shrewd or wonkish, must not be too partisan, polarizing and mean-spirited to lead a nation of distant regions and diverse opinion. It is an inescapable truth that sooner or later, such deplorable bad personality traits will do one in. A good politician serving as a party leader should stand up for principled civility in the face of the politics of contempt.

Management Ability:

Effective management should be part and parcel of true leadership; it is about engaging people, not acting heroically. Barack Obama is said to be really brilliant in his management capabilities. His election campaign was exemplary, his staff wonderfully well organized, and his management of the transition to power impressive.

Transparency and Accountability closely relates to management style and the personality of a politician. Many politicians are just too partisan, overzealously passionate, and profanity uttering prone. Others are simply egocentric, arrogant, and self-righteous. Prime Minister of Canada, Stephen Harper even after a devastating humiliation still finds it difficult to take counsel or admit his mistakes. He believes he's the smartest guy in the room and no matter what, he's never wrong.

On the other hand, Barack Obama is revolutionizing presidential communication and public consultation. He is exploiting the Web to mobilize and broaden his army of admirers, in order to validate his planned reforms. He believes the new media lower the barrier for entry of the average person into politics. This is key. It is much easier now for the average person to be informed, to be engaged, to participate, to feed back, and to take action.

Being courageous enough to publicly confess mistake is a best example of being accountable. President Obama set the latest example in this respect. To the surprise of many when watched past leaders blame others or keep mum when an error transpired, Obama said "I screwed up" after it was revealed that Tom Daschle, his pick for secretary of health and human services, hadn't paid all his taxes and was

---

[59] Liz Sidoti & David Espo, "Gregg Withdraws as Commerce Secretary Nominee", *Yahoo Finance*, February 13, 2009.

forced to withdraw his candidacy.

The Grand Hall of Politicians: the Role and Responsibility of the Congress or Parliament

If morality of duty and morality of aspiration of a politician are important to a good legal system and good law, then politicians working collectively in the capacity of the most important law-making entity should be expected to embody no less a strong sense of institutional responsibility, high ideals, and impeccable morality. Both the United States Congress and the Canadian Parliament have rules of procedure governing how these bodies conduct their business and an code of ethics guiding how a representative or senator behaves professionally in his or her conducts in decision-making process. Yet, how should politicians, either individually or collectively behave themselves in dealing with each is unfortunately largely unsaid and unregulated.

However, whenever how politicians conduct themselves in dealing with each other and working as a member of the collective body in the grand hall of representatives, reports or comments are rather mostly critical. Unfortunately, a recent commentary serves to casts a pall over the high hope and expectation of citizens on the people representing them and working for their benefits.

Despite the rhetoric of the leader of a party in power to improve the respect, civility, and the tone of debate, and to restore dignity to the "House of Commons", it is said, I quote, "no one [is] crusading to stem the vicious tide of rudeness and grandstanding that passes for parliamentary debate. But were there one, he or she would be bringing a mop and pail to sponge up a vast Atlantic of pettiness, cheap shots, ill-phrased insults and ego-stuffing bluster." "The cause is hopeless. The dove of peace has limped featherless, squawking in despair, from this scene before, ... with a similar delusory ambition that would transform the Commons from a brawling pit of nasty sub-literates to a sweet symposium of high-minded exchange." It is in the very nature of elected assemblies that what is called "debate" is really a verbal masquerade for the continuous struggle for power between contending factions. These factions, we called them parties, exist to do each other in. Debate is, in this context, a knife, a cudgel or a gun. Opposition parties do not debate to advance a truth, refine a policy or scrutinize a proposal. They take every action of a government, every statement of a minister, and by any means necessary—by shock, shout and contention—make of either a weapon to hurl at the heart of the government.

"In this war—for war it is—all the petty arts of innuendo, exaggeration and allegation, refined to the highest degree by the stagecraft of scrums and question period, are called into play. Partisanship magnifies disagreement into zealotry. Personal rivalries metastasize into raging hatreds."

"Governments play an identical game in reverse. Slay the opposition from the moment it arrives in Parliament. Mock the leader, traduce the idea, and demonize the eccentric."

"People outside politics cannot fully appreciate how total this game is, how swiftly partisanship twists otherwise benign and decent human beings into angry spouts of bluster and recrimination. Politics shrinks the human soul."

"Opponents become enemies; rivals decline into rascals. Every motive is questioned; nothing, to the true partisan, is ever what it seems. Caricature rules. Take recent history. The Prime Minster is portrayed as a sullen conspirator whose dark heart houses a hidden agenda. He is—most dreaded of slurs—a clone of George Bush. Poor Stephane Dion was still adjusting his sash as the newly crowned liberal leader when the Tories were buying ads portraying him as a bungling dreamer, simultaneously a babe in the woods and a monster of unbridled willfulness. No adult on the Hill really believed these ludicrous projections but all retailed them with the frenzy of salesmen about to lose their jobs."

In this world of constant conflict, rampant ambition and raging egos, what hope is there for the graces and restraint of civility, for the simple decencies of plain good manners and mutual respect? That code in this world is less then a nullity. It is a self-defeating and useless excrescence. To empathize, to give the other guy a break, to try to see—oh, the horror! —the good points an opponent is making, that to resign from the war, desert your party, and forgo the sweet mean pleasures of doing in the side that did in your side. Worse, it is seen as both stupid and a folly. [60]

The most recent example of partisanship runs wild manifests itself in the economic update of the Conservative Party of Canada. Instead of having concerned itself with rallying the people and the Parliament of Canada behind a vigorous response to the global economic crisis, the proposals put forward by Jim Flaherty,

---

[60] Rex Murphy, "A Mop, a Bucket and Civility", *The Globe and Mail*, November 22, 2008, p. A27.

the Minister of Finance, amounted to fiscal gerrymandering. It purports among other things, to emasculate the power, strength, and the viability of opposition parties by withdrawing public funding for political parties, since the Conservative party alone traditionally is blessed and supported by private donation. Action of this nature is the most flagrant violation of Canadian constitutional democracy in ensuring the existence and vibrancy of meaningful political opposition.

However, it must be submitted that by and large, partisanship in politics does serve like the constitutional system of checks and balances to ensure the overall good of a country.⁶⁰ The congress or the parliament is the most important arena where decisions that impact on the country as a whole are made. As such, it is only natural that the highest degree of openness and transparency is expected in how it works and how its decisions are made. Yet, openness and transparency cannot be taken for granted. Citizens must be constantly vigilant and ready to identify and expose any violation these of requirements, and take necessary political moral action to effect its correction or its elimination. One of such violation of these basic moralities of duty is the shameful and dishonest practice known as "earmarks."

Earmarks are funds provided by the Congress for projects or programs where the congressional direction (in bill or report language) circumvents the merit-based or competitive allocation process, or specifies the location or recipient, or otherwise curtails the ability of the Executive Branch to properly manage funds. Congress includes earmarks in appropriation bills—the annual spending bills that Congress enacts to allocate discretionary spending—and also in authorization bills.

Office of Management and Budget (OMB) (管理与预算办公室) Guidance to Agencies on Definition of Earmarks

OMB defines earmarks as funds provided by the Congress for projects or programs where the congressional direction (in bill or report language) circumvents Executive Branch merit-based or competitive allocation processes, or specifies the location or recipient, or otherwise curtails the ability of the Executive Branch to manage critical aspects of the funds allocation process.

- Earmarks vs. Un-requested Funding. At the broadest level, un-requested funding is any additional funding provided by the Congress—in either bill or report language—for activities/projects/programs not requested by the Administration.

---

⑩ "Partisanism Trumps the World Crisis" Comment, *The Globe and Mail*, November 28, 2008, p. A22.

Earmarks are a subset of un-requested funding. The distinction between earmarks and un-requested funding is programmatic control or lack thereof of in the allocation process.

- Earmarks and Programmatic "Control." If the congressional direction accompanying a project/program/funding in an appropriations bill or report or other communication purports to affect the ability of the Administration to control critical aspects of the awards process for the project/program/funding, this IS an earmark. Note: The definition of "control critical aspects" includes specification of the location or recipient or otherwise circumventing the merit-based or competitive allocation process and may be program specific. However, if the Congress adds funding and the Administration retains control over the awards process for the project/program/funding, it is NOT an earmark; it is un-requested funding.

Earmarks Include:

- Add-ons. If the Administration asks for $100 million for formula grants, for example, and Congress provides $110 million and places restrictions (such as site-specific locations) on the additional $10 million, the additional $10 million is counted as an earmark.

- Carve-outs. If the Administration asks for $100 million and Congress provides $100 million but places restrictions on some portion of the funding, the restricted portion is counted as an earmark.

- Funding provisions that do not name a recipient, but are so specific that only one recipient can qualify for funding.[162]

Earmarks are designed to cater and benefit special interests mostly for companies and entities with business and activity in the constituency of a congressman. These earmarks are usually secretly inserted at the last possible moment in the committees and disguised in obscure languages of double speak of the George O'Well world, and they are very hard to detect. Unfortunately, these earmarks are parasitic on otherwise laudable programs and activities. And proposals to reform and heighten congressional ethical standards purporting to minimize, if not eliminate, the earmarking practices, have repetitively failed in the past.

Earmarks of pork are so prevalent and notorious that despite what Obama said, special interests spending have found its way into the landmark 2009 $787 billion

---

[162] "Earmarks Details". For more information, check at http://www.earmarks.omb.gov.

stimulus package in massive doses. And the package is ridiculed as the lobbyists' enrichment act. What is wrong with earmarks or pork for special interests is that earmarks are self-dealing that operate to decimate the fair, competitive system based on need, value or merit. As a result, politics becomes a business, not a mission. In his 2010 state of the Union address, Obama proposes that all earmark requests be published and made know to the public. This is a good start in the right direction.

Character, Personality Flaws, Personal Traits or Unscrupulous Conducts Disqualify or Undo a Politician

What is most deplorable is that there is no lack of politicians who brazenly abandon their morality of duty, let alone morality of aspiration, and blatantly embrace power and wealth by committing criminal acts or unscrupulous, immoral conducts.

George W. Bush, the former President of the United States has been consigned to the dust heap of awful presidents because of his attitude of self-righteousness and unbridled sense of superiority.

The former Illinois Governor Rod Blagojevich was impeached and forced to resign for his attempt to corruptly peddle the Senate seat of Barack Obama, for abuse of power, and for letting ego and ambition drive his decision. And he was also barred from ever holding public office in the state of Illinois. Not a single legislator rose in his defense.

Illinois politics is said to be not about good government, it is not about ideology, it is about who gets into office so they can help the guy who got him there. Government become a venue in which to pursue one's own private interests. The state has a long history of brazen political back-scratching that has made it ground zero for corruption in the United States. This is similar to the Chinese saying of getting rich through political office, not that of studying hard to getting into politics to serve the people.

Some politicians, for reason of self-aggrandizement, power grapping, or narcissism, would resort to any possible means for self-protection or to destroy oppositions. In a burst of bombast and fury, the Prime Minister of Canada, Stephen Harper filed a libel lawsuit for $3.5 million defamation suit again the Liberal Party. The Liberals accused Harper of having knowledge of alleged unethical and even illegal behavior by the Conservatives in the so-called Cadman affair. At the centre of the lawsuit were the bombshell allegations in a book that two Conservative officials offered Independent MP Chuck Cadman, who had terminal cancer, a million-dollar life insurance policy if he agreed to return to the Conservative Party before a May 2005 non-confidence motion that could have toppled Paul Martin's minority Liberal government and forced an election. In their legal defence, the Liberals charged that Harper's lawsuit was a deliberate attempt to keep opposition Mps from exploring "alleged improprieties" within the government and to muzzle opponent critics. And the action constitutes a fundamental attack on freedom of political expression. The unprecedented legal action was eventually dismissed without costs. Reasons for the abrupt ending to the lawsuit were not disclosed.⑥

Stephen Harper has even been accused of fanning the fires of national disunity and betraying the fundamental obligation of a prime minister: to build and strengthen national unity in possibly the world's most difficult federation to govern.

If leadership is defined as tough, clear-headed decisiveness, Mr. Harper scores well. If it's defined in terms of honour and ethics and goodwill, his record poses a rash of problem. Some regard him as a dishonest, unprincipled, untrustworthy, manipulative, and calculative leader—a cynical operator who occupies the moral low ground. His government was almost overthrown on account of an opposition parties' non-confidence vote on his budget. He survived that crisis through a prologuing of the Canadian Parliament ordered by the Governor-General—a questionable constitutional act. Will Mr. Harper suffer another non-confidence vote soon? It will all depend on if he can live up to the requirements for a good politician.

The Magnificent Seven Great Politicians

Princeton University historian Theodore Rabb identifies seven great political leaders in history. They are:

Augustus (63 BC-14 AD) is a Roman emperor, a superb administrator, and creator of the Pax Romana, which bestowed peace on the Mediterranean world for more than two centuries.

Charlemagne (742-814) is the Creator of the Holy Roman Empire and the catalyst for the Carolingian Renaissance revival of art, religion and culture.

Frederick William (1688-1740) transformed Prussia from a second-rate power into an efficient and prosperous state. He introduced major civil-service(文官制度)* reforms and compulsory schooling, improved the lot of the serfs, overhauled

---

⑥ Bruce Campion-Smith, "Harper's Libel Lawsuit Settled", *Toronto Star*, February 7, 2009, p. A6.
* 指基于功绩制而非分赃制来确定公职人员的任命和任期的文官制度。

the military, and resettled and made prosperous eastern Prussia, which had been devastated by plague.

George Washington (1732-1799) presided over the convention that drafted the U. S. Constitution, established the new government's executive department, funded a national debt, created an effective tax system, a national bank and a nation that stayed clear of conflict in a world being torn apart by war.

Abraham Lincoln (1809-1865) led the U. S. through its greatest internal crisis, the Civil War, abolished slavery and sought to reunite his nation through generous reconciliation with the defeated southern states.

Franklin Delano Roosevelt (1882-1945) is a central figure of the 20th century during a time of worldwide economic crisis and war. He created the New Deal to provide relief for the unemployed, recovery of the economy and reform of the financial system.

All seven came to power at times of great crisis. All came with high expectations. All created political stability and a positive way of handling and structuring politics that long outlasted them.[64]

Why Good Leaders Make Bad Decisions is the title of a book by Sndney Finkelstein, Professor of leadership at the Tuck School of Business of Dartmouth University and two British Colleagues that they have been researching for a decade. They together reveal that assumptions about past experiences and deep-seated blind spots that can make leaders cling to the belief that they are right even in the fact of evidence that they are completely wrong. In their view, personal factors are behind many leadership blunders. In the majority of decisions our brains are able to recognize patterns and our emotions help us make reasonable decisions quickly. If our ancestors had to sit down and debate what to do when a sabre-toothed tiger was attacking, rather than making a fast exit, we wouldn't be around today.

They identify four "red flag" conditions that leaders should strive to recognize and avoid. And they associate the red flags with four contemporary leaders as follows:

Except George W. Bush, the other three are all from the financial field. Those in the financial field also fit well with the section below where the downfall of corporate leaders is discussed.

---

[64] Michael Valpy, "Not Everyone Thinks He's so Great: America's New President Is Still an Image and We Don't Yet Know What's Behind It", *The Globe and Mail*, January 24, 2009, p. F3.

a. Misleading prejudgments—Sticking to an initial decision, to the point of ignoring or rejecting evidence that it was flawed. Case in point: Former U. S. president George W. Bush pressing ahead with the invasion of Irag. He sought out data that confirmed his belief and continually played down contrary information. Red flag: Despite a lack of confirming data about weapons of mass destruction and a chorus of doubters, the former president continued to try to convince critics that they were wrong and he was right.

b. Misleading experience—Having done something successfully before, leaders assume that they can repeat the success by doing the same thing again, but fail to recognize that conditions have changed. Case in point: Bank of America Corp.'s chief executive officer Kenneth Lewis has been sharply criticized for failing to disclose the level of losses at Merrill Lynch & Co. Inc. before barreling ahead with the purchase of the troubled brokerage. Mr. Lewis pushed on, blindly believing that, because past mergers had worked, this one would, too. Red flag: He failed to adapt his strategy even as it became clear the market was tanking.

c. Inappropriate self-interest—We all make decisions that are in our own interest, and this can blind us to issues, even when someone else points them out. Case in point: Former Merrill CEO John Thain pushed multimillion-dollar bonuses to many of the brokerage's executives even as it was suffering crushing losses. He continued to defend lavish offices and big bonuses in his new executive role at Bank of America, which is receiving government bailout funds, leading the bank's board to force him to resign. Red flag: Despite facing the risk of insolvency and denouncement by politicians and taxpayers, Mr. Thain saw no need to waver from a deep-seated sense of entitlement.

d. Inappropriate attachments—We may not realize how being personally top corporate executives who should have had doubts invested in fund manager Bernie Madoff's scheme. Red flag: The return was too good to be believed, but, because they thought he was their friend, investors were happy to give Mr. Madoff their money without doing due diligence and questioning how he was investing it. ⑯

---

⑯ Sydney Finkelstein, Donald C. Hambrick, & Albert A. Cannella, Jr.
"Strategic Leadership: Theory and Research on Executives, Top Management Teams, and Boards", New York: Oxford University Press, 2009. Also "Think Again: Why Good Leaders Make Bad Decisions and How to Keep It From Happenings to You."

F. Condition and Requirements of A Good Legal Scholar(法学学者) or Jurist

What is legal scholarship? Is it description of the law as it is—what is knowns as declarative jurisprudence or prescription of the law as it ought to be? —what is known as prescriptive jurisprudence. Could description and prescription be clearly separated? Are they one and the same?

(1) Legal Scholars as Expositors of the Law

In the history of Western law, there was a prominent and influential tradition of exposition orthodoxy. This is true in both the civil law system(民法法系) and the common law system(普通法系). In France, the works of Pothier has a notable influence on the formulation of the French Civil Code. In English, Coke's Institutes of the laws of England and the Commentaries on the laws of England by Sir William Blackstone all had considerable influence on the development of English law and greatly facilitated its expansion and reception in the United States. Presently, the Restatements of law may be regarded as the model of the exposition of the Common law in the United States and exerts considerable influence on its making, study and further development.

Exposition of law by nature is supposed to be descriptive. It purports to provide a true representation of the state of legal authority(法律效力). It is not meant to be critical. Exposition is supported to be objective. However what is objective is what the expositor perceives it to be, not something to be measured by whether it is commonly shared in the legal community(法律界). As a consequence, what is presented as an objective exposition of the law may very well turn out to be what the expositor considers the law ought to be. For if the law is readily accessible to objective inquiry and exposition, there should be no need for so many different versions of exposition. If any one version can claim objectivity and be accepted as such, all other versions must be redundant. This is true unless of course objectivity in exposition and description does not necessarily lead to an identical result or conclusion due to difference in identification, choice, and evaluation of authority.

Is legal scholarship supposed to be truth seeking, and thus value-neutral, impartial, non-partisan, apolitical?[69] Anthony Kromman distinguishes legal

---

[69] William L. Twining, *Theories of Evidence: Bentham and Wigmore*, London: Weidenfeld and Nicolson, 1985.

scholarship from advocacy that aims merely to persuade.[67] Nancy Bourke disputes strongly such differentiation.[68] There are a host of competing views and visions or schools of law on almost all of the major concepts and notions of law. All of these schools claim to speak the truth. None so far has established itself unchallenged. In a society of moral pluralism and polyjurality, though conflicting visions may be shared, they may or may not completely converge. This is the problem of the so-called "mutually repellent solipsism." In trials, jury decides the truth of fact. In some cases, judges do. This is the closest we can get.

(2) Jurists as Makers of Scholarly Law

Jurists are free souls in the universe of law. The institution of academic freedom of law teachers is a deep-rooted and honored tradition. Law teachers, either individually or collectively, take upon themselves the task and responsibility to expose and criticize the gaps, inconsistency, contradictions, inadequacy, mistakes, wrongs, and other vices in the law. At the constitutive level, the very debates on what counts as law, the concept of law, and various other notions, ideas, etc., manifest the critical endeavors and commitment of legal scholars.

Jurist and reason are synonymous. The Roman jurists qua jurists owed their prestige and influence to their skill in handling abstract legal problems. The jurist individually would increase his stature and distinguish himself by inventing or crafting new solutions or compelling alternatives to either existing or potential problems and producing convincing arguments for them.

To criticize is to analyze, compare, and evaluate. The stance and perspective for critical analysis, comparison and evaluation may come from any known philosophical orientation. Explicitly or implicitly, all scholarly criticism purports to propose and recommend for change or improvement on existing law.

Jurists or legal scholars are expositors, critics, and "juridifiers" of the law. The material sources or bases used for exposition are traditionally limited to those belonging to the genre of the so-called established sources, texts and materials. These include legislation, regulations, and judicial decisions in the official camp as well as treatises, legal writings, and other materials of the so-called secondary

---

[67] A. T. Kromman, *The Lost Lawyer: Failing Ideals of the Legal Profession*. Cambridge MA: Harvard University Press, 1993.

[68] N. E. Bourke, *A Difference of Reason: the Difficulties and Deficiencies of Scientific Inquiry of Social Practice*. University Press of America, 1997.

sources of law. Hardly any legal scholars have ever attempted to explore the normative submerged legal landmass representing the action, reaction, and interaction of persons, physical and corporate in society with respect to their social, economic, professional, working, life. What is badly needed is for legal scholars to study and "juridify" the law in action in both the state domain and the non-state spheres.

The most interesting, significant and tremendously challenging function of a legal scholar is not exposition, or criticism of the law, especially of a positivist source, but "juridification." This in the context of the intellectual, recommendation and prescription function of legal scholars is their propositions of law as both it is and it ought to be. Exposition being mainly descriptive, value and moral neutral representation of the law as a given is supposed to be the easiest task. Criticism of law tends to be based on one or more theoretical or philosophical perspectives or orientations. As such, criticism of law is without exception partisan, exclusive, or incomplete that can be quite challenging. "Jurisdification" on the other hand proceeds from the foundation of exposition and criticism to advocating an integrative or combined version of the law as both it is and ought to be.

Unfortunately, there is a glaring mismatch or misfit between the scholarly law today and the law in action, the real world law. This disconnect has been criticized by Judge Edwards in "Indictment of Impractical Scholars: a Need for a Bill of Particulars."[169] Bourke sees this as a systemic weakness not simply a fault of any single piece of scholarship.[170] This failure of legal scholars to "juridify" the real world law has been noted by Llewellyn in drafting the Uniform Commercial Code.

New events, phenomena, trends, and decisions by elite powers in society are ever emerging. To "juridify" on the basis of all authoritative and effective decisions is a gigantic, daunting undertaking. It requires the most comprehensive empirical research and study of all possible disciplines: politics, economics, sociology, social and policy sciences.

Besides, every authoritative and effective decision has a unique set of variables in terms of objectives, participants (decision-makers), past trends, conditioning factors of both a temporal, spatial, or environmental nature, etc. Any particular

---

[169] 91 *Mich L Rev* 2010 (1993).

[170] Nacy E. Bourke, *A Difference of Reason: the Difficulties and Deficiencies of Scientific Inquiry of Social Practice*. University Press of America, 1997, p.103.

situation is a complex field of multiple, interdependent, and conflicting forces.

To "juridify" in the face of such complexity is much like the formulation of the holding or ratio decidendi of a case. Formulation may range from the most restrictive type limiting the content of the holding to the facts specific to the case at hand to the broadest conceptualization to cast the proposition in general and abstract terms thus causing the case to provide little precedent value. In other words, to focus or to emphasize too much on the fact situation of the case in "rulifying" (i. e. rule-making) tends to lose sight of the forest of the underlying principle of law. Perhaps, principled statements informed by highly selective representative fact situations would offer a better compromise. What ends up much resembles a judicious integration of rules and principles.

For discussion on the role, contribution, and place of legal scholarship in the collective normative enterprise of the law, please refer to the following sections of the previous chapter dealing with legal scholarship as a source of law(法律淵源), role and contribution of legal scholars in the formation of leading cases, comparative study of scholarly law and judicial law, and scholarly exposition and study of legislation.

G. Conditions and Requirements of a Good Citizen

What is the concept of a good citizen? Does a good legal system requires good citizens? What makes a good citizen? Must a good citizen be virtuous, honest, and live by a high moral standard? Must these conditions be of a political, social, legal, economic nature that is conducive to the nurturing and development of good citizens?

A good citizen should be politically and morally active and engaged. This requirement goes much beyond the quality of kindness, compassion, integrity, and gratitude for what others do, authenticity, humility and humor. Lon L. Fuller's morality of duty, in this case, the morality of civil duty, goes much beyond voting at the ballot booth on election day. Nor must one become a committed member of a political party. One should be concerned and adequately informed and knowledgeable of the constitutional structure of the country, and current developments in the present state of public affairs of all nature and kinds, locally, nationally as well as internationally.

A recent survey by The Dominion Institute taken in Canada in the aftermath of the Constitutional crisis involving Governor-General, Michaelle Jean's decision to prorogue Parliament at the request of the Prime Minister Stephen Harper suggested that Canadians had a woeful ignorance when it came to the system of government and lacked in many cases the basic knowledge to form informed opinions—knowledge that citizens need to function in a democracy.

People are the center of the normative universe. The teaching of Confucianism is that people are primary and officials are secondary. In the post-modern world, it is people power that the government must be reckoned with. What people give, what people take away. In all countries of constitutional democracy, the decision-making power and process must be open and inclusive. There are in the U.S. as well as in many other Western countries, a number of entities and organizations, such as the Advocacy Institute of the U.S. that is dedicated to capturing and disseminating learning about citizen advocacy in order to strengthen the capacity of all citizen groups effectively to pursue heir own visions of truth and justice.

The advance of the digital world with the internet and "facebook" and others providing online networks of information-sharing, organizing, and mobilization has never before leveled the playfield of politicking and empowering citizens at large.

The only person known to have advanced an observation on the possible attitude or perspective of a citizen toward the law and the legal system is O.Q. Holmes Jr.'s "bad man." Holmes' badman is a sophisticated, pragmatic, prudent, seasoned, and smart man who cares more about the material and practical impacts and value-indulgence and value-deprivation of authoritative and effective decisions than their moral quality. In other words, he is a realist who takes an external viewpoint of the law and his perspective is that of legal instrumentalist(法律工具论).

On the opposite pole to Holmes' bad man is a good citizen. A good man is a man of principle who care very much and zealously the moral quality of the law, such as equality, justice, fairness, and other human dignity values. A good man is no less sophisticated, prudent, seasoned, pragmatic, and smart. Instead of being opportunistic, manipulative, and fixated on the value consequences of authoritative and effective decisions, a good man invokes and applies the rule of law as a guide to conduct and a standard for criticizing fellow citizens who deviate from the requirements and standards of law. Most important of all is that a good citizen is an activist agent in the law making and application process or what generally termed as the process of authoritative and effective decision.

In The People Rising, Michael Pertschuk and Wendy Schaetzel orchestrate the virtues of dedicated selfless men and women of uncommon vision in terms of wise, brilliant, warm, direct, pragmatic, adept and prudent. These men and women constitute a guerrilla band of citizens lobbying for liberty that includes many of Washington's most seasoned political operatives, the leadership of powerful national organizations, leading members of the bar, and many of the Senate's most influential members. [171]

Can a good legal system accommodate O. W. Holmes Jr's' "bad man"? Must a good citizen take an internal viewpoint of the law as H. L. A. Hart advocates?] One would be very wise to establish a set of "internal morality" of a good citizen comparable to the requirements of internal morality of law as prescribed by Lon Fuller.

Two comparable notions, rule authoritarian(独裁主义者) and role authoritarian that have been advanced by jurists can be invoked in this connection to clarify the requirements for a good citizen. Rule authoritarian obeys political authority to avoid punishment but is generally alienated from authority. A role authoritarian obeys out of a sense of obligation and identification with his or her position and status in the polite or society. Role authoritarians want to be and to perceive themselves as good citizens and support policies and governments that contribute to enhancing their sense of status. [172] In doing so, they can be quite supportive of and active in authoritarian oppression of others. Both types of authoritarian adhere to consensual submission to authority. They consider this a functional way to abdicate moral responsibility and choice. As such, neither meets the stringent moral requirements for a good citizen.

An authoritarian individual is preoccupied with hierarchy, power, and obedience. He is rigid, inflexible, ethnocentric, intolerant, distrust of anything different, and punitive. In contrast, anti-authoritarian tends to be economically and socially egalitarian, trusting of others, tolerant, flexible, empathetic, non-stereotypical in thought, and ready to take moral responsibility for choices and actions.

People are the center of the legal universe and the fountain of all powers in a polity. As such, people must be fully aware of their importance and place. The conception of a free, responsible individual is embedded in the language and

---

[171] M. Pertschuk & W. Schaetzel, The People Rising: the Campaign Against the Bork Nomination (1989); Terrance Sandalow, "Supreme Court in Politics", 88 *Michigan L R* 1300, 1302-1303 (1990).

[172] Lynne Henderson, "Authoritarianism and the Rule of Law", 66 *Indiana L J* 379, 395 (1991).

pervades practices, in codes, and beliefs in all constitutional liberalism.

The highest Confucian morality of aspiration for a man is an ordered and ascendant undertaking of efforts and commitment: one must first and foremost cultivate and discipline one's own character and personal quality, must be able to control and harmonize one's own family; and only then one can process to govern the state well, and equalize and pacify the world at large. But the Confucian five virtues of moral imperatives for maintaining a harmonious and equilibrium hierarchical social and political relationship of loyalty, filial piety, benevolence and righteousness are largely anachronistic. Kant admonishes that we should treat our fellow man as an end, and not merely as a means. Eugene Pashukanis, the only Soviet thinker who can be said to having made a distinctive contribution to social philosophy, regards Kant's admonition as the natural law of exchange in a market economy. Lon L. Fuller expounds the implicit principle of reciprocity. [73]

A good citizen should take the responsibility for (1) his or her own conduct and decision, (2) ensuring that there is no unjust encroachment of any kind and from any source on his or her rights, freedoms, and other human dignity values, and (3) the promotion of the optimal moral quality and justice of the law, and the integrity of the legal system.

A good citizen must be both active and committed. From an internal perspective, law must be used as a standard for one's own conduct and the criticism of others. Generally speaking, law is whatever subject to the constraints of the constitution comes out of an open and transparent, non-discriminating democratic process. Being responsible for one's own conduct and decision means that one must be willing to take whatever consequences coming from one's violation of what is required by the law. A good citizen who takes Hart's "internal view of law" acts on the presupposition of "a living contract with one another, either through an explicit reciprocity or through relations of tacit reciprocity embodied in the forms of an organized society."[74] A good citizen is a man of good will, honest, conscientious, active, committed, and brave. A good citizen aspires not only to live up to his duty of ensuring the survival, security, order, and other demands of the minimum moral requirements for a good legal system, but also to strive for the improvement and prosperity of the polity whenever and wherever needed and possible. For the former,

---

[73] Fuller, *The Morality of Law*, New Haven & London: Yale Univ. Pr., p. 19.
[74] Id., at 183.

the minimum duty, one should willingly abide by the law of authoritative and effective decisions. For the latter, the optimal moral aspiration, one may on occasions have to engage in normative context breaking. What this means is not just active engagement in constructive criticism of the legal and political structures, institutions, culture with the aims to expose their weaknesses, inadequacy, injustice, and wrongs and operations, but also mobilizing civil disobedience to invalidate, de-legitimize, and dethrone the unjust and immoral law. In this connection, it is fitting to be reminded of what the United States Declaration of Independence implies:

Whenever any form of government becomes destructive of the ends and values as embodied in the Declaration, it is the right of the people to alter or to abolish it, and to institute a new government. The foundation of the new government will be laid on such principles and its powers organized in such form as to them shall seem most likely to enhance their safety, prosperity, liberty, and happiness.

There is a logical tension between these two opposing duties. In practice, how should one choose in a given situation and circumstance is a personal, informed, conscientious moral judgment.

People are the central attitudinal force of constraint in the normative enterprise of the law. Attitudinal constraint working together with institutional constraint holds all elite powers to act within the confine of the constitutive framework, and the law and the legal system develop the way they ought to be.

A good citizen is a committed, activist individual who care very much about both the process and the substance of the public, political affairs and who aspires to the image and action of prominent citizen activists, such as Gandhi, Dr. Martin Luther King, Jr. A good citizen would emulate Dora Bouboulis and her fellow town representatives in Vermont, who decided to vote on a resolution directing their local member of Congress to file articles of impeachment against the U. S. President in the House of Representatives for lying about weapons of mass destruction in Iraq, the mismanagement of the budget, the illegal wiretapping.

It is interesting to note that Forbe's celebrity power lists annually most influential persons on the life of people. Time Magazine also has a list of 100 most influential individuals in the world in terms of their ability to shape and transform views, opinions, and decisions.

A Reasonable Man in the Enterprise of Law:

Can a good legal system accommodate O. W. Holmes Jr's' "bad man"? Must a good citizen always take an internal viewpoint of the law as H. L. A. Hart advocates? Could it be even desirable, fair, and just that a good man at times becomes and behaves like a bad man and vice versa?

In the fields of private law, the virtues of a reasonable man are highly orchestrated and cherished. Shouldn't the concept of a reasonable man be equally applicable in all fields of political morality? In other words, whether or not citizens take an internal or external viewpoint of law depends very much on the circumstance, the needs, and aspiration in a given time and space.

Individualist(个人主义者) vs. Collectivist(集体主义者):

Must an autonomous moral agent be an individualist? Could a collectivist individual be compatible with the quality and requirements of a good citizen? An individualistic moral person is wary of all authority, hostile to every whiff of subordination, believes individual freedom would guarantee a rough social equality, and that the best government is one that governs least.

Yet, the influence of individual decision and action in the public domain is fairly limited and insignificant. To forge together the minds and ability of many into collective entities is a wise, necessary choice.

To be united and organized is the best path to power. The marvelous thing is that unity and organization do not exclude decentralized, spontaneous, confluent decision of people acting individually. For example, Friedrich Hayek, the Nobel Prize-winning Austrian economist is of the view that knowledgeable people with global perspectives don't determine prices. Ignorant people with household budgets determine prices. Prices result from human action but not human design. In final analysis, unity and organization are the form of human action, not the material content of human action.

A Good Citizen is a Politically and Morally Activist:

Victims of crime, violence, repression, or injustice may sometimes reject all legal processes, formal and informal, to choose unmediated political confrontation with their adversaries. In many instances, the targets for complaint(控告), grievance, or justice seeking may very well be the state or the Crown itself or governmental bodies. Workers being compelled to operate under dangerous conditions are not content to sue for damages after injured, to submit their grievances to arbitration, or to invoke the intervention of an oversight regulatory agency. They simply choose to walk off the job. Citizens who suffer from police violence refuse to depend on the police or the courts to correct such outrages but demand civilian control and back that demand with violence. ⑮

Such direct political confrontations with the wrongdoers and adversaries are not taking the law in one's own hand as understood in the traditional, received sense. Instead, such acts signify citizens' engaging in political, moral action and posit their best, intended legal normativity into the authoritative and effective decision-making process.

Citizen activism takes many forms. The possibility of activism only challenges imagination. One of the latest forms is a proposal dubbed "say on pay." During the most severe economic woes, financial crisis, the housing bubble burst, and subprime mortgage meltdown in 2008 and 2009, a debate was brewing about whether top bankers continue to deserve fat pay packages while write-downs, and credit losses pile up on financial statements, battering stock prices. The "say on pay" proposal was designed to seek to give shareholders an annual "advisory" vote on executive compensation.

An activist citizen aspires to "change the world." Private morality cannot be regulated. But it may very well be the precursor of the law of political morality. For example, the "Free Hugs" movement can entail important and far-reaching social consequences and political implications.

Normative Messaging and the Power of Social Norms:

Humans are social beings. Whether we admit it or not, we love to conform. The most important influence on our behaviour is not the media, as we think, it's actually other people. Though what I am doing are trivial things, if other people see me doing it, I am therefore participating in the establishment of a social norm, which encourages and invites other people to change. It's about knowing that and trusting that that is a very powerful social force.

The CBC and the Canadian arm of internet technology giant Cisco Systems Inc., have discovered the power of social norms. The One Million Acts of Green campaign, a social-networking website, hit its target after barely three months—five months ahead of schedule. The site uses the collaborative strengths of Web-based technology to get people and communities to tally up their climate-conscious behaviours, set targets and compare them with others. Many individuals, schools,

---

⑮ Richard L. Abel, "The Contradictions of Informal Justice", *Politics of Informal Justice*, Volume one edited by R. L. Abel. New York; Toronto: Academic Press, 1982, pp. 267, 309.

universities, municipalities and businesses all have joined.

Superheros:

Are you a superhero who carries out vigilante patrols in their neighborhoods? Superheros are do-gooders or vigilantes, Friends of the homeless and enemies of Bin Laden. They are donning costumes and prowling their streets, looking to fight crime—or at least shovel a senior's walk. To be fair, it seems like some of these people have their heart in the right place and even make a positive impact on their community outside of crime fighting.

From an active, positive perspective, the virtues of a good political, moral activist citizen should answer the inspirational call of greater leaders, such as Abraham Lincoln in his second inauguration in the midst of the Civil War exhorting Americans with such famous words: "with malice towards none, with charity for all." John F. Kennedy at his 1963 inauguration famously exhorted: "Ask not what your country can do for you, but what you can do for your country."

"I"law or I am the law, even in a world of the ubiquitous "I", as exemplified by iPot, iPhone, iReport, iTrade to suggest, let alone advocate, iLaw or the more preferred concept "I am the law," would appear inappropriate or misguided, if not presumptuous, insane, ridiculous or funny. Yet, upon further reflection and analysis, the concept "I am the law" is not only rational but also extremely realistic, democratic, and empowering. It reflects and captures, better than any other theory of law, the multifarious, dynamic reality of the political moral life of a polity. It is the most inclusive and comprehensive theory of law ever advocated. Just stop and think of these real life activities: iJudge, iLawyering, iLegislate, iRegulate, iApply, iInvoke, iInterpret, iAct, iDecide, and iPrescribe, in the established arena of law, you will quickly become a believer. The list goes on.

An activist citizen, whatever his or her position, role, responsibility, value system, belief, must cherish and protect his or her individuality and personal integrity. He or she must be his or her own man or woman morally committed to assert and defense his or her individuality, belief, values, action and decision.

There is a "let your life speak movement." This is very much like the "free hug" movement, Camp Obama and even Superheros. These are small groups of people gathering together, organized or spontaneous confluence of the likeminded telling stories and relating personal stories to large stories of the community. The beauty of this is from narcissism to benevolence, and in the end, making significances in the normative lives of people and the nation.

The concept of "I am the law" is fully consistent with the view and proposition of the crucial importance of the human factor in the establishment of a good legal system and good law. This is exactly what we advocate in the discussion in Chapter Seven of the conditions and requirements of a good lawyer, judge, politician, citizen and corporate citizen. In our public and political lives, we all invoke, interpret, apply, appraise, and prescribe the law. Above all, only the individual person in coordination and cooperation with the like-minded others are likely to bring about social, political, and legal changes.

In Chapter one, Section one dealing with the political, moral perspective, we have already elaborated the same theme that I am the law. Please result there for more details.

To give a timely example, saying "I made a mistake," Republican Sen. Judd Gregg of New Hampshire abruptly withdrew as commerce secretary nominee on Thursday and left the fledgling White House suddenly coping with Barack Obama's third Cabinet withdrawal. Gregg cited "irresolvable conflicts" with Obama's policies, specifically mentioning the $790 billion economic stimulus bill and 2010 census in a statement released without warning by his Senate office. Gregg was one of three Republicans Obama had put in his Cabinet to emphasize his campaign pledge that he would be an agent of bipartisan change. Being a strong fiscal conservative, Gregg searched his heart and had a second thought. "For 30 years, I've been my own person in charge of my own views, and I guess I hadn't really focused on the job of working for somebody else and carrying their views, and so this is basically where it came out. Gregg, 61, said he changed his mind after realizing he wasn't ready to 'trim my sails' to be a part of Obama's team. " "I just sensed that I was not going to be good at being anything other than myself." He foresaw conflicts over health care, global warning, taxes, the census, and economic stimulus plan. [179]

H. Conditions and Requirements of a Good Corporate Citizen

In the modern world of free market capitalism, economic power and commercial muscle play a major role in the international status of a country and in the prosperity of its people. The laws and regulations that govern the activities of corporations,

---

[179] "Gregg Withdraws as Commerce Secretary Nominee", *Yahoo Finance*, February 13, 2009, 6:56 am ET.

their size and management, their influence, their impact on society and social customs have served essentially to define the environment within which people live: some argue that this is even more so than that of the state. The force of companies in shaping society far outstrips that of educational institutions and the Church. Companies influence directly or indirectly the lives of most citizens. Companies are ubiquitous in civilized capitalistic societies. And it has been painfully witnessed world-wide and proved beyond any doubt that that large scale economic disruptions, such as the devastating events that have occurred and are occurring as a result of the economic meltdown and financial and banking crises, cause political and social unrest and even violence.

Fuller's insightful distinction of the morality of duty and the morality of aspiration is equally relevant and applicable to the issue of a good corporate citizen. Morality of duty in this respect refers to other-imposed or regulatory conditions, framework, guidance, constraint, or sanction, primarily coming from the state. Morality of aspiration finds its expression in any voluntary measures, actions, or undertakings initiated and put in place by corporations themselves. The U.S. Sarbanes-Oxley act enacted on the heels of the surge of notorious practice of corporate misconduct(企业失当行为), irregularity(不正当行为), fraud(欺诈), scandal(中伤) is a typical example of regulatory measure to impose morality of duty on American corporations. This law is primarily concerned with public accounting oversight board, auditor independence, corporate responsibility, enhanced financial disclosures, analyst conflicts of interest, commercial fraud accountability, white-collar crime(白领犯罪) penalty enforcement, and corporate fraud and accountability, among other things.

The financial and banking crisis, if not disaster, brought on by irrational exuberance and unbridled greed of sub-prime mortgage lending, notoriously gross inflating housing value, excessive leveraging borrowing, etc. have proven beyond doubt regulatory and enforcement failures and prompts the need for transparency, accountability, and tough regulation of corporate citizens even more and urgently to the fore front.

Yet, few corporate citizens have taken any political moral action of an aspiration nature out of own initiatives. Critical assessments and reports, internal or external, on corporate governance, social responsibility and financial and environmental accountability are only slow in coming. But there are encouraging signs. Many companies in response to consumers' environmental and green expectations have started to launch internal eco-sensitive programs, manufacture organic or biological products, or provide environment-friendly services.

Social and Environmental Responsibility

Another measurement for good global citizen is corporate social responsibility. This is the new buzz-word for the morality of corporate duty and responsibility. The old concept of being a good corporate citizen has grown into the all-encompassing notion of corporate social responsibility, with businesses aiming to be socially aware, eco-friendly global citizens. But companies need to be seen as credible, not simply spouting rhetoric or trying to greenwash their public image. There is now a lot of scrutiny on how companies operate, more media reporting and increased Internet information. GlobeScan, a Toronto-based research company, studies corporate social responsibility and publishes an annual Corporate Social Responsibility Monitor report. Today, companies need legitimacy, a social license to operate. The route to such legitimacy lies in measurable activities and transparent reporting. Bottom-line financial accountability in the face of rising public and governmental expectations is not enough in and by itself.

Launched in 1997, Global Reporting Initiative is made up of thousands of experts, in dozens of countries worldwide, who take part in working groups and governance bodies to develop a detailed set of guidelines to measure and disclose corporate behavior. The guidelines cover economic, environmental, social, human rights, labour practices, product responsibility and governance

The finite nature and increasing diminishing of natural resources spur companies to explore and find new ways of doing business. The alarming rates of environmental pollution and globe warming have made this a pressing task. Sustainable business becomes a vogue of the day. And there are sustainability experts available in a variety of fields can help companies realize the profit in this shift. The environment is the economy. The economy is the environment. To make the distinction is old world. The long-term relationship with the client is very high. And at the same time, the reputation as a good corporate citizen is ensured.

In Canada, Ecojustice, formerly Sierra Legal Defence Fund, a Canada's leading non-profit organization of lawyers and scientists, is devoted to protecting the environment. Since 1990, Ecojustice has helped hundreds of groups, coalitions and communities expose law-breakers, hold governments accountable and establish powerful legal precedents in defense of air, water, wildlife and natural spaces.

Responding to a financial crisis of historical proportion, Barack Obama plans to usher in a new American era of financial ethics and corporate responsibility as part of an economic recovery plan to deal with the catastrophe by instituting strict new financial regulations for banks, credit-rating agencies, mortgage brokers and "a whole bunch of folks... having to be much more accountable and behave more responsibly." This aims at ensuring corporations living up to their morality of duty for the interest of all Americans. External-imposed morality of duty on corporations comes also and even more so from the private sectors and general public.

In today's digital age, Facebook, Myspace, Twitter, Brogospher (bloogers/bloggging) with increased media reporting and scrutiny, online information dissemination and sharing, civil society has become increasingly more sophisticated in leveraging information.

Accompanying the growing public awareness of the importance of corporation's social responsibility. "ethical funds" are borne. These funds are designed to nudge businesses toward more fully embracing their corporate social responsibilities, especially in areas such as preserving the environment. Mercer (Canada) Ltd., led by pension funds, institutions and ethical mutual fund companies, shareholders are increasingly using annual meetings, proxy materials and old-fashioned public relations to nudge public companies into action over everything from environment protection to employment practices. Such movements are based on hard-edged economics and long-term sustainability—the understanding that embracing high standards on the environment, employment and other social issues reduces risk and ultimately leads to improved financial returns for corporations. The methods resorted to include writing letters on special issues, meetings to persuade companies to make changes in their policies, and incorporating proposals into proxy materials for annual meetings.

Microsoft founder and philanthropist Bill Gates has called for a new creative capitalism. There are three emerging alternatives to the shareholder-value model which could help companies avoid ethical mishaps. These are the stakeholder-owned companies—a co-operative model of ownership that has been existing for customers, farmers, homeowners, and employees, etc; The mission-controlled companies that have a long-term commitment to some mission that is expected to transcend the normal concern with profitability whose governance structure reflecting both the need for ongoing sufficient profit and a broader social priority; The public-private hybrids. A prime example is Grameen Danone Foods with a mission to feed the world's poor with a fortified yogurt. Google-.org is another model which manages an annual philanthropy budget of $2-billion (U.S.). This is not a foundation and, as a division of Google, it is expected to operate with business principles but strives to further social causes.

Public interest and convenience is a well-established standard or criterion for judging the necessity and rationality of corporate activity and decision. Public interest and convenience is the anchor of corporate social responsibility. Some sort of study or review entity, such as a group, board, or panel, is set up either in house or on an ad hoc(特定的) basis. Public interest and convenience is also the regulatory criteria employed by licensing and oversight regulatory bodies to make sure the objectives and actions and decisions of corporations serve the common good.

Corporate Transparency and Accountability

The executives and directors of all public companies are directly accountable to the employees and stocks and stakes holders of a public company. To disseminate all information of a material nature is therefore crucial for executives and directors to fulfill this morality of duty.

One of the issues that came to public attention is, whether or not and to what extent, the health condition of a CEO should be made public promptly and accurately. In a broader context, the matter concerns the ethical and legal requirement to respect privacy against a company's onus to disclose material information. The crux of the issue is the definition of "materiality." If there is news in hand that can affect whether a reasonable investor would buy or sell certain stocks or stacks in question, then the information must be disclosed according to the United States securities law. With respect to Mr. Jobs, the CEO of Apple Computer, the fact he stepped down makes it unquestionable that the information is material.

Recently, the issue of compensation for CEO and other executives and officers of corporations has made the front-page news. This issue during good times when a corporation is profitable and employees and all stake-holders share the profit does not draw much attention of either the government or the general public. Unfortunately, the devastating economic meltdown and financial and banking crises have changed everything. The decision by companies to secretly award executives and high-ranking employees with excessive amount of compensation, especially by using taxpayers' bailout money and subsequently attempted to resort to evasive measures to avoid accountability have alarmed and angered both government officials, the Congress and the general public.

A good discussion of the issues and problems relating to greed, compensation, and other perks have been made earlier in the book. Please refer to Chapter four, Section three, J (American Greed) and K Corporate Bonuses, Compensations, and Other Perks) for more details.

It is important to note that a more comprehensive study of the requirements and conditions for a good corporate citizen must include the requirements, role, responsibility and functions of not only the chief executive officer, the chief financial officer, the board of directors, but also other high ranking employees whose work significantly impact the company.

Shareholders(股东) Activism:

Shareholders activism takes many forms. Mergers and Acquisitions may be motivated by attempts to satisfy shareholders.

But there are limits imposed by law to both the nature and the scope of shareholders activism. When a company consistently underperforms its peers, a consortium of a certain major stakeholder may in collaboration with other interested parties, such as private equities, mutual funds, or hedge funds to file what's known as a schedule 13D, notifying the U.S. Securities and Exchange Commission(证券交易委员会) that it has become an activist investor. The move purports to lead a proxy battle and ultimately to form a new board of directors in order to take over the management of the company. In the case of Petro-Canada, the Petro-Canada Public Participation Act prohibits any group form owning more than 20 per cent of the voting shares. The merger of Petro-Canada into Suncor Energy may put the prohibition in danger.

White-Collar Crimes:

Unfortunately, white-collar crimes are not dissimilar to criminal wrongdoings of other nature.

It is one thing to boast that one's company aims to maintaining "an unblemished record of value, fair-dealing and high ethical standards that has always been the firm's hallmark," it is totally another thing one stays free of being accused and convicted of any white-collar crimes, such as fraud, embezzlement, or other criminal wrongdoings.

The latest and the most notorious example of this is the $50-billion (U. S.) Ponzi (pyramid) scheme—a fraud of epic scope perpetuated and ripped off clients for years by Bernard Madoff, the former Chairman of the Nasdaq Stock Market and founder of the investment firm in his very name. This giant Ponzi scheme is the largest financial scandal in history and bigger than Enron, bigger than Boesky, and bigger than Tyco. It attacks at the very core of investor confidence. The detailed stocks trading claimed by Madoff for his numerous clients are pure fiction; They are all made up; It was just money in and money out, a pure Ponzi scheme. This has to top what any dictator ever siphoned out of a banana republic. It has put the soundness of the U. S. financial system in question. One cannot simply blame for this fiasco of historical proportion on a few "bad apples". Nor it is just the fault of those who were asleep at the switch. The supposed meticulous supervision by (US financial watchdog) the Securities Exchange Commission (SEC) has failed in the task of preventing massive fraud. It is a systemic weakness and defect of regulatory and enforcement scheme. A growing criticism and suspicion point to the close relationship between the Wall Street and federal regulators. Madoff himself has boasted of his ties to the SEC. Connivance, collusion, intentional torts as well as criminal wrongdoings were at core. Systemic weakness and regulatory defect are further aggravated by unscrupulousness and evil of man. [177]

It was a blistering escalation of criticism of the SEC, which has been blasted by lawmakers and investor advocates over its failure to discover Madoff's alleged $50 billion Ponzi scheme despite the credible allegations brought to it by Markopolos over a decade. Against the backdrop of the worst financial crisis since the 1930s, lawmakers of both parties are calling for a shake-up of the agency.

Backdating stock options granted to executives and employees of a company may constitute a white-collar crime. The practice is not always illegal, however. In many cases in the United States, the illegality arose from the way companies broke accounting and tax rules in reporting the grants. Since 2000, many executives have to resign as a result of backdating scandals.

Stock options give company employees the right to buy shares at a set price, typically the price at the end of the trading session on the date a grant is made. Backdating happens when companies set the grant date retroactively to align with a

---

[177] Charles Ponzi devised in the 1920s a scam offering abnormally high profits to investors out of the money paid in by subsequent investors.

stock's low point, creating an instant paper gain.

In Canada, the Ontario Securities Commission alleges that the co-founders of Research in Motion, Jim Balsillie and Mike Lazaridis made use of a stock option time machine, retroactively matching up the date that options were granted with lows in the stock price. Executives and directors at Research in Motion, including co-CEOs Jim Balsillie and Mike Lazaridis, were slapped about $77 million in fines and restitution under a negotiated settlement with the Ontario Securities Commission. Balsillie will also be prevented from being a director of any company for a year—although he'll be allowed to remain an executive of RIM. Kavelman, who was RIM's chief financial officer from 1995 to 2007 and has been chief operating officer since then, is prohibited from acting as a director or officer of any Canadian reporting issuer for five years.

On Friday, January 23, 2009, Google Inc. (NASDAQ: GOOG) said it was resetting more than eight million stock options at lower prices to reflect the current market meltdown, where shares of the company are well below the option prices set a few years ago, making such options worthless in today's financial markets. The resetting has irked shareholders still stuck with agonizing losses on their investments. Google is giving option holders a break on the stock that has plunged 57 per cent since its peak at $747 a share in 2007.

Such practice grabbed the attention of regulators in the early 1990s. In the United States, the Securities Exchange Commission ruled that companies were required to report stock options in full detail for both their financial reports and in regulatory filings. However, that didn't necessarily mean that companies actually stopped using the practice to reward their executives.

Nearly three years ago the SEC began placing about 200 companies under investigation for their options accounting, including RIM.

The cases stretched to other major tech companies like Apple Computer, which restated its earnings to reflect US $84 million in expenses tied to options awards. Executives at the company, including chief Steve Jobs, were cleared of any wrongdoing.

Another area proven to be futile ground for white-collar crimes is accounting fraud. Indian police arrested two partners of an Indian arm of accounting giant PricewaterhouseCoopers LLP on charge of criminal conspiracy and cheating in connection with the fraud investigation at Satyam Computer Services Ltd.⑱

Corporate Fraud:

Swiss banking giant UBS has agreed to pay 780 million dollars to the US government and cooperate in a tax fraud probe, including naming scofflaw clients.

UBS AG, Switzerland's largest bank, has entered into a deferred prosecution agreement on charges of conspiring to defraud the United States by impeding the Internal Revenue Service (IRS)(国内收入署).

As part of the deferred prosecution agreement and in an unprecedented move, UBS, based on an order by the Swiss Financial Markets Supervisory Authority (FINMA)(瑞士金融市场管理局), has agreed to immediately provide the United States government with the identities of, and account information for, certain United States customers of UBS's cross-border business.

UBS's agreement "to pay 780 million dollars in fines, penalties, interest and restitution" was accepted subsequently by a US federal judge in Florida.

In light of the bank's willingness to acknowledge responsibility for its actions and omissions(不作为), its cooperation and remedial actions to date, and its promised continuing cooperation and remedial actions, the government will recommend dismissal of the charge, provided the bank fully carries out its obligations under the agreement.⑲

One of the agreements reached on April 3, 2009 by the leaders of the 20 most rich or influential countries in London is to crack down on tax havens(避税港). The age of bank secrecy as encouraged by market fundamentalists under excessive banking deregulation is over. Sanctions will be slapped on any sponsor country that refuses to sign international agreements to exchange tax information

Aspiration and Prospect of a Good Legal System

The very concept of a good legal system admits the possibility and reality of the existence through history of systems that have gone or are presently going through different phases of development. On the spectrum of morality, procedural or substantive, some systems have found their place at the very bottom of moral development, while the achievement of others is highly appraised. The moral quality

---

⑱ Jackie Range, "Pricewaterhouse Partners Arrested in Satyam Case." *The Globe and Mail*, Jan. 26, 2009, p. B7.

⑲ "Swiss Bank UBS to Pay 780 mln drs in US Tax Fraud Probe", *Rogers Yahoo News*, February 18, 2009.

and success of a legal system is believed to be intractably dependent on the moral quality and aspiration of the elite powers in a polity. Rule of law must go hand in hand with rule of man. In no cases can the legal achievement outrun the aspiration and endeavour of the human beings who guide it. Only when both perform as desired, a good legal system can be built, sustained, and progressively developed. Perceived in this perspective, it would be so much natural to expand Fuller's "internal morality of law" to include both its procedural and its substantive aspects.

A good legal system finds a strong foundation in democracy. Democracy in terms of basic social and political structure informs and is informed and strengthened by polyjurality or political moral pluralism. Either by explicit constitutive design or through implicit institutional building and practice, multiple or layered systems exist side by side in all society. State system operates along and in mutual deference with non-state autonomous systems. Fuller observes that in the United States alone, "systems of law" number in the hundreds of thousands. The existence and healthy development a legal system does not "require a neatly defined hierarchy of authority with a supreme legislative [or a judicial] power at the top that is itself free from legal restraints". There is a tacit and reciprocal expectation and recognition of authority between the state organs and non-state sectors. [18]

Review and Reflective Questions

1. Is there such a thing as a good legal system as opposed to a bad one? Or there is simply an authoritative and effective one?

2. What are the formal requirements for a good legal system?

3. What are the substantive requirements for a good legal system?

4. Are good men crucial to the establishment of a good legal system? And in what way?

5. What qualities and characters does a judge, a politician, a lawyer, a scholar, or a citizen have to embrace for the building of a good law and a good legal system?

复习及提问

1. 是否存在良法体系与恶法体系之分？或者只是存在权威性和生效性之分？

2. 构成良法体系的形式要件是什么？

---

[18] Fuller, *The Morality of Law*, New Haven; London: Yale Univ. Pr., pp. 124, 125.

3. 构成良法体系的实质要件是什么?
4. 良好的人对于良法体系的构成是否十分重要? 体现在哪些方面?
5. 在制定一部良法和构建一个良好的法律体系时,法官、政治家、法律人、学者、公民都应当各自具备怎样的素质和特点?

Chapter Eight: Legal Reason and Executing Decision

Introductory Note

Reason is the armory of advocacy. Thus, the moral quality and value strength of reason decide very much the success or failure of advocacy and whether or not the normativity of a decision can be effectuated.

In this chapter, the nature, form, content of reason and its operation in advocacy are discussed in a fairly comprehensive manner. Every aspect imaginable of legal reason marshaled to effectuating decision is covered in detail. This chapter is the soul of the book that must be carefully studied by every student of Anglo-American law.

简 介

理性是论辩的武器,理性的价值及其道德对于论辩的成败具有决定性意义。此外,一项决定是否有效及其可持续性,也是由理性决定的。本章就理性的实质、形式、内容以及理性在论辩中的具体操作做了详细讨论。该章内容是整本书的核心,因此,每一位学习英美法的学生都需要仔细研读。

Not all of the normative propositions will become law. Not all the rules in statutes or regulations will become authoritative and effective. Not all of the judicial decisions will acquire the authoritative status of precedents. To acquire the privileged status of the authority of law, they need effectuation, enforcement, or implementation. Mere efficacy alone won't do. Nor authority accorded on the basis of formal or procedural validity and appropriateness suffices. For any normative proposition to be accepted as law, the proposition must acquire authority along with efficacy. In this connection, H. L. A. Hart's distinction between what is obligated and being obliged, and the internal and external statements go a long way to capture the essential nature of law.

Even a valid legal rule may not be an authoritative and binding law. Legal rules themselves may have embedded problems, such as generality, vagueness, confusion, contradiction, insufficiency, other weaknesses that make them impossible to follow. Fuller's "internal morality of law(法律的内在道德性)" discussed above must be fulfilled to obtain both.

To effect a political moral action is difficult and complex. The challenge requires much more than simple mobilization of resources. Proper and effective ways and means to put resources to use and to persuade target audiences on the merits, material as well as moral, of the action in question must also be taken.

Decision can be effectuated by means of power, force and violence as well as through reason and persuasion. Decision effected by violence and force alone may lack the normative power of the law and even legitimacy, the sine qua non(必备因素) of any power and decision. The life of a law would be quite fleeting when backed by naked power alone. President George W. Bush's unilateral attempt(单边努力), however well-intended, to force democracy on the Arab world fails miserably, because he ignores one basic element that in effecting decision successfully, one has to discuss with those directly affected and be blessed with their consent. In modern states of liberal democracy, public, rational discourse, reasoning* and persuasion are cherished distinctive characteristics. Yet, in many instances such as in areas of deep, intractable controversies as well as in conflicts of a transnational nature, communications may be strategically crafted, calculatedly planned, and forcefully executed. Such communications often proceed retaliatory actions or threat thereof.

Devising effective strategies goes hand in hand with judicious presentation and communication. The means and ways to effect decisions are as varied, complex, rich, and infinite as the power and creativity of the human mind.

George W. Bush had a plan to reshape the Arab world. But he didn't talk to the Arabs. You can't force democracy. Unilateralism is the byword for the present United States administration that seems congenitally unable to consult effectively or work within a multilateral framework(多边框架). Many of the actions taken by the United States on the international stage cannot be called a success; some may prefer to consider these actions successful, but at what costs.

One of the old standbys of liberal theory is the distinction between power and persuasion. Persuasion through reason should be made on the basis of superior knowledge, the compelling power of reason and reasoning. Persuasion with regard to

---

* reason, reasoning, rationality 三个词都有"理性"的含义。一般来说, reason 与 rationality 可以互换使用。关于 reason 与 reasoning 的区别,请参见本书下文第 350 页的脚注。

matters of political morality should be done in a political forum by public discourse (公共商谈). Superior knowledge must be demonstrated and not claimed. No individual, organization, or entities, official or private, should be allowed to claim superior knowledge and to use political power to achieve partisan ends. In this world, no one who comes into public debates having a secure possession of the moral high ground, is able to persuade but immune from persuasion by others. No one can use the ostensible mellowness or vulnerability of someone else's preferences and position to establish the indubitability of her or his own.[181]

Normative propositions, actions, and decisions can be generally divided into two kinds, namely, self-executing decisions and non-self-executing decisions.

A decision that is self-executing must meet two conditions. Either one of the two conditions alone won't do. First, in terms of the form of the decision, the words, language, and structure of the decision must be clear, precise, free of vagueness, contradiction, confusion, etc. Second, with respect to the substantive content, the quality of the moral content must be persuasive, compelling, commanding high admiration. Such decisions are willingly accepted and acted upon by all concerned; the duty and responsibility demanded by such decisions will be internalized and no external elements or forces of any kind are needed for their compliance, implementation, and in other words, efficacy.

When a decision that cannot be put into practice solely on the basis of its form and substantive content, it must resort to external, additional, supplementary, or other means to obtain the two constitutive or defining elements of law: authority and efficacy.

The United States Federal Reserve is responsible for the setting of interest rates to fight inflation and to ensure price stability. Unfortunately, the Fed has had an unusual amount of trouble talking, if not double-talking, in its policy decisions and its communication thereof. Its opaque remarks and vague commitment caused misreading, misunderstanding, confusion, damaging impacts on the financial markets, and triggered whiplash in bond yields. As a result, the Fed had to refine its messages in order to set the record straight.[182] The new chairman of the Fed apparently has been trying hard to change this unfortunate state.

---

[181] Richard A. Epstein, *Simple Rules for a Complex World*, Harv. Univ. Pr., p.312.
[182] Victoria Thieberger, "Analysts Mull Over Fed to Refine Message", *Yahoo Finance*, 9/13/03 9:49 AM.

Law and Legal Reason

The plight of reason(理性的困境) in (American) law is not an oddity or a peculiarity, but rather is as emblematic or symptomatic as some much broader cultural tendencies. Every act or decision of a public political nature* is informed and justified by some moral or value-based points. Claims of justification for what count as law made on the basis of a rule must necessarily go beyond or behind the rule to the norms that are the grounds of justification of the rule. The norms are the points or reasons(原因或理由) that serve as the criteria, grounds or bases of justification. Even the editor of a newspaper agonizes over his or her decisions. To make sure position is mature, rooted in analysis, not prejudice, he or she discusses and debates, ponders and probes, examining the arguments and evidences from many different angles.

Legal reason probably has its beginning in the conceptualization of law. Legal reason operates at two levels: the philosophical or theoretical level and the practical and decisional level. At the philosophical level, legal reason attempts at tackle the most fundamental question of what counts as law, what are its defining features, nature, function, authority, etc. At the practical and decisional level, legal reason purports to ground and justify authoritative and effective decisions. Every decision-maker or actor has a philosophical stance on law and its concomitant concepts, such as validity, authority, obligation, right or wrong, justice or injustice, etc. Thus, every decision or action is informed and shaped by a particular philosophical stance. Law is normative statement of political morality. As such, every law has certain moral or value-based points or reasons. Those who claim otherwise are nonetheless, implicitly maybe, informed by certain jurisprudential thought(法学思想) and stance by default.

Dynamic and robust "juridification(法规化)" is an omnipresent and most ambitious normative enterprise of a political society. "Juridification" has become the desired end point of all kinds of public political moral programs from the far right to the far left. All activist groups of society speak in a legalist idiom and seek to institute their propositions of political moral programs in the aesthetics of the legal code. In

---

* 在文中的含义是"种类"、"类型",如 books of a scientific nature(科学类书籍)。

short, all such political moral actions are law advocacy, "juridification."⑱

A. Nature of Legal Reason

Legal reason is a specific form of rhetoric that signifies a mode of oral address or written statement that attempts to elevate private, subjective utterances to the status of an objective, commonly acceptable meaning, knowledge, and understanding. Reason is the fundamental base of political and moral decision and action. Reason is immanent to the normative enterprise of the law: reason is the mind of law, the heart of authority, the body of legal materials and sources, and the spirit of process.

It is rather an overstatement to regard reason as a constitutive feature of law only. Reason and reasoning is a universal practice prevailing in all fields of knowledge and decision.

Legal reason is the political and moral thematization of authoritative and effective decisions.

Not all the reasons given for decisions and actions are politically commendable or morally compelling. Unfortunately, rent seeking*, power politics, outright deceit, and other questionable strategic behaviors do in fact play a significant part in the production of many laws, and masquerade as reasons of justification.

Rhetoric achieves its power by means of manipulation, strategy, persuasion, or by reference to facts and truth. The success of rhetoric or advocacy depends to a significant degree on the legitimate, right, just, effective choice of words, language, materials, approaches, and even time, space, and audience.

The most common form of legal reason is from law to facts. This is generally called application**. When reasoning from facts to derive legal propositions or conclusions as in judicial decisions to formulate the holding of a case, it may be called normative generalization of facts*** or "juridification," if you will.

Coherence, comprehensiveness, and determinacy have been advanced as important qualities for law and legal reason, and for that matter, for all of the normative rules and propositions. To a large extent, when being compared to the

---

⑱ Pierre Schlag seems to speak in the same vein in "The Enchantment of Reason" Duke Univ. Pr., 1998, p.14.

* 寻租。"寻租"是经济分析中使用的一个术语,其描述的是个人或者群体所采取的那些试图改变公共政策的行为,其目的在于以牺牲他人利益为代价而获取个人私利。

** 法律适用,意指从法律到事实的演绎推理。

*** 事实的规范性概括,一般译为"归摄"或"涵摄",意指从事实到法律的归纳推理。

substantive content, the formal qualities or characteristics are moral or value neutral (道德或价值中立).

Law, especially the positive law(实在法) of our post-modern age is made increasingly of formulaic rules, such as in legislation. In a judicial decision that epitomizes the ideal type of legal reason, the provision of reason is not always mandatory as in the case of England.

Some scholars have suggested that lawyers are trained and initiated into the legal profession to think not only alike but also formally, universally, neutrally and impersonally just like the law itself is made. This conception of the notion of thinking like a lawyer is certainly a general and sweeping statement on the "legal self."

One of the formal qualities or requirements the critics like to tout is the separation of the self from the legal artifact or object studied. By this separation, the self stands outside or independent of the various positions or views implicated in the issue, and is free to choose that which is needed or required. This is another misconception of the notion of thinking like a lawyer.

But lawyering or legal scholarship is very much a committed profession or committed intellectual enterprise. Legal scholarship represents the very best of an academic's committed views and positions in political morality. To believe otherwise is to view legal scholarship as a kind of "as if" theorization, that is to practice what Jeurgen Habermas calls "a performative contradiction."[18] When the legal self thinking formally in an abstract and detached manner, and separating itself from the object studied and represented, the legal self detaches not only from the constitutive and environmental context and forces but also from the legal self's personal, psychological, or social background and experience. But such a view and conception of the legal self and its relationship to law and reason is fictitious. It is not only counterfactual; it is also counter-intuitive. Only when committed in the most sincere and solemn manner, both professionally and politically morally, the legal self is a responsible, honest, and trustworthy one. Lawyers and legal academics think alike only in the formal sense; thinking alike formally does not always lead to same or even similar result in the substantive sense. In advocacy, lawyers think of and through the English language, terms, conceptions, methodology, techniques, sources, and processes they all share.

---

[18] J. Habermas, "Discourse Ethics: Notes on a Program of Philosophical Justification", *The Communicative Ethics Controversy* 60, Benhabib & F. Dallmayr eds. 1990.

Law is a collectively committed enterprise of political morality. The moral visions and value perspectives are necessarily embodied and represented in the various rules, principles, standards, precepts, concepts, propositions, and theories. Lawyers and legal academics who take their profession seriously are morally and politically committed selves. And the positions, theories, propositions, etc. they select or choose should aptly reflect their professional and moral commitment. What is the true and correct expression of the law is not and never was a matter of objective existence waiting to be discovered and declared, but a subjectivist manifestation of an individual or collective or organized individuals' view or stance on political morality.

Even standing on the highest perch of the subjectivist aesthetic, those that are doing law can never be above law. In Common law, there are abundant opposing and even conflicting precedents. While it is possible, and even desirable for judges or jurists to invoke and apply cases that support their propositions and reasons at the sacrifice of those opposing, it would be a misconception and misleading to suggest that the authority of applicable precedents can be manipulated at will. The authority of law does not change or lessen as one becomes more knowledgeable, more experienced, more sophisticated or has written more beliefs. Lawyers who deviate significantly from constraints of law would lose their case. Judges at the lower levels are strictly restrained to toe the authority line of the hierarchical structure of the judiciary. The Supreme Court judges must feel their way in asserting a leading role in setting the course of social development by sensing and balancing the gravitational pull of the normative forces of society. Academics only in their purely academic musings can risk doing what they wish bending and twisting the form and substance of the law. Even in such intellectual and normative speculations, they have to be ready to face the criticism, rebuke, or ridicule of fellow academics. When engaging in serious and committed scholarly writings purporting to influence and shape both the form and the substance of the law, legal academics are no less subjected to the constraints of legal authority.

B. Content or Material Bases of Legal Reason

What is reason? A better question is what constitutes reason? Or what are the material bases, sources, and content of legal reason? Few would disagree that all of the sources of law, however defined, are the raw materials to be invoked for the reason of law. From the perspective of progressive or activist legal thinkers and actors, orders, directives, and other normative pronouncements of state organs should also be counted as sources. To extend the logic further, a broader conception of law would demand that all decisions and actions of a public political morality nature including those from non-official sectors be regarded as raw materials of reason.

Rules do not expropriate and exhaust the sources or material bases of reason. Policy decisions are not made on the basis of rules. Instead, they draw heavily on factors and considerations of a social, political, economic, and environmental nature. In hard cases(疑难案件), for which none of the existing legal rules seems applicable and for which the doctrine of stare decisis is thrown out of the window, ignored, evaded, downgraded, overruled, or emasculated, judges draw upon discretion(法官的自由裁量权). The Federal Reserve sets interest rates through risk management rather than on the basis of any rule.

Reason may also be drawn from other sources such as experience, convention, tradition, ethics, and so on. In the inquiry of the nature of law and its authority, a number of resourceful notions have been submitted by legal thinkers. These include, for example, H. L. A. Hart's "internal perspective", S. Fish's "interpretive community", R. Dworkin's "Hercules* judge", and even conscience or good judgment. These are also often invoked and called upon as reason in legal discourse. Pierre Schlag, a leading critic of law and legal reason, calls these "theoretical unmentionable."

Reason is a grab bag, an agglomeration, of whatever one invokes to persuade. The material base and content of reason is infinite, all-inclusive, and evolving as society or knowledge changes. Sources of legal reasons reach and extend far beyond those of a legal nature, so-called. Attorneys use arguments that sentence-by-sentence could have been lifted from discussions of morality, economics, sociology, debates of public policy, etc.

Reason has a superior and overriding status. Reason draws upon all recognized sources and remains distinctive from them. What distinguishes reason from other sources/bases is its deliberative self-questioning character. Reason is open to and considerate of contrary or opposing arguments, and is conscious of, and attentive to its

---

* 拉丁语,赫尔克里斯,希腊、罗马神话中的大力神。

own possible biases and distortions. Reason operates like moral absolutism(道德绝对主义); it appropriates, co-opts, overrides, dominates and controls. It subjugates the many to the one, pluralism to monism, polytony to monotony, differences to sameness, etc.

In short, reason feeds possibly on all the established sources of law, authoritative and effective decisions/actions broadly defined, and other general sources of beliefs or normativity, and even facts, events, and incidences.

The quality, authority and success of reason depend largely on how the various sources of law, beliefs, faiths, practices, traditions, facts, etc. are packaged, presented, communicated, and effectuated by the art, skill, and strategy of advocacy.

This conception of reason evidently differs from that which is conjured up by those who believe that there is clear divide between reason and other sources, whatever these may be. Robert Nozick sees reason as "embedded within a context and playing a role as one component along with others, rather than as an external, self-sufficient point that judges everything."[85]

Reason per se should not be confused with good reason*. Reason as a content-neutral form and substance of public discourse may fail to persuade or to secure its set goal. Good reason, on the other hand, finds its acceptance, consideration, and success in authoritative and effective decision-making. Good reason is what is considered morally superior, compelling and politically persuasive.

Doubters of reason claim that an argument or dialogue that presupposes a commitment to reason must demonstrate it is so. This stance apparently confuses reason per se as a form of public discourse and persuasion with reason that is considered good and persuasive.

Reason has infinite potential and is inexhaustible. Reason is omnipresent in matters of political morality. Reason is also omnipotent. The sources, grounds, and bases of reason are equally infinite and inexhaustible. Even in legal discourse and argument, rule, principle, precept, standard, and doctrine do not preempt the ground. In legislation as well as in adjudication, social and empirical date, policy

---

[85] R. Nozick, *The Nature of Rationality*, N. J., Princeton Univ., Pr. 1993. pp. 71-72 as quoted in Schlag op cit at 80.

* 不能把理性本身与"善的理性"相混淆。"per se"意为"本身"、"自身"或"本质"。"reason"仅指"理性",与理性的价值目标无关;而"good reason"则指好的、善的理性,属价值理性范畴。

goals, social effects and consequences, and even storytelling can all be invoked in advocacy. Therefore, the potential and the inexhaustibility of reason depend solely on the intelligence and the power of our imagination and creativity.

Reasons supporting opposing views and positions are routinely made by parties in adversarial, adjudicative bodies, especially respecting matters and issues of a fundamental or constitutional law nature, such as abortion, collective rights to a universal, publicly funded health care system as opposed to individual rights to private care. Whether or not the reasons advanced by the parties and the reasons justifying the decision rendered by the court is good or persuasive, is an entirely different question.

Is reason reasoned? Could the form, methodology, or techniques of reason be reasoned but the material content or substance not? Doubters of reason try to make a strong case that the material bases, especially the sources of law and other law-generating acts and decisions are generally and falsely believed to be reasoned or organized in the image of reason. In fact, these are often the products of rent-seeking, power politics, outright deceits and other questionable strategic behaviors (策略性行为). As adjudication (judicial decision) is informed and grounded by these very non-reasons, how could they be reasoned?[18]

Reasoned or not, this is how the democratic process works. Until we have found a perfect polity or utopia where there is no conflicts or dissents and everything is decided by love, virtue and universal morality, that is all we have. In the meantime, we, as autonomous moral agents (作为自治的道德主体), can take deviating, opposing, countering political action to ensure that all constitutive sources of law are reasoned. This is what political dissent and legal activism are all about.

C. Distinctive Nature and Superior Status of Reason

The proponents of reason see reason, though derived from and informed and shaped by established sources of law, tradition, practice, and even belief and faith, is distinguishable from and superior to these derivatives. Reason has a superior, overriding status. This primacy of reason over sources of reasons can be attributed to the immanent ability or power to identify, select, evaluate, appropriate, co-opt, subjugate, override, control, and organize all the informing sources of information,

---

[18] R. Nozick, *The Nature of Rationality*. Princeton, N. J., Princeton Univ., Pr. 1993, pp. 71-72 as quoted in Schlag op cit at 80.

text, material employed by reason to do its work. Reason also has a deliberate, self-questioning, and self-appraisal character. Reason is accessible to and considerate to contra-opposing argument (reason) and is conscious of or attentive to its own possible bias, weakness and distortion. Reason is a meta-form or frame of persuasion in the democratic process of political morality. The operational requirement for reason to succeed is to cast all relevant bases/sources for decision-making in this frame; There is nothing that cannot be so frame, including anti-reason, irrationalities, religious fundamentalism, belief systems, faith, etc.

The word "reason"* may refer to both its form and substance. When used in the same context with the word "reasoning", reason signifies its substantive content. To be distinguished from reason, reasoning should be understood to refer to the form, process, technique, methodology, approach or operation of reason.

Is reason virtuous? This question cannot be definitely answered without knowing in advance which one of the two related meanings the question refers to.

Reasoning as a form and process of public discourse cuts both ways: the partisans as well as scoundrels of reason resort to it. There is no necessary ethical or conceptual alliance between reasoning on the one hand and the merits, justice or other moral quality of the content of reason on the other.

Proponents portray reasoning as a rightful or truthful way of gaining knowledge and understanding of the world. Though reason itself is not self-grounding, it is only by believing in and through reason that we may approximate some desired virtues such as good, right, truth, etc. In this sense, reason is meant to signify its form and process, i.e., reasoning as well as its moral quality. Whether or not the moral quality of the reason advanced is persuasive and able to successfully win over those who disagree is an entirely different question.

Thus, when doubters claim that reason is not ethically superior to other sources of beliefs, they definitely refer to the moral content of reason. Same for their claim that when reason attempt to rule in the world of beliefs, it becomes a violence.

Yet, when doubters claim that in a world of moral, religious, political pluralism and diversity, the assumption and demand for universal laws and norms are false and tyrannical, they really become radical and scoundrels themselves. For such claim would regard the Universal Declaration of Human Rights and the Convention on

---

* "理性"一词,既指理性的形式又指理性的实质。当在同样的语境中使用"reason"与"reasoning"时,前者指涉理性的实质内容,而后者则被理解为指称理性的形式、过程、技术、方法、方式或操作等。

Crimes against Humanity equally false and tyrannical.

In short, reason or reasoning is a sine qua non of public discourse. As such, reason is the sine qua none for a political society and by extension, for intelligent, legal conversation and for the fashion of a workable law. Reason or rational discourse is also the prerequisite for democracy. Through rational public discourse, justice, equality, and other human dignity values, such as those entrenched in the charter or bill of rights founded in the constitution can be secured. The value of reason can never be denied. To deny reason is a "performative contradiction." For the denial to succeed, one must employ reason to persuade—that is the doing of precisely what one claims to be impossible.

Reason has rationalizing power. Man is a rational animal. This is certainly true in public discourse. Thus, to reason is immanently human. We justify our decision and action with reason. Even decisions and actions seemingly based on intuition, faith, belief, or emotion are informed and supported by reason. To justify one's decision and action in the political moral domain seems such a logical, natural and even moral thing to do. It is thus not a surprise that reason has been praised as a moral good, a virtue.

Legal reason is informed and shaped by established sources of law, authoritative and effective decisions/actions, and other sources of belief. What is intriguing and significant is that reason is generally accorded (with) a superior and controlling status over all the sources, decisions, actions, and beliefs generally identified. Reason is distinct, transcendent, and supreme. Reason has the disciplinary power to constrain and control the bases, material and intellectual and otherwise, of reason such as power, interest, prejudice, and personal proclivities. But how could this be possible? To accord reason (with) a superior and controlling status versus its informing and constituent elements is to believe that the sum is larger than the parts. For the superior status of reason to be credible instead of being subservient to its informing and constituent elements, there must be certain additional or extra ingredients, or characteristics going into the formation of reason. What could these possibly be?

The authority, namely the superior and controlling status of reason substantially depends on that authority of the informing sources, decisions, actions, and beliefs. What is interesting is the stance that reason originated from the informing sources, etc. has the ability to assert a superior and transcendent status and authority.

One idea advanced is that reason has rationalization power. Rationalization is capable of making the other sources, materials, texts, experience, tradition, etc. more precise, more coherent, more integrated. Reason selects, organizes, and purifies. Rationalization aims to transform the manifold meanings of whatever considered as authority, into the ordered propositional aesthetic of reason.[187]

Reason operates through both inclusion and exclusion. Through inclusion, reason extends its realm by appropriating, co-opting, and neutralizing the manifold legal materials and sources. Reason serves as a "big tent". To protect the integrity and supremacy of reason, reason excludes any contamination and undesirables. Reason functions as the central command. "As central command, reason is pure, closed, formal, univocal, polyvocal, and dialogical. Much of reason and rationalization is devoted to manage the relationship and tension between these two aesthetic aspects of reason." (A very interesting and stimulating account of the nature, content, and function of reason is given by Pierre Schlag.)[188]

Using a rationalization process and techniques such as summarization, restatement, or reconstruction, legal scholars have transformed American law into various kinds of propositional systematization; there have been attempts to codify the Common law, to uniform state laws for example. The American Law Institute* has successfully been launching its most comprehensive and ambitious "restatements of law"** projects.

The drive for rationalization has been equally prodigious and profitable in the field of prescriptive jurisprudence. In the twentieth century, a number of fairly creative theorization of the law has risen to claim their legitimacy, right place, and prestigious status in the normative enterprise of the law.

Rationalization is a special form of "rulification" in the sense that law aspires to have its formal existence. In this sense, rationalization of whatever approaches and techniques is a necessary function of the enterprise of law. Reason should prevail

---

[187] Pierre Schlag, Id., at 25.
[188] Id., at 27 et seq.

* 简称为 ALI,美国法律研究院。该院成立于 1923 年,其成员为美国最杰出的法官、法学家和执业律师,近年来也开始吸收美国之外的杰出法律人士进入该院。美国法律研究院的成立初衷是对美国法进行"重述"。

** 法律重述。进行法律重述是美国法律研究院的首要任务之一。美国法律之所以需要"重述",原因在于美国为不成文的判例法国家,并且美国国内各法域实行的也并非统一法,因而为使美国国内的法律明确和体系化,美国法律研究院于 20 世纪初叶即开始启动法律重述活动,迄今已起草并公布了财产法重述、侵权法重述、代理法重述等十余部"法律重述"。

and be let to prevail in deep or most intractable social or moral conflicts. And this is not "hypertrophification" of reason or rationalist delusion as the critics like to think.

D. Reason and Discretionary Decision

Judges and governmental officials make discretional decisions routinely. A typical example is the prosecutor's discretion in plea-bargaining*. Judges are bureaucrats regardless of the various methods of their selection, though there is a different set of rules guiding their decisions and the distinct function they perform. As officials, they are to be expected to exercise discretion in making decisions. The Federal Reserve sets interest rates by risk management rather than following any rule. Management is inherently discretionary. No rule has absolute control. Every case carries with it a distinct set of fact-situation. New facts call for special consideration and innovative distinguishing.

In the management of the $700 billions authorized under the Troubled Assets Relief Program 2008, Hans Paulson, the Treasury Secretary, defended his decision to shift focus and strategy, including his decision to officially abandon the original rescue plan: buying rotten mortgages and other bad debts from banks to free up their balance sheets and get them to lend more freely.

He argued that focusing the bailout program on infusing billions into banks—and possibly other types of companies—to pump up their capital and bolster lending to customers was deemed a faster and more effective approach to stabilizing the financial system than the original centerpiece of the plan, he said.

While acknowledged that the financial crisis was caused by many factors including "government inaction and mistaken actions, outdated U. S. and global financial regulatory systems, and by the excessive risk-taking of financial institutions," he cautioned against the U. S. and other countries developing a too-onerous regulatory response.

"By proactively addressing the problems we saw coming and being pragmatic enough to change strategy in the face of changed facts and despite the inevitable

---

* 控辩交易。在美国法上,控辩交易是指在刑事诉讼中,检察官与被告人进行谈判,说服被告人做有罪答辩,以换取检察官的指控或法院判决上的让步。通常做法是,如果被告人承认犯有某一较轻的罪行,或者承认控方多项指控中的一项罪行,检察官可以对被告人降格指控,或者撤回对其他罪项的指控,或者建议法庭对被告人减轻处罚。检察官与被告人达成的协议经法院批准后即可执行。控辩交易的做法在出现之初曾引起了人们的广泛争议。20世纪60年代美国联邦最高法院宣布其为合法,此后在美国刑事司法实践中得到了广泛运用。

criticism—we prevented a far worse financial crisis," Paulson insisted.

"There was no playbook for responding to a once or twice in a hundred year event," Paulson argued, saying he needed to shift strategy to respond to worsening financial and economic conditions.

"If we do not correctly diagnose the causes, and instead act in haste to implement more rather than better regulations, we can do long-term harm," Paulson said in a speech in Simi Valley, Calif.[189]

In hard cases, H. L. A. Hart thinks judges use discretion. Hard case means, in terms of law, there is either no applicable rule or the rules potentially applicable are conflicting or opposing.* Hard cases usually involve either new facts, new subject matters, new issues, or the situation is mired in difficult, deep divisive or intractable social, policy, moral, legal problems. In hard cases, choice has to be made among the competing views and insights. Since no rule applied, discretion is resorted to.

Ronald Dworkin suggests that even in hard cases, there are principles that judges should refer to for guidance. But unlike rules, principles are much flexible, that is, manipulative or to put it differently, discretional. There may be even competing principles. In such situation, Dworkin advocates that judges resort to a technique he calls "integrative interpretation" in order to find the appropriate principle to cast the law in the best light it can be. This he said requires a Hercules' standard of knowledge, insight, and skill. This is a laudable aspiration, but hardly achievable by any mortal soul.

E. Allure and Rick of Legal Reason

Legal reason or reasoning in law is in essence a part of the rationalist tradition. Rationality is universally regarded as the major quality that separates man from other animals. Thus, to reason is human. We reason in all matters of human affairs regardless of the nature, subject matter, location or situation.

Moreover, the partisans of reason believe that only through open, transparent, and inclusive reasonable discourse, truth, goodness, and other high values could be secured. The doubters call this the enchantment of reason. The doubters regard the power of reason to obtain desired goals as an impossible dream. To obstinately hold

---

[189] Jeannine Ayersa, "Paulson: Crisis Happens Once or Twice in 100 Years," *Yahoo Finance*, Nov. 20, 2008, 2:17 pm EST.

* 法律上的疑难案件是指,要么是不存在可适用的规则,要么是潜在的可适用规则存在冲突或矛盾。

onto the phantom power of reason is the very predicament of reason. This obstinacy inevitably causes reason to become a venue of faith, prejudice, dogma, and company. It becomes a sort of deification of reason.[09]

Some legal thinkers have advanced the view that there is an "equilibrium zone of efficiently processed disputes." Where and when sharply conflicting views and positions are involved, it would be useless, arrogant, or imperialistic to reason. Deep divisive issues such as whether a fetus has a <u>right to life(生命权)</u> and certified by the state are simply not amendable to extensive rationalist analysis and cannot be successfully resolved by political scientists, moral philosophers, or the politicized lawyers called judges.

In all of such situations, reason becomes a meta-text of law and of legal argument. It ends as a text whose only message is its performance—without the power of persuasion and without meaning. Words call for more words; reasons call for more reasons. Everything else gets buried under the words of reason.

Law is Reason. No law can be founded and sustained by naked power alone. Ditto the authority of the law. The relationship between authority and reason is deep and complex. To separate and distinguish them while theoretically palpable is extremely difficult. The situation is similar to that between authority and efficacy. There is a subtle and yet evident mutually informing and shaping relationship between law and reason like that between authority and efficacy. And contrary to the belief that any cognitive dissonance between them will be internalized by legal thinkers and actors, it is more practical to think that law and authority operate at their own risk and destruction when the weakness or limitation is ignored and uncorrected.

The loss of reason is the loss of legitimacy. When reason loses control, arbitrariness, emotion, self-interest, politics, power, and force take over the legal machinery. From the perspective of the <u>rule-of-law(法治)</u> ideal, law becomes lawless. This prospect is a dread moment.[09]

Furthermore, the doubters even suggest that legal reason and law job are excruciatingly boring. In other words, what the doubters themselves are doing to ridicule and debunk those who are doing law is similarly boring. Criticism of law is an integral part of doing law just as critical reflexivity becoming frame construction as

---

[09] Schlag, *The Enchantment of Reason*, Durham [N. C.] Duke Univ. Pr., 1998, p. 16.
[09] Id., at 21.

noted by Schlag himself. Since doing law is such a dreary and boring job, why Schlag passionately goes a great length to convince us by reasoning?

Are the canonical materials of the law pathological and imagination stifling or impoverishing? And no matter how cynical legal thinkers and actors have become, we are simply incapable of finding a more interesting profession to engage in, and we are not willing to give up our nice positions, morally and professionally, but continue to police the grid and run the mazes. Is this really so as the doubters claim? Schlag notes that "reason becomes the resources of first and last resort. We expect everything to be done by reason and we lose the faculties, the capacities, and inclination necessary to perform other cognitive operations such as reconnaissance, characterization, description, apperception."[92] But one wonders what are these operations for, if not to serve reason. Aren't these prerequisite functions of reason and reasoning?

Schlag justifies his claim that law and legal reason are boring and intellectually impoverishing by the fact that intellectual and social culture including law is screened and formatted in the image of the rationalist aesthetic. As a result, we lose depth, dimension, and contrast of life and alternatives. In the view of the doubters of reason, the excessive faith in, and obsession with, reason "can come to resemble a form of mental illness."[93]

Law is the normative form of social life. How could social life be so dreary and boring unless life itself is considered so. Questions respecting legal method, the concept of authority, limits of law, efficacy, and in essence the very nature and concept of law have haunted, stimulated and challenged the most brilliant and creative legal minds throughout history. The normative life of man marches on and on for better or for worse. Doubters apparently are purposefully painting a much more bleak, impoverished, skewed, and even a false picture of our normative life. Maybe the shallowness and impoverishment that the doubters have in mind are really the intellectual representation of the law, not the law as it is. Maybe what doubters really aspire to is to construct a new philosophy, and a new paradigm of law that truly reflects, represents, and describes the normative life of a society, and at the same time, to enrich and liberate the intellectual and professional life of all legal thinkers and actors. It would be hard to dispute that life has much more than the

---

[92] Id., at 142.
[93] Paul E. Campos, *Jurismanias: the Madness of American Law*, Oxford Univ. Pr., 1998, p.72.

normative or the rational. Emotion, feeling, happiness, suffering, etc., are all integral parts of human life. Surely, these are not boring; these are beautiful. But these have little if anything at all to do with the normative aspects of public life.

F. Evaluation and Balancing of Reason

Since the authority of the law rests fundamentally on the content and quality of reason that informs and justifies it, to evaluate the authority of the law is tantamount to the evaluation of legal reason itself.

How to evaluate legal reason? Are there objective standards or tests that one can resort to assess its quality and strength? Are there any special approaches or methodologies designed or useful for the evaluation of legal reason? What does evaluation of legal reason mean? Is it to ascertain the very existence, the quality, the nature, the strength, etc of legal reason?

First, could it be possible that law as authoritative and effective decisions is not informed and justified by reason at all? Put it differently, law is simply anti-reason, arational or irrational as doubters claim. In other words, the real base or ground of the law is nothing but emotion, power, preference, or faith.

As in the case of evaluating the authority of the law, both formal criteria and substantive tests can be envisaged.

Formal criteria are used to test coherence, comprehensiveness, appropriateness, suitability, form, style, organization, characteristics, and communication of reason. Formal evaluation does not concern the immanent nature, content, and quality of reason. Substantive criteria directly deal with moral content of the reason, such as justice, fairness, goodness, etc. The persuasiveness of reason depends on both its formal quality and its substantive content. As legal reason is mainly made of the various sources, bases, or materials of law, the acceptability and persuasiveness of legal reason depend wholly on the merits of these elements provided that the quality of the formal criteria is not in question. In other words, the question "is it a good legal reason becomes the question is it a good law."

Method, technique, and approach are important to the success of reasoning. To effect decisions requires more than just mobilization of available resources. Devising effective strategy as well as judicious presentation and communication to the proper audiences must also be attended to. Means and ways to effect decisions are as varied, complex, rich, and infinite as the power and creativity of the human mind.

The form of reason includes potentially all the established as well as possible methods and theories of analytic and critical study of the law. In fact, the form of reason extends to analytic or critical study of the law.

Generally speaking, there is no correlation between method, technique, and approach and a good result. Even when a particular method that is privileged, widely practiced, and accepted as paradigmatic, it may not lead to desired result because the materials, grounds, content presented may be flawed. A rational procedure may be applied in a very systematic, purposeful, conscientious way, yet the outcome obtained may be irrational. Garbage in, therefore, garbage out. Methodology and technique are neutral and value-free(价值无涉)* of and by itself. Only in specific context and with respect to particular subject matter, the appropriateness and suitability of method and technique employed may be put in question.

One loudly orchestrated and vigorously advocated method of reasoning is multi-factor test and balancing. This inevitably involves the identification, clarification, weighing, measuring, and prioritizing of all relevant or applicable sources, texts, authorities, values, and beliefs. The language or wording used to accomplish these seemingly difficult and challenging functions includes "precedence taking", and "overriding", "predominating" etc.

The notion of balance, not too much, not too little, is a characteristic of normal human beings that they pursue a plurality of ends. Yet, unless there exists an ultimate end for human life to which one is committed, the shift from on particular end to another would go on forever if one is not guided by some highest end. Balancing somewhat is like Aristotle's "just mean" that demands on insight and intelligence that sound economic management does.⑲ One might even add in this respect that taking the middle of the road approach of Confucianism to guide one's conduct is ultimately the most rational and reasonable thing to do.

John Rawls provided an example of the balancing of reasons. In the context of abortion, he advanced three public reasons, namely, due respect for human life, the ordered reproduction of political society, and the political equality of women. Upon consideration of the three reasons, he concluded that at the early stage of pregnancy,

---

* 该概念是由德国哲学家马克思·韦伯提出的,倡导在进行一切社会科学领域研究时,研究者不带有课题之外的取向,坚持学术本身之价值。

⑲ Fuller, *The Morality of Law*, New Haven & London: Yale Univ. Pr., pp.18-19.

the political value of equality of women is overriding.⑲

Is Rawls' conclusion the outcome of some rational deliberation and reflection, an ineluctable product of reason, or in fact mere personal belief that is familiar, comfortable, and even widely held and long-standing, and that is skillfully incorporated into the categories, the idioms, and the grammar of reason?

G. Authoritative and Effective Decisions and Justifying Reason

Reasoning is possible and good, and is required in the midst of diversity. The notion that truth is an unachievable ideal must be rejected, for it can easily become an excuse for sloppy reasoning or inadequate methods.

Reason may be invoked to justifying any authoritative and effective decision. To blame reason being hijacked to aid a political or normative program is simply a misconception. It is perfectly legitimate and proper to invoke reason and other justification in the process of authoritative and effective decision-making or legal discourse.

Reason informs and justifies authority; good reason enlightens and strengthens authority, while bad or weak reason weakens and is derogatory of authority. Whether or not a reason given to justify a decision or an action is good is a matter of judgment. The distinction between reason of authority and authority of reason mostly rests on such judgment. *

Not all of the authoritative and effective decisions are reasoned. Not all reasons are authoritative. Both Dworkin and Raz believe the legal arguments gain persuasive power as they demonstrate that they have some connection with legally authoritative materials. Dworkin forges this connection with his interpretive theory of "fit." Raz does this by means of his "sources thesis." Unfortunately, to confuse reason with authority and to conflate one into another are routinely made by both the proponents and doubters of reason alike. Strategic scheming, seamy motivations, fortuity, happenstance, sloth, power politics, and general human blundering may on occasion inform and effect decisions, the authority status of such decisions does not logically or naturally follows but is to be decided in the hand of authoritative and effective decision-makers coming along on a continuing basis. The relationship between reason and authority is quite tenuous and even opaque. Whether or not and to what extent

---

⑲　John Rawls, *Political Liberalism*, New York, Columbia University Press (1993), p. 243, note 32.
*　权威的理性与理性的权威之间的区别主要就是基于这样的判断。

reason attributes to authority may very well defy intellectual analysis and articulation. Reason by and in itself is not authoritative; reason must be effective and persuasive in the sense of guiding decision and action to become authority.

H. Truth and Myth of Judicial Reason

Legal reason is the central core of the body and spirit of the law. In its fundamental and jurisprudential sense, legal reason is synonymous with law. Judicial reason epitomizes the purest and ideal form of legal reason. It is comprehensive, coherent, tough, argued in an adversarial fashion and it is richly and soundly referenced. In both form and substance, if not in authority, it symbolizes a good law and a good legal system.

Judicial decisions by nature imply judgment of choice. A judicial decision can be understood as comprised of three elements or stages: the trial, the act of judging, and the written judgment. In the trial stage, the judge is institutionally and necessarily open to persuasion by others. It is marked by multiple perspectives, multiple potential legalities. In the act of judgment phase, the judge reduces plurality to singularity, replaces the fecundity of alternate visions and alternative arguments to a single "right answer." In the final stage, the judge seeks to justify his or her conclusions in ways that will persuade others.[96]

Among judicial reasons, the opinions of the appellate courts are most highly regarded and studied. Much to one's chagrin, the praise of appellate courts opinion is not universal. Critics claim that: "appellate opinions are a kind of extended brag sheet through which the judge gets to report on how well he or she did his or her job."[97] Scholarly commentary, in turn, is a second-order rationalization(第二顺位的理性化). But what one must be reminded of is that rationalization cuts both ways. Whether or not an appellate opinion will grow to become a leading case possessing enormous precedent power or fade gradually with time is also very much decided by scholars' rationalization and criticism.

Yet, the Common law form of analogous reasoning from precedents is always fraught with ambiguities and dangers. The task of determining the relevance, comparative value and the significance of similarities and differences between cases is inherently problematic. As a species of legal conceptualization, it has been criticized

---

[96] Sandia Berns, *To Speak as a Judge: Difference, Voice and Power*, Aldershop, Ashgate, 1999.
[97] Pierre Schlag, *The Enchantment of Reason*, Durham [N.C.] Duke Univ. Pr., 1998, p.119.

as an elaborate form of question begging.[98]

Judicial reason is constitutive of three distinct core elements: ratio decisis, obiter dictum, and legal principle. The definition, identity, ascertainment, and application of these constitutive elements determine the form, content, and persuasiveness of judicial reason. In the Nature of Judicial Decision, Cardozo said that judicial reasoning is based on principles, precedents, and common sense presented in syllogistic, analogical or philosophical form. At bottom and in its underlying motives, it is inspired by a yearning for consistency, for certainty, for uniformity of plan and structure. It has its root in the constant striving of the mind for a larger and more inclusive unity, in which differences will be reconciled and abnormalities will vanish.[99]

The entire chapter five on case law should be studied for more details.

When studying and analyzing any common law doctrine, such as the finder's law in property, one is very likely to be confronted with a mass of conflicting formal rules, instrumental concerns, policy goals, and ethnical norms and expectations. This is in addition to the challenge of disentangling the complexity of the factual situations in relevant cases. Short of the wisdom and capability of a Hercules judge, how can one identify and compare the relevance, significance, weight, merits, order of priority, etc of these deeply involved and potentially opposing factors and considerations? No wonder, reasons marshaled in support of the decisions in hard cases, that is, all appellate court decisions, are often dismissed as partly amateur sociological speculation, partly basic folk psychology, and partly seat-of-the-pants intuition.[20]

Hard cases are understood to be disputes or conflicts that take place in a social and legal equilibrium zone. Social and legal equilibrium zone is defined as an area of moral and political judgment in which various powerful, widely held, and rationally irrefutable beliefs—beliefs not amenable to either rational confirmation or rebuttal—can be adduced for holding contradictory positions regarding controversial issues. Seemingly impassioned moral and political debate as well as reason for decision with respect to issues or conflicts of this nature will tend to devolve into the bald assertion

---

[98] Paul E. Campos, *Jurismania: the Madness of American Law*. Oxford Univ. Pr., 1998, p. 83.

[99] Benjamin Cardozo, *The Nature of Judicial Process*, New Haven CT: Yale University Press, 1921, pp. 48-49.

[20] Id., at 86.

of intuitive belief masquerading as rationally compelling argument.

A retired Supreme Court of Canada justice once confessed that judges often decided the outcome of cases (hard cases no doubt) before setting foot in the courtroom for the hearing; they came to a conclusion beforehand by reading and discussing the written legal briefs and case history. This was done despite the possibility of missing out the crystallized arguments of the appellants that didn't register with the judges beforehand. Nevertheless, it is rightly pointed out that what is important is not whether the court has made its decision before a hearing—what matters is the reasoning behind its rulings, which often takes several months to complete.

The judicial process, like, if not better than, other decision-making process at the state level, is adequately supported by all the views and opinions of experts deemed relevant; the process is meticulously structured to ensure <u>procedural justice</u> (程序正义) and fairness. And the adversarial system of reasoning provides a reasonable guarantee for the outcome to be rational, practical, and fair. The reason of the court reflects and captures the essence of all the views, opinions presented.

Unfortunately, the doubters of reasons prefer to appraise the courage and honest of judges who render decisions without justifying reasons in hard cases. In their view, when reason fails or has exhausted itself, "the demand for more reasons from decision makers amounts to an invitation for them to indulge in analytical pointless—yet ideologically potent—form of juridical rationalization."[20]

In the face of such an irrational demand from American legal and political thought, "the system reacts to the cognitive dissonance the demand generates by producing artifacts of rationalist excess that simultaneously deny and illustrate the limitations of reason: the decade-long appeal, the 100-page appellate court opinion, the 200-page law review article, the 1,000 page statute, and so on. These sorts of legal artifacts are the fruit of futile, hypertrophied exercises in forms of argument that call themselves 'reason,' but that in fact must conclude with the assertion of axiomatic or circular propositions."[22]

"For the uninitiated lay public, the massive bulk of the endeavor combines with the technical obscurity of its language to provide a vague assurance that, surely, these people must know what they are talking about. As for lawyers, who are

---

[20] Id., at 100.
[22] Id., at 101.

supposed to know better from experience serving as advocates, they just continue to fake it at the way.

The appellate court opinion is not studied in the same way as investors pore over the stock tables. While both may serve as a base for prediction of trends, there are however significant differences between them. We do not just study or analyze in a number of ways the opinions, we criticize, evaluate, and improve these opinions in terms of form and substance. In the case of the stock tables, we take them a given, never question.

Sir William Blackstone's dictum that the determination and sentence of the court are not those of the judges but those of law has how become a shame. The law does not go from case to case; it changes with social and economic policy set by judges.

Criticism of judicial reason is abundant. The doubters of reason believe that the opinions of the appellate courts which are generally regarded in the legal community (法律共同体) as the very embodiments of the law, and indeed, the purest form of the tough law(严格法), represent in fact the very core of an excessive faith in the power of reason. In attempt to resolve deep social conflicts, courts in fact mince absurdity in their reason and justification.

It seems the Supreme Court has been caught in the throes of various methodological obsessions. It has provided a set of three or four prong tests everywhere and for everything. It has an almost medieval earnestness about classification and categorization; has a theological attachment to the determinate power of various "levels of scrutiny"; and it provides with an amazingly fine distinctions that produce multiple opinions, designated in parts, sub-parts, and sub-sub-parts.[203]

Judges are the oracles of the law. Judicial reason epitomizes the optimum quality or zenith of legal reason. But judges do not speak with one voice in most of the highly controversial and far-reaching cases(疑难案件). Instead, the opinions of the court are badly and deeply fractured. In plurality decisions there is no longer the reason of the court. Each judge may write his or her own opinion concurring in one part and dissenting in another from the opinions of other judges. In many cases, we are now talking about the reason of individual judges and their theoretical view and jurisprudential standpoint of the law. Consequently, there is no longer a correct

---

[203] Id., at 72.

reason for decisions. What we have is very much like "political correctness" a temporal, fleeting force which changes unexpectedly and drastically. When reasons for decisions are full of dissenting views and competing and divisive insights, the law itself becomes a shame. It fosters uncertainty, instability rather than informs authority. Not surprisingly that Justice Marshall had long proclaimed that "power, not reason, is the new currency of the Supreme Courts' decision-making."[204]

With respect to constitutional law issues, everyone from the most self-consciously critical thinkers to the most traditionally minded doctrinalists, more or less toes the same basic rhetoric path. It goes like this: "The extant law on the subject matter is an incoherent mess made up of conclusory and muddled doctrines embodied in methodologically useless multifactor tests that decide nothing and that no one even pretends to take seriously; All the previous attempts to derive a coherent and workable theory from this materials have failed miserably. Therefore, here's mine."[205]

In the view of the doubters of reason, the constitutional law issues are a disaster area; it is a categorical dumping ground for everything the normal political process can't digest.[206] It is true that for political expediency or other strategic considerations, people often prefer to refer issues or disputes of deep social, moral divisive nature to the Supreme Court for opinion or decision. But this fact by or of itself does not have any thing to do with the nature and quality of the reason given for supporting the decision or opinion.

If judicial activism usurping legislative prerogative is an issue, launch a frontal attack on that. If judicial supremacy should not be valued, reconstitute the basic political structure of the polity. The courts are well advised to strive to emulate the almighty Hercules judge in crafting their reasoned opinion to cast the law in the best light it can be. For the advancement of the collective normative enterprise of the law, the contribution of the court through judicial discourse or reason if you will is an indispensable ingredient.

Are doubters prepared to suggest that none of the so-called "intractable social or moral issues or conflicts" should be referred to the court for disposition and that the court should not even bother offering justifying reason for its decision? If not, they

---

[204] Payne v. Tennessee. 111 S. Ct 2597; 791 S. W. 201 (1990).
[205] Campos, *Jurismania: the Madness of American Law*, Oxford Univ. Pr., 1998, p. 71.
[206] Ibid.

are better advised to accept the fact that judicial law is tough law and scholarly renditions on judicial decisions are tough law intensified and beautified. Moreover, legal education informs and shapes the thinking and critical faculty of the future and quite probably the present members of the legal community. And the opinion of the appellate courts constitutes the very core of legal landmass that determines the outcome of the disputes efficiently processed.

I. Moral, Epistemological Pluralism, and Incommensurability

What is incommensurability? Are there incommensurable things? Is it possible to choose among the incommensurable and give reason for the choice? Can one make a reasonable choice between, for example, eating apple pie and reading Wittgenstein? Could one reduce these values to, and measure them on, a single metric or criterion? Or when choose one thing not the other, do we have to place them on the same scale?

Are there "radical incommensurabilities?" Could one choose among incommensurable options on rational grounds? The doubters ironically believe that "the world is organized in various regions or sectors or modes of cognition or kinds of discourse that are radically different and they do not all fit within a single frame."[207] The world is irreducibly plural in character.

The proponents of reason insist on the other hand that radical incommensurability is very rare and people who face incommensurability often think rightly that their judgments are based on reason. The doubters dismiss that as conflating a belief about something with the thing itself—a pre-Kantian kind of confusion. But to the thinker who reasons, I think therefore I am, and belief and being are the same thing until otherwise demonstrated beyond doubt.

The doubters of reason have committed a series of intellectual contradictions in their attack on reason. For example, doubters' attempt to attack reason is resulted from some kind of rational deliberation and choice. These are the very products of reason. The doubters advocate that we jettison reason, when deciding issues that involve deep, intractable, divisive social conflicts. No doubt, such advocacy for not to reason or unreason is also a choice of outcome coming from rational deliberation and reflection. There is nothing more incommensurable than the decision to reason

---

[207] Schlag, *The Enchantment of Reason*, Durham [N.C.] Duke Univ. Pr., 1998, p. 42.

and the decision not to reason. Yet, doubters have no difficulty in making their desired choice.

Instead of being a bane of or denying the plausibility of reason, moral and epistemological pluralism is the necessary premise and fertile ground for reason.

Reason feeds on, flourishes, and triumphs in diversity. Doubters believe that truth is an unachievable ideal. And to believe otherwise becomes an excuse for sloppy reasoning or inadequate methods and displaces the traditional dichotomy of subjectivity and objectivity with an integration of part and whole. Harmony, unity and sameness respecting political morality are fleeting and transitory, even those dealing with issues of human dignity value. Diversity, dissenting and conflict are all integral parts of human development.

We reason to persuade precisely because we hold divergent, opposing, or sharply different views or understandings of things. Reason will never be necessary when everyone agrees. Short of power or violence, what alternatives to reason do we have to resolve disagreements, disputes and conflicts? Love and compassion alone would not solve disputes and conflicts. Even god with its almighty love cannot pass un-challenged. Force and aggression always prove futile in the long run. How to do them necessarily requires reason and justification.

This is why Sunstein says that incommensurability is rare and why S. Sherry claims that the primary failing of epistemological pluralism is that it leaves no way to resolve disputes except by recourse to power. Schlag disputes such stances and argues that such claims are only true if the initial condition is met—namely that argument and dialogue presuppose a commitment to reason. Doubters prefer to equate reason with violence and power. It is unquestionable that in this connection, Schlag appears to focus on the moral content of reason rather than reason as a form and means of communications and persuasion which Sunstein and Sherry seem to have in mind.

Reason informs law. The issue of political, moral incommensurability collapses onto the very heart of law. Incommensurability of political, moral stance means the incommensurability of law. Divergent and conflicting reason generates divergent and conflicting law. Here we are revisiting the issue of legal and moral pluralism and polyjurality. While it is true that dissenting views and opinions may exist in many authoritative and effective decisions, there is but only one statute, one judgment and one executive order. We act and decide one thing at a time. Legal pluralism or polyjurality obtains and flourishes only when and where competing, conflicting or competing views or claims exist in harmony: They are operating at a different plane of political morality and at a different time and space. When competing public political moral actions clash, there is only one emerging as authoritative and effective in time, space, person, subject, etc. Of course, when and during the gestation process of a law struggling to be born, there may be contradiction, uncertainty, and indetermination.

To a significant extent, to evaluate the quality, strength, persuasiveness, etc of reason is tantamount to the evaluation of the law or source of reason itself. There is no universally applicable reason just as there is no universally applicable law, universal declaration of human rights notwithstanding. Even this historical document has not commanded the recognition of all countries in the world. Rationality of law cannot be ensured by a priori, formalist account. Nor could rationality be guaranteed by any cross-historical, cultural study.

There is simply no objective or impartial standards or criteria one can resort to for assessing the quality, strength, or persuasiveness of reason. The only sensible thing one can do is to hawk back to the constitutive authority of a political community to anchor one's footing. Decisions are made, laws are enacted and pronounced, and reasons are given, whether or not objectivity, impartiality and truth, are at assistance.

Doubters of reason question the rationality of reason because doubters of reason question the legitimacy and authority of the law. From the perspective of the doubters, it is perfectly logical to say that the attempts of legal academics to rationalize decision and the law "as best as it can be" are largely pathological. Doubters even view as absurdly comical the admonition of the Legal process school that "in interpreting statutes, courts should construe them reasonably by presuming that they have been drafted by reasonable men acting reasonably."[209]

Ultimately, the test for reason is authority. When reason becomes the ground or base of decision and action taken on issues of public political morality, reason achieves the elevated status of authority. Before reason earns this privileged status, it remains academic or theoretical.

The popular belief that everything has a price and money is the ultimate base for

---

[209] Schlag, *The Enchantment of Reason*, Durham [N.C.] Duke Univ. Pr., 1998, p.119.

evaluating the worth of things strongly refutes the incommensurability thesis. In all practical affairs in life, we negotiate, compromise, and reach agreement. The emerging constitutional agreement reached post Saddan Hussein results from a long, hard, and painful process of hard negotiations, bargains, and compromises of seemingly intractable opposing views, beliefs, and value systems. In the democratic process of rule-making at the U.S. Federal Reserve, public hearings, roundtables are held, comments are solicited from the public, professionals, corporations, government bodies, and other interested parties, and divergent views and stances are considered and coalesced into a rule that accomplishes prescribed objectives. [209]

J. Limits of Legal Reason and Limits of Knowledge

Law is reason. Authoritative and effective decision-makers are "reasoners" of law.

As such, the authority and power of reason is inherently qualified and limited by its constituent bases, materials, and sources. The authority of reason can not and should not be simply presumed and accorded without question. The finiteness of knowledge is the main factor. In any efficient process of collective reasoning, no reason can be invoked and furthered without being forced and unduly stretched. Beyond a point, any further investment of intellectual capital and labor to strengthen reason is subject to the law of diminishing marginal utility. [210] Difficult and intractable political and moral questions or disputes defy rational analysis and persuasion. To suggest or to proceed otherwise is to engage in rationalist frivolity. Yet, no judge or jurist would readily admit this truism. They would rather be content with more rhetorical tricks or stylistic devices and begging the question in extremely abstractive, oracular language, and assertions of non sequitur. Such are the doubters' claims

It is a truism and banal to suggest that reasons are partial, partisan, subjective, and limited as to time, space, person, and thing. All reasons are made by a situated self—a person conditioned in history, culture, experience, or personal quality, etc. There is simply no such thing as a universal reason applicable across-history, across-culture, across-thing (subject matter) and across-person. The limitations of reason

---

[209] "SEC Could Water Down Plan to Boost Shareholders' Powers." Reprinted with permission from Wall Street Journal. The Globe and Mail, April 19, 2004.

[210] Paul E. Çampos, *Jurismania: the Madness of American Law*. Orford Univ. Pr., 1998, p.57.

strictly reflect the limitations of law as this informs and constitutes the foundation of reason of law. If law is conceived as the collective normative enterprise of a polity, law becomes an on-going, progressive intellectual force and intention. Then, the reason of law will be unlimited. What is limited is the scope and reach of its application.

Limitations of knowledge go beyond the problem of ascertaining truth, factual or theoretical, and its meaning and implications. Useful and crucial information and knowledge is difficult and expensive to acquire. To a significant extent, great efforts and valuable resources need to be mobilized. Besides, there is the problem of processing acquired information and knowledge efficiently, rationally, and persuasively.

In short, reason is limited by four factors; the authority of law, truth, the material content informing reason, and language and communication. Except the authority of law, the rest of the factors are all limited by knowledge. We act and decide on the basis of what is known, in other words, out of ignorance and folly if you will. Truth may be uncovered or uncoverable.

K. Reason Runs out

To the doubters, weighing, balancing, and choice of decisions ultimately are made on the ground of preference, faith, or self-evidence truth(不证自明的事实), etc. By such a view, they seem to claim not only that the moral quality and persuasiveness fail but also that reason as a form or means of discussion and persuasion is impossible and implausible.

One example given for the doubters is the choice between strawberry ice cream and vanilla ice cream. To them, a choice between tastes in essence is not different from the choice between freedom of speech and the right to equal protection. Ultimately, such choices are all founded on preference. What this claims is that reason or reasoning has no immanent morally or other rational base or footing. In the final analysis, reason of whatever nature and kind invoked to justify choice between competing or different views, stances, things, etc., rests on non-rational ground, such as belief, preference, faith, etc. Therefore, reason suffers the same flaw of infinite regression as most of the constitutive notions of law and the concept of law itself.[21]

Both internal and external factors or considerations may cause reason to fail to persuade. Internally, reason fails due to the inherent defects, weaknesses or inadequacy of its methodology, the process or the logical nature of its presentation or the truth or compelling quality of the substantive components or elements embodied.

Other factors or obstacles that preclude reason from performing its crucial operations include gaps, paradoxes, discontinuities, disjunction, undecidability, ambiguities, and ambivalence.

Externally, the failure of reason is caused by the fact that the target audience holds deeply entrenched, intractable value system or sharply diametrically opposing view. This is the situation in all hard cases. The reasons advanced to support a decision or a choice are ultimately post-hoc rationalizations designed to justify axioms and intuitions that are not worth arguing about.[22]

The failure of reason may also be caused by its irrational, hard sale. Excessive and overly attempts to vanquish its opposition may turn out to be <u>self-destructive of reason(理性的自我毁灭)</u>. Pursued long and hard enough, these tendencies can lead to a metamorphosis of reason into its very enemies or anathema. For example, the doubters accuse the proponents for referring to rhetoric tricks and insults, imperial assertions to short circuit the discourse.[23] On occasions both the proponents and doubters of reason are guilty of this.

"Keeping talking" will never last forever. Decision must be made sooner or later. In trials, further evidence must be foreclosed, testimony ceased, argument curtailed and proceeding ended. This does not signify the failure of reason, nor it runs out.

To the doubters, reason runs out whenever starkly conflicting views or positions clash.

Non-frivolous appellate court cases are all hard ones stuck in the social and legal equilibrium zone infested with intractable and insoluble conflicting interest, belief and value systems and moral conceptions. One of the abiding vices of rationalism is the assumption that reasoning about difficult question is always reasonable. To demand for reasoned decision in cases falling in the social and legal

---

[21] Schlag, *The Enchantment of Reason.* Duke Univ. Pr., 1998, p.32.
[22] Campos, *Jurismania: the Madness of American Law.* Oxford Univ. Pr., 1998, p.70.
[23] Schlag, *The Enchantment of Reason.* Durham [N.C.] Duke Univ. Pr., 1998, p.146.

equilibrium zone amounts to an invitation for indulging in analytically pointless, yet ideologically potent forms of juridical rationalization. At this point, any further deployment of reason becomes superfluous and unreasonable.⑭

To proponents of reason, reason displays its potent power and brilliantly shines just in situation of deep, seemingly intractable social conflicts.

Failure to persuade does not doom reason in any way. Nor does failure signify reason runs out. That H. L. A. Hart's "rules of recognition"(承认规则), Ronald Dworkin's "best moral theory" or John Rawls' principles of justice such as "original position"(原初状态) and "veil of ignorance" does not find receptive ears among certain legal thinkers does not diminish the originality, compelling nature, and insight of their thought. Ditto the reason and reasoning of the doubters.

The arguments of doubters are patently counterfactual. Even in situation of sharply polarized politics, people change loyalty. In religion, pagans, Jews, Muslims, and atheists have been known to having been converted to Christians.

The equilibrium zone of efficiently processed disputes which is so dear to doubters' hearts and central to their arguments is just a fiction or a trumped up presumption. It never existed, nor is it existing, or will arise and last. The simple truth is that technology, information, and knowledge advance continuously. And no one can claim that these sources of reason have ever been sufficiently and completely marshaled and processed in the most optimum manner. There is always more room for new, more robust, and powerful reason to be created as the mainstreamed legal thinkers advocate.

When preference or choice was made with respect to matter or issue of a political moral nature, decisions were seldom grounded on emotion, arationality or irrationality. The fact that reason advanced to justify decision may be not accepted or even vigorously disputed does not disprove its irrationality. We would submit that even Holmes' "cannot help" dictum(情不自禁规则), though appearing irrational, is based on reason. The factors, consideration, experience, or conditions that caused Holmes to entertain his assertion are his background reasons.

Even the unfolding of an infinite regress of asking why, why, why and answering because, because, because signifies the continuous search for better and stronger reason rather than exposes the failure or run-out of reason as chided by the

---

⑭ Campos, op cit at 101.

doubters.

What is rationality, arationality, or irrationality? Would it be ever possible to reach a consensus on their definition in a society where citizens hold diverse, pluralist political and moral visions and views? This shows how the arguments of the doubters can easily backfire.

Any attempts to define or clarify the substantive content of rationality would encounter the same problems, issues, difficulties associated with inquiries about the substantive content of good law, good legal system, and good reason. And suddenly, we find that we are revisiting the debates between the legal positivists and the proponents of the natural law and entering the seemingly ever-lasting debates about the very concept of law and its philosophical foundation.

A reasonable compromise is to jettison any inquiry of the substantive content of rationality and to concentrate our efforts on the systemic and procedural features or characteristics of rationality and by implication, irrationality. In this respect, what constitutes arationality remains a challenge. Either arationality can be simply dismissed as a misnomer or the meaning of arationality has already been well taken care of by the systemic and procedural approach.

L. Subjective versus Objective Reason

In the final analysis, most if not all of the contentions between the doubters and the proponents of reason concerning questions such as the incommensurability, balancing, comparison, choice, etc of reasons boggle down to a distinction and debate between subjective reason and objective reason.

The doubters of reason in the strong and radical camp allege that all reasons are subjective, that is, reasons are advanced from the special perspective of one's own epoch, perspective, understanding, and culture, etc. Those who reason can only do so based on their own knowledge and local conditions. All of us who reason are specially situated and uniquely conditioned. Taking into consideration of the testimony of human experience from all epochs and cultures would not avoid " the fallacies that come from allowing special authority to the judgments of any one milieu. "[219] In its strong and radical sense, this view denies the very existence of objectivity in reason. In the context of political morality, this view would also deny

---

[219] Schlag, *The Enchantment of Reason*, Duke Univ. Pr., 1998, p. 82.

the possibility of widely if not universally shared and cherished human dignity values.

In a strict sense, such a widely or if not universally shared value, normativity, and law need not necessarily come from any one base, culture, history. In a society of ethical and legal pluralism, not only fundamental constitutive values are shared, common grounds and consensus are routinely established through the democratic process of making authoritative and effective decisions.

The doubters not only are fond of questioning the vigor and cogency of reason and of dwelling excessively on its weakness and limitation but also loathe and hate reason. Thus, Schlag accuses reason, reasoning, persuasion, agreement and unity as advocating monism as opposed to pluralism, monotomy as opposed to polytomy, sameness as opposed to difference, monojurality as opposed to polyjurality. Could it be possible that the doubters even question our commonly shared and cherished histories, traditions, cultures, values, and whatever stand for the people of a polity as a whole? Like law, these are the collective normative intention of the people.

M. Reason, Faith, and Other Belief Systems

Faith and belief influence decision and action. The Conservative Party of United States posits policy often and especially on issues of deep social conflict on the basis of evangelist Christian faith. Social issues such as abortion, gay rights, stem-cell research and "faith-based" delivery of government programs are some of the well-known examples.

It has been rightly observed that public disputes implicate powerful competing ideological visions that are themselves the products of axiomatic, diverse political and moral beliefs. What is curious is that little has been said explicitly, especially in the context of legal reason with respect to the material sources of beliefs. Richard Posner thinks beliefs live below reason. Does that mean that beliefs actually inform and sustain reasons? If not, then what are the material bases of beliefs? Is it possible that the source or base of belief be simply divine or spiritual revelation?

A whole legal system may be based on religious beliefs. Both the Talmudic law and the Islamic law are such example. The draft constitution of Iraq post the U. S. - led invasion agreed upon by the Shiits and the Kurds without the Sunnis unequivocally enshrines the Islam as the source of all law. No legislation can be enacted in contravention of the basic teachings and principles of the Koran*.

Could it be possible that faith is born out of, informed, and sustained by, reason? Faith or religious belief is never a monolithic unity. There are faiths within faith; all are born and flourish in the name and image of God. The existence of the mainstream, moderate, and radical strands of faith attest to this truism. There is nothing on Earth that could not be the object of reason. Question respecting the time and space of the existence of God is even in the hand of the court, as the ruling of Supreme Court attests in the case of the pledge of allegiance in public schools. Another example of beliefs, faith, or God being the object of reason is the battle between observant Jews and secular Israelis over the religion in daily life, in this case over the sale and consumption of pork. The Israeli Supreme Court ruled Israeli municipalities must permit the sale of pork where a majority of residents demand it. In the landmark 1976 right-to-die** case of Karen Quinlan, for example, it was the Roman Catholic bishop of New Jersey, Lawrence Casey, who argued before the court in support of Quinlan's parents' request that her respirator be turned off. The reason is that to use artificial modern medical devices to prolong a naturally unsustainable life—particularly that of a brain-dead person who has, arguably, lost that "image of God" raises fundamental and serious theological and ethical questions and complications. It is hardly deniable that in the U.S. to hijack religion for political, strategic purposes has become a fact of life. The contentious Terri Schiavo debate was to be all about political gain with an eye on the next election by the Conservative members of the Congress attempting to trample into the most private, personal and painful decisions families must make. The Florida state law prescribes that in cases in which a patient has not signed a directive about life-prolonging care, the patient's spouse—unless there is a court-appointed guardian(法庭指定监护人)—makes the call. The patient's parents are listed third, behind reasonably available adult children.

While it is true that we use reason to select, test, monitor, advocate, and promote beliefs, it is equally undeniable that beliefs are often invoked and applied to evaluate, judge, and trash reason.

What is most crucial is to ascertain and clarify the relationship between reason and belief. Unless this is done and widely shared criteria are identified to distinguish

---

* 又拼作 Qur'an,《古兰经》,又译作《可兰经》,伊斯兰教经典。

** 死亡权,即请求安乐死的权利。

one from the other, it would equally be irrational or unreasonable to brand reason as belief or vice versa.

Only political or moral disputes arising and coming from divinity or spirituality informed and sustained beliefs and faiths post severe evidentiary problems and radically incommensurable conceptual understandings and thus are not amenable to rational analysis and solution.

It is true that divergent, competing, and even conflicting interpretation and application of legal materials, rules, or doctrines frequently happened due to their notoriously vague and contradictory nature and the law appeared to be of little real guidance to a harried decision-maker. And the uncertainty or unpredictability of the law may be a systemic problem. But it would be wrong to quickly attribute this problem to radically incommensurable conceptual understandings or beliefs.

The belief that this reason is sound is different from one's believe in God. Belief in reason is essentially rational, while the belief in God is pure spiritual and cannot be demonstrated. To equate secular affairs with the business of God is highly blasphemous. Reason does not depend upon belief. Nor reason is special or a kind of trans-contextual belief.

Thus, based on their misunderstanding or faulty understanding of reason, the doubters accuse the proponents unthinkingly equating belief with reason. In reverse logic, the proponents of reason may charge the doubters unthinkingly equating reason with belief.

Public political, legal, moral discourse and reasoning are a continuing normative enterprise; theoretically never should it be ended. However, due to limitations in resources and time, the reasoning process must be cut short, except where the issues, problems, conflicts are of such a nature that delay can be postponed and tolerated infinitely.

Thus, for almost all social, political, moral, legal issues, soon or later reason must stop. And choice among competing reasons must be made. At the point of choice, reason that stops can not be further deployed to form the base of choice. Choice must be made on the basis of what among the competing reasons is deemed and accepted to be most just, fair, appropriate, desirable, good, etc. Admitted that whatever choice is made, it is the product of contingent human decision, however fallible it may be. This decision of choice is not in any sense formally or substantively circular or self-referential. Nor is it based on belief. To argue otherwise is to admit that in the final analysis all arguments and reasons are circular and self-referential.

When reason and choice among competing reasons are viewed this way, it will not be so surprising that protagonists of reason deploy at the end of a discourse and persuasion strong, axiomatic, conclusive rhetoric and language to end the argument. Thus, it is simply not fair to accuse the deployment of axiomatic and conclusive language as eloquently seductive, ideological distorting, or axiom-ridden, etc.

N. Belief in Disguise of Reason

The doubters of reason seem to believe that in any modern society of moral and political pluralism, choices are always made on the ground of preference and faith rather than reason. Preference and faith are advanced and justified in <u>disguise of reason(理性的伪装)</u>. Preference and faith skillfully and effectively transposed and incorporated into the sober categories, idioms, and grammar of law and legal argument. By thus attacking the authenticity, purity, and legitimacy of reason, the doubters attempt to weaken and erode the validity and authority of law and legal argument. For example, John Rawls posited three public reasons in the context of abortion, namely due respect for human life, the ordered reproduction of political society, and the political equality of women. And he concluded upon consideration of these values that at the early stage of pregnancy, the political value of equality of women is overriding. The doubters brand Rawls' conclusion not an ineluctable product of rational reflection but his deep and long held personal belief in disguise.

The proponents of reason rightly pointed out that as reason is informed and shaped by the various sources of law, and that authoritative and effective decisions and actions are advanced and advocated as such, there is hardly any metamorphosis. Admittedly, in the process of presenting sources and authoritative and effective decisions and actions as reasons in legal arguments, there are certain subtle but transparent transformation in form. The doubter's attack should be directed at these law-generating decisions and actions, rather than at reason, if the former are made on the basis of preferences, tasks (as in gastronomic jurisprudence), W. Holmes' "cannot help or intuition."

In this substantive sense, sources, preferences, beliefs, faiths, etc. are the very reason they constitute. Notions such as "basic norms," "secondary rules," "the very best moral philosophy," "justice trumps efficiency," or "fidelity to precedent are more compelling than policy arguments." And after being incorporated into legal arguments, such notions count as reasons of law, regardless of whether or not these "unthoughts" remain unquestioned, unnoticed or undisturbed.

If these are not reasons, what are they? What are the grounds or criteria the doubters are able to advance to objectively distinguish reason from belief, faith, or other arationalities or irrationalities? In other words, a complete new species of reason is required. When reason is challenged, neither the nature nor the authority of reason changes. Only the efficacy of reason versus the non-persuaded is weakened. Otherwise, one would be always free to brand reason as belief or vice versa.

Are the doubters prepared to advocate and argue for the view that one should give up reason outright and simply utter or assert arationality or irrationality in public discourse?

The alarming phenomenon of political evangelism in America speaks voluminously for the political nature of religion and faith in public life. The orthodoxy of the Roman Catholicism (罗马天主教传统) has been increasingly asserting its place and influence in the realm of political morality. Religion and faith has simply become part and parcel of public discourse. The rhetoric of political evangelism is weaved in sophisticated theology, philosophy, history, and whatever found relevant and useful and presented in impeccable argument.

"That is my belief" or "I believe that is right or wrong" is such a cliche that we say it in opining matter in our daily lives as well in politics and discourse in law. In fact, the word "belief" employed in this connection is simply a convenient wrap-up or substitute for all the reasons and justification embodied.

Admittedly, reason does suffer instability and vulnerability in some context due to its incompleteness, disjunction, or some other weakness. But this does not in any way change the nature and way of how we reason. It is simply a natural thing to do that in the face of challenges, we process and even double our efforts to fortify, purify, and perfect reason by attempting to eradicate tensions, paradoxes, contradictions, etc. rather than to admit defeat, to give up, and to run away. This in no way would transform reason into its traditional enemies: faith, dogma, and prejudice.[216]

---

[216] Schlag, *The Enchantment of Reason*, Durham [N.C.] Duke Univ. Pr., 1998, p.79.

The doubters of reason are right in pointing out that at some specific point in the decision-making process, reasoning must stop for one reason or another. And a choice must be made among competing reasons. And it is belief that in fact dictates the choice of the version of reason that considered more beneficial, right, desirable, etc. But here the belief is not the same sort as that in spiritual beliefs. It is the force of the gravitating pull of all reasons advanced and combined.

In short, faith is a convenient package of reason in the name of God. * Faith, unreasoned, becomes moral absolutism and is what ails the world. And reason without faith is dangerous. Law is a normative package of public reason in the name of political and moral authority. It appears that the doubters' understanding about the enchantment or predicaments of reason is just a misconception, a fiction, and a straw man.

O. Legal Reason is a Noble Scam: The Self-Referential Nature of Law and Legal Reason

Does law and legal reason have distinct features? Could purely legal argument be made to the exclusion of argument of a "non-legal" nature? Is not law just a formulaic rendition of the normative statement of a political, moral nature?

Law and legal reason suffer a great deal in the hands of many of post-modern legal theorists. The Critical legal studies'** indetermination thesis and view of an inherent contradictory nature of law mount a frontal, if not fatal, attack on legal reason. Stripped of the false pretense of reason and justification, it is alleged that what judges and other legal actors do in fact is tantamount to a practice of the ritualized form of violence. And the legal academics are virtually demoted to the status of thug-trainers. ⑰

The doubters believe that legal decisions and reasons are founded on the ground

---

* 简言之,信仰是一个以上帝之名的便利袋。

** 批判法律研究(CLS)。批判法律研究是一场激进的法律批判运动,它活跃于20世纪70年代早期至80年代后期的美国(在其他国家也有一些追随者和支持者)。批判法律研究结合了左翼政治观和最早由美国法律现实主义发展起来的激进版的批判命题。批判法律研究的主题包括:法律的彻底的不确定性、批判公与私的区分、论证法律为权力服务。他们认为法律是彻底的不确定的,法律推理仅仅是不同利益群体或不同意识形态冲突的遮羞布。这些观点有时用"法律就是政治"这句口号来总结。批判法律研究内部的紧张和对这场运动施加的压力导致了它的分崩离析。目前不再有一个以批判法律研究命名的自我认同的群体或运动。虽然许多以批判法律研究而闻名的法学家继续以同样的方式从事法律研究,批判法律研究发展起来的许多批判已经被其他的批判进路取代了,例如,种族批判理论、女权主义法律理论和后现代法律理论。

⑰ Id., at 20-21.

of preference, taste, faith, or other arationality or irrationality. Legal reason and argument is a noble scam. The doubters compare and in fact equate reason to dogmatic assertion, rhetoric bluster, political posturing, and ethical bullying. The doubters ground their distaste for reason on the specious logic that reason can never prove its rationality rationally. To deploy reason to defend reason, though laudable and mandatory, is logically redundant and absurd. One can prove that a particular argument is valid or rational within the criteria of rationality or validity a priori established and recognized. One cannot prove by referring to or using the same set of criteria the rationality of those criteria themselves. Like the argument for the autonomy or the autopoiesis of law, the exercise purely becomes an internal self-referential operation, a shallow circularity that is at odd with the idea of reason. This is what is called "Munchausen trilemma": infinite regression, circularity and dogmatic assertion.[218]

The noble scam is built on a continuous stream of infinite regression and circularity of reasoning and argument for the validity and authority of the law. Cleverly crafted gimmicks or fictions such as H. L. A. Hart's "secondary rules(次要规则)", H. Kelsen's "Basic norms(基本规范)", and Ronald Dworkin's "the very best moral philosophy", amply illustrate their noble scam.[219] What is curiously interesting is that the doubters concede to the institutional efficacy of the scam. And reason successfully finds it place in the "real law," because the legal institutions are full of royal believers and followers, rather than those who hold different or divergent political and moral views and opinions. What is of particular importance is that reason figures prominently in the real world of authoritative and effective decisions of a political, economic, and social nature.

But to the dismay of the doubters, the "noble scam" found in the "real law" works effectively where it counts. From the perspective of the law of authoritative and effective decisions and actions, the noble scam is law just as the law it informs and justifies.

There is a fundamental and deep philosophical and biological question with respect to the self-referential phenomenon. It may be cogently argued that all biological beings live and operate in a self-referential, circular fashion. If reason is unique to man, then circular reasoning is human. I think, therefore I am. Niklas

---

[218] John Searle, *The Construction of Social Reality*, New York, Free Press, 1995, p. 178.
[219] Schlag, *The Enchantment of Reason*, Durham [N. C.] Duke Univ. Pr., 1998, p. 34 et seq.

Luhmann's autopoiesis of law may be the most significant insight on this issue.[20]

Even Schlag himself has admitted that the self-referential nature of the mainstream legal thinkers' reasoning is understandable and reasonable. The very notion that law is autonomous conceives the seed of infinite regression, circularity, and self-reference. These internal operations are the constitutive features of the normative idea of law and legal reason.

The doubters severely criticize the monistic aesthetic of law and legal reason. The fatal fault of the mainstream law and legal reason, they argue, is that it subjugates the many to the one, pluralism to monism, polytony to monotony, difference to sameness, and so on.[21] One wonders if the crimes listed above by the doubters really exist in the real world or they are in fact what fictionalized or conjured up as a sort of straw-man. Even in dictatorship, such political and moral absolutism hardly obtains.

The doubters may have their particular conception and version of the law. Certainly any credible conception of law and legal reason requires more than simply hosting up legal reason as a straw man to attack its "short-circuiting any thoughtful consideration of the grounds of [legal] reason and its "smug dismissals" of opposing views and reasons. Nor would it suffice by branding the mainstream mode of aesthetic of understanding as impoverished and abstract and by charging the proponents of reason for "misprision of all that is not reason."[22] The doubters of reason criticize the validity, legitimacy, and advocacy of the reason of law because they disagree with the existing institutions of law, legal system, and/or the rule of law. No where is this thinking more clearly revealed than in the context of Schlag's piece regarding laws and reason as "divine deceptions." [Legal] "[r]eason and thus law itself become vehicles for the rule of the dominant forms of life... the rule of technology, bureaucracy, and the commodity form." The doubters despise the dominant forms of law because they spiritualize and venerate the profane and the vulgar, vulgarize the spiritual and the sacred, and they materialize life, choice, and values.[23] In the hands of the doubters, the study and evaluation of the humanistic

---

  [20] There are numerous writings tackling this issue that are either authored by Luhmann himself or scholarly comments thereon. A concise introduction to Luhmann is found in *The Philosophy of Law: an Encyclopedia*. Ed. Christopher Berry Gray. New York & London: Garland Publ., 1999, pp. 527-528.

  [21] Schlag, *The Enchantment of Reason*. Durham [N.C.] Duke Univ. Pr., 1998, p. 44.

  [22] Id., at 47.

  [23] Id., at 92 et seq.

Chapter Eight: Legal Reason and Executing Decision 381

and spiritual dimensions and features of law become an unabashed glorification of law. The approach of law espoused by the law and literature school ends up poeticizing the dreary, mechanistic side of law, deadening of ethical and aesthetic awareness, worshiping the bureaucratic machine.[24]

Under the pen of the doubters, social science study and police analysis of law are fatally constrained within the fundamental categories, concepts, and grammar of the established sources, and remain hopelessly scientifically unredeemed and unredeemable. The conflating and synthesizing strand of the legal scholarship as championed by the neo-pragmatists naively disregards irreconcilable differences between science and spirit.[25]

The doubters of reason accuse legal academics as compulsive solution mongering by insisting on possibility of rational resolution of deep intractable social, moral conflicts. And the general public in the face of a reality full of intolerable webs of uncertainty surrounding their most difficult choices, has happily found in the person of an army of bureaucratic lawyers certain paternal figure who are willing to dictate conduct and life. In the view of the doubters, the tendency of the legal community and the legal academics in particular, to continuously orchestrate and over-generalize the power of reason, is rooted in professional vanity. Reason and reasoning is the very weapon that sustains the myth and the livelihood of lawyers, academics, and judges who are just loath to the idea or suggestion that to continue to engage in rational analysis of issues or controversies of a deep intractable social or moral nature would lead to hyper-trophification of reason verging on rationalist delusion.

Of course, nothing can be further from the truth. Issues, controversies, conflicts of any nature, social, moral, political, cannot be left unsettled for long with the rights of people left in limbo. These issues, controversies, conflicts must be resolved. And the best way to do it is through public and rational discourse that is open and transparent and the participation in such discourse is free, equal, and inclusive. To suggest otherwise is just pure delusion, anti-intuition, anti-democracy, and anti-reality.

P. Beyond Reason, beyond Law; without Reason, without Law

The doubters' cynicism goes much beyond the nature and function of reason in

---

[24] Id., at 94.
[25] Id., at 94-95.

the legal process. They in fact question the objective existence of fundamental constituents, formal features, as well as the basic concepts of law. For example, they accuse the proponents of reason look upon rules, principles, doctrines, standards, precepts, etc. as if they were physical objects or mindful subjects like "dropping objects" or "bee-stings," and having stabilized identity and status. The apprehension of the legal artifacts in this way—called the objectivist aesthetic—is counterpoised with the legal thinkers and actors' subjectivist aesthetic by endowing upon the legal artifacts qualities and characteristics of a mindful life, such as will, intention, purpose, and even personality.

The objectivist aesthetic is the very constitutive elements of the law of authoritative and effective decision. And the subjectivist aesthetic is the life and blood of law in terms of its operation and performance. By questioning and ridiculing these fundamental elements, the doubters deny the very possibility and existence of law—the most fundamental social normative elements of a political community. Language, concepts, rules, principles, doctrines, etc. are just as real as the physical world. Without the aid of language and linguistic representation, neither the physical world nor human artifacts, such as law, will be known or meaningful.

There is no need for legal thinkers and actors to deny the utility let alone the very existence of either the subjectivist or the objectivist aesthetic. Whatever the insights, constructive or deconstructive, the criticism of the legal realists and the critical legal studies may embody, they have failed to bankrupt the institutions, concepts, functions of the law. Law as the most fundamental normative enterprise of a political community along with its accompanying reason lives on with continued vitality. The doubters rightly observe that these "aesthetics remain sedimentary within the discourse, the vocabulary, the grammar of [American] law." Nor is it necessary for the proponents of reason to recognize the weaknesses and sillies of either the objectivist or the subjectivist aesthetic when putting on their philosopher's cap and embracing these very aesthetics in engaging the normative enterprise of the law. A morally and politically committed thinker and/or actor lives and excels with a reasonable combination and balancing of the law's objective existence and subjective aspiration.

Yes, something called "the law" is confirmed, affirmed, and carried forward in each and every authoritative and effective decision as manifested in public political moral action. The objective components of the law never remain static and

Chapter Eight: Legal Reason and Executing Decision   383

unchanged in the face of new perspective, use, or interest. On the contrary, law and its constitutive parts change and are keeping abreast with social change.

It is necessary to clarify the doubters' criticism of law's aesthetic representation in factual terms. The subjectivity of the law comes not from its objectivist aesthetic, such as rule, principle, doctrine, precepts, etc. It emanates from all the authoritative and effective decision-makers who ascribe to widely shared interpretation and application of the rule, principle, doctrine, etc. and who confirm and bring forward the interpretation and application through their own public political moral actions. It is their effective base power as formalized and reflected in the rule, principle, doctrine, precept, etc., that binds, requires, obligates, constrains, compels, guides, etc. Similarly, it is the decision-makers' will, intention, and purpose working in the same way in action. In a way, the personality of Justitia who holds the scales of justice represents the aggregation of the effective power, will, intention, purpose of all authoritative and effective decision-makers.

This coming of the subjectivist will, intention, purpose, etc from authoritative and effective decision-makers rather than emanating from inanimate conceptual legal artifacts can be called "re-imagination of authority." What the doubters call "theoretical unmentionables," such as the "interpretive community," R. Dworkin's "Hercules," H. L. A. Hart's "internal perspective," are conceptualizations of such re-imagination of authority.[29] And these theoretical unmentionables may very well represent the collective expectation of authority in a liberal democracy. Interpretive community is constituted of jurists, judges, and legal practitioners by virtue of their formal legal training and professional responsibility. The collective internal viewpoint of the interpretive community exerts a direct and powerful influence on law's formation and transformation.

Neither the objective aesthetic nor the subjectivity in authoritative and effective decisions is any kind of hypostatization, reification, illusion, or fetishism. They are very much the fact of the life we live politically, or morally. It seems the doubters must have conceived or envisaged a kind of life that does not belong to any political community found on the planet Earth. As a political moral community, the law we set forth in our collective life of coordination and cooperation are either what we actually live or what we aspire to live. It would be so much better if our collective

---

[29] Id., at 112 et seq.

life happens to satisfy the ideal qualities of human existence and aspiration.

It is totally nonsensical to view the objectivity and subjectivity of law as some kind of "as if" jurisprudence or metaphysics. The implications and consequences of human dignity values involved in these constituents of the law are too serious and important to be branded an "as if" hypothesis.

Legal academics by means of their scholarship are formalizers or "rulifiers." They engage as the mandate of their professional responsibility in nurturing and shaping both the form and substance of the law.

In their zealous pursuit of the agenda to discredit the institutions of law and the reason of law, the doubters of reason do not even hesitate to exaggerate their metaphors and wildest imagination. One such instance is their comparison of the ascription of the performance and effecting power to the rules, principles, etc of law and their decision-makers to the investiture of magic and miraculous power in God and his word.

The doubters have completely missed the point by consciously or unconsciously ignore the authoritative and effective decision-makers behind the law.

Q. Law, Reason and Deep, Divisive Social Issues

Is it true that deeply or sharply divisive social controversy is not amenable to or beyond rational solution? Whatever methodology of the argument one invokes, logical, empirical, rhetorically camouflaged emotive, such as elementary logic, common sense, public reason(公共理性,与"私人理性"相对), or the perennial favorite "the Constitution," it won't change an iota of an opponent's deep-held view or belief. In other words, in the view of the doubters of reason, divisive issue, such as abortion, same-sex marriage, biotechnology and stem cell research simply defies rational analysis and solution. By implication, the doubters advocate that issues of this nature be left unsolved and let laissez-faire(自由放任) rein. Critical legal studies scholars mount a frontal attack on law and legal reason by claiming that law is inherently self-contradictory and indeterminate. Thus, stripped of the false pretense of reason, what judges, lawyers, and other legal actors do in fact is tantamount to the practice of ritualized form of violence.

The doubters believe that the Constitution has become "an ideally vague set of oracular-sounding propositions, whose very vagueness comfort the devotee with a sense that the correct interpretation of an essentially magical text will provide insight into mysteries that would otherwise remain unknowable and obscure."㉗

The doubters hoist up laws against physician-assisted suicide(安乐死) as another example of a deep divisive social, moral, legal, and political controversy or an issue that lies squarely in the middle of the equilibrium zone of competing opinions, views, visions, and laws. In this case, there are two opposing forces in a mature democratic society. These are the recognition of the legal right of any mentally competent adults to refuse medical treatment on the one hand and the need to ensure equal and non-abusive diagnose and treatment for all citizens regardless of race, gender, age, social and economic status on the other hand.

It does not take much to realize that in any society of a heterogeneous nature where moral and value pluralism prevails, competing forces are a given. Instead of festering permanent intractable divisive conflicts, partisan politics and rational public discourse tend in the long run to promote understanding, tolerance, compromise, and the development of a health, progressive, and prosperous society.

In fact, there never has been or will be any social issue of any controversial or divisive nature that has not been settled one way or another for a considerable time period by reasoned decisions. Admittedly, different and even conflicting solutions may exist in different locales or societies. And the justifications advanced for these solutions are all reasoned or rational.

The idea that important values may be irreconcilably at odds with each other and that choice between them has to be made on grounds or reason not shared by all is simply part and parcel of any political community. This is just a reasonable trade-off between the various competing interests and forces in society. Hopefully, in the final analysis, advantages victoriously outweigh disadvantages. Maybe this is what Robert M. Cover called the "juripathic" character of legal decision making.

Instead of seconding Robin West's insight that "reason will not account for, or in the end meaningfully challenge, our rock-bottom moral beliefs," we believe that reason is just potentially too rich, inexhaustible, and powerful not to win the heart and mind of nonbelievers in the end. Besides, beliefs are not inborn, preordained, or held through brainwash beyond the possibility of being deprogrammed. Beliefs have their origin and are formed in reason.

No doubt, reason may be informed and reinforced by, for example, experience,

---

㉗ Campos, *Jurismania: the Madness of American Law*, p. 169.

empathy, and reflection, as noted by Robin West. But such enriched reason is still reason. Reason still has to do its work to persuade those who hold steadfast to a sharply different experiences, identifies, etc. And partisans of competing beliefs can all put up a good argument for their stances.

Critics are very much dismayed by the fact that a highly intelligent legal scholar can willingly and quickly "metamorphose into a veritable warren of rationalist rabbits, bobbling in a blissful community of agreement, as the question is begged and the magic words uttered: "justice," "principle," and of course "reason." while "fully capable of appreciating the tremendously complex and indeed fundamentally inexplicable elements involved in undertaking essentially contestable ethical judgments."㉘ One wonders what would Campos think of his own attempt and efforts to persuade us into believing the irrationality or arationality of law, reason, and authoritative and effective decisions concerning issues of in what he calls the "equilibrium zone." Is he also a happy and blissful rational idiot or an irrational one?

In hard cases, doubters would advocate that we appeal to sentimental faculties and axiomatic moral beliefs rather than commit the fallacy in trying to employ logical argument and empirical analysis.㉙

R. Critique of Cynicism, Defeatism and Self-denial of Law and Reason— "As If Jurisprudence"

Through training and indoctrination, professional initiation, and experience of practice, members of the legal professional have established and entertained a sort of double consciousness and are engaging in a kind of Orwellian doublethink. This is a sort of "as if" jurisprudence, within the context of which the lawyer both knows and doesn't know that most important legal facts are facts only to the extent we believe them to be legal fact. To ignore this intensive cognitive dissonance resulted from such double consciousness and thinking becomes a common practice.

The doubters of law and legal reason continue their assault by treating the law as a peculiar kind of psychological artifact whose existence or absence completely depend on our desires and beliefs. This is true only if what we call desire or belief is in fact the final form of reasons as crystallized.

㉘ Çampos, Id., at 172.
㉙ Id., at 173.

The doubters' notion that law as a conceptual artifact like many other legal concepts and ideas, is a psychological phenomenon that depends entirely for its existence on our desires and beliefs is utterly false and distorting. Nor legal objectivity is some kind of semiconscious illusion, or a mythical beast like the fictitious unicorns.

Law is founded on the twined notion of authority and efficacy. Efficacy is authority externalized to influence the practical impacts and consequences of decisions and actions on what is inclusively called human dignity values. Authority when internalized as binding as a standard for conduct and criticism becomes a legal objectivity. Authority whether internalized or externalized is informed and shaped by the same consideration of the impacts and consequences of human dignity values.

To criticize, debunk, deconstruct law and reason, doubters in fact are engaged in not just cynicism, defeatism but more importantly self-denial.

S. Doubters' Law and Legal Reason

There is simply no escape that by engaging extensively in the enterprise of law and legal reason along with their criticism and conclusion, the doubters commit exactly the same "mental illness" as they accuse the proponents of law commit. The failure of the mainstream legal thinkers to persuade in the discourse of issues, socially, politically, morally intractable or not, does not in any way signify reason itself runs out. Reason like knowledge and truth continues to challenge us. What the doubters appear to concern with may be called re-rationalization(再理性化). But it is still rationalization. Unfortunately, they don't even do much frame or paradigm reconstruction.

In Compas' "jurismania" rendition, he finally made an alternative proposition to cure the illness of American legal culture in his "way of renunciation." He proposed that we acknowledged and accepted the fact that judicial decisions were made by fiat, that is, all the reasons and justifications were just disguise of naked power. He advised us that we completely expunged reason and justification from decisions. Campos offered a short, simple, and cute alternative. It goes like this: "judgment for the plaintiff," or better still, "because the legislature did not intend to bar claims filed on the last day of the year, the claims are valid," or "because of the plain meaning of the statute's text, the claims fail."⑳

By adhering to Compas' admonition, it should be no doubt that the institution and doctrine of the Common law would not only be severely or rather fatally impoverished but also quickly vanish from the corpus of American law.

If reason is nothing but assertion and if the reasoning advanced by Sunstein and many others who share his view is just a rhetoric trick, one wonders what would doubters, such as Schlag and Campos, expect those who disagree with them to think about the reason they themselves advanced?

T. Truth in Law and Reason

Truth in law or legal reason differs from truth in fact. Factual truth is supposed to be observable, proven, tested, demonstrated, etc. Real factual truth should be universally accepted. If factual truth has to be scientifically proven, then factual truth is not absolute or beyond doubt since the advancement in sciences and technology may very well prove what has been accepted as truth may turn out to be not true. Scientific truth depends primarily on shared paradigm and accepted theory in the scientific community(科学共同体). Who knows the fact that the Earth is round or moves around the Sun may even be proven wrong in some distant future. If truth in fact can be really scientifically proven, why trust the task to juror to establish it on the basis of unanimity—beyond any (or reasonable) doubt in cases of disputes? This is true regardless of the stringent requirements of the law of evidence.

In George Orwell's dystopian classic 1964, power begets reality begets truth. Specific ideas and images can be systematically promoted. Documentary filmmakers no less than state apparatus, can shape the truth through a variety of styles and with an even wider range of intentions. A camera, depending on who holds it, can tell the whole, part of, or nothing of, the truth. "[T]here is no such thing as being strictly objective in anything that is at all artistic. The objectivity is just a personal integrity." With most of the truth or fact being represented third-hand, meaning of reality is manufactured.㉑ Truth is not black and white; it comes in a shade of gray. Some truth can be held to a higher standard than others. In criminal law, the standard is "beyond any reasonable doubt(排除一切合理怀疑)," while in the law

---

⑳ Ibid.
㉑ Manohla Dargis, "Documentary vs. Propaganda", *The Gazette*, Montreal, July 2, 2004, p. D14.

of torts, a preponderance of evidence(优势证据)* is sufficient. The dichotomy between and the fight for subjectivity and objectivity amply testify this problem.

Truth and Conventionalism:

Truth in law, if ever there is such as thing, is in essence based on arguable or persuasive reason. All theories are constructed; the formalist syllogism is equally philosophically framed just like all other legal theories. The factual truth established by jury is nothing but shared and consensual meaning and understanding. There is no higher standard for truth in law. Truth in law concerns political morality. The standard of proof is reasonable doubt.

Truth in reason is sine qua non of rational discourse. Thus, the persuasiveness of reason may be weakened by the nature of truth claimed. In addition to the incompleteness and insufficiency of knowledge, there is also the question of language. The predicaments of reason are also caused by the unavoidable objectifying aspects of language in terms of reformulating the reality, normative or factual, and its context in a form that it is not. Description and clarification of reality and context necessarily result in transformation of the factual context from a way of being into a set of linguistic representations.㉒ All representation occurs in language and there is no way to step outside of language in order to survey its connection with reality. Reality is a social process of convention, which are not agreed but shared.

Wittgenstein also believes that all understanding occurs in and through language. Thus, there is no way to show what is fair that corresponds with the "idea of fair." Truth is local and pragmatic. Wittgenstein's conventionalism rejects Cartesianism and Kant's transcendental idealism. Action is an unreflective reaction to the meaningfulness of the situation in which one is engrossed. Obeying a rule is not a matter of choice but is done blindly.㉓

Truth exists not just in the materialist or physical sense, but also in the mental or conceptual sense in the mind of men. Nietzsche's famous aphorism that there is no "facts" but only interpretations does not take too much of our imagination to know it

---

* 在英美法中,举证责任由轻到重分为四种程度:是的可能性比不是的可能性大(more probably than not);优势证据(preponderance of evidence),需达到50%以上的可能性,是民事案件需要达到的举证程度;清楚及可信(clear of convincing evidence);排除一切合理怀疑(beyond reasonable doubt)是刑事案件证明被告有罪时所需达到的证明程度,非证明被告人有无罪的证据只需到达清楚及可信的程度。

㉒ Pierce Schlag, *The Enchantment of Reason*. Durham [N.C.] Duke Univ. Pr., 1998, p.74.

㉓ Peter Hacker & Gordon Baker, *Wittgenstein: Understanding and Meaning*. 2ed extensively rev. ed. Malden, MA; Oxford: Blackwell Pub., 2005.

is wrong. Hutchinson is no less wrong in refuting objectivity in reality, text, and language. And this is no Archimedian point from which the truth and falsity of interpretive acts can be tested. To term this as functional essentialism or reductionism is insignificant. It is really surprising that the doubters in their rush to discredit the possibility of the existence of truth and the objectivity in law and reason regard "the notion that the perceived universe could somehow subsist autonomously from some mind's perception of it[29] as patently absurd.

There is an interesting but specious flaw in the metaphor that with each man's death, a whole universe vanishes. This is beautiful poetry but means little in intellect. It is hardly deniable that the perception and knowledge of the universe as well as countless events, happenings, activities, etc, occurred to each of us are all gone upon and with our death. But let's be very clear that even with the total destruction of the mankind along with the Earth, the sun, the moon, and the stars continue to shine. And the truth and objective existence of human victories, defeats, happiness and sufferings live on in the civilization and the minds of aliens who once visited and studied us.

Surely, social and normative truth is a different thing. In Orwell's novel 1964, power begets reality begets truth. Truth can be manipulated or fabricated. Meaning can be manufactured. There are higher and lower standards of truth. For all ethical judgment and political and moral decisions, we need no teleological basis. Our constitutional and political structure and our democratic system of decision-making provide at the present stage of civilization and moral development are all we have got until we have them changed and improved.

In the view of logical positivists(逻辑实证主义者), truth claim or true statement can be divided into two types: that which can be proved through logical and mathematical reasoning and that which can be verified empirically. The latter may be called factual or materialist truth, while the former logical or formalistic truth. The truth regarding "dropping objects" or "bee stings" can be physically or emotionally experienced and thus proven. On the other hand, whether or not "rights trump", "rules or doctrines bind" or "principles override or guide" can only socially or politically, or if you prefer, legally determined. The doubters of reason and law claim that statements about right and wrong, justice, fairness, and

---

[29] Campos, id. at 40.

reasonableness are sorts of degraded subjective truth; logically speaking, they are meaningless. The example given to support this distinction is the objective truth of the statement that the Earth revolves around the Sun, and the claim that the Haagen-Dazs ice cream tastes better than Ben & Jerry's. [235]

It seems well established that scientific truth is based on nothing more than what is generally accepted paradigm in the scientific community. Facts are themselves often nothing more than agglomerations of broad scale ideological, scientific, aesthetic, rhetorical, institutional, technological, and other formations. With the advancement of scientific inquiry and discovery and the advancement of knowledge, paradigm may change. And what is recognized as factual truth will change when paradigm shifts. It would therefore follow that a statement of truth of logical and empirical types may very well be proved wrong as time and circumstance change. Of course, normative entities or artifacts vary in meaning, application, and significance with person, perspective, interest, value system, political orientation, or philosophical bend. As a result, the certainty, determinacy, and predictability of normative entities are compromised. Some view this kind of approach to social normativity or law "protestant," which is contrary to the public and social nature of law or social rules, as Robert Cover claims. [236]

Certainly, scientific paradigms (科学示范) are established on the basis of materialist and/or logical reasoning. We belief claims of right and wrong, justice and fairness are also established in the same way through general community recognition and acceptance. Even personal preferences can be similarly objectified and believed and accepted by the general community. The phenomenon of fast food and fashion vogue amply proves this truism.

There is thus a third method which should be used, and in fact is generally employed, to establish the objectivity, or if you prefer the truth of claims, propositions, statements on political, legal, or moral issues. The doubters prefer to call these types of truth or objectivity "culturally sanctioned subjective beliefs." [237]

Maybe, the doubters are simply carried away by their zealous pursuit in deconstructing law and legal reason. What else could one make doubters' claim that

---

[235] Campos, id. at 152.
[236] Brian Bix, "Dworkin, Ronald (1931)", *The Philosophy of Law: an Encyclopedia*. Ed. Christopher B. Gray. New York & London: Garland Publishing, 1999, pp. 233, 235.
[237] Campos, op cit at 154.

the "contemporary ethical debate about right and wrong, etc. is analogous to the continuation of the passionate arguments concerning the biology of the unicorn when all belief in the unicorn as an actual biological entity has vanished."[28]

There is neither cognitive dissonance nor magic word gambit. The language, concepts, notions, modalities, doctrines (i. e. paradigms) evoked and applied in political, legal, and moral discourse and persuasion are the very stuff that advances understanding and knowledge.

As Martha Nusbaum rightly observes that the news of the death of God does not bring nihilism and the abandonment of evaluation and selection. Failure to commit ourselves "to sorting out our human and historical practices of choice and selection by flexing our knowledge and reasoning muscle only betrays a shame before the human."[29] Any transcendent ground for value, if ever there is such a thing, is just uninteresting or irrelevant to human ethics and law. We think, we reason, and we act as we have always been doing.

However, the doubters of law and legal reason stubbornly insist that ethical choices, that are meant to include law too, are not truly the product of a rational process, but the total subjectivization of ethical argument, and they amount to nothing other than a reduction of the good to beliefs about the good. In other words, in their view, truly ethical choices can only be established by reference to some kind of transcendent criteria or bases. In the mind of doubters, ethical judgment cannot be made rationally in the political community through reason. Yet, what the doubters of law and reason are doing is exactly what political and moral discourse is meant to be, that is, to make rational judgment and decision by public reason. Ironically, the doubters attempt to persuade us from doing what they have been doing all along.

Surely, it is nothing wrong to say that law is a social product of reason mediated through language. But truth can only born out and nourished on freedom of speech. John Mill believes in truth and optimism of progress. Holmes is skeptical. Yet both advocate the marketplace of idea justification of the freedom of speech. Posner sharing this view believes that constraining the marketplace of ideas would do more harm than good.[30] However, in another context, Posner appears to be retreating from

---

[28] Ibid.

[29] Quoted in Campos, op cit at 156.

[30] Richard A. Posner, *Problems of Jurisprudence*. Cambridge, MA: Harvard University Press, 1990, p. 467; Michel Rosenfeld, *Just Interpretation: Law between Ethics and Politics*, Berkeley, California: California Univ. Pr., 1998, p. 181.

absolute freedom and consistent with his pragmatism observed that nothing in pragmatism justifies the privileging of freedom of speech over other social interests. ㊶

U. Emotion Figures Large in Political and Moral Decision-Making Process

It is generally understood that reason and emotion are antithetical; Reasoning is free of emotion, while advocacy, debate, or argument may and is often emotion-loaded. Adjudication or judging should be equally free, as it is considered as pure reason. It has somehow become a common practice in our post-modern society(后现代社会) that passionate, partisan advocacy in public political discourse and especially in the court of law, such as in jury trial, is not only normal and acceptable but also highly expected and praised.

Yet, generally speaking, in the authoritative and effective decision-making process of the normative enterprise of the law, emotional or passionate advocacy or representation may not strengthen the quality of reason and ensure success of persuasion. This is true regardless of the fact that politics or public political debates often involve important value consequences. No doubt, it is generally believed that emotional and passionate advocacy can be taken to indicate one's strong commitment to the cause involved, and as a result inspire trust unless, of course, one is purely performing and faking. Still, one may dispute that passionate, emotional advocacy refers to the body language, presentation, communication, or other formal aspects of reasoning, while cool, rational, dispassionate argument rely solely one's success on the merits of the reason one advances, i. e. the substantive quality of reason.

It is extremely difficult to argue that in political and moral decisions, rationality always reigns. O. W. Holmes Jr. believes that the element of intuition, hunch, or" can't help" shapes decision. Myres DcDougal and Harold Lasswell of the Yale School of Law advocate in their political science to law, also known as the configurative jurisprudence, that in making decision, we should take into consideration of all known and foreseeable factors. It is also not unreasonable to argue that in H. L. A, Hart's "discretion" in reaching decision, there is possibly a large dose of emotion. With regard to how markets work in reality, it would be better and certainly more profitable if one bridges the divide between the supposed rationality and efficiency and the argument of a growing number of behaviorists who

---

㊶ Richard A. Posner, *Overcoming Law*. Cambridge, Mass: Harvard Univ. Pr. 1995. p.396.

argue that psychology always rules. Truth emerges from a clash of reasons in political and moral discourse. Presumably, rationality may very well arise from a confrontation of emotions. Each of us contains within ourselves the capacity for rational thought and deliberation. But at the same time, our brains are magnificent instruments of protection largely emotion motivated.

In authoritative and effective decisions, especially those of an economic nature, the tremendous influence of oration has some economists and policymakers wondering whether useful tools for dealing with economic problems might lie beyond stimulus packages and in the realm of psychology and behavior. For Nobel winning economist George A. Akerlof, a professor at the University of California at Berkeley, and Yale economist Robert J. Shiller, the idea that economic trends are linked to psychological states is fundamental. In their new book Animal Spirits: How Human Psychology Drives the Economy, and Why It Matters for Global Capitalism, they have revived the idea of "animal spirits," initially used by the great economist John Maynard Keynes to describe the period of despair that accompanied the Great Depression. They argued that it has important consequences for how we make economic decisions-and especially for consumer confidence. The very meaning of trust is that we go beyond the rational, they write. Do business decisions not involve decision-making processes that are closer to what we do when we flip a pancake or hit a golf ball? Keynes' ideal of government guidance of the market must be undertaken with an understanding of psychology applied to economics, the field is called behavioral economics. ㉔

V. Defending and Redeeming Reason

Does reason need to be defended? Could reason be defended on reasonable grounds? Is reason self-grounding? Does reason defend itself? Are such questions paradoxical? The doubters allege that to defend reason through reasoned discourse is to engage shallow circularities and infinite regression. It is similar to proving the validity or rationality of an argument within the criteria of rationality and validity.

Is the notion that law is in quest of itself logically or ontologically the same as

---

㉔ Sarah Barmak, "Tightrope: Hope vs. Fear Amid a Ceaseless Barrage of Negative Numbers, Are Leaders Obligated to Communicate Harsh Reality ... or Do They Have a Responsibility to Convey What Plato Called 'Nobel Lies' in the Name of Order and the Greater Good?", *Toronto Star Insight*, March 1, 2009, pp. IN3 & IN7.

that reason is invoked to defend reason itself? Are such questions really rhetorical trick cleverly crafted to confuse reality with theory? It does appear circular or infinitely regressive at the metaphysical or theoretical level both in the law's quest of itself and in reason's defense of reason. But in reality, the assertion is the doubters' own philosophical scam.

Is reason then redeemable? To salvage itself from the squalor of the unthinking, belief, faith, preference, prejudice and all other things that are bane of reason, reason ceaselessly engages in critical reflexivity. Unfortunately, locked in a prison of its self-imposed and tightly netted aesthetics and frame, reason is destined to find no door of escape.

Reason's critical reflexivity has both its anti-formalizing bent and a formalizing aspiration. In anti-formalizing, critical reflexivity is context-breaking; it dismantles the existing aesthetics and frame of law and moves beyond them. In its formalizing ambition, critical reflexivity engages in rebuilding aesthetics and frame to replace existing ones. Thus in the continuous process of reason's critical reflexivity and rational frame construction, they collapse onto one another, becoming one.

In American law, "nothing destroyed the Common law quite so well as the advent of the constructive contribution of consequentialist reasoning, policy analysis, and ultimately, law and economics."[93]

Instead of perceiving the circularity and infinite regression in the working and operation of reason, we see critical reflexivity and frame construction in a new light that enriches and strengthens the Common law by keeping it abreast with social change and legal philosophizing. And the importance and moral judgement of what is destroyed and built are a matter of evaluation—an issue continuously fought between subjectivity and objectivity.

To further discredit reason and to expose its limitation, the doubters of reason invoke the skeptical and cynical views of Nietzsche, Gadamer, Foucault, Derrida, Lyotard, etc. to finish the job. The argument is that the self is fatally situated, mediated, and contextualized; understanding is forever limited and partial; and construction is a work in process. As Schlag points out that "[t]here is no unmediated access to the unthought." Truth is elusive and an illusion. Decision is nothing but political preference.[94] Reason feeds on belief, nurtured and shaped by

---

[93] Schlag, op cit at 66.
[94] Id., at 69 et seq.

belief. Reason is belief. Such view is in essence similar to that which denies the autonomy of law without defining what law is and how law differs from its constituent elements or materials.

There is however no denying that the doubters' radical, cynical views and conceptions have found few followers and are failing to radically change and slow down the task of reason and the process of reasoning. And these facts speak volume about the anti-factual, counter-intuitive nature and orientation of doubters' views and conception of the world, the political community, and the politically moral self. Such radicalism and cynicism that reason is fatally indebted to belief or to something other than reason itself without even offering a reasonable definition of what counts as reason is simply a hyperbole.

Neither law nor legal reason necessarily needs to be infinitely regressive. A forwarding looking and infinitely progressive definition of law and legal reason by implication could be equally persuasively constructed and shared widely. Such a conception of law and legal reason can be founded in the notion of what is tentatively "the law of authoritative and effective decisions." And the notion of the law of authoritative and effective decisions necessarily conceives an element of "displacement", an iconoclastic component we called "public political moral action."[23]

Instead of seeing the specter of disciplinary solipsism as the doubters of the legitimacy and autonomy of law(法律的自治性) and legal reason see, we see the legal structure's working in appropriating and coupling the external world—the assimilation of critical reflexivity and frame construction into the main corpus of the law. In the same vein, instead of finding the working and operation of law and legal reason in self-reference, we witness the normative integrity and closure of the concept of law.[24]

The normative enterprise of the law and its accompanying reasoning are a continuous and progressive collective effort of all members of a political community. Rather than unduly being preoccupied with its incompleteness, we stress and draw

---

[23] Displacement is defined to mean "every attempt to articulate the context within which one is writing or speaking establishes a new context." Schlag. op cit at 71 et seq.

[24] Structural coupling and normative closure are the essence of law's autonomy as elaborated by Niklas Luhmann in his Autopoiesis of law. Detailed account can be founded in "Closed Systems and Open Justice: the Legal Sociology of Niklas Luhmann". *Cardozo L Rev.* 13 (special issue) 1419 (1992); Niklas Luhman. Das Recht der Gesellscht. Frankfurt, Suhrkamp, 1995.

strength from the best interpretation and application of the law manifested in each and every authoritative and effective decision.

In its struggle to have a formal existence in terms of essentialization and abstraction as manifested in both judicial pronouncements and legal scholarship—a sort of the "rulification" of the law of authoritative and effective decisions, law is fulfilling and completing its aspiration at every corner and turn.

Whatever the limitation or inadequacy of our language and linguistics, these would not retard or thwart the progressive development and "purification" efforts of the law.

W. Re-imagine and Re-conceptualize Law and Reason

Just like the proponents of reason believe that reason is a sine qua none of public discourse, a necessary virtue for all authoritative and effective decisions, the doubters believe probably even more fervently that reason is a professional scam fatally infested with irrationality, shallow circularity, infinite regression, and self-reference, etc. Both are deeply confident of the rationality or truth of their beliefs. Neither would be easily persuaded otherwise.

It is admitted that the arguments advanced so far to defend reason are mainly culled from the armory of legal reason itself as informed by the law itself. As doubters of reason no less vigorously attack the law and the conceptions of law per se, it is no surprise that they would not take proponents' arguments seriously and rather dismiss these arguments in the most repulsive manner they know.

Therefore, to redeem and reinvigorate reason, we must re-imagine and re-conceptualize law itself. We suggest that there is a really new, sufficiently different, and highly innovative perspective and exposition with respect to law and its conceptualization. Neither law nor reason needs to be defined in a self-referential, circular manner. There are credible, practical criteria for testing what counts as law and consequently the reason of law. Such criteria are outside or external to law, and can be established rationally, widely accepted, and successfully tested in the reality of the collective normative enterprise of political morality. Legal reason informed by such law is free standing, vigorous, and forward-looking. Authoritative and effective decisions "juridified" on the basis of political moral actions are these criteria.

Review and Reflective Questions

1. Why and why not reason is different from legal reason?

2. Does legal reason have any particular form and content? Whether you answer affirmatively or not, please give your reasons.

3. Is law and reason the same? Discuss your answer.

4. Do you think legal reason is all-inclusive and superior? Please discuss it in detail.

复习及提问

1. 为什么推理不同于法律推理?

2. 法律推理是否有特别的形式与内容? 无论回答是与否,请给出你的理由。

3. 法律和推理是否可以等同? 对你的回答进行讨论。

4. 你认为法律推理是包罗万象的还是具有优越性? 请详细讨论。